Inside the Wigwam

Inside the Wigwam

Chicago Presidential Conventions
1860–1996

R. Craig Sautter and Edward M. Burke

Foreword by Richard M. Daley

 **Wild Onion Books**

an imprint of Loyola Press
Chicago

About the Authors

In August 1968 Edward M. Burke was a Chicago police officer assigned to the Democratic National Convention at the Chicago Amphitheatre. R. Craig Sautter was a philosophy student at Indiana University and an anti-Vietnam War and civil-rights protester during the infamous "Battle of Chicago" of August 28, 1968, when violence raged in the streets and on national television.

In 1969 Burke was elected alderman of the Fourteenth Ward and for the past twenty-seven years has served on the Chicago City Council. As chairman of the City Council Committee on Finance, Burke is, in accord with a long-standing practice, de facto leader of the council. Acting also as the council's unofficial historian, Burke has produced a wide array of public historical exhibits in city hall. He has been a delegate to seven Democratic national conventions. In addition, Burke is a partner in the Chicago law firm of Klafter and Burke.

Sautter began teaching third graders from New York City's Harlem in 1969. He later traveled across the nation as a field coordinator for the National Urban League's voter registration/political education program. Sautter then spent several years in New York and Illinois as a poet-in-residence, conducting creative writing workshops with twenty thousand students in grades kindergarten through twelve. An award-winning education journalist with numerous newspaper and magazine articles to his credit, he is also author and co-author of several books including: *Smart Schools, Smart Kids*, with Edward B. Fiske and Sally Reed; *Wicked City: Chicago from Kenna to Capone*, with Curt Johnson; *Expresslanes through the Inevitable City*, a collection of poetry; and editor of *Floyd Dell: Essays from the* Friday Literary Review *1909–1913*. For the past fifteen years, Sautter has taught courses in philosophy, politics, history, literature, and creative writing at DePaul University's School for New Learning in Chicago. He also writes and produces radio and television media campaigns for Sautter Communications: Political Media and Strategy with his brother Chris Sautter, a Washington, D.C., attorney and political consultant.

Sautter and Burke were introduced to each other in May 1995 during an informal storytelling discussion on Chicago presidential conventions while at a black-tie DePaul University fund-raising dinner in the grand ballroom of the Chicago Hilton and Towers, site of so many convention events over the years. *Inside the Wigwam* is a collaborative effort arising from that meeting. The authors hope the book becomes a magnet for further convention stories.

Wild Onion Books
an imprint of Loyola Press
3441 North Ashland Avenue
Chicago, Illinois 60657

Wild Onion Books publishes provocative titles on Chicago themes that offer diverse perspectives on the city and surrounding area, its history, its culture, and its religions. Wild onion is a common nickname for Chicago.

Wild Onion Books staff:
Editorial director: Joseph F. Downey, S.J.
Imprint editors: June Sawyers, Jeremy Langford
Interior design and production coordination: Jill Mark Salyards

Cover design by: Juanita Dix

Library of Congress Cataloging-in-Publication Data

Sautter, R. Craig.
    Inside the wigwam: Chicago presidential conventions. 1860–1996 / R. Craig Sautter and Edward M. Burke.
        p. cm.
    Includes bibliographical references and index.
    ISBN 0-8294-0911-4
    1. Political conventions—United States—History. 2. Political conventions—Illinois—Chicago—History.
I. Burke, Edward M. II. Title.
JK2255.S28 1996
324.5'09773'11—dc20   96-14360
                                                                    CIP

Dedication

We dedicate this book to all the voters, delegates, and candidates, past and future, who make our democracy work, and to the great city of Chicago, the capital of American presidential conventions.

R.C.S./E.M.B.
Chicago 1996

The term *wigwam*, initially an Algonquin word for a dwelling made of bent tree poles overlaid with bark, was later used to refer to any temporary shelter. Chicago's early presidential convention halls were often called wigwams.

Contents

Foreword

American democracy has never found a more fertile place to thrive than in Chicago, home to more political conventions than any other American city. The process by which Americans choose their candidates for the nation's highest office has enriched our city with countless tales of political conflict and compromise, courage and cowardice, and with each retelling, the stories get better and better. Starting in 1860, with the convention that nominated Abraham Lincoln, Chicago has hosted twenty-five national political conventions. For the first time, an account of all of Chicago's political conventions has been set down in one place, for the pleasure of historians, students of the democratic process, and interested citizens alike.

Inside the Wigwam sets the drama and intrigue surrounding the conventions into the larger political context of the times, the tragic wars abroad and at home that both defined us and divided us, and the compelling social upheavals, such as the labor and civil-rights movements that reshaped America's political, economic, and cultural landscape. Lincoln's nomination takes on its fullest meaning in the context of the impending Civil War. Eleanor Roosevelt's dramatic speech on behalf of her husband in 1940 shimmers brightly against the backdrop of fascism sweeping through Europe and Asia. The Vietnam War and the assassinations of Dr. Martin Luther King Jr. and Robert F. Kennedy so colored the events of 1968 as to make conflict in Chicago almost inevitable. Today our city prepares to host another political convention amid a historic debate in Congress and in the public arena over the appropriate role of government in our society.

Let the debate proceed here in Chicago, a glorious showcase of America's diversity, ambition, and achievement. From our magnificent architecture to our breathtaking lakefront, our tree-lined neighborhoods, and our emerging industries, Chicago remains the leading example of how American cities can prosper and thrive in the century ahead. And for those who wonder where we came from, how we got here, and why people keep coming—whether to live, work, or simply choose a president—this book is a good place to start.

Richard M. Daley
Mayor of Chicago

Acknowledgments

The authors wish gratefully to acknowledge the assistance of several people in the preparation of this book: for research, writing, editing contributions, advice, and especially encouragement, Curt Johnson, Michael J. Tynan, Thomas O'Gorman, and Dennis McSweeny; for additional research and observations, Benjamin Mednick, Timothy Hill, Peter Goodman, Amanda Cochran, Andrea Miller, Allan Feldman, and Peter Cunningham; for editing and manuscript preparation, Sally Reed, Kriss Marion, Anita Lauterstein, Connie Amon, and Louis Coronel; and, of course, our editor, June Sawyers.

Thanks also to the staff of the Chicago Public Library; the Newberry Library; the DePaul University Library; the Chicago Historical Society; the Denver Public Library's Western History Division; the Maine Maritime Museum; the Edmund S. Muskie Archives at Bates College, Lewiston, Maine; and the Nebraska State Historical Society.

And special thanks to Joel Weisman, David Rosenberg, David O. Justice, Virginia Sautter, Ted Sautter, Father George A. Lane, Judge Anne Burke, Sandy Hazel, and Jill Mark Salyards.

Introduction

"Friends, delegates, the convention system itself is the greatest expression of freedom in all the history of the world," the Democratic Party National Chairman John Moran Bailey told the 1968 Democratic National Convention in Chicago. "I see a system that has never produced a tyrant, which has never produced a despot, which has never produced a demagogue, but a system which has always produced the right leader for the right time."

Well, perhaps not always. Herbert Hoover might be an example of the right leader for the wrong time, and perhaps so was the nominee of the convention to which Chairman Bailey spoke, Hubert Humphrey. But the former senior adviser to President Kennedy was, in the main, correct. America's democratic national party conventions have produced many great leaders, a few mediocre ones, but never a dictator, rarely a demagogue, never a despot, and most often a candidate who expresses the beliefs and aspirations of a large segment of the people of this great nation at a particular moment in time.

America's presidential nominating convention is an enduring social institution that serves a serious purpose and offers entertaining democratic rituals. Sometimes trivial, sometimes electrifying, the convention is a symbol and instrument of the nation's contentious freedom. Perhaps that's because presidential nominating conventions exhibit several basic tenets of our democracy: freedom of voluntary assembly; freedom of competitive speech; freedom to propose guiding policies and principles for the Republic; freedom to use influence, money, and power; and freedom to select a candidate for national leadership; in short, to lead the United States of America through good days and bad.

Yet the nominating convention is not without serious flaws. At times it has been manipulated by the parties; other times it has been trivialized, for example, as television entertainment. Although it seeks to be democratic, it is often dominated by political bosses and the national organizations that require compliance. Thousands of party members may attend and create great noise and excitement, but a privileged few speak for the record and make enduring statements. And although the convention, at its best, expresses the idealistic richness of the nation and its people, its decisions are often made in a manner reminiscent of crude ward politics and old-fashioned deal cutting. Given all its negatives, though, the presidential nominating convention endures, as Chairman Bailey exclaimed, as one of the greatest expressions of our freedom, and it is likely to remain so for years to come.

The U.S. Constitution, adopted in 1789, makes no provision for political parties or presidential nominating conventions. In fact, the founding fathers feared political parties might degenerate into "factions," like the extremist Jacobins of the French Revolution who butchered their own ideals of "life, liberty, and fraternity," and brought about as an antithetical consequence a dictatorship in the military figure of Napoleon. The framers of the U. S. Constitution abhorred political parties, believing they would splinter the national unity and purpose that had emerged during the American Revolution.

Despite their misgivings, parties did evolve in the new Republic, founded, as it was, on the division of power between the states and the federal government and among the branches of the government. Parties were needed to consolidate power and support legislative agendas around common political goals and ideals. After a few decades, power bifurcated into two dominant parties, the one in power and a strong, articulate legislative opposition.

The American political party also helped to organize and deliver support before the election and reward loyalty afterward. At the local level, people needed practical help and parties needed votes to gain control of the resources to fund the constituency and its interests. They exchanged favors. At the national level, parties grew stronger as fundamental social splits emerged in the new nation: disputes over the scope and purpose of the central government, over economic growth, over states' rights, over agrarian versus urban interests, and, of course, over slavery. Presidential candidates represent the highest expression of a party's national principles and ambitions.

Voters do not directly select the president of the United States. Presidential electors do. The nation's founders had little trust in the "people," whom they associated with the "mob." Voting privileges were at first entrusted only to white, property-owning men. This, indeed, was a radical and revolutionary step forward in the march of human freedom, away from the dominance of kings and tyrants, but it represented only a beginning. One of the great democratic achievements of the past two centuries in the United States has been the struggle to enlarge political participation to universal suffrage and representation.

Enfranchisement of all white men led to all men—black or white—then all men and women twenty-one or older, and finally all citizens at least eighteen years of age. A similar situation has happened in the delegate selection process to national conventions. These advances came only through great political effort and personal sacrifice. (Yet only a quarter of the eligible U. S. population takes advantage of its hard-won voting rights.)

In the beginning, each state legislature, not individual voters, selected electors to the electoral college. The electors were expected to cast their ballots for the best man, using their best judgment. During the first election of 1789, electors selected by the state legislatures unanimously chose the popular George Washington as president. John Adams, next in line of trust, was picked by the electors as vice president.

By the second election, two contentious political parties had emerged in Congress and the country.

The Federalists of John Adams represented the commercial interests of the industrial Northeast, who were in favor of a strong central government and protective trade agreements. The anti-Federalist Republicans (later called Democrat-Republicans and finally Democrats) endorsed the agrarian democratic idealism of Thomas Jefferson, but were embraced by the Southern slave aristocracy as well. After Washington, who while opposed to parties was a Federalist in temperament, John Adams was elected to the presidency by the electors. Democratic-Republicans Thomas Jefferson, James Madison, James Monroe, and John Quincy Adams were next elected to lead the nation.

By the election of 1800, presidential nominees under consideration by the electors were selected by congressional caucuses of party members or in secret meetings in undisclosed locations. The congressional caucus system brought top congressional leaders to the fore as qualified and preferred candidates and narrowed the field, from thirteen candidates for president in 1796 to five in 1800. But the process was far too self-serving for the growing American democracy. Caucuses excluded almost all citizens and smacked of aristocratic rule. Then, during the early 1820s, known as the Era of Good Feeling, political parties temporarily disappeared, as most members of Congress followed the leadership of James Monroe.

By 1824 voters in several states rebelled against caucus nominations of presidential candidates. Protests forced potential candidates for the presidency to seek nomination from state legislatures or to submit directly to popular election. Finally, in 1831, fifty-five years after the Declaration of Independence, the Anti-Masonic Party held the first national presidential nominating convention. The National Republican Party met later that year in Baltimore, nominating Henry Clay. In May 1832 the Democrats met in Baltimore. (The Democrats' next five conventions were also staged in Baltimore, host to a total of ten conventions by Republicans and Democrats, the second highest total next to Chicago's twenty-five.) The Democrats renominated Andrew Jackson, who beat Henry Clay in November.

Since one prime purpose of the convention was to bring together leaders of the far-flung national party, Chicago proved to be a natural choice, and the city became the mecca of political conventions. Because of its central location and excellent transportation system, the rapidly growing prairie giant attracted both major parties, and many of the third parties, over the decades. Delegates by the thousands rolled into the dynamic metropolis on the iron tracks that converged in the city's hub. Also, Chicago's location suggested political neutrality to both the East and the West, and the city government and businesses were almost always eager to play the gracious hosts. Indeed, Chicago has erected a strong economic pillar on its convention trade, serving everything from hardware to electronic equipment to conventioneers.

Chicago's first national convention, the River and Harbor Convention of 1847, attracted three thousand delegates from twenty-nine states, including a new Whig congressman named Abraham Lincoln. The deliberative body met in a large canvas tent on the grounds of city hall. Delegates were entertained by local bands and parades in a spectacle that Horace Greeley, editor of the New York *Tribune*, called "magnificent." The convention petitioned President James Knox Polk and Congress to fund Northwestern waterway improvements as a way to promote the region's development. By 1996, 149 years later, Chicago's convention trade has blossomed into a nearly $1 billion a year business.

But it is the presidential nominating conventions that have most captured the city's enthusiasm and been shaped by its politics. Both Republicans and Democrats have written their political histories on the shores of Lake Michigan. After the disintegration of the Whigs, a coalition of Eastern and Western reformers—united against the spread of slavery to the territories—founded the Republican Party in Ripon, Wisconsin, in 1854. The Republican's first national convention was held in Philadelphia in 1856. The new party then came to Chicago four years later in 1860 to nominate its first president, a dark horse named Abraham Lincoln, in its Wigwam constructed along the Chicago River.

The Democrats, the world's oldest political party, have convened presidential nominating conventions every four years since 1832. The Democrats first arrived in Chicago for their national presidential nominating convention in 1864 amid demands for a peace candidate and criminal charges of conspiracy. They met in the second Wigwam along the shores of Lake Michigan near Park Row (Eleventh Street). The "Democracy" (as the party was called back then) first

nominated a president in Chicago in yet another Wigwam further north in Lake Park (now Grant Park) along Michigan Avenue at Washington Street in 1884. Grover Cleveland won the popular vote in three consecutive national elections, but lost once, in 1888, in the electoral college, to Chicago-nominated Republican Benjamin Harrison.

The term *wigwam* was not alien to American politics when it was first used as the name of the early Chicago presidential convention halls. The word was initially an Algonquin one and referred to a dwelling made of bent tree poles overlaid with bark. In the American West, the label later was used for any temporary shelter. But it had a peculiar political lineage. In the days preceding the Revolutionary War, Pennsylvanians celebrated Saint Tammany Day to honor Tammany, a legendary Indian who had paved the way for peaceful relations with early colonists. Saint Tammany was invented to replace the English patron Saint George, who colonialists despised.

The Tammany Society of New York, which began in 1787, called its meeting hall the Wigwam. Even though the colonies launched a war of displacement against the many Native American tribes, Tammany members admiringly called themselves "braves" and emulated their political structure inside the Wigwam, as the U.S. founding fathers had emulated the Iroquois federation of the seven nations in their own Federation of States. The New York Tammany hierarchy featured thirteen "sachems" or board directors, a scribe, a "wiskinsky" or sergeant-at-arms, and a "sagamore" or chief. At the head of the secret organization stood a Council of Sachems with a "Father of the Council" and the "Grand Sachem," at the pinnacle of political power, as a tribal leader.

If the Tammany tradition didn't exactly travel with settlers of the open prairie, of which Chicago was the great commercial gateway, at least the notion of the wigwam did. In 1860 the Republican wigwam held ten thousand delegates and spectators, while twenty thousand more citizens crowded close by in the streets to hear the proceedings repeated by shouters from the doorways. In 1996 the Democratic wigwam is a multimillion dollar sports arena, the United Center, and the proceedings inside this modern wigwam will be watched on television by tens of millions around the globe.

Despite the fears of the founding fathers, there was no splintering of the parties into tiny or violent factions. When it came time for fundamental political changes in America, a party such as the Federalists simply faded out of existence to make room for another. In a realignment of political allegiance, the Federalist Party gave way to the Whigs, which eventually yielded to the Republicans. The splintering took place at the fringes. Third parties defined alternatives but never attracted mass followings. Yet they still introduce radical and unpopular ideas that ultimately have impact, an essential role for the health and progress of the democracy as a whole.

Instead of turmoil, the two parties ushered in continuity and narrowed choices to "either-or" leadership and policy alternatives. Thus, with the exception of the Southern Democrats of 1860, U.S. political parties have been patriotic and differed primarily over notions of how to shape the social democracy and economy and the leaders they offer to the voters. None have been revolutionary parties intent upon political destruction and reconstitution. All have abided by the ballot, not the gun. This political continuity is remarkable. The presidential convention every four years is a gateway to the national election and both a contributor and beneficiary of its stability and focus.

The presidential nominating convention is a political invention answering the democratic pressures of a geographically diverse and growing nation. The quadrennial event has the virtue of bringing party members of like persuasion from across the land into face-to-face contact with one another, often after months of correspondence; in olden days through the mails, then the telegraph and telephone, and in the 1990s by computer and teleconferencing. National conventions also provide a national forum in which the ideas and problems of the party's constituency can be debated and brought to bear on the platform. Conventions also supply a national stage for the great party orators to let loose their verbal bombast, as readers will herein encounter in the likes of Roscoe Conkling, Frederick Douglass, William Jennings Bryan, and Adlai Stevenson.

Conventions serve, as well, to motivate party members at the state level as they jockey for position for the right to attend, or involve voters in the selection of delegates and candidates in the primaries. They focus interest and electoral activity and generate enthusiasm as a warm-up for the presidential contest. What's more, the conventions set the occa-

sion for the celebratory traditions associated with all the excitement and hoopla of deal making and fighting for a particular candidate while the band plays on and the chair pounds the gavel for order.

The convention has endured all these years, in large part because it has served as a stage for the national drama of presidential nominations and the rhetorical excitement of policy debate. It remains a pressure-packed conduit for decision making about who will lead the United States during times of peace and prosperity, war and want. After 165 years of service, the presidential convention continues as a grand civic spectacle of pomp and circumstance, of rhetoric and debate, a ritual that likely assures continued political vibrancy for the United States in the years ahead.

Not only has the convention system not produced a tyrant or a dictator, as Chairman Bailey boasted, its very existence, along with the system of direct primaries that select delegates to the convention, has made the rise of tyranny in the United States extremely unlikely because the major nominees must submit themselves to popular review. Most are also forced into a kind of moderation that contributes to social stability.

In 1932 *Baltimore Sun* scribe H. L. Mencken, who had attended every presidential convention since 1900, doubted conventions accomplished much good. "The selection of a president is obviously the concern of every American," he said. "Well, two things deserve to be noted. One is that it is done by professional politicians and by professional politicians exclusively, and that at least nine-tenths of them can be bought, if not with downright money, then at all events jobs."

On Mencken's first point, there appears to have been some progress. Thousands of ordinary Americans now run in primary elections, along with the professional politicians, for the right to attend the convention. And campaign donations have been greatly regulated in recent years by criminal laws and campaign reform, although individual millionaires are often found blowing their money to the wind. On the other hand, paid television advertising attempts to influence election outcomes. The system is indeed in dire need of reform.

"The other point," Mencken continued, "is that [conventions are] a purely extra-legal proceeding, that there is no mention of it in the Constitution, and that even the laws take little notice of it. The last fact is very curious. We live in the most law-ridden country on earth, and yet we manage to select our candidates for its highest office in a wholly informal manner, without the slightest aid from courts and the policeman. A national convention is as free to change its rules as it pleases. It may expel a delegate at will and seat another. It may increase or decrease the representation of a state."

Again, things have changed a little since Mencken came to Chicago. In 1974 Congress passed the Federal Election Campaign Act, although the rules and procedures of the convention remain predominantly self-prescribed and regulated. But there is a more serious complaint against conventions, expressed to the Democratic Party of 1892 that met in the temporary wigwam on Lake Park at Washington Street. General Patrick Collins of Massachusetts wanted to revise the convention process entirely:

I feel free to say, in the presence of the small fraction of the great American public outside of ourselves as delegates, that a mistake has been made. The time has now come when a Democratic convention should be a deliberative body, not governed by outside influences. If we could be on exhibition in the view of 65 million of our people, and seven million of Democrats who will vote for the Democratic Party, well and good. But what is the use? What is the sense of having fifteen thousand people who can hardly see, and who cannot hear, prolong the proceedings of a Democratic convention and prevent it from being deliberative?

His resolution was referred to committee, and never to be heard from again. But clearly the intrusion of television negates much of his concern that conventions are cut off from the people. Indeed, television has done much to preserve and expand the convention, although the attempt to script and manage the proceedings to please television entertainment standards diminishes its authenticity and purpose. The relationship between television and politics continues to evolve in fascinating ways. Television need not wreck the political purpose of the convention any more than TV time-outs need to

wreck a basketball game, but the parties must demand political integrity or be overwhelmed by the threat of technology.

Finally, the sage of Baltimore, H. L. Mencken, was less than charitable in his conclusions, but right in tune with today's political minimalists of both parties when he argued:

A gathering of a hundred or even two hundred, reasonably sensible men and women could select the two candidates in an hour, and have the rest of the day left to visit the speakeasies. But instead of a hundred, there are more than a thousand, and instead of a few officers who suffice for an ordinary meeting there are hoards of bombastic and futile functionaries, all of them the most stupid and degraded sorts of political hacks. And the proceedings are dragged on for long days and nights simply and solely to give a gang of slightly superior mountebanks a chance to posture and perform. Not one man in forty who addresses a national convention has anything worth hearing to say, and not one in twenty is worth seeing and meeting for any other reason.

Somewhere between the accolades of Chairman Bailey and the cynicism of Mencken rests the truth. Certainly at most of the Chicago conventions, we find more than a little genuine political drama, human excitement, passionate oratory, and significant decision making critical to the nation's future, from the debate over slavery to the war in Vietnam. Inside the Chicago wigwams, the fate of the everyday millions of people who proudly called themselves "Americans" was often determined by delegates trying to do their best for their party and nation.

More than a few of the conventions described in the following chapters represent the grand social experiment of democracy in action that is the history of the United States. Delegates from every hamlet, village, and city, with differing experiences, backgrounds, ideas, beliefs, and objectives here gathered together for one week every four years to chart the course of action and choose the leader they deemed best for themselves and their fellow citizens. It was and is an awesome responsibility and a difficult task, one that is done in chaotic conditions, but, for the most part, with the best of intentions.

Out of the chaos of Chicago's presidential conventions have emerged candidates that led a nation, men who have manifest the hopes and fears of millions: Lincoln, McClellan, Garfield, Blaine, Harrison, Cleveland, Bryan, Theodore Roosevelt, Taft, Hughes, Harding, Hoover, Franklin Roosevelt, Dewey, Truman, Eisenhower, Stevenson, Nixon, Humphrey, and Clinton—men whose ideas and actions have defined our nation.

The convention is thus a ceremony of the democracy that endures, even as it ebbs then thrives. It is reminiscent of the citizen assemblies of Athens and the American Revolution, of the town hall meetings, county fair debates, and the Fourth of July parades. The convention is an expression of both major political parties and is embedded in their distinct and often glorious histories. It is so powerful a model of democracy that it has been duplicated by most third parties. Short of the direct electronic democracy that will probably be adopted by twenty-first century Americans, in which advanced computer and media merge to give every citizen the opportunity to instantaneously nominate, debate, consider, and

then elect presidents and decide issues, the convention is likely to survive many more elections. It is a grand political tradition whose home has been Chicago. And Chicago, despite its occasional dry spells, will be at the center of these deliberations.

"Chicago is a city of Conventions, but not a Conventional city," wrote the *Chicago Times* in 1884. "It draws to itself the great gatherings of the country, not necessarily by sympathy, but because it has become the great center of the country . . . and the probability is that as long as political Conventions are in fashion, Chicago will be the location for them."

Inside the Wigwam is an attempt to convey some of the circumstances, personalities, issues, debates, and decisions of these historic meetings that have shaped our past and present and to preserve and further that history. Here then is a record of our democracy in action, of the rise and fall of great leaders, of the conflict over platforms, of grand oratory and parliamentary maneuvers, a quadrennial trip through the growth and transformation of a nation in search of its democratic destiny.

Abraham Lincoln
1860 Republican Presidential Nominee

Hannibal Hamlin
1860 Republican
Vice Presidential Nominee

Facts-at-a-Glance
★★★

Event:	Second Republican National Convention
Dates:	May 16–18, 1860
Building:	The Wigwam
Location:	Lake and Market Streets
Chicago Mayor:	"Long John" Wentworth, Republican
Candidates for Nomination:	Edward Bates, Missouri; Senator Simon Cameron, Pennsylvania; Salmon Portland Chase, Ohio; Abraham Lincoln, Illinois; Senator William Henry Seward, New York
Presidential Nominee:	Abraham Lincoln
Age at Nomination:	51
Number of Ballots:	3
Vice Presidential Nominee:	Hannibal Hamlin, Maine
Number of Delegates:	465
Number Needed to Nominate:	A majority, 233
Largest Attendance:	10,000
Critical Issues:	Slavery, tariffs, water and harbor development, a transcontinental railroad
Campaign Slogan:	"Honest Abe, the Rail Splitter"
Convention Song:	"Ain't You Glad You Joined the Republicans?"

I
★★★

The 1860 Republican National Convention
Powwow in the Wigwam

On May 18, 1860, inside a jam-packed, two-story, pine-plank riverside hall dubbed the Wigwam, the Second National Republican Convention met to nominate an unlikely candidate for president of the United States, Abraham Lincoln. On that date a great and glorious convention history began for the Gem of the Prairie, as the thriving new town of Chicago was called.

Yet the historic presidential election of 1860 did not really begin with the surprise May nomination. Rather, the momentous election that led almost inescapably to four bloody years of the Civil War began to unfold three years earlier in a Washington, D.C., courtroom. Indeed, in some ways, the decisive election of 1860 was fated with the very founding of the United States itself as a nation "half slave and half free."

On March 6, 1857, the Supreme Court of the United States announced the Dred Scott decision. Just two days after the inauguration of President James Buchanan, a Pennsylvania Democrat who supported slavery in the West, Chief Justice Roger Brooke Taney issued the lethal ruling: Slaves were property, not citizens with rights, the court held, and hence could not sue for their own freedom. Further, the judges ruled that slaves could be transported anywhere in the nation an owner so desired. Finally, the ruling deemed that the Missouri Compromise of 1820, which prohibited slaves in some new Western states, was unconstitutional.

Dred Scott fueled the antislavery fervor sweeping the North. Free-Soilers knew that the slightest expansion of slavery increased the legislative power of proslavery states in Congress. Ultimately, those states could declare the entire United States a slave nation, if they gained control. The Scott decision also hastened a national political reorganization, including the breakup of the old Whig Party of Henry Clay and Zachary Taylor and the realignment of the Democratic Party of Thomas Jefferson and Andrew Jackson into northern and southern factions. Into the fray came the new Republican Party. Thus, Dred Scott set the stage for the most crucial electoral contest in U.S. political history.

To the majority of Chicagoans—whether Whig, Republican, or Native American (Know-Nothing)— Dred Scott was the latest evidence that the forces of slavery were winning. A decade earlier, in 1850, the Chicago City Council had condemned the Fugitive Slave Law that required the capture and return of African Americans who had managed to escape the South via the Underground Railroad that ran through Chicago and nearby villages on its way to Canada. In the wake of the Scott decision, thousands of Chicagoans, many of them immigrants whose jobs were threatened by the slave-based Southern economic rival, turned out to hear antislavery radicals call for open defiance of the law. The scent of distant war tainted the air.

Chicago had been outraged when one of its favorite sons, Democratic Senator Stephen Arnold Douglas, brokered the Kansas/Nebraska Act of 1854 that repealed the Missouri Compromise of 1820. Douglas persuaded Congress to permit a state-by-state option on slavery based on a vote in the territory when it petitioned for entry into the Union. Douglas argued that Kansas/Nebraska was the most democratic solution, the only way to maintain legislative balance and keep the Union together. But his critics shouted "not another inch" for slavery.

A mob of eight thousand assembled outside Douglas' *Chicago Daily Times*, the city's chief Democrat newspaper, and threatened to burn it to the ground. But others, particularly in the East, who saw him as a wise and courageous patriot, defended the "Little Giant" and hosted lavish banquets in his honor. Still others simply swore when they learned his young Mississippi wife had inherited slaves.

Meanwhile, a pre–Civil War conflict broke out in Kansas as a result of his compromise.

Douglas, always expedient, subsequently moved away from the radical slave expansionists but defended his state-by-state position in the famous Lincoln/Douglas debates of 1858 (the first of which was staged on the balcony of the Tremont House in Chicago) and then again during the 1860 presidential election. It was in the 1858 debate that Lincoln declared, "A house divided against itself cannot stand . . . this government cannot endure permanently half slave and half free." The '58 debates ended in Douglas's election to the U.S. Senate by the Illinois legislature, which at that time still selected senators, even though Lincoln won the popular vote in a tight race. Both Illinois and Chicago maintained divided loyalties all the way through the subsequent war.

The Dred Scott decision also angered Free-Soil papers, such as the *Chicago Daily Tribune*, which was under the new and aggressive owner-and-editorship of Dr. Charles Ray and Joseph Meharry Medill. The *Tribune* charged that Dred Scott made slavery national. Now nothing could prevent "opening a slave pen and auction block for the sale of black men, women, and children right here in Chicago," the paper warned. "Freedom has no local habitation nor abiding place save in the hearts of Freemen. Illinois in law, has ceased to be a free State!"

Medill had cofounded and even named the Republican Party in 1854 while he was a Cleveland newspaper editor, before moving to Chicago to buy the *Tribune*. His party was a coalition of Free-Soilers, Whigs, and Anti-Nebraska Democrats united by their burning opposition to human bondage. Now, seven years later, Medill and other key antislavery Republicans realized they had to unite once and for all. Only then could they put an end to Democrat rule and its Southern sympathies. Only then could they elect a president who would forever put an end to slavery in the territories. They had to find a leader who would free new states like Kansas that already had fallen into proslave hands and was gripped in a murderous war. Such a man would probably need to abolish slavery in the nation as a whole, no matter what the cost.

Most Republicans looked to the senator from New York, William Henry Seward. He had the stature to lead the new party to victory over the despised Democrats of President Buchanan. After all, as first Whig governor of New York, Seward had resisted the Fugitive Slave Law by giving runaway blacks a trial, with state-paid counsel. In the Senate of the United States, Seward had fought against the Kansas/Nebraska Act, appealing to a "higher law" than the Constitution in his arguments for the abolition of slavery. Seward further predicted that an "irrepressible" conflict awaited the nation over the ancient evil. He had the courage to speak the truth, his admirers crowed, and the resolve to enforce a solution. But for every northern admirer, Seward had a sworn enemy in the South.

The slender, red-haired fifty-nine-year-old statesman had the added advantage of power that came not only from his office but from other sources as well. He was a representative of the huge monied interests of the East whose investments flowed from sea to shining sea and who often found themselves in fierce combat with the slave economy of the South. As thousands of Seward supporters stepped off the hundreds of trains that poured into Chicago for the Second National Republican Convention in mid-May, all the straw polls showed the New York senator easily outdistancing his most prominent rivals. Horace Greeley, editor of the New York *Tribune*, called Seward "unbeatable." His bands played the theme song "O, Isn't He a Darling?" as they marched through the streets of Chicago, and everyone had a grand time in the wide-open town.

Other contenders included Salmon Portland Chase, the potbellied, two-time Ohio governor, who was newly elected to the U.S. Senate. Chase was a vociferous abolitionist whose credentials were well-established. As Ohio's favorite son, Chase threatened the solidity of Seward's overwhelming dominance. But detractors charged that Chase's nomination meant the party had no chance of winning in border states.

Edward Bates of the slave state Missouri offered delegates still another option to Seward, whose Western support was weak. Bates, a sixty-seven-year-old former Free-Soil, Whig congressman, was favored by those who were particularly worried about Southern secession. Bates, by virtue of geography, was thought to have the power to hold the Union together. But Bates had endorsed the Know-Nothings in 1856 and alienated Republican immigrants who were not likely to vote for him.

Many delegates considered Supreme Court Justice John McLean from Ohio, who had dissented on Dred Scott, to be the perfect candidate, if only he were in better health. But at age seventy-three he

The 1860 Republican Wigwam. Chicago Historical Society. Photo by Alexander Hesler.

was failing, and his voice on the court was almost as important as the presidency. Pennsylvania was ready to stand by its native son, Senator Simon Cameron. A staunch supporter of the tariff, Senator Cameron's reputation as a spoilsman and consummate machine politician would inhibit him from receiving any votes other than those he controlled.

Although he had gained some national notice for his speeches in a losing 1858 senatorial campaign against Stephen A. Douglas, the favorite son of the Illinois delegation, Abraham Lincoln, a private attorney, was not seriously considered for the office, except in the public-relations campaigns of western papers like the *Chicago Daily Press and Tribune* and on the pages of Mayor "Long John" Wentworth's *Chicago Democrat.*

Lincoln had been a Clay and Seward Whig in the state legislature and a one-term congressman. In hypnotic speeches that transfixed his audiences, he declared, "Slavery is found in the selfishness of man's nature, opposition to it in his love of Justice." Lincoln made himself available for the Senate sev-

eral times without success. He was against slavery as well as the Know-Nothings and their anti-immigrant fervor. By 1856 Lincoln was calling himself a Republican. Through his spellbinding speeches, he leap-frogged to state party prominence. At the First National Republican Convention in 1856 held in Philadelphia, Lincoln even received 110 votes for vice president on the first ballot, losing to William L. Dayton. Senator John Charles Fremont, the "pathfinder" who brought California into the Union as a free state, was the Republican presidential nominee. He was beaten in 1856 by Democrat James Buchanan and his vice presidential candidate, John Cabell Breckinridge of Kentucky.

Supporters reissued Lincoln's speeches as booklets to bolster his standing. He became known as the man who said, "A house divided against itself cannot stand." The *Lincoln/Douglas Debate Book* sold for fifty cents. Lincoln's "Cooper Union Speech" went for one cent. In that speech Lincoln succinctly defined the national crisis as a chasm dividing North and South on moral principle: "All they ask, we could readily grant, if we thought slavery right; all we ask, they could readily grant, if they thought it wrong. Their thinking it right, and our thinking it wrong, is the precise fact upon which depends the whole controversy."

Voters by the tens of thousands all across the land read his words. Lincoln hinted he would leave the slave states alone, but block any expansion westward. Despite the growing legend of the six-foot four-inch tall, log cabin-reared, flatboating country lawyer, Lincoln was still a backwoods voice to the delegates from the East, where the wealth and power of the nation and the party resided. Indeed, Lincoln was such a dark horse that several papers printed his name as "Abram."

The real Lincoln was far from provincial. During the year preceding the Chicago convention, he traveled nearly four thousand miles to deliver twenty-three Republican speeches, trying to fashion a powerful new political party that could put force behind his ideas about slavery and the Union. Indeed, in his fifty-one years, Lincoln had traveled from New Orleans to New England and had lived in both New York City and Washington, D.C., as well as a log cabin. Yes, he had split rails, but he had also split fees with the nation's richest railroads. He knew America far better than it knew him.

Just a week before the national convention, on May 10, the Illinois State Republican Convention in Decatur had stampeded for Lincoln. Even though a third of the delegates favored Seward, the party locked all of them in a unit vote for their favorite son, "Honest Abe." Now like zealous disciples, Illinois Republicans jawboned delegates and visitors from other states as they arrived in this strange boom town, trying to switch votes wherever possible for Lincoln. Usually when out-of-state delegates were approached by Lincoln disciples and heard the arguments for the Springfield attorney, they acknowledged that he would make a good candidate—for vice president, if that would make the West happy. For as Horace Greeley pointed out, Lincoln had "no national experience." Because he called for restoration of the Missouri Compromise, many delegates agreed the Rail Splitter was "too risky."

The Chicago of 1860 that the five hundred convention delegates and forty thousand visitors beheld as they stepped from their trains at the huge Illinois Central station was a brash, energetic town, growing by the day. Noisy with the sound of construction, young Chicago was a hard-drinking, carousing kind of place on call twenty-four hours a day, with hundreds of saloons and dens of iniquity. Willow and cottonwood estates fronted the lake along Michigan Avenue behind which trembled a dreary and mud-stained hive of yellow-pine, three-story buildings, and shacks of every shape, size, and purpose.

In less than thirty years, Chicago was overtaking the older river trading posts of St. Louis and Cincinnati as the major metropolis of the West. Its population had swelled to 109,000, up from 16,000 just thirteen years earlier. Its streets were jammed with wagon, pedestrian, and horse traffic. It boasted five hundred factories, scores of mills, lumberyards, docks, and slaughterhouses. Jobs went begging. The decade-old Illinois and Michigan Canal made Chicago the great hub of waterways from the Atlantic to New Orleans. More than ten thousand schooners, barges, and boats bobbed in its harbor, more rigs than docked in Boston, New York, and New Orleans combined. By land, Chicago was the trading post to the great North and West, supplying all the tools of frontier civilization. In return, the bountiful harvests of the plains were shipped East and transformed into speculative fortunes in Chicago trading pits. Thousands of newcomers arrived daily from the eastern and southern states, eager to partake in the chaotic creation of a new kind of Western culture and, if possible, to become rich along the way.

Chicago had already withstood its first big fire. In 1849 Lake Street, the center of commerce, was reduced to ashes. Now five-story marble buildings lined the main business concourse. A new court house, the center of civic pride, graced the tree-studded square block at the intersections of LaSalle, Randolph, Clark, and Washington Streets. Fine New England-style houses stood just down the street. Chicago boasted forty-two hotels, including the sumptuous Richmond House, the elite St. James, and the exclusive Burlington. Yet much of the city had a raw, ragged, and squalid frontier town look.

But Chicago was also a city of miracles. In 1855 it had lifted its entire central district eight feet high out of the mud and cholera-plagued lowlands (three thousand died in the epidemic of 1857). The entire business district between the south branch of the Chicago River and Lake Michigan flooded every spring, and customers would sink to their knees in sludge. George Pullman made a name for himself by elevating the fashionable Tremont House, at the corner of Lake and Dearborn Streets, with five hundred

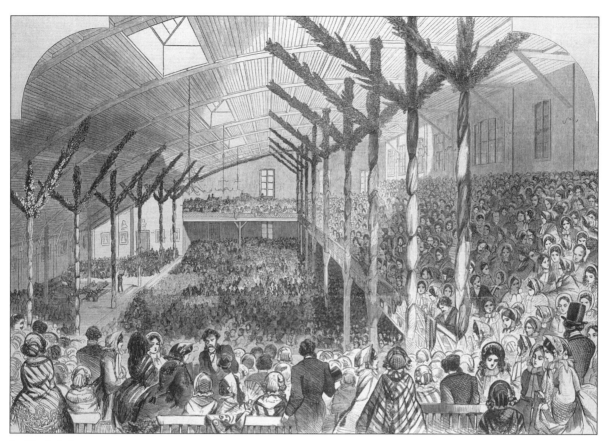

Inside the Wigwam. May 1860. Chicago Historical Society.

men and five thousand jackscrews without breaking a dish. Chicago indeed was a technological marvel rising out of the empty prairie. Even a horse-drawn trolley now moved up and down the new State Street owned by Potter Palmer. Yet, the town's sidewalks were still uneven, rickety boards that sometimes required the use of a ladder. Nonetheless, incredible fortunes were being made by real estate speculators who banked on the city's expansion.

Since its founding, the town had voted for free-wheeling Jacksonian Democracy. Democrat Stephen Douglas was Chicago's man in Washington, making the city rich by bringing the railroads its way with free federal land when other frontier outposts might have been connected. By 1860 Chicago was America's rail center, and the Illinois Central Railroad station along the lakefront at South Water and Lake Streets was the largest in the world.

Even though they controlled the city council, the Democrats had lost the mayor's office as the national party tottered on the slavery issue. With the exception of the Irish, who remained loyal Democrats, Chicago's immigrant population was ready to vote

Republican. The former Democratic congressman, "Long John" Wentworth, was now the city's first Republican mayor. He had publicly broken with Douglas on the slavery question and counseled Lincoln. Despite Wentworth's support for Lincoln, his newspaper endorsed Sam Houston of Texas for president, with Lincoln in the second spot.

Wentworth was a typical Chicago success. In 1836, at age twenty-six, a penniless young Wentworth walked into Chicago from New Hampshire and made a fortune as a publisher. In 1860 the 300-pound, hard-drinking, red-haired mayor still rode his white stallion through the center of town, scandalizing the more genteel society north of the river with his foul mouth and debauchery. His wife was so revolted by Chicago's coarseness that she refused to live in the city where her husband was mayor. So Wentworth traveled east monthly to visit her in Troy, New York.

The Lincoln campaign strategy was worked out in the offices of Joseph Medill's *Press and Tribune* at a meeting of the Republican state committee during the summer of 1859. Lincoln wondered if he should seek the vice presidency instead, but was told by Medill, "It's the presidency or nothing." (Medill's paper formally endorsed Lincoln on November 19, 1859.)

In December 1859 Lincoln's close associate Norman Judd, a powerful Chicago railroad corporate attorney and former Republican state chairman, and Medill, who had been added to the state central committee, plotted to bring the Republican convention to Chicago instead of Indianapolis or St. Louis. It was an important first step in Lincoln's campaign. Judd and Medill met party leaders at New York City's Astor House and argued that the party was in danger of "losing the West" if Republican leaders did not locate the meeting in the "Garden City," especially if they were going to nominate an Easterner like Seward. The party leaders fell for their ploy, and besides, it gave Easterners a chance to see this new boom town everyone was talking about with its grand hotels and railroad connections on the great inland sea.

As the delegates converged on Chicago, the *New York Commercial Advertiser* summed up the situation: "The probabilities are strong that, if, a wise discretion is exercised, the man whom the Chicago Convention nominates, will be the next President of the United States, and the probabilities will become moral certainties if the present breach in the Democratic Party remains unrepaired . . . The future of that [Republican] party to a great extent hangs on the proceedings and decisions of this Convention."

Chicago's first national presidential convention was housed in the Wigwam, an impressive new meeting hall constructed only a month earlier on the site of an old civic landmark, Mark Beaubien's Sauganash Tavern and Hotel at the south fork of the Chicago River. The Wigwam would soon howl with its own "powwow" and war cries as Republican fever swept the city. After all, Chicago's settlers had their own Indian tales to tell.

Back in 1835 the last big powwow of five thousand Potawatomies, Chippewa, and Ottawa, who inhabited the site they called "Chicagou" before white trappers and soldiers drove them out, was held just north of the river where the Wigwam was erected. (They received a million dollars for five million acres of land.) Then the Indians, enraged and sorrowful, crossed the river and snaked a torch-lit dance through the city streets, stopping at each house before they departed at dawn. The wary citizens of the newly incorporated village, fearing another mas-

sacre, cringed at the shrieks and screams of tomahawk-toting warriors as their cries rose like smoke from ceremonial fires.

Chicago's first Wigwam was a two-story, rectangular, pine-board assembly hall, twice the width of other large warehouses scattered along the south bank of the Chicago River. It was hardly a hut, but it took only five weeks to build. The barn-like edifice featured long rows of arched entrances nearly twenty-feet high and even loftier rectangular windows designed to allow air circulation for the ten thousand delegates and supporters who gathered inside. It was wooden on three sides; and the brick fourth wall was shared with a neighboring structure. When the sessions convened, the party activists jammed noisily into the hall, packing it to the rafters, sealing the doors, and overflowing into the dirt streets. The gallery stretched around three sides overlooking the movable stage that was built on wheels. Republicans had made a public appeal for the chairs on which the delegates and spectators sat. Crowning the long, flat roof at the grand entryway arched a fluted wood crescent bearing the name "Republican Party Headquarters." Square turrets stood at each corner topped with flagpoles flying Old Glory. A cupola graced the apex. In front, along the river bank, was a brass cannon ready to fire when the nominee was confirmed. The Wigwam cost $5,000 and withstood the stress of tens of thousands of feet stomping on its floorboards.

Truly, the convention hall—decked out in red, white, and blue garlands, ribbons, streamers, banners, flags, and bunting by the Republican women's club—stood as one of the finest architectural feats in town. Inside, each state's coat of arms was attached to the front of the galleries. Busts of great men and of "Liberty," "Justice," and "Plenty" adorned the stage, supported by figures of Atlas. Some even called it the best political hall in the nation. The wooden edifice was a prefire work of frontier simplicity and political pragmatism. At night, when the gas lights were turned on and all the decorations took on a new luminescence, everyone "fell in love with the great Wigwam . . . and its praises were on more than half a thousand tongues," said one observer.

As the convention neared, Seward shouters rolled in by the thousands on the 150 trains that terminated in Chicago every day. A thirteen-car train from New York was jammed with champagne, oysters, and thousands of hard-drinking, boisterous Seward sup-porters, led by Thurlow Weed, the tall and refined editor of the Albany *Evening Journal* and manager of Seward's campaign and his substantial war chest. Every room in town was booked. Those who found beds paid between $1.50 and $2.50 a night.

Marching bands from New York and Pennsylvania paraded through the dry and dusty streets carousing up the crowds as they toured from saloon to saloon boosting their candidate to the local skeptics. The thousand Seward "irrepressibles" from New York, many dressed in red and green uniforms with beaver hats, staged torchlight processions through Chicago streets, picking up support as they surged forward. They were led by the heavyweight boxing champion of the world, Tom Hyer. But New York's ranks were overshadowed by Pennsylvania's fifteen hundred marchers. To add to the civic celebration, many transplanted Easterners greeted old friends and made new acquaintances. Chicago had never roared before like it did for those three days in May 1860.

Thurlow Weed set up operations in the opulent Richmond Hotel, one of the city's first-class estab-lishments that featured ornate Victorian rooms and marble parlors within its five-story wooden frame. Weed had been in attendance at Chicago's first national convention in 1847, the River and Harbor Convention. Back then he predicted greatness for the small town. Now Weed, who had spent months preparing for this week, was in contact with hun-dreds of political editors and party men from around the nation. (None of the candidates came to the con-vention themselves, although they stayed in eager contact by telegraph.)

Other Seward supporters lodged at the Adams House at Lake Street and Michigan Avenue. All week, spirits were high and the champagne flowed as dele-gate leaders from Michigan, Wisconsin, Minnesota, Massachusetts, and California regularly reported to Boss Weed. They walked away with wads of cash with which to amuse themselves, as the Richmond House rollicked with prenomination celebrations. Chicago proved to be a town of limitless energy.

Lincoln's manager was the formidable Judge David Davis, a downstate Illinois millionaire farmer and jurist, who adjourned the Eighth Circuit Court for a few weeks so "his boys" could work full-time for his candidate's nomination. Davis paid $300-plus to set up operations on the third floor of the newly-built brick Tremont House, the third hotel by that name constructed on the same site. Fifteen hundred slept at the Tremont on the night before the opening ses-sion, many on billiard tables. Other Lincoln support-ers bunked at the Briggs House at Randolph and Wells Streets. During that fateful May week, hundreds of Lincoln allies filed through Davis's quarters where the liquor also flowed. Yarns were spun, free cigar smoke hung thick, and deals were hammered out just as they were by old frontier traders.

Jesse Dubois, Illinois's state auditor, was Davis's wily lieutenant. Chicago lawyer Norman Judd cut deals with the big Eastern railroad men. Lincoln's old Springfield friend Jesse Fell worked the Pennsylvania delegation. Lawyer Leonard Swett tried to break loose Seward votes in Maine. Richard Oglesby, a Whig Free-Soiler, caucused with delegates from his former home state of Kentucky. Lincoln's law partner William Herndon hustled Know-Nothing and Whig delegates from wherever he could find them.

Admission for the convention's opening session was twenty-five cents, in hopes of repaying some of the $2,000 debt. The *Chicago Daily Journal* on May 16, 1860, depicted the scene outside the Wigwam on opening day. "The streets in the vicinity of the Wigwam were thronged by thousands of people who crowded around the doors and windows, congre-gated upon the bridge . . . inside it was standing room . . . The side galleries were filled with ladies . . . The front of the platform was filled with delegates, the alternate delegates, and editors." Women, accompanied by men, were escorted to the bal-conies. Many enterprising Chicago ladies went in several times at the expense of the men on their arms, walking stylishly under colorful parasols, wearing hoop skirts of expensive silks and tafettas, and donning bonnets bold enough to cause a stir.

At 12:10 P.M., Wednesday, May 16, 1860, (Seward's birthday) beneath the garlanded rafters of the Wigwam, the Second Republican National Convention was called to order by Edwin Denison Morgan, governor of New York, and head of the Republican National Committee. In his opening remarks, Morgan affirmed the earnest sense of duty of every delegate. "No body of men of equal number was ever clothed with greater responsibility than those now within the hearing of my voice."

The temporary president of the convention was David Wilmot of Pennsylvania, a founder of the party and an energetic veteran of bitter sectional debate. He had been the author, back in 1846, of a congressional proviso to prohibit slavery in the territories acquired from the Mexican War. Wilmot now took the chair and declaimed the cardinal purpose of the assembly: They must stop the extension of slavery into the territories as endorsed by a patently Southern-controlled administration, and so recently reinforced by the pernicious Dred Scott decision.

Often interrupted by the enthusiastic and animated response of the delegates to his soaring oratory, Wilmot proclaimed, "A great sectional and aristocratic party, or interest, has for years dominated with a high hand over the political affairs of this country. That interest has wrested, and is now wresting, all the great powers of this government to the one object of the extension of slavery. It is our purpose, gentlemen, it is the mission of the Republican Party and the basis of its organization, to resist this policy of a sectional interest . . . It is our purpose to restore the Constitution to its original meaning; to give it its true interpretation; to read that instrument as our fathers read it." Bringing his fist down on the podium, Wilmot insisted, "Slavery is sectional. Liberty national."

Permanent convention president George Ashmun of Massachusetts called on the delegates to "impeach the administration of our general government of the highest crimes which can be committed against a constitutional government, against a free people, and against humanity." The skilled and blazing speeches of Morgan, Wilmot, and Ashmun infused the delegates of the convention from the start with a sense of fiery purpose. And it delighted the spectators who crowded outside the open doors of the Wigwam to listen to shouters repeat each word relayed from the podium. The temporary chairman assigned committees to address procedural rules, delegate credentials, voting protocol, and the all-important platform. The delegates then adjourned to meet again at 10:00 A.M. the next morning.

The second day, May 17, opened with the report on the Committee for Credentials and the convention's first real dissension. Wilmot moved to reconsider the legitimacy of the committee's accepted delegates from Virginia, Maryland, Texas, and Kentucky, the only slaves states represented at the convention, along with the District of Columbia (where slavery was legal) and the territories of Kansas and Nebraska, to be sure they represented a bona fide Republican constituency.

Charles Lee Armour of Maryland rebuffed Wilmot's motion. Living in a slave state as an avowed Republican, Armour declared that he had "dared more than he [Wilmot] had ever dared. I have periled more than he has ever periled. He lives in a free state . . . I faced the mob at Baltimore . . . if ever we expect Republican principles to prevail over all of this land, we must organize, and you who live in the Northern states must fraternize with us, and not despise the day of our small things."

In response to this and other claims of delegates from challenged states and territories, Wilmot replied, "I cast no imputations upon their integrity . . . It was from the purpose of inquiry, not to proscribe or disenfranchise anybody, that my motion was made." Whatever Wilmot's intentions, his motion was clearly not supported by most of the delegates, who chafed at this blot on their unity of purpose and fervor. The debate did force the issue back to the committee, but when it returned to the afternoon session it recommended that the challenged delegates be admitted. This recommendation was promptly adopted by the convention.

Afterward, the rules committee settled the total voting members at 466 (during the nominations, 465 would actually be cast). A simple majority would elect the candidate for president. Outside, crowds swelled to twenty and thirty thousand, all wanting news of what was going on inside, while pickpockets and pamphleteers peppered their midst.

The second session of May 17 was devoted to fashioning a Republican Party platform. The platform, read by William Jessup of Pennsylvania, endorsed the fight against slavery in the new territories. "We deny the authority of Congress, of a territorial legislature, or of any individuals, to give legal existence to slavery in any territory of the United States," it asserted, but added, "We affirm the right of each state to order and control its own domestic institutions according to its own judgment exclusively." Thus, the Republican platform did not call for an end to slavery in the states where it currently was legal.

The new Republicans also called for higher tariffs to protect farmers and workers, protection of states' rights, for a commitment of the federal government to public works, and the pressing necessity for a transcontinental railroad. The platform opposed "any change in our naturalization laws, or any state legislation by which the rights of citizenship hitherto accorded to immigrants from foreign lands shall be abridged or impaired." Strong denunciations of the Dred Scott decision and secessionist ravings topped off the polemic. "We hold in abhorrence all schemes for disunion, come from whatever source they may."

"Of all the manifestations of enthusiasm that we have ever witnessed, anywhere or on any occasion," exclaimed the *Chicago Daily Journal*, "that in the Wigwam immediately succeeding the adoption of the platform . . . was the wildest, the most spontaneous, and the most exciting . . . men waved their hats, women their handkerchiefs, reporters their written pages, and all screamed with joy. This wild excitement was kept up for some ten or fifteen minutes. It was a scene that can never be forgotten by those present, a spectacle that was worth a man's lifetime to witness. It made one feel good all over . . . Its very spirit breathes life and hope and patriotic ardor into the souls of men."

With the platform gloriously completed, Seward's supporters were anxious to march forward. Now it was time to nominate a candidate for president. Tension rose across the floor and in the balcony. The Seward forces were in control, and their chants for their candidate were strong and regular. The delegates decided that they might as well vote now and anoint their man. Seward was their clear choice. It was time to get it over with so the real celebrating could start.

But in an instant, Lincoln's Chicago leaders, who were ever at the podium directing events, convinced party chairman Ashmun that the final tally sheets had not yet been delivered from the printer. Tomorrow was the day for a scheduled vote, they argued. Why disrupt the carefully planned schedule? The Seward supporters were restless but felt no challenge and no real threat. A quick adjournment was pushed through by the Chicago leaders. Seward's followers returned to the plank-board streets and resumed their revels, though most were tiring from a full week of festivities. The quick adjournment would haunt them and change the history of freedom.

Lincoln supporters went to work. The Indiana delegation was solid for Lincoln, its former resident. Radical Republican Henry Lane, who was called the "Liberator of Kansas" because he fought the slave owners, was running for Indiana governor. He warned other delegates that Indiana could lose with Seward at the head of the ticket. There were similar rumblings in Pennsylvania, Maine, and even in the New York delegation. New Jersey might go for Lincoln. Meanwhile,

Horace Greeley had broken with Seward and was backing Bates, who was gaining some support. "Anybody but Seward," Greeley insisted. An opening appeared for the Lincoln strategists.

In the heat of the debate, Lincoln telegraphed Davis and his other top supporters that "I authorize no bargains and will be bound by none." With Davis in charge, Lincoln's words were like a legal disclaimer, just in case something went wrong. Lincoln knew that Davis and his partisans were prepared to give away whatever it took to gain votes. And time was running out.

Davis shot back, "Lincoln ain't here and don't know what we have to meet, so we will go ahead, as if we hadn't heard from him, and he must ratify it." With that as a guiding philosophy, Davis kicked and cajoled and shared his best bourbon and cigars with the Pennsylvania delegation into the late hours before the final day of the convention.

Now they were locked up in conference in the upstairs rooms of the Tremont House. Their opposition meeting broke up after midnight, and Horace Greeley came downstairs to send a telegram back to New York that read "Seward Will Be Nominated on the First Ballot." Desperate, the Lincoln strategists got down to the final hours of exhausting deal cutting.

As darkness deepened and the Seward forces staggered off for some rest, Ward H. Lamon, one of Lincoln's Springfield friends and a former prosecutor, paid a special visit to a Chicago printing house, one of many in town. All night before the third and final session, Lamon directed a crew that forged signatures of convention officials on counterfeit tickets that looked just like the originals.

Early in the morning, Davis, future supreme court justice and U.S. senator, came down to the Tremont lobby, his face flushed with victory. They had done it. He put out the word to a score of ward leaders to organize the Lincoln men. All week the Lincoln forces had laid low, a tactic that Lincoln himself had learned from the Indians during the Black Hawk War back in 1832. Now as the sun rose, thousands of Lincoln supporters who had been routed out of bed suddenly appeared at the Wigwam with their newly-issued tickets. (Norman Judd had arranged with the railroads for a special cheap rate for thousands of Lincoln shouters to travel to Chicago.) All across the city they were reporting ready for action.

By the time Seward's "irrepressibles" arrived after breakfast, the Wigwam's main floor and balconies were packed with excited Lincoln supporters, shouting their admiration for the Rail Splitter. Try as they might, only official Seward delegates could squeeze in. Fights broke out at the entrances, tempers flared. The entire proceedings were delayed for two hours and didn't get under way until noon. Wide Awake Clubs of Lincoln supporters in Illinois and Indiana marched through the streets outside the Wigwam.

Meanwhile, the Seward delegates on stage were isolated between Lincoln supporters and could barely hear each other amid the chants. Lincoln's organizers had recruited one thousand of the loudest shouters in the state. One Lincoln man reputedly could be heard all the way across Lake Michigan. (It was probably a story Lincoln made up himself.) All were organized to take their cues from the Lincoln managers on stage. Unsuspecting delegates whispered, "I didn't know Lincoln was so popular."

Nominating speeches that day were short and sweet, just a sentence long. William Maxwell Evarts, a prominent New York attorney, rose to place Seward's name before the convention. Incredibly, his words were met with a stony silence and only the cheers from the New York delegation broke the hush. Weed knew big trouble was brewing. Norman Judd nominated Lincoln, and on cue the Wigwam broke loose in "immense applause, long continued," with the "Lincoln yawp," as ten thousand vocal chords shook the Wigwam. Lincoln's nomination was seconded by Indiana.

When it was time for the 465 delegates to cast their votes, it would take 233 votes to win the nomination. On the first ballot, Seward was strong, but not as strong as his supporters had thought. Favorite son voting blocked his path to the nomination. Seward rounded up 173 1/2 votes to Lincoln's 102. Cameron polled 50 1/2; Chase, 49; Bates, 48.

Earlier in February, Mayor Wentworth had advised Lincoln, "When it is certain that none of the prominent candidates can be nominated then ought to be your time." Now, his words seemed prophetic. Throughout the week, Lincoln's supporters had argued, "Why go with Seward? He can't win. What will our party be with its second loss? What of our Great Cause? Cannot Lincoln represent it best in his unique way? Lincoln is not a radical like Seward." Suddenly in the pressure cooker of the Wigwam, that argument was making sense to more and more delegates as they switched over to Lincoln on the second and third ballots.

The Chicago floor managers had made sure to seat the Pennsylvania delegation on the stage as far away from New York as possible. Pennsylvania found itself snuggled between Illinois and Indiana, Lincoln's two strongest proponents. Momentum began to shift when suddenly Pennsylvania switched its forty-eight votes to Lincoln on the second round. Judge Davis had cut a deal, and now they were keeping their end of it. Seward's levee began to spill over with Lincoln votes. Out of spite, Greeley convinced Oregon to withhold its forty-eight votes from Seward. Other delegates in Maine and Kentucky and even New York jumped to Lincoln.

At the end of the second ballot, Seward's support rose to 184 1/2, Lincoln had 181, Chase, 42 1/2, Bates, 35. For the first time, the Lincoln delegate leaders knew they could win with Abe. For all their enthusiasm, shrewdness, and money, the arrogance and rowdiness of Seward's New York supporters antagonized undecided Westerners, who felt that they themselves represented the true wellspring and grassroots organization of the new Republican fervor. They associated Seward's men with the corrupt monied interest of the East.

On the third ballot it was Lincoln 231 1/2 to 180 for Seward. Lincoln was short just 1 1/2 votes. Medill, an old Buckeye, turned to the leader of the Ohio delegation and said, "Vote for Lincoln, and Chase can have anything he wants." Chase eventually became Lincoln's secretary of treasury. The convention had in the madness of the moment nominated the darkest dark horse in American political history. On the third ballot, Abraham Lincoln, the former one-term congressman and private attorney from the frontier of Illinois, had received 364 votes to 121 1/2 for the great Free-Soil senator from New York.

Now Chairman Ashmun rose to call for unanimous consent, which quickly followed. Lincoln supporters jumped for joy. Women dropped their fans in the galleries to embrace. Hats were flung in the air, the Wide Awake bands blared on. Outside a scuffle took place around the cannon brought along by the Seward "irrepressibles." But when Captain Elmer Ellsworth of Chicago arrived with his marching Zouaves, they relinquished it. The cannon fired for Lincoln. As it boomed its announcement, all Chicago let out a grand old cheer for the most illustrious moment in the city's short history.

Lincoln was fifty-one at the time of his nomination. The *Chicago Daily Journal*, a Seward supporter, on May 18, 1860, said of the new nominee, "We have long since learned to love him as a true and good man." As almost a second thought, the convention confirmed former Senator Hannibal Hamlin of Maine as vice president over Cassius M. Clay of Kentucky, on the second ballot, to add a shade of experience and to pay for some early Maine support for Lincoln. Then the happy crowd of Lincoln celebrants poured out of the Wigwam and promptly took their turn tearing up and down Chicago's wooden sidewalks, displacing Seward's "irrepressibles" and bragging about how they pulled off the most unlikely of victories. Wide Awakes tramped through the streets in their gold-trimmed blue uniforms and with American eagle oil torches singing their theme, "Ain't You Glad You Joined the Republicans?" Chicago celebrated all night. Fireworks lit up the sky. Several cannons on the balcony of the Tremont House boomed away every half hour until dawn.

Many wondered why Pennsylvania switched so suddenly to Lincoln instead of backing Seward or Bates. Davis later admitted he paid Pennsylvania's price, which was an agreement that Lincoln would nominate Simon Cameron as secretary of the treasury. Cameron became Lincoln's first secretary of war but, because of inefficiency and corruption, he was replaced by Edwin M. Stanton. Chase was appointed to the treasury and in 1864 to the Supreme Court.

Dr. Charles Ray, the *Chicago Daily Press and Tribune* coeditor and owner, had argued, "We want the presidency, and the treasury is not a great stake to pay for it." And what was the total cost of the Lincoln campaign for nomination? The final week rang up at just $700, far less than the estimated half-a-million dollars handed out by the free-spending Weed. But Lincoln later complained that, "I cannot begin to fill all the pledges made in my name."

Downstate in Springfield, Lincoln waited anxiously by the telegraph, following each ballot, trying to relieve the tension in the newsroom of the *Journal* with a folksy tale or two. When news of his nomination arrived, the room broke into cheers, and a hundred guns were fired in the streets beyond. All night Springfield rang triumphantly with the sound of brass bands and parades of local Wide Awakes who stopped outside Lincoln's Eighth Street home. Torches lit up the street. Lincoln filled the doorway and quietly thanked them for their help before going to bed while the crowds celebrated.

The national Democrats had held an April 1860 convention in Charleston, South Carolina. But Stephen Douglas, even with a strong majority, could not muster the two-thirds vote needed for nomination. Then a Dixie Democrat splinter group walked out over the slavery plank. The Northern Democrats reconvened in Baltimore in June to nominate Douglas. The Southern faction nominated Buchanan's vice president, John Cabell Breckinridge of Kentucky, as its presidential candidate, with Senator Joseph Lane of Oregon as his vice president, thus siphoning away Southern votes from Douglas and opening the way for a Republican victory.

A fourth political party joined the 1860 election as well. The Constitutional Union Party nominated John Bell, a former Whig senator from Tennessee over Texas governor Sam Houston. Edward Everett of Massachusetts, who would later be the keynote speaker in 1863 at the ceremony where Lincoln delivered his Gettysburg Address, was Bell's running mate.

Lincoln never left Springfield to campaign during the presidential canvass. Instead, he greeted visitors by the thousands. Neither did he utter provocations on slavery or other issues, merely saying to the press and those who wrote him that, "Those who will not read, or heed, what I have already publicly said, would not read, or heed, a repetition of it." Instead he devoted his attention to the details of how he would run the country if elected. But the Lincoln forces across the nation worked tirelessly, and millions read his words. The price for pieces of a log fence he cut as a boy rose to $20 each.

Seward, always a fighter, crisscrossed the East and West for Lincoln. Weed threw in all of his considerable support and resources, too. When the time came, the new president in turn appointed Seward as secretary of state. Seward did not disappoint Lincoln and performed well during the bitter Civil War.

Douglas campaigned mightily for his state-by-state solution to the slavery issue. But with the Democrats split, he knew his dream of the presidency was gone forever. In the North, he campaigned against Lincoln, in the South against Breckinridge. But Douglas was not yet done. On the election's eve, he rushed South to use his powers of persuasion to try to save the Union. He knew that, if Lincoln were elected, plans for secession had already been drawn up. Douglas spent all of his last energy for his cause and for the Union. Months later, exhausted, he died of typhoid and pneumonia in his room in Chicago's Tremont House in June 1861. He was only forty-eight.

Lincoln dined at the Republican Ladies Club in Springfield on election night, November 6, 1860. The crowds outside were swelling. Soon the news broke: Lincoln had won the key states of the North and was to be the sixteenth president of the United States. The final popular vote gave Lincoln 1,866,452 to Douglas's 1,376,957. But the electoral college vote looked much different, with Lincoln winning 180, Breckinridge, 72, Bell, 39, and Douglas only 12. Lincoln was a minority president, garnering a million less votes than the combined total of his opponents. In fact, as a protest, not a single Lincoln vote was recorded in the South. The United States had a new president, and the bitter winds of civil unrest began to howl across the land.

General George Brinton McClellan
1864 Democratic Presidential Nominee

George Hunt Pendleton
1864 Democratic
Vice Presidential Nominee

Facts-at-a-Glance
★★★

Event:	Ninth Democratic National Convention
Dates:	August 29–31, 1864
Building:	The Amphitheatre, also called the Wigwam
Location:	Lake Park, Michigan Avenue and Park Row (Eleventh Street)
Chicago Mayor:	Francis Cornwall Sherman, Democrat
Candidates for Nomination:	Former President Franklin Pierce, New Hampshire; General George Brinton McClellan, New Jersey; Senator Lazarus W. Powell, Kentucky; former Governor Thomas Hart Seymour, Connecticut
Presidential Nominee:	General George Brinton McClellan
Nickname:	"Little Mac"
Age at Nomination:	37
Number of Ballots:	1
Vice Presidential Nominee:	George Hunt Pendleton, Ohio
Number of Delegates:	231
Number Needed to Nominate:	Two-thirds, 151
Largest Attendance:	10,000
Critical Issues:	The defeat of Lincoln, negotiation of peace between North and South, restoration of the Union, and constitutional rights
Convention Song:	"Hooray for Little Mac"

2
★★★

The 1864 Democratic National Convention
The Copperhead Conspiracy

The first antiwar "conspiracy" surrounding a Chicago Democratic convention did not take place in 1968, but 104 years earlier, in late August 1864. That year the Ninth Democratic National Convention didn't attract idealistic demonstrators and youthful Yippies who came to "freak out" a city, but rather agents of insurrection and arson on a mission to free Southern war prisoners and to burn Chicago to the ground, thus striking a mortal blow against the industrial heart of the North.

In the four long and despairing years of Civil War that followed the election of Abraham Lincoln, millions of Northerners had grown weary, bitter, and uncertain about the wisdom of the president's steadfast course. The North had not won the war. The conflict had not been as short and decisive as everyone had forecasted. The shock of new technological warfare, with its enormous loss of life, and destruction of southern and northern rural culture disoriented everyone. On the battlefield, General Ulysses Simpson Grant had only recently been repulsed at Cold Harbor and Petersburg, Virginia. He shuddered at the "prospect of new rivers of human blood." Southern general Robert Edward Lee dispatched twenty thousand troops to surround Washington, D.C. A chill descended upon the nation. Northerners by the millions were tempted by the peace demands of the discredited and divided Democrats. Horace Greeley grieved in the New York *Tribune* over "our bleeding, bankrupt, and almost dying country."

Many Republicans believed Lincoln could not be reelected. Greeley, in a letter to the mayor of New York, declared, "Mr. Lincoln is already beaten. He cannot be elected. And we must have another ticket to save us from utter overthrow." New York lawyer and staunch Republican George Templeton Strong scribbled in his diary, "Lincoln manifestly loses ground every day. The most zealous Republican partisans talk doubtfully of his chances."

By 1864 Northern Democrats believed voters were ready to turn on Lincoln. He had gone too far, they declared, with his Emancipation Proclamation of January 1, 1863, and his usurpations of constitutional rights. They had been sacrificing and fighting for the Union, yes. Now suddenly they were expected to die, as well, to free slaves who might take their jobs at lower wages. In the process of engineering its war, the government had made slaves of them all, the Copperhead faction of the party charged. Others were angry over random suppressions and denials of constitutional liberties.

Reporting on a party strategy meeting at the White House, John Nicolay, one of Lincoln's private secretaries wrote, "Everything is darkness and doubt and discouragement." The beleaguered president also saw himself already defeated. In a folded letter Lincoln presented to his cabinet less than a week before the Democrats met in Chicago, he asked each to sign it without revealing its doleful contents. It read, "This morning, as for some days past, it seems exceedingly probable that this Administration will not be reelected. Then it will be my duty to so cooperate with the President-elect, as to save the Union between the election and the inauguration; as he will have secured his election on such ground that he cannot possibly save it afterwards."

Chicago of 1864 was divided about the war as well, just as it had been split between Lincoln and Douglas in the years before the agonizing conflict. Though pro-Union sentiment usually prevailed, many Chicagoans hailed from the South or had Southern sympathies that were often expressed openly. The *Chicago Times*, Douglas's old paper, now under the inflammatory editorship of Wilbur Fisk Storey, had been temporarily shut down by General Ambrose Everett Burnside in 1863 for "repeated expression of disloyal and incendiary sentiments." (The general's ample side whiskers gave rise to the term "sideburns.") A mob of twenty thousand came to the rescue of the paper, threatening to burn down the *Tribune* if the *Times* was harmed. Republican Senator Lyman Trumbull, an old friend of Lincoln's, and Chicago's congressional representative, Isaac Arnold, led an appeal to the president himself to rescind Burnside's order or face public discord. Lincoln did so. The next night a mob of abolitionists of equal size and temper turned on Trumbull and Arnold and branded them traitors.

By the end of the war, twenty-six thousand Chicagoans had taken up arms for the Union, and over the front doors of hundreds of Chicago homes draped wind-worn black memorial crepes commemorating a son fallen in uncivil battle. Funeral processions daily wound their way through the jammed city streets. A "draft riot" had even taken place down in the "Patch" at Twelfth Street and Fourth Avenue, where a lawless and defiant group of gamblers, thieves, and roustabouts refused to give their names to marshals taking a poll for military duty. The defiant mob attacked and drove the authorities out. How long could the public be expected to back Lincoln, especially when Union and rebel armies were stalemated in deadly balance? Had not the South already been taught a lesson? Had not the North? If a solution could not be found on the field of battle, perhaps it could be won at the ballot box.

The first political convention of 1864 had been convened in May in Cleveland by a rump group of radical abolitionist Republicans who nominated John C. Fremont, the military hero of California's liberation from Mexico, for president. Fremont was the Gold Rush State's first senator, and the Republican Party's first presidential candidate in 1856. John Cochrane, attorney general of New York, won the vice presidential nomination. Within days the regular Republicans opened their third national convention in Baltimore by renaming themselves the National Union Party. The party sought to distinguish itself from the radicals and to create a home for prowar Democrats, such as Andrew Johnson, the military governor of Tennessee, who would become Lincoln's running mate. The convention solidly advocated the abolition of slavery, to be insured by a constitutional amendment and the unconditional surrender of the South. The platform included a call for more immigration, confirmed the Monroe Doctrine, and demanded the completion of the transcontinental railroad. Controlled by the administration, the delegates renominated Lincoln on the first ballot.

Originally, the Democrats of 1864 scheduled their convention for the week of July Fourth. Then they delayed the gathering as long as possible, hoping to gauge the antiwar sentiment growing throughout the North. Their delay seemed to work. General Grant was repelled at Richmond, General William Tecumseh Sherman stalled outside Atlanta. The press was bitter in its attacks on Lincoln. As the heat of August inevitably rose, so did the pleas of millions who yearned for peace and restoration of the Union as a loose confederation of states. The Democrats answered with a plan for immediate relief.

As the Ninth Democratic National Convention approached, Chicago surged again, as it had four years earlier. Tens of thousands of Democratic Party members, political activists, con men, schemers, gamblers, operatives, Confederate soldiers out of uniform, spies, agent provocateurs, and spectators arrived in town demanding peace, even if it took violence to make their point. It was "cot accommodations" only at hotels, such as the new Sherman House at Clark and Randolph, owned by Mayor Francis C. Sherman. At the Richmond House, guests received a free copy of the Emancipation Proclamation from owner and abolitionist Thomas Richmond. Finding room for the crushing stream of newcomers was all but impossible.

To local businessmen, downtown property owners, and strident prowar voices like the *Tribune*, the wave of political immigrants looked sinister. Many of the men who gathered in threatening groups about town were clearly Southern ruffians ready for trouble. Bowie knives and guns were flashed on the streets, and belligerent visitors took their arguments from saloon to saloon stirring up unrest. "The Union element was compelled to stand passive, and let the whelming wave of opposition sweep over it," residents complained. The city fathers knew well enough that their wooden town was terribly vulnerable. With almost all its military might out of town and engaged in war maneuvers and an overcrowded prisoner-of-war camp just outside its limits, the young city lay virtually defenseless.

Camp Douglas was a constant source of concern. Constructed on the estate of the late Senator Douglas at Thirty-Third Street and Cottage Grove Avenue, the camp was just east of land owned by John Wentworth. As an induction center for northern recruits, it was initially erected as a tribute to the Little Giant. Now it was a hideous curse on the city. Its twelve thousand "Johnny Reb" prisoners, ill-clothed and sparsely fed, anxiously awaited freedom. They wanted out. In the face of inadequate security, citizen patrols stood vigil each night as the convention approached. Tension was building all around town.

Rumors of a violent conspiracy, of an armed jail-break from Camp Douglas, of arson, looting, rape, and plunder sent the fashionable North Side residential neighborhoods into a state of near panic over the "rebel invasion." Men armed themselves. Women and children left for Wisconsin. Chicago itself stood in peril before the elaborate criminal plan designed to destroy it.

Or was it just self-induced fear? Democrats argued they were convening to do nothing more than nominate a president who would lead the nation to peace. The name of General George Brinton McClellan, hardly a rebel sympathizer, was on their lips. One Republican noted, "The shibboleth of the house was 'peace at any price.' And when one side charged that such an attitude was treason to the nation, the other retorted that coercion was treason to the Constitution." Throughout the week, Copperheads and Republicans hurled insults and provocations at one another in their newspapers and in the city's saloons where political life was its most lively.

If the rumors were true, Chicago had much to lose in the conflagration. The war had not only bereaved the city of its valiant, patriotic sons, but it had, as if by some countervailing force, also made many of its leading citizens incredibly wealthy. As the second leading war supplier after New York, Chicago drove the Union war machine with arms and material from its burgeoning industrial base. The McCormick reaper, by itself, freed up thousands of farm workers to fight for the cause. Chicago's stockyards kept the army and civilians well fed. Shipping lanes from Chicago supplied the troops with ammunition.

During the war years, the city's population almost doubled from 109,000 in 1860 to estimates as high as 180,000 in 1864. Thousands of immigrants and Americans had arrived by train, horse, and foot. Buildings were going up on every street in town, and new streets were being marked off every day. The young town now sprawled more than twenty-four square miles. Finding shelter for the crushing stream of newcomers was extremely difficult. Real estate values and rents soared. Wages for skilled working men doubled every few months; so did prices. Millionaires were made each year. Opulence abounded in residential and business dwellings in which the successful lived and worked. The central

The Amphitheatre, Michigan Avenue and Eleventh Street, site of the 1864 Democratic National Convention. Chicago Historical Society.

business district showed off new marble facades featuring stylish squares of plate glass windows. New five-story buildings even featured elevators manufactured of wood and metal, as the city thrust upward, as well as outward.

But the war left others destitute and hungry. The *Tribune* confessed, "We probably have a greater number of poor to care for now than ever before, not only because our population has greatly increased, but we have here hundreds of soldiers' wives, with families of children, who will be unable to gain a livelihood from their own efforts at labor, with greatly enhanced rates of all living expenses."

Along with human desperation and economic growth came the first sludge of industrial waste. The *Tribune* now called the Chicago River "the vilest cesspool in the West." Its pungent smell drove Chicagoans indoors during the hottest days. The lakefront reeked with stacks of horse manure that had been dumped there by street cleaners who found the alleys already stacked to the hilt with the stinking debris.

On the city's wooden sidewalks, along with dignified representatives of Chicago society and business, strolled hundreds of gamblers, thieves, and prostitutes. Years earlier Mayor Wentworth had burned down their scalawag haunt, called the Sands, on the river east of Michigan Avenue. Now they congregated in the downtown district bounded by Clark and Wells, Van Buren and Madison. Crime of every sort was rampant. Murders, burglaries, and railroad accidents all grabbed daily news headlines. The streets were packed with crowds lured by the excitement, the opportunities, the necessities of survival. In the eyes of all comers, Chicago represented a chance to strike it rich.

Despite the city's shortcomings, Chicagoans of 1864 had done their best to raise themselves above its more primitive aspects with a full-scale embrace of "culture." McVicker's Theater (where John Wilkes Booth thrilled audiences), Mabie's Winter Garden, Bryan Hall, and Metropolitan Hall put on extravagant productions featuring the most popular plays and shows of the season. Scores of concerts, balls, masquerades, and festivals all kept the leisure classes well entertained during the frontier town's long and raw winters.

Chicago had the nation's attention. The city was a dynamo, a prairie fire, a place to marvel and behold. Even European royalty visited the "Urbs in Horto,"

the City in a Garden, as it was called because of the oak, ash, maple, elm, birch, hickory, and cottonwood trees that lined the streets. Famed artists and lecturers put on nightly displays to educate and inspire the public. Frederick Douglass, the escaped slave, abolitionist, and author exhorted a crowd against the error of the Underground Railroad. He praised the brave people who ran the operation, but condemned their methods. (In 1863 Chicago's African-American population numbered only several hundred people.) Just as parts of the city were shabby beyond belief, other parts were wonderfully elegant and fabulously ornate, attracting thousands to its exotic intrigues. For the rebels to commit Chicago to flames, and inflict upon it significant fear and damage, would hamper the war effort itself and destroy the morale of Northern soldiers who had left their home defenseless.

All that last week of August, poorly dressed rogues rode into town on horseback, in wagons, and on foot from southern Illinois, Indiana, Kentucky, Ohio, Michigan, and the East to assemble at a huge, new amphitheatre called the second Wigwam, named after its 1860 predecessor.

The second Wigwam was built with money from private subscriptions and resembled a giant circular barn. It had a low, sleek, sloped canvas roof flaring upward at the edge like a colossal saucer looming against the green-blue lake water. The wooden building was located in Lake Park, the narrow man-made park along Michigan Avenue and Park Row (Eleventh Street), fronting a lagoon that lay beyond Lake Park (later known as Grant Park). The Democrats had to initiate a lawsuit to get it built across from the luxurious homes on lower Michigan Avenue. They won since it was a temporary structure.

By the time the national assembly opened on August 29, 1864, the Democratic Party had shed its Southern faction that had wrecked Douglas's presidential chances and driven the South toward secession. The Northern Democrats now had new issues dividing their party. The Copperhead faction, an epithet originally coined by their Republican opponents after the deadly snake of the same name, were by 1864 proudly wearing in their lapels the Liberty head cut from a copper penny as a symbol of their affinity to states' rights and their aggressive disdain toward the heavy-handed policies of the Lincoln administration. Copperheads favored an immediate end to hostilities and a negotiated peace with the South. Other

Democrats still supported the war effort but were vehemently opposed to Lincoln and his abrogation of constitutional rights and liberties for states and individuals. A third and much smaller faction supported both the war and Lincoln and boycotted the Chicago convention, joining with the National Union Party.

After the attack on Fort Sumter, the Democratic Party, so long identified with Southern sympathies, became the orphan child of the political North. Literally torn asunder by the war, it was losing much of its strength and leadership to the South. While professing to support preservation of the Union, it found itself too often in the ticklish and embarrassing position of defending the South's odious institution of slavery and the rebellious and blatant treason of its masters. Particularly in the border states, Democratic Party members had suffered censorship and arrest by an administration vigorous in its desire to quench rebellious dissent through any means necessary, constitutional or not.

With all these disadvantages, however, the Democrats—ever resilient and ably led—managed to survive, and, in some states like New York, flourish. Ironically, the party's survival was helped by the very conflict that almost destroyed it, for this cruel and fratricidal war, with all its economic and emotional instabilities, grim casualty lists, heartaches, and tragedies was inevitably linked to the administration in power. The Democratic Party was a natural haven for dissent and a well-organized sounding board for the many honest and patriotic Northerners disgusted with the corruption and abuses of the burgeoning bureaucracy necessary to prosecute a huge and costly war. In fact, an active party of dissent, well-placed to readily denounce the excesses and unjust policies of the administration in power, was a decided advantage the North possessed over the one-party South.

So the Democratic Party did not limp into Chicago but rather arrived surefooted, determined, and with a confident swagger. With the right platform and the right candidate the presidency would be won, they believed. But obstacles lay before them. The Democratic Party was not without its factions and tensions. Two opposing groups were marshaled by moderate Democrats into a tenuous coalition. The Purists, known for their peace-at-any-price stance, were ever faithful, but extreme. They burdened the party with the many avowed Copperheads in their ranks. The Purists were opposed by the

Legitimists, or War Democrats, who while crying foul about the administration's inefficiencies and repression considered the Union paramount and would attempt no reconciliation with the South until she acquiesced, preferably by negotiation, but if necessary through the continued force of war.

To win, the Democrats needed a national leader to succeed Douglas—the Little Giant had died in 1861—who could unite all factions. Ironically, they found their peace leader in a trained though tarnished warrior, General George B. McClellan, who had been dismissed from his command of the Army of the Potomac in 1862 by Lincoln and replaced by Ambrose Burnside. McClellan was nothing if not precocious. A West Point cadet at age fifteen, he graduated near the top of his class to the elite Corps of Engineers at nineteen. He returned to West Point as a twenty-one-year-old veteran of the Mexican War after serving with distinction under General Winfield Scott, alongside fellow engineer officer Robert E. Lee.

After several routine and a few plum stateside appointments, McClellan, an ardent student of military history and a freshly appointed captain of twenty-nine, was sent abroad in 1855 by Secretary of War Jefferson Davis to study Europe's armies. He witnessed the Allies' siege of Sevastopol during the Crimean War. Fluent in French and German, he immersed himself in the Continent's military texts and even taught himself Russian and became the American authority on that army's organization. In addition to being serious, bright, and well-connected, his published reports of his European experience marked him as a rising star in the United States army.

However, the peacetime army proved too stagnant for McClellan's animated ambition, and he resigned his commission in 1857. Equally successful as a civilian, he became, at the ripe age of thirty-two, vice president of the Illinois Central Railroad. Posted in Chicago from 1857 to 1860, he energetically directed the railroad's expansion and entertained former army pals at his lakefront home. At the outbreak of war in 1861, he was naturally considered for high command by General Scott. As a major general in command of troops in western Virginia he achieved some small but widely-reported victories.

After the first debacle at Bull Run, he was called east to command and reorganize what became known as the Army of the Potomac. A master at organization and morale and looking every bit the Young Napoleon the adoring press called him, McClellan became, at age thirty-four, commander-in-chief of all Union armies. After providing for the defense of Washington, he brilliantly forged a formidable and impressive force. Convinced of the enemy's even greater strength (numbers documented by reams of misinformation gathered by former Chicago private detective Allan Pinkerton, his intelligence chief), McClellan was hesitant to engage his forces in battle.

Lincoln thought his young general suffered from a case of the "slows" and patiently, but firmly, prodded him to action. In the spring and summer of 1862, McClellan ponderously moved his army by way of the James Peninsula to within sight of Richmond only to be outgeneraled and intimidated by Lee and his army. By late summer, he was forced to retreat back to Washington. Here, his clumsy and tardy support of Union troops engaged with Stonewall Jackson near Manassas contributed to the Union defeat at the second battle of Bull Run. Cabinet members, led by Secretary of War Edwin McMasters Stanton, called for his dismissal, but Lincoln, while admitting Little Mac was "good for nothing" in an offensive campaign, knew the general had the confidence of the now beaten and disorganized troops. McClellan conducted one more campaign to resist Lee's invasion into Maryland. The resulting battle of Antietam in September was an awful and bloody stalemate, but enough of a Union victory to enable Lincoln to announce his Emancipation Proclamation.

After McClellan allowed Lee to retreat back to Virginia unchallenged, Lincoln, having "tried long enough to bore with an auger too dull to take hold," was convinced McClellan would not fight and replaced him with Burnside. McClellan was ordered to Trenton, New Jersey, to await further orders, while Lincoln and his cabinet decided what to do with him. Little Mac was serenaded and applauded at every train station on his way to Trenton, a clear signal to leading Democrats of the general's undying popularity.

Lincoln knew McClellan, as a longtime Democrat, was a potentially formidable political rival and even considered offering him a high command if he would remain out of politics. But McClellan, his ego deeply wounded, ignored any attempts by his friends at reconciliation with the administration except on his own terms. In the summer of 1864, on indefinite leave and still drawing his general's salary, the short, handsome thirty-seven-year-old awaited his party's call.

The crowds outside the second Wigwam were even more passionate and reckless than those who assembled inside to demand peace. The most extreme of the Copperhead Lincoln-haters and race-baiters set up operations at the Sherman House. Former Ohio congressman Clement Laird Vallandigham's pro-Southern, antiwar statements were considered so seditious that Lincoln had banished him to the South. He had just circuitously returned by way of Canada and was running for governor of Ohio. From the Sherman House balcony, favorites of the radical wing of the Democratic Party, many of whom had served jail time in the "Lincoln bastille," harangued crowds that surged into the tens of thousands, whipping them to a fever pitch.

Lincoln's observer at the convention, Noah Brooks, a Maine journalist turned Washington correspondent for the *Sacramento Union*, wrote the president: "The assemblage of Democrats here is very large indeed and they appear to manifest a great deal of enthusiasm." According to Brooks, one word beat in their pulse, "Peace, Peace, Peace." To Union newspapers, the entire week was nothing but a "Copperhead Orgy."

It fell upon Chicago's quixotic former mayor, "Long John" Wentworth, now serving as police commissioner, to stand fearlessly alone in defense of the Union against the firebrands who invaded his city. Wentworth, in official attendance at a Copperhead rally, brazenly challenged Vallandigham to an open debate on the courthouse's north stairs across from the Sherman House on the evening of August 26. The Courthouse Square itself had declined considerably in grace during the war years. But the circular balcony on top of the Courthouse still attracted plenty of sightseers. From this day, the Courthouse would become the center of civic pride for generations to come. Wentworth loved the give-and-take of a brawling debate and was used to swinging it out with an opponent.

Before a huge crowd, the former mayor pulverized Vallandigham's narrow constitutional arguments with patriotic fervor and rhetorical appeals. As an old Chicago pro, he knew enough to use a megaphone to address the distant and rowdy gathering so his arguments could be heard. His opponent, used to the luxuries of a legislative assembly, was unheard by most of the throng.

Wentworth proclaimed that "while he was thus deprecating war and violence, I listened in vain for one single breath of censure, one word of reproof from his lips, of those who first madly unchained the ugly demon, and let loose the storm of deadly hate . . . Why this omission, why this studied silence on the part of Mr. Vallandigham?" The Copperheads tried to shout him down, but his powerful and commanding voice routed them. " . . . [Let] us push on in the race of civilization and progress, and reach the summit of greatness and glory. . ." Wentworth won the exchange and soon thereafter was nominated for his sixth term in Congress.

At noon on Monday, August 29, 1864, the turbulent throng was called to order by August Belmont, a wealthy New York banker and chairman of the Democratic National Committee, with a blistering speech as hot as the midday crowd: "Four years of misrule, by a sectional, fanatical and corrupt party, have brought our country to the very verge of ruin." Belmont warned that Lincoln's reelection could only end in "the utter disintegration of our whole political and social system amidst bloodshed and anarchy, with the great problems of liberal progress and self-government jeopardized for generations to come."

Temporary chairman William Bigler of Pennsylvania highlighted the small, but potentially fatal rift between the Purists and the Legitimists when he argued that the party's purpose was "the overthrow, by the ballot, of the present administration, and the inauguration of another, in its stead, which shall directly and zealously, but temperately and justly, . . . bring about a speedy settlement of the national troubles on the principles of the Constitution and on terms honorable and just to all sections, North and South, East and West . . . one which shall have no conditions precedent to the restoration of the Union."

There was the rub. The Legitimists thought it was political suicide for the party to accept reconciliation with the South without at least one very important concession: The enemy must acknowledge the irrevocability and sanctity of the federal union before any talk of armistice or reconstruction. The Purists felt no terms were necessary for readmittance except the laying down of arms. Whichever way the convention went would be settled in its platform fight. And when the committees were established shortly after Bigler's address, the platform committee would lean decidedly in the direction of the Purists, if Vallandigham, a member on the committee, had anything to say about it.

For it was policy more than the candidate that would be debated by this convention. McClellan

was a sure thing going in. There was dissent from Maryland delegates, where Little Mac had declared martial law, closed the legislature and arrested more than a few political leaders, but everyone realized that McClellan was the most popular Democrat of the day and eminently electable. The convention's hardest task was drafting a platform that McClellan, a strict war Democrat, would not repudiate.

New York Governor Horatio Seymour, the permanent president of the convention and longtime peace advocate, opened the second day with a florid denunciation of Lincoln and a call for peace that was cheered vociferously by the delegates. "If the administration cannot save this Union, we can. Mr. Lincoln values many things above the Union; we put it first of all. He thinks a proclamation worth more than peace; we think the blood of our people more precious that the edicts of the president."

Seymour, who would be the party's candidate four years later, claimed the Republican Party was responsible for the nation's woes and a cruel, divisive war. He called for its overthrow. "Four years ago it had its birth upon this spot. Let us see, by our action, that it shall die here where it was born."

Ohio Congressman Samuel S. Cox charged, "Abraham Lincoln has deluged the nation with blood, created a debt of four thousand million dollars, and sacrificed two million human lives. At the November election we will damn him with eternal infamy. Even Jefferson Davis is no greater threat to the Constitution." After tumultuous applause, Seymour called for the report from the Committee on Resolutions.

Six resolutions were heartily endorsed. The second declaration charged, in part, that "the Constitution itself has been disregarded in every part, and public liberty and private right alike trodden down and the material prosperity of the country essentially impaired—justice, humanity, liberty, and the public welfare demand that immediate efforts be made for a cessation of hostilities, with a view to an ultimate convention of the states, or other peaceable means, to the end that at the earliest practicable moment peace may be restored on the basis of the federal union of the states."

As the peace plank was read into the record, thousands of voices drowned it out with wild cheers of affirmation. After the turmoil subsided, the plank was read again, this time to a totally silent, somber sea of tired and hopeful faces. When the chairman's voice quieted, a dozen more vocal demonstrations followed on the floor. The convention had, in the spirit of compromise, adopted the policies of the peace wing of the party in order to agree to the nomination of the War Democrats' candidate, McClellan. Then the second session adjourned, and the invaders slipped into the darkness of Chicago streets and the glow of its saloons.

Long before the convention began, federal authorities collected evidence that Confederate diplomat Jacob Thompson, formerly President Buchanan's secretary of the interior, had smuggled $250,000 in sterling silver into Canada to organize a Camp Douglas escape. Informants further alleged that Colonel G. St. Leger Grenfell and J. T. Shanks were coordinating a plot to free the twelve thousand prisoners and set them loose on Chicago during the Democratic convention. The insurgent army would then turn South to free more prisoners in Indianapolis. Two secret organizations sympathetic to the rebel cause, the Knights of the Golden Circle and the Sons of Liberty, meanwhile had stockpiled weapons for just this uprising. Armed delegates to the convention were to be cued to join in the planned insurrection. Despite the discovery of weapons and ammunition, the authorities did nothing to counter the threat.

But on the second day of the convention, Camp Douglas Commandant General J. B. Sweet himself feared the worst and wired for reinforcements. Some 8,350 rebel prisoners captured at Fort Donelson and Fort Henry were guarded by just 736 Union soldiers. To his relief, one thousand reinforcements from the 109th Pennsylvania Infantry rode in from Milwaukee. Word of their timely arrival spread quickly through the tense city and abruptly broke the fever of anticipation and fear. Conspiracy leaders quietly passed the word that their assault would be delayed until the element of surprise could be regained. The city would not burn.

On the last day of August, the Democrats moved swiftly to endorse their candidate. Against McClellan stood three others: former President Franklin Pierce; Kentucky Senator Lazarus W. Powell; and former Governor Thomas Hart Seymour of Connecticut. Before the first ballots were cast, both the names of Pierce and Powell were withdrawn to allow for a two-way horse race. Surprisingly, criticism of McClellan was severe among Seymour supporters.

Congressman Benjamin Gwinn Harris of Maryland caught the convention off guard when he shouted, "Do you want McClellan because he is a great general? Why, he has never won a battle. Does he stand for liberty? Why, the military oppression under which Maryland suffers was instituted by him . . . All the charges I can make against the Lincoln administration, I can make against McClellan." Suddenly a fight broke out at the podium, and Harris knocked down an assailant who rushed to stop him. Harris was armed and threatened to kill anyone who interfered with his right of free speech. How could the Democrats offer McClellan as a real peace alternative? What loyalty would he have for the party or its positions? His questions would haunt the Democrats.

Most of the four hundred delegates derided Harris's remarks. On the first ballot, McClellan secured the nomination, 202 1/2 to Seymour's 28 1/2, after some last-minute horse-trading and switches. The nomination was in deference to the War Democrats, who controlled the party. A fifteen-minute celebration, a cacophony of boisterous voices, musical instruments, and even a ceremonial cannon outside the Wigwam greeted the nomination. McClellan's executive committee rushed the stage carrying a large portrait of the general, hoisting it high for all to salute. The band played "Hail to the Chief" to an empty chair beneath the general's portrait. The delegates and party partisans waved their handkerchiefs in adulation.

Congressman George Hunt Pendleton of Ohio, well-known as one of the country's most ardent Copperheads, was designated to join McClellan on the national Democratic ticket of 1864. Then the great Democratic horde dispersed into Chicago's streets where it lit fireworks, torches, and bonfires along the lake to celebrate through the night in what a French visitor called a "political saturnalia." The *Tribune* denounced the entire affair as the "most unblushing and shameless utterances of treason, unveiled incitements to revolt against the Government." On the night of McClellan's nomination, crowds of Democrats sang in the streets as they tramped from the Tremont House to the Sherman House: "Hurray for Little Mac . . . Ol Abe's a Tyrant, Mac's for Us."

A full week passed before McClellan received the official mail notification of his nomination, though his executive committee was already hard at work putting together a national campaign to defeat Lincoln. Just as Harris had warned, McClellan accepted the nomination, but repudiated the peace plank that had represented the convention's spirit. The convention had failed in its central purpose of giving voters the choice of a peace candidate, and it had failed as a shield for a demoralizing Copperhead assault. Perhaps it made no difference, because the long summer of military stalemates suddenly came to a dramatic halt as David Glasgow Farragut's navy closed Mobile Bay, and Sherman's army, filled with many Chicago recruits, set fire to Atlanta. A month later, General Philip Henry Sheridan won successive victories in the Shenandoah Valley. As a political consequence, Fremont quit the presidential race, seeing now that Lincoln's victory was certain.

With desperate hopes of demoralizing Lincoln voters and saving the election for McClellan, many of the original Chicago convention conspirators regrouped and prepared again for a Camp Douglas breakout before the November election. A thousand armed men were clandestinely poised to storm the vulnerable facility that had again let its guard down. The regiment of rebel escapees was scheduled to join the Sons of Illinois outside the Courthouse, before they spread out in all directions setting fire to the city's wooden structures. They would stuff the ballot boxes and steal the election for McClellan along the way. Simultaneous rebellions were allegedly planned for Missouri, southern Illinois, Indiana, and Ohio.

Before the conspirators could act, the plot was again foiled by informants. The U.S. Judge Advocate issued arrest warrants served by soldiers against leading coconspirators. On the eve of the November election, a dozen men were arrested, including two former mayors: Judge Buckner S. Morris, the city's second mayor, who secretly served as treasurer for the Sons of Liberty; and Levi Boone, the city's fourteenth mayor who had been an anti-immigrant Know-Nothing. Along with leaders of the various factions, the two luminaries were hauled into court on conspiracy charges.

Cynics cried "foul." After all, it was well-known that Judge Morris was a War Democrat who supported the Union, they said. He ultimately was found innocent, but his reputation was ruined. Five of the ringleaders, including Mayor Boone and Charles Walsh, who was a Sons of Liberty brigadier general, were convicted and jailed. Colonel G. St. Leger Grenfell was sentenced to death. (The sentence was never carried out.) Others were acquitted. Whether or not the conspiracy had been real or simply feared, the danger passed. The Democrats, who left Chicago with high hopes, were overwhelmingly defeated at the polls. On the eighth of November, four million Northerners voted for president. Lincoln garnered 55 percent of the popular vote and an electoral college landslide of 234 to 21 for McClellan.

Then, for another five tormenting months, the nation endured more fighting. Soldiers died, and families grieved. Finally, Robert E. Lee surrendered to Ulysses S. Grant at the Appomattox Courthouse on April 9, 1865. Lee had been overwhelmed by the superiority of the North and its bountiful resources and yielded to the methodical and orderly military campaign of Grant of Illinois, the man who would be hoisted to the presidency by Chicago's next national political convention. Within a week after the surrender, amid the strange and exulted relief, a lonely and enigmatic president whom Chicago loved and celebrated was assassinated by John Wilkes Booth, a man the city had cheered on the stages of its theaters and whom the president himself had applauded six months earlier. Though none had thought it possible, the nation now mourned in peace as it had in war.

Ulysses Simpson Grant
1868 National Union Republican
Presidential Nominee

Schuyler Colfax
1868 National Union Republican
Vice Presidential Nominee

Facts-at-a-Glance
★★★

Event:	National Union Republican Party Convention
Dates:	May 20–21, 1868
Building:	Crosby Opera House
Location:	Washington Street between State and Dearborn Streets
Chicago Mayor:	John Blake Rice, Republican
Candidate for Nomination:	Ulysses Simpson Grant, Illinois
Presidential Nominee:	Ulysses Simpson Grant
Age at Nomination:	46
Number of Ballots:	1
Vice Presidential Nominee:	Speaker of the House Schuyler Colfax, Indiana
Number of Delegates:	650
Number Needed to Nominate:	A majority, 326
Largest Attendance:	3,000
Critical Issues:	Reconstruction, impeachment of Andrew Johnson, repayment of debts, lower interest rates and taxes, immigration
Campaign Slogan:	"Let Us Have Peace"

3
★★★

The 1868 National Union Republican Convention

To the Victors Belong the Spoils

With the end of the Civil War came the enormous problems of reuniting a badly scarred nation and adjusting to the new industrialism that was radically transforming American life. Voters, who now included male blacks in both the North and South (there were four million African Americans in 1868), faced the task of choosing a new national leader to replace the martyred Lincoln and his ill-fated successor, War Democrat Andrew Johnson, who was still in the middle of his senatorial impeachment trial.

Johnson had inflamed Congress with his moderate Reconstruction policies and by dismissing Lincoln's Secretary of War Edwin M. Stanton. Johnson had further declared that the sitting Thirty-Ninth Congress was illegitimate because it only represented northern states. He therefore denied that it had the right to enact the Fourteenth Amendment of the Constitution that granted full citizenship rights to ex-slaves, as well as other laws of Reconstruction.

Four days before the Republicans gathered for their fourth convention, Johnson had been exonerated by only one vote (thirty-nine in favor of impeachment, nineteen opposed, two-thirds required for conviction), on the critical Article 11 of the Articles of Impeachment for his alleged "crimes and misdemeanors." Illinois's two senators split on the issue, with Lyman Trumbull, a Lincoln stalwart, denouncing Johnson's policies, but casting a decisive vote for acquittal.

"The question to be decided," Trumbull told his senatorial colleagues, "is not whether Andrew Johnson is a proper person to fill the presidential office, nor whether he is fit to remain in it; nor indeed whether he has violated the Constitution and the laws in other respects than those alleged against him. As well might any other fifty-four persons take upon themselves by violence to rid the country of

Andrew Johnson because they believed him to be a bad man, as to call upon fifty-four senators, in violation of their sworn duty, to convict and dispose him for any other causes than those alleged in the articles of impeachment." Trumbull felt the president had full authority to remove Secretary Stanton, though he thought it ill-advised.

In response, Senator George Henry Williams charged, "I shall vote for conviction. Whenever the Chief Magistrate of this country makes a public blasphemer of himself, and, going about the country, in speeches excites resistance to law and defends mob violence and murder, I think he ought to be removed from office." The senator bellowed, "I have been sorrowfully and reluctantly brought to the conclusion that Andrew Johnson is a bad man; that the policies of his administration have been to rule or ruin; that he has endeavored, by usurpation and the abuse of his veto, to subordinate the legislature to his personal views and purposes; and that his official career and example have been to injure, degrade, and demoralize the country; and I believe that his removal from office will invigorate the laws, vindicate the Constitution, and tend greatly to restore unity and peace to the nation." Court was adjourned until May 26.

To select a man to succeed Johnson, the Republicans returned to the land of Lincoln. The national convention convened on Wednesday, May 20, in the ostentatious Crosby Opera House on Washington Street between State and Dearborn. It was considered by some "the most imposing art temple in the country" and was the jewel of Chicago's cultural life.

The giant edifice was the brainchild of Uranus H. Crosby, a one-time Massachusetts brewer, who had anticipated war taxes on liquor and stored enough before their imposition to become fabulously wealthy.

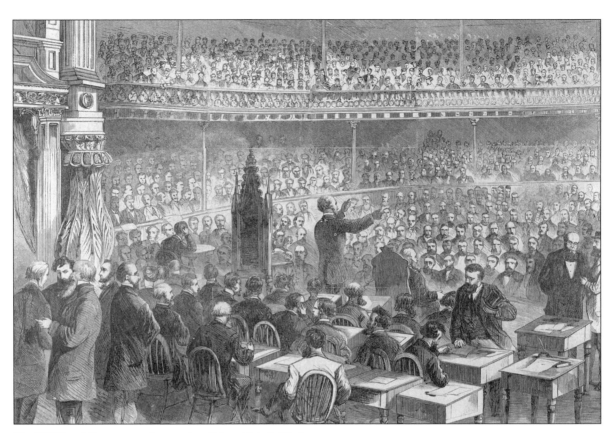

The 1868 Republican convention session. Chicago Historical Society.

The $700,000 grand opera house brought the city new cultural distinction, though its owner was later caught in a scam to auction it away, with the winning ticket going to one of his fronts. At street level, the building housed W. W. Kimball's piano store and John Wright's (Chicago's "first schoolmaster") restaurant. Suites of offices occupied the second floor, while a first-class art gallery, with ten artists' studios, filled its third level. An immense auditorium in the rear of the giant structure, with sixty-five private boxes, could entertain three thousand spectators. It was here that the Republican delegates gathered. A smaller concert hall for music lovers had a State Street entrance.

Once again the new party offered voters a new name, the National Union Republican Party. General Daniel Edgar Sickles, who had lost a leg at Gettysburg, led the procession into the opera house. New Jersey Governor Marcus L. Ward, chairman of the national committee, gaveled the 650 delegates and thousands of spectators to order. The party, he shouted, was here assembled to "declare your unswerving attachment to the Union and liberty, and to pledge you will take no steps backward in the work of reconstructing the rebel states and re-estab-

lishing the Union." Ward continued, "An emancipated race has been lifted from the debasement of slavery, and today, with the Union men of the South, reorganizes in the name of liberty the government and institutions of the rebellious states."

This was a generals' convention in which the nation's military leaders were hailed as conquering heroes and rewarded for their valor on the field of battle. The convention's first act was to appoint General Carl Schurz, now a Missouri newsman, as its temporary chairman. He made a few perfunctory remarks. Then, as a gesture of openness, delegates from all states, including those from the South, not just those represented in the current Congress, were voted convention seats. Colorado, although denied statehood by President Johnson's veto, was also given delegate votes and promised entry into the Union under the next administration. In all, thirty-eight states and four territories joined the deliberations, with each given two delegates for every congressional member.

After his ceremonial duties, General Schurz turned the gavel over to the convention's permanent chair, Connecticut's former governor, General Joseph R.

Hawley. In reviewing the course of history since the party's last Chicago convention, Hawley asserted that "God then ruled our council. He made our declaration of principles manly and severe. He gave us Abraham Lincoln for president." Hawley paused, "May He send us like wisdom and success today." The delegates responded with ovations as the chairman predicted further success for the party's divine mission.

Next, General Lucius Fairchild of Wisconsin and representatives from the Soldiers' and Sailors' Convention that was concurrently meeting in Chicago appeared before party delegates, asking for permission to address the assembly. Their request was granted, and they presented a resolution to the National Union Republicans calling on them to adopt their recommendation for president. The entire auditorium echoed with shouts of approval as the veterans offered up the name of the nation's greatest living hero, General Ulysses Simpson Grant of Illinois. That recommendation, along with others from the Soldiers and Sailors, was accepted into the official convention record. An attempt to nominate Grant by acclamation was turned away with shouts of "too early."

It was then the turn of the vanquished to speak. Joseph E. Brown, the Confederate governor of Georgia heading a Republican delegation from that state, stood reconstructed before the victorious congregation. In illustrating his long and trying path to Chicago, he explained,

> I was an original secessionist . . . born in South
> Carolina, in Mr. Calhoun's district . . .
> I early imbibed his states' rights doctrine . . .
> [I foresaw] that the issues which divided North and
> South must ultimately be settled by the sword . . .
> Secession was the result. I went into it cordially.

Brown, whose strident advocacy of states' rights had lead him to obstruct Jefferson Davis's policies for a more centralized war effort, continued:

> I will not attempt to review [the war's] history, and
> you of the great North were the conquerors; and I
> think I had sense enough at the end of the struggle
> to know when I was whipped. The president of the
> United States, after the surrender of General
> Johnston, ordered my arrest and imprisonment . . .
> I still love my own native land the best. And, with
> your construction of the Constitution, established by
> the sword, I still preferred the government of the
> United States to any other recognized government.

But some doubted Brown's sincerity. He was a political chameleon who forever served his own self-interests. Hardly an advocate of black equality, he envisioned a reconstructed South ruled by whites only. He would later run as a Redeemer candidate when Reconstruction was abandoned by the North. A few Union men rose on the convention floor to argue that the vision of a better and more just country should not be compromised in the name of unity, and the convention should be aware of the reality of what was happening in the South. Mr. Hassurek of Ohio, in a very long and eloquent speech, cautioned the delegates, "There must be no riots, no mobs, no burning of school houses and churches, no Ku Klux Klan."

Hassurek clearly foresaw the unfortunate fate of the South. "The Union men of the South, who risked their all, by their devotion to the old flag; the Negroes of the South, who rushed to our rescue, fought under our flag, saved our prisoners from starvation, and harbored, fed, and piloted our refugees, with a self-sacrificing devotion which stands without a parallel in the history of mankind, must not be coolly, cruelly, and heartlessly abandoned to the hatred and vindictiveness of those who seek to reestablish slavery in fact, after its abolition in name." With that in mind, the convocation then adjourned until the next day.

When the assemblage reconvened on Thursday, May 21, it was with the purpose of adopting a platform on which their candidate could honorably run. Twelve "Declarations of Principle" were put before the body and unanimously adopted. The first reaffirmed the congressional policies of Reconstruction in the rebellious states. The second guaranteed equal suffrage and safety to all loyal men of the South, but left the decision of suffrage in the Union states to those individual states. The third declaration denounced all forms of repudiation of public debt and demanded that it be paid in full according to the laws under which it was incurred. The fourth principle called for the equalization and reduction of taxation as rapidly as the national debt allowed.

The party's fifth principle called for the national debt to be extended over a fair period of redemption and for Congress to reduce the rate of interest whenever it could fairly do so. The sixth called on the government to improve its credit worthiness so that capitalists would lend to the government at a lower interest rate. The seventh principle called for the strict economic administration of the national government. The eighth deplored the death of Abraham Lincoln and the ascension of Andrew Johnson, who, they believed, had been "justly impeached of high crimes and misdemeanors and who has been properly pronounced guilty."

The ninth principle asserted the right of expatriation and the protection of U.S. rights of citizens abroad. The tenth confirmed that the pensions provided to sailors and soldiers and the widows and orphans of those who died are "a sacred legacy bequeathed to the nation's care." The eleventh encouraged a "just and liberal policy" of immigration. And the last principle universally declared "sympathy with all oppressed peoples which are struggling for their rights."

General Carl Schurz, who would be elected Missouri senator later that year, then claimed the floor to offer two additional principles, which were unanimously adopted by the convention. The first commended the magnanimity with which former rebels were aiding in the Reconstruction of Southern state governments upon the basis of impartial justice and equal rights and therefore recommended the removal of restrictions on them wherever it was safe to do so. Schurz's second resolution reasserted "principles laid down in the Declaration of Independence as the foundation of democratic government" and hailed "every effort toward making the principles a living reality on American soil."

With that done, the delegates launched into their final business, the nomination of their presidential candidate. In the year prior to the convention, Supreme Court Justice Salmon P. Chase, who was presiding over the impeachment trial, was frequently mentioned, along with Grant, as a possible nominee. But on this day, only one name was presented to the body. General John Alexander Logan, now an Illinois congressman, stood to nominate General Grant to calls of "Bully, John!"

Logan was brief:

> Then, sir, in the name of the loyal citizens, soldiers, and sailors of this great Republic of the United States of America; in the name of loyalty, of humanity, of justice; in the name of the National Union Republican Party; I nominate, as candidate for the Chief Magistracy of this nation, Ulysses S. Grant.

The delegates shouted their approval. A pigeon, painted red, white, and blue, was released and flew frantically about the hall.

Former Governor Henry Smith Lane of Indiana, who had presided over the first Republican convention in 1856, called for nomination by acclamation. But Chairman Hawley followed convention rules in a Roll Call of the States and Territories. Afterward, Hawley gladly announced, "Gentlemen of the convention, you have 650 votes, and you have given 650 votes for General Ulysses S. Grant." The celebrations began and would continue through November.

At the time of his nomination, Grant was serenely at work at his army desk in Washington. In reality, the general had little political experience. He had voted only twice for president, in 1856 for General Fremont, "because he knew him," and in 1860 for Lincoln. He had served in Mexico under the greatly respected Whig candidate General Zachary Taylor, "Old Rough and Ready," who ran for president in 1848. A year before the 1868 conventions, Grant had been wooed by both Democrats and Republicans. "General Grant does not wish to be president," his second-in-command, General John A. Rawlins, told the press, "but thinks the Republican Party may need him, and he believes, as their candidate, he can be elected and reelected."

Grant had almost destroyed his chance a year earlier. In April 1867 he accepted President Johnson's invitation to replace Stanton as secretary of war, ad interim, against the wishes of radical Republicans in Congress, and then had broken a promise to the president to stay there until the Supreme Court ruled on his dismissal of Stanton. Grant stepped down in January 1868, on the night Congress reinstated Stanton. But the Man of Appomattox, who his opponents thought "a dullard," had managed to stay silent during the impeachment trial and thus gained in popularity while others were tarnished.

In the forty-six-year-old, five-foot eight-inch Grant, the Republicans gained a national hero who could unite the party and was high-minded and personally honest. But he was also self-reliant and slow to trust party insiders. It is a great irony of war that strewn among its grisly fields of death and destruction can be found the seeds of life and renewal. So it was for U.S. Grant. Pulled from obscurity and failure by the tides of war, he rode its stormy seas to fame and success.

When the war began, Grant was thirty-nine years old and working as a clerk in his father's harness shop in Galena, Illinois. A graduate of West Point, Grant had capably served with Robert E. Lee and George B. McClellan in the Mexican War (a conflict he regarded in his memoirs "as one of the most unjust ever waged by a stronger against a weaker nation"). He later stayed on in the small peacetime army, eventually making the grade of captain. Transferred from one remote Western outpost to another, he finally succumbed to the tedium and loneliness of frontier life and resigned from the army in the summer of 1854. Reunited with his wife, Julia, and his children he returned to his Midwestern roots and thus began a series of failures as a farmer on a small farm called Hardscrabble outside of St. Louis, as a bill collector, and as a woodcutter.

At thirty-seven, broke and humbled, he moved his family to Galena to work for his father. Two years later, after the fall of Fort Sumter, his military background secured him a command in Cairo, Illinois. As the war progressed, his reputation as a bold and determined fighter was recognized by his superiors, who promoted him to higher and higher command. His victories in the Tennessee and Mississippi Valleys, concluding with the capture of Vicksburg, made him a national hero. On March 8, 1864, Grant, accompanied by his fourteen-year-old son Fred, checked into the Willard Hotel in Washington. He came to consult with Lincoln and assume command of the entire Union army.

Of all Lincoln's generals, Grant most understood the true nature of the war and the effort needed to win it. His tenacious and grinding use of the North's advantage in men and resources made him appear, to some, a butcher, but his brutal war of attrition led inexorably to Appomattox and victory. When the war ended, and Lincoln was dead, this taciturn and unassuming man who cherished his children and displayed an almost uxorious devotion to his wife could no longer return to obscurity in Galena. He was the most popular man in the North. Its citizens wanted him for their president.

The National Union Republicans now turned to the task of selecting a vice presidential candidate who would not pose the threat that Johnson had. Ten men were nominated: Schuyler Colfax of Indiana, Speaker of the House of Representatives; Senator Henry Wilson of Massachusetts; Senate president Benjamin Franklin Wade of Ohio; Governor Reuben Eaton Fenton of New York; former attorney general James Speed of Kentucky; Congressman William Darrah Kelley of Pennsylvania; Lincoln's former vice president, Hannibal Hamlin of Maine; Senator James Harlan of Iowa; and John Angel James Creswell of Maryland, who would become Grant's postmaster general.

Wade had been the preconvention favorite, but the failure to convict Johnson a few days earlier had seriously harmed his candidacy. After six ballots, Speaker Colfax, a radical Republican who Grant had called "the most popular man in the country," emerged victorious, with only a few delegates from New York holding out for Fenton and from Ohio for Wade. With this decided, the Grant/Colfax ticket was saluted with a grand finale of enthusiastic demonstrations. Governor Hawley pounded his gavel for the final time, and the convention adjourned in high spirits.

On May 29 a party delegation headed by Hawley greeted Grant in his Washington army office. "I have a policy of my own," Grant told them, "not to interfere against the will of the people." And in his formal letter of acceptance to the national committee, he concluded with the words that would become the National Union Republicans' slogan, "Let us have peace."

The Democrats, meeting in New York City in early July, nominated former New York Governor Horatio Seymour for president and Francis P. Blaine of Missouri for vice president. Blaine had served as a commander under Grant. The campaign took Grant across the land, including out West where he traveled by train and stagecoach to survey the treatment of Indians. He came away making a strong commitment to their fair treatment, "civilization, and Christianization." On November 3, 1868, the nation's male voters, black and white in North and South, spoke. Grant underwhelmed his opponent. He won by just 306,000 popular votes out of the 5,715,000 cast, yet the electoral college tally of 214 for Grant compared to Seymour's 80 made his election seem more like a landslide.

On March 4, 1869, Grant was inaugurated on the steps of the Treasury Department, a fitting place for the beginning of an administration that was continuously embroiled in financial scandals, from the Crédit Mobilier stock bribes to the Whiskey Ring. At the end of his first term Grant complained, "I have been the subject of abuse and slander scarcely equaled in political history."

Despite his problems, Grant was reelected to a second term in 1872, which he took as vindication by the people. More scandals followed. What was ultimately worse, during his two terms, Grant would oversee the implementation and, reluctantly, the dismantling of the congressional Reconstruction of the South. At first he did not hesitate to use the army to shield voters from Southern terrorists. Determined to "protect the colored voter in his rights," he sent General Philip Sheridan to subdue violence in Louisiana. But eventually Grant claimed the "whole public are tired out with these annual autumnal outbreaks in the South . . . [and] are ready now to condemn any interference on the part of the government."

Although Grant believed in Reconstruction and sympathized with the plight of Southern blacks, by 1874 the mood and resolve of the North toward black equality had changed. Support of Reconstruction policies became a political liability. The country's exponential growth and financial headaches during the Gilded Age were now considered the nation's first business. Whites, North and South, wanted to put the war behind them. Freedom was no longer the shibboleth of the Republican Party. Money and "progress" had replaced the ideals of Lincoln.

Having reached its apogee with the Fifteenth Amendment and the Civil Rights Act of 1875, the electoral crisis of 1876 would, in the name of national unity, effectively end Reconstruction. But the amendment, which prohibited federal and state governments from excluding voters on racial grounds, would be circumvented in the South by poll taxes, literacy tests, and property qualifications. In 1883 the Supreme Court would declare the Civil Rights Act of 1875 unconstitutional, leaving African-American men and women at the mercy of an uncaring nation and a Jim Crow South.

In 1876, with his reputation and popularity plummeting, Grant decided against a third term. One potential rival had been General George Armstrong Custer, "the most hated and beloved man in America." Months earlier, Custer, who had presidential ambitions of his own, testified in Congress against corrupt practices of Secretary of War William Worth Belknap. To rub salt in Grant's wound, Custer also implicated the president's brother Orvil. When Custer left town without authorization to rejoin the Seventh Cavalry, Grant had him arrested in Chicago. He later relented under a barrage of newspaper criticism. The vain general rushed out West to claim a big victory to help his political career. His charge at Little Big Horn may have been a political ploy to get the Republican convention to nominate him by acclamation. The *New York World* claimed that Grant's policy of peace for the Indians was "what killed Custer." So, instead of seeking a third term, Grant sailed around the world and ultimately spent his last dying days writing his memoirs, published by Mark Twain, who knew a great story when he heard one.

James Abram Garfield
1880 Republican Presidential Nominee

Chester Alan Arthur
1880 Republican
Vice Presidential Nominee

Facts-at-a-Glance
★★★

Event:	Seventh Republican National Convention
Dates:	June 2–8, 1880
Building:	Interstate Industrial Exposition Building
Location:	Lake Park, Michigan Avenue from Van Buren to Monroe Streets
Chicago Mayor:	Carter Henry Harrison Sr., Democrat
Candidates for Nomination:	Senator James Gillespie Blaine, Maine; Senator George Franklin Edmunds, Vermont; former President Ulysses S. Grant, Illinois; Treasury Secretary John Sherman, Ohio; former Congressman Elihu Benjamin Washburne, Illinois; Senator William G. Windom, Minnesota
Presidential Nominee:	James Abram Garfield, Ohio
Age at Nomination:	49
Number of Ballots:	36
Vice Presidential Nominee:	Chester Alan Arthur, New York
Number of Delegates:	756
Number Needed to Nominate:	A majority, 379
Largest Attendance:	15,000
Critical Issues:	Party unity, victory over Democrats, strong federal government, tariffs, federal support of education, civil service reform, reduction of Chinese immigration
Campaign Song:	"Rally Round the Flag"

4
★★★

The 1880 Republican National Convention
Grant's Waterloo

When Ulysses S. Grant stepped off an ocean liner in San Francisco in September 1879 from his two-and-a-half-year, round-the-world tour, he was hailed by the cheers of adoring crowds who had followed his travels in the daily newspapers. Surveying the enthusiastic throng, the general felt certain that after a four-year rest and a careful public relations campaign to restore his image, he could win a third term as president of the United States in the 1880 election. Grant was still America's greatest military hero and his global travels gave him an air of expertise on international affairs. He was a national idol and a world leader. What other candidate, Democrat or Republican, could block him from his goal? Grant's handlers knew now that the 1880 Republican nomination was theirs to lose, and they hungered after the spoils of office once more.

During Grant's absence abroad, most memories of his administration's greed, payoffs, favoritism, criminal indictments and convictions, and of the resignation of cabinet officers were swept aside by more dramatic national events. First, the election of 1876, in which Grant did not run because of his low public standing, confirmed that the Civil War had not ended in 1865. Indeed, the nation stood at the brink of a second internecine conflict over the results of the 1876 Tilden/Hayes contest. Later, while Grant visited royalty from Europe to Japan, the federal government's protection of African-American voters in the South was under constant assault by congressional Democrats and hooded vigilante groups. Finally, after hard economic times, the public longed for the "good ol' days" under Grant. He represented stability and constitutional enforcement of the law.

In 1876 Governor Samuel Jones Tilden of New York, the Democratic nominee, and his running mate, Governor Thomas Andrews Hendricks of Indiana, won the national popular vote. The country was sick of sixteen years of Republican self-righteousness and graft. The Democrats campaigned on Tilden's strong state reform record against "Boss" Tweed of New York City's Tammany Hall and with hard-hitting charges against corruption in the Grant administration. Horrified Republicans acted quickly to nullify the election results in the South by certifying their own vote totals. They pointed to previously Republican districts that suddenly voted lopsided Democratic returns. In the end, the Republicans "stole" the election back and called it the "Great Compromise." Democrats called it the "Great Fraud."

President Grant appointed an extraordinary electoral commission of fifteen senators, congressional representatives, and members of the Supreme Court to investigate ballot box tampering and voter intimidation in South Carolina, Florida, and Louisiana, and to certify the final electoral results. The commission found African-American voters in the three southern states had been terrorized by an assortment of "rifle clubs." Other vigilantes whipped and murdered blacks bold enough to try to cast ballots insured by the new Fourteenth Amendment to the Constitution.

House Minority Leader James Abram Garfield, a former president of Hiram College, an abolitionist, Civil War general, and Republican congressional leader, convinced the commission to reverse the results in those disputed states, thus giving Governor Rutherford Birchard Hayes of his home state of Ohio an electoral college victory of just one vote. Congressional Democrats threatened to filibuster past the March 4 inauguration date and leave the nation without a president. When at the last moment, Congress, as final arbiter, ratified the Hayes "compromise," a riot nearly broke out on the floor of the House of Representatives as "wild-eyed" Democrats stormed the podium shaking their fists shouting "Tilden or blood." Republicans smugly replied, "We whipped you once, we'll do it again." Democratic newspapers like the New York *Sun* called the new president, "Rutherfraud B. Hayes."

The Hayes vote stood and the former Ohio governor assumed office on March 4, 1877. But by 1878, Democrats controlled both houses of Congress for the first time since 1860. They used their new power to try to eliminate the few remaining Reconstruction laws through legislative riders to Hayes administration appropriation bills for the army and other government functions. Senator James Gillespie Blaine of Maine and Garfield in the House stood against those subversive efforts. Garfield charged that the Democrats had launched a "revolution against the Constitution and the government." Garfield's defense made him a national Republican hero, almost as imposing and spirited as Blaine himself. However, Garfield, a conservative money man, then tried to smooth the South's wounds with economic development appropriations. He hoped to redefine the Republican Party around issues of economic conservatism rather than race and thereby make the South Republican. His efforts in this direction failed.

The "hard money" practices of Hayes weaned the nation from the inflationary "Greenback" era of the Civil War, even though it brought economic hardship to millions with declining markets, plunging real estate values, scarcity of capital, unemployment, reduction of wages, strikes, and lockouts. (The Greenback Party polled a million votes in the 1878 off-year elections, but after Hayes's monetary success, slipped into insignificance.) However, the Hayes administration alienated friend and foe alike with its civil service reforms, while distributing spoils to ex-army veterans and preaching the high road for all others. Then Hayes infuriated radical Republicans (who called him a traitor) by announcing that federal troops were no longer needed to protect African-American enfranchisement at the polls in South Carolina and Louisiana, even though, ironically, his own election was based upon charges to the contrary. The Republican presence in the South was swept away along with the safety and freedom of African Americans. The Republican Party was now at war with itself as well as with the Democrats. After four tumultuous years, Hayes scornfully announced he would not seek a second term.

Thus once again, hundreds of coal-burning iron horses huffed and puffed into Chicago's Union and Dearborn stations carrying ten thousand convention delegates and visitors. All were eager to settle party business as well as see the miraculous "Second City"

that had risen like the proverbial phoenix from the ashes of the Great Chicago Fire. The blaze had reduced the old, overgrown frontier town to cinders just nine years earlier. In the business district alone, 460 acres, 1,600 stores, 60 factories, and 28 hotels had been consumed. Some seventy-five thousand people were left homeless and more than three square miles incinerated.

Now, a booming metropolis of taller and taller buildings lorded over the disappearing prairie. The new Chicago boasted not only saloons and gambling joints but also scores of elegant homes on South Michigan Avenue, the exclusive Prairie Avenue, Rush Street, and Lake Shore Drive; restaurants like Chapin and Gore's, theaters like McVicker's, music halls, parks, race tracks, even popular natatoriums like the one at the corner of Michigan Avenue and Jackson Boulevard where swimmers could practice their strokes all winter long. Sears and Montgomery Ward were rewriting the rules of commerce and profit.

But times were also difficult for thousands of families, mostly new immigrants, who worked in the factories and slaughterhouses. Although Chicago caught onto an urge for "genteel" culture and style during "The Elegant Eighties," poverty was growing along with wealth, and tensions between capital and labor were escalating. Still a vibrant artistic and architectural creativity was reinventing the city as a midland metropolis, an industrial dynamo leading the world in unimagined directions.

The Crosby Opera House, the previous convention hall, had been destroyed by the Great Chicago Fire of 1871. Hence, when the rains suddenly cleared on a wet June 2, 1880, fifteen thousand delegates, spectators, newsmen, party operatives, and hangers-on who had jammed Chicago's Lake Park dropped their umbrellas as they sought entrance to the grand, three-story, turreted Interstate Industrial Exposition Building, popularly called the "Glass Palace," in reference to London's Crystal Palace. The fire brigade and a force of seventy-five police officers put up ropes for crowd control to prevent accidents and guide what the *Chicago Daily News* called "the mass of moving humanity." Tickets were scarce, even at the "exorbitant price of 30 dollars" and there was "great trouble in seating the immense multitude" with tickets.

The proceedings were held in the south half of the immense structure. The giant hall with its arched iron girders sweeping across rounded glass ceilings was designed by William Boyington in 1873 to declare Chicago's recovery from the conflagration of 1871. The gigantic assembly hall, which cost $250,000, measured one city block wide and two blocks long, running from Van Buren to Monroe Street on the east side of Michigan Avenue. A 280-foot American flag was draped across the ceiling. The hall was so big that orators on the speaker's stand at the semicircle southern end of the building could barely be heard, and resolution after resolution had to be shouted several times through megaphones before votes could be taken. At each end of the hall were giant paintings of Lincoln and Washington, as well as portraits of Republican and abolitionist leaders Dix, Chandler, Yates, Wade, Stevens, Lovejoy, Morton, Chase, Fessenden, Giddings, and Sumner, while scores of flags hung from the balconies.

On stage a flag-draped Statue of Liberty stood behind the chairman's swivel chair. The furniture on the platform was crafted of walnut and leather. A quote of Lincoln's, "A government of the people and for the people shall not perish from the earth," hung from one wall. Seated among the Republican chieftains was ex-slave and abolitionist orator Frederick Douglass. One hundred reporters sat between the stage and the delegates. The presiding officer's desk stood forty feet away from the delegates, so it was difficult to understand how any human voice could be heard throughout the great cavity or how deliberation was possible. The band struck up the "Old Red, White, and Blue" as delegates marched to their seats behind each state's standard.

The convention's goal was simple. Republicans had to find a successor to Hayes who could unite the party and stem the rise of Democratic power in the North and South. The candidate's victory had to be large enough to survive any vote fraud or Democratic congressional interference. The party had to save the Republican gains of the Civil War, a conflict that America did not want to fight again.

The Seventh Republican National Convention was called to order at noon by Senator James Donald Cameron of Pennsylvania, chairman of the Republican National Committee, a Grant supporter, and close friend of Senator Blaine. The head of the gavel he loudly banged was hand-carved wood from Lincoln's Springfield home, its stem from Washington's Mount Vernon. But he could barely be heard fifty feet beyond the speaker's platform. Shouts of "louder" filled the hall, but to no avail. As the delegates gathered, Grant remained the overwhelming favorite, though his critics joked that he had come home a year too early and had run out of diplomatic hands to shake and now was just making old-fashioned political deals again. The anti-third-termers who opposed Grant had failed to pick up steam or find an alternative candidate with his stature. Most delegates believed no one could stop the general, but that Grant's nomination meant no party unity.

Grant's convention brain trust was commanded by three stalwart Republican senators. Most notable was the arrogant, burly, blond orator and machine boss Roscoe Conkling of New York, known as the "King of Patronage." Conkling had battled Blaine and Hayes for the 1876 nomination and held a deep grudge against the Maine senator. Assisting Grant from the podium was Donald Cameron, son of Simon and inheritor of his father's senate office. General, now senator, John A. Logan of Illinois, war hero and defender of veterans' pensions, was a close Grant friend. Chicago's "Long John" Wentworth chaired delegate meetings for Grant. All were united in their hatred of Hayes and his "snivel service." Hayes had gone so far as to remove Conkling's associate, Chester Alan Arthur, from his powerful position as collector of the Port of New York. Conkling knew from experience that Grant would make no such blunders.

Grant, now back home in Galena after excursions throughout the United States and Cuba, was very worried under his stoic calm. He desperately wanted another chance as president to clear his name. Weeks before the convention, he visited his son, Colonel Fred D. Grant, assigned to General Sheridan's staff, to supervise his strategy and count potential votes. He felt his campaign stagger and slow as the June assembly approached. But when his wife, Julia, suggested that they stop in Chicago at the Republican convention on their way from Galena to Milwaukee to attend the Soldier's and Sailor's Convention, Grant balked. He would rather die than disgrace himself by appearing actively to seek the nomination, he told her. Instead, the Grant brain trust maintained daily telegraph contact with the general.

As the convention opened, Grant's managers counted their strength at three hundred delegates, seventy-nine short of victory. But they had a strategy to boost their total over the top. If they could quickly enact the unit rule that required all delegates in a particular state to vote as one, Grant could gain eighty dissenting votes, most of which were committed to Blaine in key states. Other delegations would follow. Thus Grant could win on the first or second ballot. They planned to strike before delegates knew what hit them. Chairman Cameron was instructed to entertain nominations for the convention's temporary chairman and invoke the unit rule in that vote, thus setting a precedent for the entire meeting. A Grant supporter could recognize Grant delegates and ignore others.

But the forces representing Senator Blaine and Treasury Secretary John Sherman, the younger brother of General William T. Sherman, were ready for the Cameron/Conkling ruse. Garfield, a Sherman supporter who chaired the rules committee, denounced the tactic as straight out of the Democratic "Tammany Hall" bag of tricks. In preconvention decisions made in a suite of smoke-filled rooms at the Palmer House, built in 1875, two blocks from the Exposition Building, the anti-third-termers fought and beat the unit rule. Then, on the convention floor, the anti-Grant coalition installed its own man, Massachusetts Senator George Frisbie Hoar, as temporary chairman. (He was made permanent chairman on the second day.) The anti-Grant coalition's first-day victory was enough to blunt the rush to Grant, for the moment.

Hoar rose to set the tone for the gathering:

It is twenty years since the Republican convention met in this city, and after a stormy but friendly contest, put in nomination Abraham Lincoln and Hannibal Hamlin. Lincoln has gone to his rest. His companion upon the ticket, in fresh and vigorous age, is present with us today. [Hamlin rose to accept applause.] Douglas and Breckenridge, his two competitors for the great office of the presidency, sleep by his side. But the parties which confronted each other then, confront each other now, unchanged in purpose, in temper, and in character. The Democratic Party was ruled then, as now, by the South. The single purpose of its being was to give political supremacy to the oligarchies of the South, and office, without influence to their subservient Northern allies . . .

The crowd grumbled in agreement.

Chairman Hoar continued triumphantly, "The keynote of every Republican platform, the principle of every Republican union, is found in its respect for the dignity of every individual man. Until that becomes the pervading principle of the Republic, from Canada to the Gulf, from the Atlantic to the Pacific, our mission is not ended . . . [until] every man within our borders may dwell secure in a happy home, may cast and have counted his equal vote, and may send his child at the public charge to a free school."

That night thousands of delegates and influence seekers roamed through the crowded corridors of scores of Chicago hotels, restaurants, and saloons, trading rumors and strategic information, and looking for open hospitality suites stocked with cigars and liquor, plenty of which were consumed as the week wore on. But the convention, under the influence of a growing temperance movement, passed a prohibition resolution for the Exposition Building itself.

The June 3 session started promptly at 11:00 A.M. with a prayer. The invocation was followed by a confusing assortment of delegate challenges. The Grant forces desperately searched for questionable delegates they could replace with their own men. Senator Conkling, despised by many, feared by many more, dominated the morning session. He demanded to know the results of the Committee on Contested Seats and Credentials. Since it was not ready to report, he offered a motion to adjourn until the evening session. His delaying tactic was rebuffed by voice vote. The Committee on Permanent Organization then introduced a list of convention vice presidents from each state. "Long John" Wentworth, again congressman of the First Congressional District and Chicago's aging statesman, was the Illinois representative as convention vice president.

The Committee on Rules and Order of Business, chaired by General Garfield, was also embroiled in disputes over a minority report devised by Grant's followers. Again the Republican National Committee met feverishly at the Palmer House to resolve the procedural problems. At one o'clock on Thursday afternoon, the convention was forced to recess until five o'clock that evening. The delegates were becoming restless, even angry, tempers were flaring, and arguments broke out across the floor.

At 5:00 P.M., Mr. Henderson of Iowa and Senator "Black Jack" Logan broke into acrimonious debate over the credential committee report. Logan demanded fairness for himself and five other at-large delegates who had been replaced by the credential committee that agreed with the charge that these delegates were appointed by a secret state convention committee. They were also Grant supporters. A disturbance broke out among the hissing spectators in the gallery above, and Chairman Hoar called on the sergeant-at-arms to clear the section. The credential skirmishing lasted until 7:00 P.M., when Mr. Metcalf of Illinois moved again for adjournment, so the final issues of the various committees could at last be settled in private and the convention could, in its third day, finally get down to business.

On Friday, June 4, the delegates gathered again at 10:00 A.M., hoping to adopt a platform and nominate a presidential candidate. Senator Conkling opened the session on the offensive with a call for a loyalty oath in support of the 1880 nominee, whoever he might be, to enforce party discipline. His resolution was overwhelmingly adopted. But Conkling was forced to back off when he tried to expel three West Virginia dissenters.

"I fear this convention is about to commit a great error," Garfield warned, "and before they act, I beg leave to state the case." Soon his reasonable discourse mollified the agitated assembly. Garfield henceforth became perceived as the convention's champion of party unity, a role he had perfected in the House of Representatives. Senator Conkling passed a note to Garfield, "I congratulate you on being the dark horse."

The credential fight began again with state-within-state combat. The minority report protested the way Grant delegates had been dislodged in a number of delegations, including Illinois, where Logan and others charged the Cook County Republican Party with gross "fraud and conspiracy."

The delegate debate dragged on for hours, becoming more and more unruly. First, the credentials of competing delegations from Alabama were disputed. Then the case of the Louisiana contingent, a state that only recently elected competing legislatures, took up a few more hours.

The convention itself was tightening into a deadlock that could fatally shatter at any moment as the Democrats had done in 1860. The mass gathering, so large, unruly and hard to hear, was veering out of control. To Garfield, who battled Conkling on every issue from its front ranks, the whole spectacle seemed like "Paris in the ecstacy of Revolution." In all credential cases, the majority report, filed by the anti-third-ter-

mers, was accepted. The convention decided to abide by the authority of each state convention and its certification of delegates. Then the question of Illinois's delegates-at-large, Logan among them, was debated. Logan spoke forcefully:

> I am aware of the impatience of this convention; I am impatient myself . . . Now, let me say to the Sherman men here, to the Blaine men, to the Edmunds men, . . . if you can beat the old soldier, all right. For him I claim nothing that is not due to each and every citizen of this grand Republic; he asks nothing that he will not grant to others . . . We that support him do it because we think him worthy, and you do the same for the candidates that you support. No one word has ever been lisped by the Grant men against any of your candidates. You have never heard a Grant man say that he would bolt your nomination—not one—and you never will. But do not beat the old soldier by tricks; do not, by chicanery, beat the soldier that led your armies and saved your country; do not, by such means, beat the man that has been recognized by every civilized nation of the earth as the grandest citizen the world knows today . . . Do not by tactics . . . prevent the old soldier from having his share of votes.

As a result of Logan's stature and appeal, his at-large delegation was seated amid Blaine allies. A motion then was made to divide the majority report so the convention could hear district-by-district disputes in Illinois. Finally, after several more hours of bitter wrangling, the majority report was accepted by a 384 to 356 vote. Several Grant supporters, in Illinois and other states, were denied official seats, despite the fact that Illinois was overwhelmingly for its adopted son. At last, the third session adjourned at 2:20 A.M. The Grant campaign had been dealt another serious blow.

"Work of Convention Proceeding Very Slowly" announced a *Chicago Daily News* headline. Yet the show continued to attract throngs of curious spectators, among them Prince Leopold and Princess Louise of Belgium. On Saturday, June 5, the fourth day of the 1880 convention, weary delegates gathered at 11:00 A.M., to the beat of the brass bands. To avoid future disputes like the credentials battles of the first three days, Mr. Boutwell of Massachusetts offered a resolution empowering the Republican National

Committee to prescribe definite candidate selection procedures for subsequent conventions. Meanwhile, delegates who were concerned about return trains home were assured by the railroads that their tickets would be honored. Then the convention took up more arguments over credentials, this time in Kansas, West Virginia, and the Utah Territory.

At last the convention moved sluggishly forward, to the rules debate. It fell upon Congressman Garfield (though elected, he still hadn't been sworn in as U. S. senator), chairman of the rules committee, to carry forth the battle, particularly over rule eight, which eliminated the unit rule. After a few more hours of arguments, the Majority Report on Rules was formally adopted, and the unit rule was permanently scrapped by a floor vote of 449 to 306. It was another blow to Grant.

The convention suddenly picked up momentum and passed a platform of resolutions submitted by Edmund Pierrepont, the chairman. Despite their deep divisions, Republicans endorsed the accomplishments of the Hayes administration, and agreed, with little debate, that the federal government must exercise its power to enforce the supreme law of the land, the Constitution, and protect the safety and enfranchisement of all its citizens. The platform's third plank noted, "The work of popular education is one left to the care of the several states, but it is the duty of the national government to aid that work to the extent of its constitutional power." The party's fourth resolution warned that states must "forbid the appropriation of public funds to the support of sectarian schools."

The 1880 Republicans insisted that tariffs were needed to protect American labor and industry. They also demanded "no further grants of the public domain should be made to any railway or other corporations;" and argued that "slavery having perished in the states, its twin barbarity, polygamy, must die in the territories." The convention sought to limit Chinese immigration in the manner of the Chinese Exclusion Bill vetoed by Hayes in 1879. Mr. Baker of Massachusetts offered an additional platform amendment that endorsed the "declarations of President Hayes, that the reform in the civil service shall be thorough, radical, and complete."

Considerable debate followed the civil service resolution. Mr. Flanagan of Texas found the amendment particularly objectionable, complaining, "There is one plank in the Democratic Party that I have ever admired and this is, 'To the victors go the spoils' . . . What are we up here for? I mean the members of the Republican Party are entitled to office, and if we are victorious we will have office. I, therefore, move to lay the amendment on the table." He also pointed out that of the fourteen hundred officers appointed by the president in Texas, only 140 went to Republicans under Hayes. His objections were voted down by indignant delegates at the urging of Mr. Codman of Massachusetts, and the party had its civil service plank. At 5:25 P.M., the convention again recessed until seven o'clock.

That evening when Chicagoan Emory Storrs mentioned the names of Grant and Blaine in his speech, a three-quarter hour demonstration of support, particularly from the galleries, followed utterance of each name. Delegates waved hats, jackets, banners, and handkerchiefs. They even ripped off articles of clothing and tore American flags from the walls as they leaped to tables and chairs in delirious dances. First Grant's men shouted, then Blaine's. Neither was prepared to yield to the other.

Grant was a national hero and former president. But the dashing and eloquent James G. Blaine was the Republican Party's senatorial star. Blaine, born in Pennsylvania, had been a journalist in Maine before coming to the House of Representatives in 1860. He was acknowledged to be the greatest Speaker of the House since Henry Clay. Next to Grant, the spellbinding orator was the most popular and sought-after figure in the Republican Party. He had come within a few votes of the 1876 nomination in Cincinnati, before the dark horse Hayes, using his home state influence, overtook Blaine, and broke his heart. He became a senator later that year. Several months before the Chicago meeting, his presidential ambition led him to sponsor a bill to stem "The Yellow Peril" of Chinese slave labor immigration. His efforts were fought by Garfield and vetoed by Hayes. But Blaine was now satisfied with his power in the Senate and somewhat disgusted with American politics. Yet, he disliked Grant and believed his nomination would doom the party in the November canvass. So he agreed to stand as nominee at the head of the anti-third-term movement and perhaps win the office he thought worthy of his own achievements and abilities. Blaine refused to come to Chicago to direct his forces, fully expecting Grant would eventually prevail at the convention and would take the party down in November.

John Sherman of Ohio, Grant's other leading opponent, had retired from the Senate to become Hayes' secretary of treasury. He made his reputation during the Kansas War and as a radical Republican in Congress. Sherman took credit for the recent prosperity and the reestablishment of the gold standard to replace the Greenback. But Sherman, who was nicknamed "The Ohio Icicle," was rigid and cold and attracted little support beyond his state's delegation, headed at Sherman's insistence by Garfield. Sherman had supported Garfield for the Senate and extracted a promise in return from Garfield to support his own presidential campaign. Other presidential hopefuls included anti-Grant reformer Senator George Franklin Edmunds of Vermont; Minnesota's favorite son, Senator William G. Windom; and former Congressman Elihu Benjamin Washburne of Illinois, a confidant of Lincoln who had demanded that Congress make Grant the general of the Army of the Potomac and then served as his secretary of state.

Finally, during the June 5 evening session, the factions stood face to face, ready to make their official nominations. The drama reached its apparent apex as Blaine's name was offered first. But instead of a stirring defense, the kind Blaine gained in 1876 from Illinois Congressman Robert Green Ingersoll, the moment was wasted with a barely audible speech by Michigan millionaire industrialist James F. Joy who condemned himself by confessing, "If, therefore, words of mine are important for the candidate, who shall be proposed, they will benefit him little." He did manage to compare Blaine to Henry Clay. The inept speaker's ultimate humiliation came when he concluded by nominating "James S. Blaine." "'G!' 'G. Blaine', you fool!" one of the horrified Blaine supporters yelled back. Then the Blaine forces staged their demonstration again.

Next came the nomination of Senator William Windom. Mr. Drake introduced him as one who, "in his course, he has ever sustained the cause of the oppressed and supported the government loyally." Then strutted out New York Senator Roscoe Conkling, a figure who fascinated Chicago journalists. "Conkling's manner has thousands of times been described," the *Chicago Daily Tribune* wrote. "But [this] was the first time he had ever been seen in the vicinity of Chicago. He has behaved with some recklessness for the past two or three days; owing to the late hours he has kept, the disappointments he has encountered,

the defection of a large part of his delegation, and the apparent collapse of his political program."

Senator Conkling now took the occasion to make one of his greatest and most flamboyant speeches. Jumping on top of a reporter's table next to the speaker's stand to get a height advantage over all opponents, Conkling's golden throat burst forth with a stanza of doggerel calculated to set Grant supporters into pandemonium.

And when asked what State he hails from,
Our sole reply shall be,
He hails from Appomattox,
And its famous apple tree.

The Exposition Building rocked with approval, particularly the galleries that were packed with Chicagoans in favor of the state's adopted son. Senator Conkling, always overly theatrical and haughty, continued: "I rise, Mr. President, in behalf of the state of New York, to propose a nomination with which the country and the Republican Party can grandly win. The election before us is the Austerlitz of American politics. It will decide, for many years, whether the country shall be Republican or Cossack. The supreme need of the hour is not a candidate who can carry Michigan," he said, mocking Michigan's Joy, "All Republican candidates can do that . . . The need which urges itself on the . . . convention is of a candidate who can carry doubtful states. Not the doubtful states of the North alone, but also doubtful states of the South . . . New York is for Ulysses S. Grant."

He hesitated as a giant cheer erupted from the crowd, then lunged on in animated gestures, "Never defeated, in peace or in war, his name is the most illustrious borne by living man." Again Grant supporters burst into vociferous agreement. Among Grant's greatest triumphs, Conkling said, was curing inflation with a single declaration to keep America's money sound by basing it on the gold standard. After praising his virtues, "his integrity, his common sense, his courage, his unequaled experience," Conkling turned to his enemies. "Vilified and reviled, ruthlessly aspersed by unnumbered presses, not in other lands, but his own, assaults upon him have seasoned and strengthened his hold on the public heart." Conkling pegged Grant's opponents as hypocrites who were as reliant upon patronage as Grant ever had been, calling them, "charlatans, jayhawkers, tramps, and guerrillas." Blaine and Sherman supporters booed and hissed as Grant's men hooted with amusement. When Conkling finished, the demonstration following his performance lasted nearly an hour. William Bradley of Kentucky seconded the Grant nomination.

Then Sherman's name was placed in nomination by Garfield, whom the treasury secretary had forced into reluctant duty. Incredibly, during all the convention strategizing and infighting, Garfield had forgotten to write an official speech. Undeterred, he leaped to the same tabletop that Conkling had made his stage an hour earlier. The former house minority leader spoke in a clarion but calm voice that commanded a different kind of attention than accorded Conkling. He seized upon a sea metaphor used in the nominating address for Blaine. "I have witnessed the extraordinary scenes of this convention," Garfield began, "with deep solicitude. Nothing touches my heart more quickly than a tribute of honor to a great and noble character." His rhetoric flowed smoothly like waves lapping the shoreline after Conkling's storm.

When Garfield asked of the assembled party, "And now gentleman, what do we want?" a voice from the gallery shouted back, "We want Garfield." The general ignored it and forged ahead, but did not, until the very end, put Sherman's name before the delegates. The smallest of the three major demonstrations of support followed. Mr. Winckler of Wisconsin seconded Sherman, as did Mr. Elliott of South Carolina, calling Sherman a "champion of human rights everywhere."

Then followed the nomination of liberal Republican Senator George F. Edmunds, "a candidate far better than the platform, because known everywhere throughout the length and breadth of the land as the very incarnation, long tried and never wanting," as Mr. Billings of Vermont reminded the delegations. Mr. Cassody of Wisconsin entered the name of Elihu B. Washburne, arguing "what we want most just now, is unity of purpose through the entire party, for the public good . . ." Washburne was seconded by Augustus Brandegee of Connecticut, who argued that with 150,000 Germans in New York and Illinois, Washburne could turn the tide back toward the wavering Republicans.

It wasn't until 11:45 P.M. that the Republican delegates pulled themselves back through the city streets in a driving cold thunderstorm to their hotels to get a few hours sleep before the official balloting began on

Monday. The convention adjourned for a sabbath of political deal making.

The anti-third-termers had a problem. Neither Blaine nor Sherman were willing to yield to the other, even as it was apparent that neither could win against Grant. Their momentum wilted with the sudden burst of late spring heat. Benjamin Harrison of Indiana began searching for alternatives. Late Sunday night Harrison visited Garfield in the new Grand Pacific Hotel at Jackson Boulevard and Clark Street. Harrison asked for the conditions under which Garfield would accept the nomination.

"My name must not be used," Garfield protested vigorously, as he had all week whenever the newspapers promoted his case. For years Garfield had thought privately that the presidency was his destiny. But now he was honor bound by his promise to support Sherman. He tried to deflect any draft movement.

When the fifteen thousand Republicans thronged back into the Exposition Building on the Monday morning of June 7, they looked like they had "slept in the lake." Grant took a big lead on the first ballot with 304 against Blaine's 284, Sherman's 93, Edmunds's 34, Washburne's 30, and Windom's 10 votes. With the exception of Garfield, who received a stray vote from the Pennsylvania delegation and from Maryland on a number of ballots and an occasional vote for General William T. Sherman, who declined to run "against his best friend," the respective forces sat deadlocked ballot after tedious ballot. Political operatives of all camps shot back and forth among the delegations trying to break the stranglehold. Even Hayes got a vote to relieve the boredom.

"Who Will It Be?" the newspapers wondered. "Preparations for the Portentous Struggle of Today," "Conkling, Cameron, and Logan Visiting Southern Colored Men," "Serious Defections in Alabama, Kentucky, and Mississippi," "Rumors of Agreement between Grant and Sherman Men," "A Friendly Feeling Toward Mr. Washburne in the Indiana Delegation"— so the headlines continued to speculate on the outcome. All morning and afternoon the tiresome polling of delegations and official roll calls continued.

A record eighteen ballots were taken in four hours. After twenty-eight tries the exhausted delegates broke for the night. It was nearly 10:00 P.M., and the convention had completed its fifth day without a nominee. None of the anti-Grant factions would budge. Blaine clearly had the greatest claim, but

Sherman would not concede defeat. The fruitless negotiations continued in the baroque suites of the Palmer House almost until dawn, with every kind of official and unofficial inducement dangled in front of the delegates who were gripped in a political fever.

At 10:00 A.M. on Tuesday, June 8, the sixth official day of assembly, the Republican delegates from across the land could stand the deadlock no longer. They frantically looked for a way to break the tension, for a new direction, for a leader to save the party. Realists like Garfield now expected General Grant to have his victory, having laid the convention to a week-long siege. Grant's operatives were trying to sell cabinet seats to southern delegates, but with few takers who could deliver votes. The political armies stood stalemated. Then on the twenty-ninth ballot, Massachusetts switched to Ohio's John Sherman, trying to dislodge other Blaine delegates. When the tactic failed, Sherman faded altogether. Then on the thirty-third ballot, nine votes from Wisconsin switched to Washburne. (Grant would always resent Washburne's candidacy.) Still, no followers.

The excitement of the delegates was growing. They felt a mysterious change come over the hall, perhaps the cold mist from the lake seeping into the Exposition Building as the Chicago June turned suddenly chilly with a northern wind. Something was about to happen. They could sense it, they later claimed. On the thirty-fourth ballot, Wisconsin threw sixteen votes to Garfield. The general, stunned and "dumbfounded," rose to object, but was gaveled out of order by Chairman Hoar, who was a Garfield admirer. On the thirty-fifth ballot, Indiana's Harrison followed Wisconsin's lead with twenty-seven more votes for Garfield. Garfield totaled fifty-nine. All at once, the floodgate broke, and Blaine delegates jumped on the bandwagon. Within moments the convention was cheering Garfield's name, and the Grant forces couldn't hold back this unexpected, last assault against the old general. Suddenly, the convention was delirious with the solution that had stood before them all along, "Garfield, Garfield for president," they whooped.

Despite Garfield's protests, Ohio itself switched from Sherman to Garfield, as the new nominee sat now alone, possessed of calm, "white as death." Soon Garfield was on his feet with a newsman avowing his support for Sherman, but he was too late. Wisconsin, which had started the stampede, ended it on the thirty-sixth ballot. Garfield stood victorious with 399 votes to Grant's loyal 306. Blaine collected 42, Washburne, 5, and Sherman, 3. Garfield was over the top. A junior general had triumphed over his army commander. Grant had met his Waterloo.

Maryland demanded a recount of its delegates, as did Mississippi, South Carolina, and Tennessee. A stunned Conkling took but a moment to recover from his disappointment, then moved, with Logan's second, to make Garfield the unanimous nominee. Conkling added, "I avail myself of the opportunity to congratulate the Republican Party of the United States on the good nature and the well-tempered rivalry which has distinguished this animated contest." Garfield was escorted in haste back to his Grand Pacific Hotel room in order not to break the tradition of protecting a nominee from the rumble-tumble of a convention that nominated him.

After a final half-hour demonstration in favor of their new party hero, the Republicans again followed the tradition of giving the vice presidency to the losing side and nominated a Conkling supporter, the impeccable Chester A. Arthur of New York. Mississippi's Senator Blanche K. Bruce, a former slave who became rich in real estate, became the first African American of either party to receive convention votes for a national office. Washburne, Thomas Settle of Florida, Horace Maynard of Tennessee, and Edmund J. Davis of Texas also received votes.

"The Luck of a Dark Horse from Ohio," the *Tribune* announced. How had an undeclared candidate swept the convention with such surprise and force? One observer recalled that on that sixth and final day, the assembly was overcome by a kind of mystical trance when Garfield's name swept across it. Suddenly, it felt "like a mist come down from the mountain" to direct the convention to a divinely inspired pick. All Republicans knew and respected Garfield. The forty-nine-year-old general had served ably as the House leader when Blaine moved to the Senate. But Garfield did not have the personal drive of a Blaine that brought him to the fore on his own behalf. Instead, 250 of Blaine's delegates propelled him to victory. In the end, the nomination was really no surprise to Garfield himself. He had long ago entrusted his future to a spiritually inspired force that transported him forward and protected him throughout his life, whether on the battlefield of war or politics. He eschewed ambition as the route to his position.

Garfield became a definer and defender of ideas and policy, a man of moral and political courage. He left the gab and gossip of politics to others.

Like Lincoln, Garfield had been born in a log cabin and grew up in severe poverty. And like Lincoln, as a day laborer, learning on flatboats and through books read by candlelight, Garfield found his way to greatness. In his early fights against slavery, and again during his army tests as a young general at the Battle of Chickamaunga and in his repeated congressional victories, Garfield felt destiny at his back. He was fated for greatness, his wife had equally prophesied. He was comfortable with her verdict.

Garfield was the new Republican leader. In national policy, Garfield believed that after human rights, all other issues were related to the question of money—its value, its use, its stability. Inflation, depression, even the recent outbursts of labor agitation, such as the Great Railroad Strike of 1877, were related to how the government regulated its money. Garfield preached what would become Republican doctrine, "laissez-faire" (let the market alone), enforce the gold standard, and pay all debts with hard currency. On the announcement of Garfield's nomination, delegates felt a great sense of relief, but stocks fell 2 percent nevertheless.

A convention delegation brought Garfield official notification of his nomination in the Club Room of the Grand Pacific Hotel on the evening of June 8. In his letter of acceptance dated July 10, 1880, Garfield announced that until "every citizen, rich or poor, white or black, is secure in the free and equal enjoyment of every civil and political right guaranteed by the Constitution and its laws," the Union would not be healed. "Next in importance to freedom and justice," Garfield wrote, "is popular education, without which neither justice nor freedom can be permanently maintained. . . . Whatever the nation can justly afford can be generously given to the States in supporting the common school; but it would be unjust to our people and dangerous to our institutions to apply any portion of the revenues of the Nation to the support of sectarian schools," and so on in support of his party's platform, which he had helped to draft.

During the campaign, Garfield never left his Mentor, Ohio, farm. As with Lincoln, streams of visitors, newsmen, and others of influence came to visit him. But the battle ahead looked difficult. Republicans were hemmed in with little chance of winning a single southern electoral vote. The Democrats cleverly nominated another national war idol, General Winfield Scott Hancock of Pennsylvania, who had destroyed Pickett's charge at Gettysburg. But as military commander in the postwar South, Hancock had endeared himself to southern Democrats by failing to defend vigorously the rights of former slaves. The general still suffered from war wounds. His vice presidential running mate was William H. English of Indiana. The Democrats made the "Great Fraud" and a call for decentralization of the federal government their main issues. Garfield counterattacked by citing the Democrat's barren congressional record.

Without the heroic effort of Roscoe Conkling, who gave up $25,000 in legal fees to campaign vigorously for Garfield, or Grant, who joined the popular orator in his barnstorms of New York and Indiana, Garfield certainly would have fallen to defeat. Later it was alleged that in a "Treaty of Mentor," Conkling had extracted a promise from Garfield to pass all federal nominations in New York before him and the Republican state party first. In exchange the golden-throated orator made twenty-six speeches to enthusiastic crowds from Madison Square Garden to Indianapolis. Garfield won a narrow victory of just 7,018 out of the nearly nine million votes cast. He had broken the momentum of the Democrats and kept the Republican presidency.

After his triumph Garfield made Blaine his secretary of state, much to Conkling's disgust. Garfield continued to fight Conkling over civil-service reforms, even as thousands of bureaucratic office seekers streamed into the Capitol in a pathetic procession. Conkling was so enraged at the president's rebuff that he resigned from the Senate in protest and failed to get reelected by the New York legislature.

Then on July 2, 1881, just four months after Garfield's inauguration, Charles J. Guiteau, a failed Chicago lawyer, now a disgruntled, desperate, and deranged job seeker, took out his anger at failing to secure a government appointment by shooting the fifty-year-old president as he strolled through Washington Station. Garfield died of his wounds two agonizing months later to the solemn grief of the entire nation. As a monument to the slain heroic leader, Congress enacted, and President Arthur signed, the vigorous civil-service bill Garfield had fought so hard and long in Congress and during his brief presidency to secure.

In his eulogy of Garfield, delivered before both houses of Congress and the justices of the Supreme Court, James G. Blaine, Garfield's closest political friend, explained:

> As the end grew near, his early craving for the sea returned. The stately mansion of power had been to him a wearisome hospital of pain, and he begged to be taken from its prison walls, from its oppressive stifling air, from its homelessness and hopelessness. Gently, silently, the love of a great people bore the pale sufferer to the longed-for healing of the sea, to live or die, as God should will, within sight of its billows, within the sound of its manifold voices . . . Let us think that his dying eyes read a mystic meaning which only the rapt and parting soul may know. Let us believe in the silence of the receding world he heard the great waves breaking on a farther shore, and already felt upon his wasted brow the breath of the eternal morning.

James Gillespie Blaine
1884 Republican Presidential Nominee

John Alexander Logan
1884 Republican
Vice Presidential Nominee

Facts-at-a-Glance
★★★

Event:	Eighth Republican National Convention
Dates:	June 3–6, 1884
Building:	Interstate Industrial Exposition Building
Location:	Lake Park, Michigan Avenue from Van Buren to Monroe Streets
Chicago Mayor:	Carter Henry Harrison Sr., Democrat
Candidates for Nomination:	President Chester Alan Arthur, New York; former Senator James Gillespie Blaine, Maine; Senator George Franklin Edmunds, Vermont; Senator John Alexander Logan, Illinois; Senator John Sherman, Ohio; General Joseph R. Hawley, Connecticut; Secretary of War Robert Todd Lincoln, Illinois; General William Tecumseh Sherman, Illinois
Presidential Nominee:	James Gillespie Blaine
Age at Nomination:	54
Number of Ballots:	4
Vice Presidential Nominee:	John Alexander Logan, Illinois
Number of Delegates:	820
Number Needed to Nominate:	A majority, 411
Largest Attendance:	15,000
Critical Issues:	Party unity, defeat of Democrats, reasonable tariffs, support of labor, education, human rights
Campaign Slogan:	"Blaine from Maine"

5
★★★

The 1884 Republican National Convention
"Blaine from Maine"

The summer of 1884 was the first in which Chicago hosted both national conventions of the major parties. Republicans gathered again in early June at the Interstate Industrial Exposition Building, which was constructed to handle 9,500. Republicans packed it with an estimated fifteen thousand conventioneers. The Democrats came to town in July and attracted even bigger crowds. The Republicans had held the White House for twenty-four years, since Lincoln's day. But the Democrats had recaptured both houses of Congress in the 1882 midterm election. The 1884 campaign to win the canvass of ten million male voters, set in motion by the two conventions, was one of the most exciting in American history. Dominated by accusations of scandal, adultery, bribery, and secret opposition funding, its outcome changed the course of American history and speeded new political alignments among voters.

The Chicago of the mid-1880s that delegates encountered was a magnetic metropolis teeming with well over half a million diverse people and many tongues. It boomed with industries and dazzled with inspiring architecture. Its recovery from "the most terrible conflagration known in modern times" had been called "one of the wonders of the world." Its new post office, courthouse, and city hall were counted among the finest public buildings in the land. The city boasted a system of elaborate parks and boulevards. Its hundreds of factories, lumberyards, and giant, sprawling stockyards stretched for miles. Millions of bushels of wheat, corn, oats, rye, and barley were shipped to Chicago elevators and warehouses to be sold in the East. All these provided jobs to the thousands who continued to pour into the city, from the farms and towns of the Midwest and East, and from lands beyond the seas. Chicago had become breadbasket, not only to America, but to Europe. Major rail systems terminated in its coal-choked yards. On the business

front, Chicago's speed was probably the fastest in the world. Unlike in New York, telephones already linked most of the offices across the business district, saving companies thousands of dollars in delivery fees, and accelerating the pace of commerce. The city was also a powderkeg of labor unrest. Immigrants, anarchists, and native-born workers violently clashed with police and company goons over livable wages and an eight-hour work day.

After the assassination of President Garfield, his secretary of state, James Gillespie Blaine, confronted with the sudden ascension of his arch-enemies from New York, left public office for the first time in twenty-three years, hoping to pursue a peaceful private life. He claimed he couldn't be "dragged back" to politics. But his supporters and the newspapers would not allow him the luxury of completing his dream book, *Twenty Years of Congress*. "Before leaving this world I want to see a man of genius in the White House, and you are the only chance I know," wrote Illinois Congressman Robert G. Ingersoll (who had nominated him at the Cincinnati convention of 1876, calling him the "Plumed Knight.") His sentiment was widely felt, especially among Republicans.

Blaine had been Garfield's secretary of state, already prosecuting an aggressive and robust "American" policy with other nations, particularly in Latin America. Blaine also stood up to the British and championed Irish independence. He had been the president's prime adviser, upon whom Garfield relied perhaps too much. He had been at Garfield's side in the Washington railroad station when the assassin Guiteau gunned down the president. The evening before the tragedy, the two friends had walked together, arm in arm, from Blaine's Fifteenth Street home to the White House, the assassin on their heals.

Blaine had stayed with the wounded president during the long months he lay in agony while the

Delegates entering the Interstate Industrial Exposition Building, 1884. Chicago Historical Society.

nation prayed for his recovery. By all rights of reason, Blaine was the natural successor to Garfield. But there was a problem or two. The vice president, not the president's most trusted adviser, succeeds him by constitutional order. The inauguration of President Chester A. Arthur meant new influence for New York "stalwarts," party professionals and their system of spoils. Blaine balked and resigned, his long public career brought to a sudden and disappointing halt.

President Arthur defied the pundits' predictions. He was not a cheap and tawdry party hack whose lifeblood was patronage, kickbacks, and skims. He quickly grew into the presidency and usually stood up to his old cronies. That of course wasn't the case when he offered a seat on the U.S. Supreme Court to his old mentor, Roscoe Conkling of the New York Republican machine. Conkling haughtily refused Arthur's offer, and as with most cases of hubris, faded from the political scene, although not before inflicting severe damage on Blaine. Conkling became a handsomely-paid private counsel to railroad magnate Jay Gould, who was robustly for Blaine. Yet Conkling had other thoughts.

Arthur followed Garfield's lead and fought for civil-service reform. He signed the Pendleton Act of 1883 that brought widespread change in the selection of government employees. He also worked to reduce tariffs sensibly, in part to balance the government's growing surplus. Arthur angered Congress when he vetoed pork barrel bills and anti-Chinese immigration legislation. He assumed the dignity of his office and pursued sound national policies. That wasn't enough, though, for the party stalwarts who thought Arthur had double-crossed them, or the Republican liberals who never believed he was out of the grip of the Republican New York State machine.

It didn't help Arthur that 1881 brought another economic depression or that his justice department had prosecuted Republican National Committee Secretary Stephen W. Dorsey, an Arkansas senator, for fake mail contracts and fraud against the federal government. When Dorsey was acquitted, party support for Arthur evaporated. Between Arthur and Blaine there was only cold formality. Then in the 1882 congressional elections, Democrats gained back the House of Representatives that Garfield had reclaimed for Republicans. None of the party factions wanted to see Arthur reelected, though the stalwarts gave him modest backing to oppose Blaine.

His only reliable support was from the army of federal workers, particularly in the South, who owed him loyalty. But no Republican had a hope of winning southern electoral votes and all the delegates knew it, so while Arthur was numerically strong, politically he was weak.

Excitement filled the sidewalks of Chicago as the crowds outside the ornate building pushed into the "glass palace." The Eighth Republican National Convention opened the Exposition Building doors onto Lake Park along Michigan Avenue at 10:15 A.M. on June 3, 1884. The crowds rushed into the huge cavern that had been designed for industrial expositions. Its ceiling arched two hundred feet above. The speaker's stand rose twelve feet above the platform, and above that was a large sounding board to project the speaker's voice to the crowd, something new since 1880. The 820 delegates responsible for deliberations were swallowed in a sea of fifteen thousand political operatives, lobbyists, party officials, dignitaries, and spectators. The two hundred ushers did all they could to hold back the crowds. Two tiers of boxes overlooked the floor. Naturally none of the candidates were present, but their strategists were hard at work. Arthur and Blaine were the clear frontrunners for the nomination, a sitting president challenged by the party's spokesman of two decades. Could the Republicans hold onto the White House, or would they give it up to the party of rebellion? Everything counted on the nomination.

Distinguished guests, politicians from all locales, packed the front rows. Many women filled the galleries, of whom the *Chicago Daily News* noted, "it goes without saying that they were handsomely costumed." The convention was called to order at 12:28 P.M. by Dwight M. Sabin, chairman of the national committee. Sabin addressed the attentive assemblage. "This city, already known as the city of conventions, is among the most cherished of all the spots of our country, sacred to the memories of a Republican."

Blaine's men controlled the party apparatus and in the first test of delegate strength, Sabin proposed former Alabama Governor Powell Clayton for temporary chairman. But before they could call for a vote, Henry Cabot Lodge of Massachusetts interrupted and nominated John R. Lynch, an African-American delegate from Mississippi and an Arthur supporter, for the post. In 1872 Lynch had become Speaker of the Mississippi House of Representatives at the tender age of twenty-four. The motion was seconded by a nervous twenty-five-year-old Theodore Roosevelt, attending his first convention as a first-term New York State assemblyman committed to cleaning up corrupt government. Lynch won the position 424 to 384, and once again the Blaine forces were worried about a repeat of 1876 and 1880 when other candidates ganged up to stop "Blaine of Maine."

The *Daily Inter Ocean* described the situation as Lynch approached the podium: "When the Mississippi negro, a man who had already distinguished himself in the Congress of the Nation, walked up the aisle to mount the Chairman's stand . . . a burst of magnificent applause . . . rang through the hall like a roar of winds, and was twice repeated before the enthusiasm aroused by an act so significant could be controlled."

Everyone wanted to avert another six-day convention like the one of 1880, now legendary in its duration, but the anti-Blaine delegates needed to keep the votes going as long as it took to force an alternative. In 1884 the Committee on Credentials, aided by rules set down four years earlier, the Committee on Rules and Order of Business, and the Committee on Resolutions worked without major disputes. While the convention delegates awaited their final reports, a number of planks were read to the gathering.

W. G. Donnan of Iowa spoke on behalf of Frances Willard and the Women's Christian Temperance Union, headquartered in nearby Evanston. "I hold in my hand a memorial of the women of the United States," he somberly proclaimed, "the Women's Christian Temperance Union: a memorial representing twenty-eight states and territories, asking for a constitutional prohibitory amendment to the national Constitution." David McClure of California instantly moved that the memorial be referred to the Committee on Resolutions where it could do no harm, a decision Republicans would later regret. Then at 11:00 A.M., with no business to conduct until the committees finished, the convention took an early recess, and delegates scattered into the streets of Chicago.

On Wednesday, June 4, the convention reconvened to hear more resolutions, starting with state temperance alliances. Another resolution called for a constitutional amendment to limit the presidency to one six-year term. It too was sent to committee. Then Republicans turned to procedure. S. W. Hawkins of Tennessee moved that all delegates needed to pledge prenomination support for the party's candidate,

whomever it might be, or be expelled. The issue, objected to by E. L. Pierce of Massachusetts, was the same one introduced by Senator Conkling in 1880. George A. Knight of California, a Blaine man, supported the motion, warning: "There are already whisperings in the air, of men high in the Republican party, or that once stood high in the Republican party, openly and avowedly declaring that they will not support one man if he is nominated by this convention, a convention of the most intelligent men of this nation." Knight was rebuffed by New York reformer, George William Curtis, "A Republican and a free man, I came into this convention," he shouted back, "By the grace of God, a Republican and a free man I will go out of this convention." Curtis won the day, and Hawkins withdrew his resolution. It was yet another rebuff to Blaine.

Other resolutions were introduced. George F. Hoar, Massachusetts senator, introduced a plank on female suffrage, reading, "Whereas, the women of this country are citizens, producers, and taxpayers, and are amenable to all the laws of the land, civil and criminal, which they have thus far had no part in making; therefore Resolved, that we favor the right of the women of the country to vote." The matter was immediately referred to the Committee on Resolutions, and the convention broke until 7:00 P.M. when it again tended to minor credential business, before recessing again until morning.

On June 5 the convention reconvened at 10:50 A.M., when it finally heard the report of the Committee on Credentials, which it accepted with a unanimous vote. It then dispensed with the report of the Committee on Rules and Order of Business, after some debate on procedures to pick delegates to the next convention. A minority Report on Rules was debated but withdrawn. Then William McKinley of Ohio, chairman of the Committee on Resolutions, loudly announced the 1884 platform to the attentive assembly that strained to hear: "The Republican Party has gained its strength by quick and faithful response to the demands of the people for the freedom and equality of all men; for a united nation, assuring the rights of all citizens; for the elevation of labor; for an honest currency; for purity in legislation; and for integrity and accountability in all departments of the government, and it accepts anew the duty of leading in the work of progress and reform." Naturally, McKinley pointed out, the party lamented "the death of President Garfield, whose sound states-

Interior view of the Exposition Building. Both the 1880 and 1884 Republican conventions were held here. Chicago Historical Society. Photo by C. D. Mosher.

manship, long conspicuous in Congress, gave promise of a strong and successful administration." The platform also gave a nod to President Arthur, who gave the country "wise, conservative and patriotic policy, under which the country has been blessed with remarkable prosperity; and we believe his eminent services are entitled to and will receive the hearty approval of every citizen." Arthur delegates and many in the galleries gave hearty approval.

McKinley condemned "the so-called economic system of the Democratic Party, which would degrade labor to the foreign standard . . . The Democratic Party has failed completely to relieve the people of the burden of unnecessary taxation by a wise reduction of the surplus." Among its many stances, the Republican platform of 1884 demanded that "the imposition of duties on foreign imports shall be made, not for 'revenue only,' but that in raising the requisite revenues for government, such duties shall be so levied as to afford security to our diversified industries and protection to the rights and wages of the laborer . . ." On Chinese immigration, the party denounced "the importation of contract labor, whether from Europe or Asia, as an offense against the spirit of American insti-

tutions; and we pledge [ourselves] to sustain the present law restricting Chinese immigration . . ."

The convention, seeking the vote of working men, endorsed "the establishment of a national bureau of labor; the enforcement of the eight-hour law; a wise and judicious system of general education by adequate appropriations from the national revenues, wherever the same is needed." Additionally, Republicans called for regulation of the railroads to help farmers. "The principal of public regulation of railway corporations is a wise and salutary one for the protection of all classes of the people . . ." And the platform noted, "Reform of the civil service, auspiciously begun under Republican administration, should be completed by the further extension of the reform system already established by law." The resolutions were adopted by acclamation and enthusiastic applause as the convention recessed until 7:00 P.M., when nominations for president would be entertained.

The parade of nominating states began with Connecticut. Augustus Brandegee nominated favorite son General Joseph Hawley. "General Hawley," said Brandegee, "believes in the morality of practical politics," striking a discordant theme against Blaine. Years earlier, Blaine had been tarnished by charges he accepted $150,000 in Arkansas and Fort Smith Railroad stock in exchange for legislative favors while he was Speaker of the House. The House cleared him of the charges, but they remained a potent campaign tool in the hands of his enemies.

When the call came to Illinois, the land of Lincoln nominated General John Alexander Logan, the "Black Eagle." Former Illinois governor and now Senator Shelby Moore Cullom came to the podium amid much applause. After calling Chicago a "political mecca," Cullom noted that Logan was a "gallant son of the Prairie State," who at the start of the Civil War had retired his seat in Congress. His "history is a part of the history of the battles of Belmont, of Donelson, of Shiloh, of Vicksburg, of Lookout Mountain, of Atlanta, and of the famous march to the sea. He never lost a battle. I repeat again," Cullom shouted, "Mr. President and my fellow citizens, he never lost a battle in all the struggles of the war."

Then it was Blaine's turn, and the convention went wild with anticipation of his nomination. Blaine, whose popularity continued to soar after he left office, had lost close nomination fights in 1876 and 1880, both times to the men elected president. But that was no matter now. A career as the party's chief spokesman, as an elegant and eloquent leader, entitled him to this moment. The delegates rose to their feet chanting Blaine's name, over and over. Ohio's blind orator Judge William H. West called for order so he could commence, but the turmoil lasted an additional ten minutes.

West began exuberantly:

> Gentleman of the convention, as a delegate in the Chicago convention of 1860, the proudest service of my life was performed by voting for the nomination of that inspired emancipator, the first Republican president of the United States.

The convention saluted his good works and after reviewing the struggle of five successive campaigns, West noted that,

> Political conditions are changed since the accession of the Republican Party to power. The mighty issues of struggling freedom . . . which convulsed the continent and rocked the Republic . . . have ceased their contention . . .

Who could command the new conditions? the judge asked his listeners.

> Who shall be our candidate? Not the representative of a particular interest or a particular class . . . Gentleman, he must be a representative of American manhood, a representative of that living Republicanism that demands the amplest industrial protection and opportunity whereby labor shall be able to earn and eat the bread of independent employment. . . . Through all the conflicts of [the nation's] progress, from the baptism of blood on the plains of Kansas to the fall of the immortal Garfield, wherever humanity needed succor, or freedom needed protection, or country a champion, wherever blows fell thickest and fastest, there, in the forefront of battle, was seen to wave the white plume of James G. Blaine, our Henry of Navarre.

Once again the applause was so thunderous that the gas lights trembled, and the walls shook as the delegates stamped and shouted. In the galleries women gave way to loss of decorum and joined the delirious pandemonium. The hysteria lasted for several minutes more before Blaine was seconded by Cushman K. Davis of Minnesota.

President Chester Arthur's name was submitted for consideration by Martin I. Townsend, a representative of the business interests who supported him: "America is proud of her great men; the Republican Party is proud of her great men; and the great men of America are in the Republican Party." Arthur was seconded by Henry H. Bingham of Pennsylvania, who added, "The unknown man of four years ago has become the best known within the confines of the Republic. What a man can do is best determined from what he has done." Winston of North Carolina and Lynch of Mississippi also seconded. Another African-American delegate, P.B.S. Pinchback, former governor of Louisiana (for one month) also stood to second "General Arthur." The nominating speeches and demonstrations continued for five hours. The delegates were exhausted, but motions to adjourn were voted down. Ohio's Republican candidate for governor, Joseph Benson Foraker, nominated John Sherman.

George Franklin Edmunds of Vermont, a senator since 1866 and now perennial candidate of the liberal Republicans, was presented by former Governor John

D. Long of Massachusetts. George W. Curtis of New York, once a resident of the utopian Brook Farm community, now an essayist and editor for *Harper's Weekly*, seconded Edmunds. He contrasted Edmunds to Blaine. "Incorruptible, unassailable, a Republican whom every Republican trusts to the utmost; whom every Democrat respects with all his heart . . ." Delegates were now too fatigued and too dazzled by a night of high-blown Republican oratory to argue, but Mr. Foraker of Ohio moved for the first ballot anyway. The crowd refused and after a dispute at the podium that lasted another half hour, exited at 1:45 A.M.

The convention reconvened at 11:00 A.M. June 6 for its crowning performance. When the president called the Roll Call of the States, Blaine jumped to an imposing lead with 334 1/2 votes from the thirty-five states and territories with 411 needed to win. Arthur trailed with a surprisingly strong 278. Edmunds tallied just 93, Logan, 63 1/2, John Sherman, 30, General Hawley, 13, Robert Todd Lincoln, 4, and General William T. Sherman, 2. (General Sherman had earlier telegraphed the convention saying, "If nominated, I will not run. If elected, I will not serve.")

The chair announced, "No nomination having been made, according to the rules of the convention, the convention will now proceed to another vote." The Arthur and Edmunds men caucused in the aisle. Arthur's people offered a full commitment to reform and whatever else the Edmunds supporters wanted. But the hardened Republican reformers were more than skeptical. They scornfully resisted any deals with the president and stood in contempt of both Arthur and Blaine. It was a standoff Blaine hadn't been fortunate enough to see in 1876 and 1880. It meant he would at last win the nomination. While the other contenders searched for alternatives, Blaine gained. The ballots came in rapid succession.

The second ballot proceeded, and Blaine gained ground over his competitors at 349. The third ballot followed without hesitation, with Blaine inching forward to 375. A motion to recess was offered by Foraker of Ohio, so anti-Blaine forces could again confer. Roosevelt jumped on his chair, "I demand a roll call of the states upon the motion." It was defeated 364 to 450. On the fourth ballot, Illinois read the chair a telegram from General Logan instructing his name be withdrawn from consideration. Then the land of Lincoln switched to Blaine. So did Ohio. At last James G. Blaine, one of the greatest

Speakers of the House of Representatives and pride of the Republican Party, had won his nomination. Blaine surged to 541. Arthur fell back with 207, while Edmunds limped in at 41, Logan retained 7, and Lincoln settled at 2.

President Arthur sent a telegram to the convention asking for unanimous approval of the nominee. Then, the chair read another telegram from the president, to Blaine, "As the candidate of the Republican Party you will have my earnest and cordial support."

Illinois once more had the honor of a national nominee, as the convention, on the first ballot, almost unanimously elevated General Logan, who now commanded a national army of veterans who voted, to the second spot. A few weeks later, Eugene Field, a Chicago newspaper poet and author of "Little Boy Blue," penned a poem about Logan that ended:

> And 'neath the burning Southern sun,
> where e'er your standard waved,
> We found a glorious victory won,
> Our soldier honor saved!
> We live on history's page, and yet,
> They ask us at this time,
> To furl our banners and forget,
> Those days and deeds sublime!
>
> Nay! Sound the trumpet, beat the drum,
> And call the roll again!
> A million soldier boys will come,
> A million Logan men!

The Blaine legions were still enthusiastically demonstrating as they filed out of the Exposition Building in anticipation of a victorious campaign. But within a week trouble was brewing. Before the Democrats even met in Chicago in July, Blaine was fighting a battle at his Republican rear. The Massachusetts and New York backers of Edmunds could hold no countenance with James Blaine, the man who allegedly had compromised his position as Speaker of the House in exchange for stock and who was allegedly under the spell of Jay Gould and the Union Pacific Railroad. The liberal Republicans reconvened on June 7 at the Massachusetts Reform Club in Boston to denounce Blaine and Logan and declared their willingness to create an alliance with the new anticorruption wing of the Democrats that was making a run at the nomination.

The bolters were called *mugwumps,* an Algonquin word for "chief," and were led by George W. Curtis and Carl Schurz, who had been a radical Republican soldier and senator from Missouri before coming to New York to join Curtis on *Harper's.* The liberal Republicans had bolted the party in 1872 in protest against "Grant's devils." Their candidate, publisher Horace Greeley, became a fusion candidate with the Democrats, a party he had spent his career castigating. Now an "honest government" campaign was gaining strength among voters who were sick of seeing their revenues wasted on party spoils. Democrats who had been out of power since the Civil War were beneficiaries of the discontent. Mugwumps let the Democrats know of their interest in fusing. Blaine was in trouble.

Grover Cleveland
1884 Democratic Presidential Nominee

Thomas Andrews Hendricks
1884 Democratic
Vice Presidential Nominee

Facts-at-a-Glance
★★★

Event:	Fourteenth Democratic National Convention
Dates:	July 8–11, 1884
Building:	Interstate Industrial Exposition Building
Location:	Lake Park, Michigan Avenue from Van Buren to Monroe Streets
Chicago Mayor:	Carter Henry Harrison Sr., Democrat
Candidates for Nomination:	Senator Thomas Francis Bayard, Delaware; Speaker of the House John Griffin Carlisle, Kentucky; Governor Stephen Grover Cleveland, New York; former Governor Thomas Andrews Hendricks, Indiana; George Hoadly, Ohio; former Speaker of the House Samuel Jackson Randall, Pennsylvania; former Senator Allen Granberry Thurman, Ohio
Presidential Nominee:	Stephen Grover Cleveland
Age at Nomination:	47
Number of Ballots:	2
Vice Presidential Nominee:	Thomas Andrews Hendricks
Number of Delegates:	820
Number Needed to Nominate:	Two-thirds, 683
Largest Attendance:	15,000
Critical Issues:	Reform of corrupt government, lower tariffs
Campaign Slogan:	"Public Office Is a Public Trust"
Campaign Song:	"For He's a Jolly Good Fellow"

6
★★★

The 1884 Democratic National Convention
Mudslingers and Mugwumps

With a formidable Blaine nominated by the Republicans a month earlier, Democrats met in Chicago on July 8, for the first time in twenty years. In the two decades since the "Copperhead Convention of 1864," the Democrats had taken on an entirely new look. In the last election, they had piled up electoral victories in northern states that were tired of a quarter century of Republican rule that had degenerated into corruption and machine control. Republican reformer George W. Curtis, editor of *Harper's Weekly*, described the New York State Republican machine as "an odious and intolerable oligarchy which menaces the very system of our government . . . [with its] flagrant decay of official faith and integrity." The new Democratic Party of 1884 was called "country democracy." It was fast attracting a younger set of urban professional and business men with its avid "honest government" agenda.

In New York, reform governor Stephen Grover Cleveland had already begun to dismantle the old system of contracts to cronies and kickbacks. Cleveland was said to be clean and courageous. He did what he thought was right and stood ground on principle. He brought a different kind of feel to a party that no longer dwelled on old Reconstruction issues or states' rights. In 1882 Cleveland, mayor of Buffalo, had catapulted to the governor's office with the largest plurality in New York State history, tossing out the remnants of the Conkling/Platt state Republican machine and challenging its patronage army. Cleveland's rise was meteoric. Now the presidency beckoned.

Rain had fallen heavily the night before the Chicago gathering and as it let up, the few paved streets of the city were running with muddy water. The city was bustling, but amid the commotion on the street were the marks of hardship. Unemployment was high, and homeless men, women, and children wandered Chicago's streets. Industrial strikes for the eight-hour day were more frequent than ever. None of that deterred though the thousands of delegates,

spectators, and bands marching in procession into the Interstate Industrial Exposition Building, its impressive towers topped with an abundance of American flags flapping in the warm lake wind. The First Illinois Regiment, in scarlet coats, played the theme songs of entering delegations. New York City's Tammany Hall with "flags and banners made the finest showing of all," noted one observer. More than fifteen thousand packed into the giant Exposition hall, with the humidity rising. When the band played a rendition of "Dixie" the eager crowd leaped up with wild hand clapping and foot stomping.

The Fourteenth Democratic National Convention was gaveled to order that Tuesday morning, July 8, by William H. Barnum of Connecticut. The convention picked a temporary chairman, Richard B. Hubbard, former governor of Texas, who got the delegates wound up again by blasting Republican corruption. He summoned memories of the "stolen election of 1876," which he called "the greatest crime in history," and concluded that now was the time for a reformer to lead the Democratic party, a hint at Cleveland.

All this reform talk frightened old-time Democrats like former Congressman "Honest" John Kelly and Thomas F. Grady of Tammany Hall, the heirs of "Boss" Tweed. They held half of the New York State contingent under tight control. "Cleveland is the enemy of the working man," "Honest" John told reporters. "Tammany wants candidates who are honest men and able men and statesmen who have been tried in the crucible and not found wanting." Cleveland, who had not yet been endorsed by the evenly split New York delegation, had already attacked the Hall's interests from the governor's mansion in Albany. Tammany wanted to stop him cold, before he gained the power of the presidency.

The Tammany contingent of seven hundred, all sporting white hats, left New York on the Fourth of July with high hopes. Tammany's strategy was to undermine Cleveland's support in the New York delegation. Elsewhere they sought to block his nomination in whatever way possible. But once in Chicago, Tammany was swallowed in the sea of 820 delegates and thousands upon thousands of observers, reporters, well-wishers, and jobbers, all fever hot in their short sleeves, with their fans flapping furiously. Chicago conventions, in the throes of summer, were always hot, sultry affairs. New York State Democratic chairman Daniel Manning backed Cleveland and had put his career on the line standing up to Tammany Hall. E. K. Apgar of the Albany *Evening News* also spread the word for Cleveland. Tammany Hall was isolated, but not without its own power and convention savvy.

In fact Grady had headed out to Chicago a week early with some of the boys to line up opposition to Cleveland. The first place he lit upon was Chicago's large Irish community, which had a vocal interest in freeing Ireland from British control as soon as possible. Grady sold a bushel of apples to the local press, convincing them that Cleveland was anti-Irish and anti-Catholic, producing his veto of a Catholic home for delinquents as proof. In truth, Cleveland vetoed it because public monies could not, by law, go to religious institutions. Quickly Grady stirred up fervent anti-Cleveland feeling. Cleveland was a Know-Nothing back in 1856 and 1860, Grady told Chicagoans, and he still was a Know-Nothing, an anti-Irish, Protestant bigot.

When the Cleveland forces reached Chicago, they met strong opposition. They tried to prove Cleveland had been defamed and that indeed he had three trusted Irish-American Catholics in his top administration. But Tammany's men were everywhere—in the hotel lobbies, the barrooms, and the delegate caucuses—spreading their poison. When asked why he did it, "Honest" John piously replied, "It is not on either personal or political grounds; it is because I believe him to be a moral leper." With that kind of talk, the pragmatic men of the party began to look elsewhere for a candidate. "I would regard Cleveland's nomination," "Honest" John pontificated, "very much in the light of a party suicide, and hope it will not be done. It would kill us. The laboring classes are not with him and cannot be made to support him." Some of "Honest" John's friends feared he might "lose his mind" if Cleveland won. True or not, Tammany was out to demolish Cleveland, and that could wreck the election for the Democrats. But as Tammany knew, if

you knock a man down, you must have one in his stead. But who? Tammany had a name. Trot out Tilden again and stampede the convention, overwhelm Cleveland before he picked up speed.

As soon as Chairman Hubbard finished his keynote speech on that first day, a motion was made to adopt the same rules used by every Democratic convention since 1832. Grady of Tammany Hall jumped to his feet, moving an amendment to abolish the unit rule, something the Republicans had already done to make their party more representative and something that Tammany Hall never wanted in the past. Grady's real motivation was to break loose New York votes that state chairman Daniel Manning was ready to cast for Cleveland.

Grady's protest set the delegates and galleries into rival hissing and cheering for the well-known ward heeler. Roll was called on the unit rule, and New York cast all its seventy-two contested votes in favor of the unit rule. Grady's motion failed. Tammany's Bourke Cockran immediately challenged the count, but with no change. Someone made a motion to adjourn to calm nerves, and it carried. Delegates marched out to loud communal choruses of "Dixie."

That night the New York delegates took their final vote in their clubrooms at the Palmer House. The delegates were split thirty-five for Cleveland to thirty-five against the governor, with two still uncommitted. But where were the two? They had been missing for hours. Both Kelly and Manning had been working them for their price. Outside the clubroom a tide of delegates and operatives passed back and forth. Finally, the two delegates who held the balance in their hands showed up and voted for Cleveland. Price? Nomination for state office. Tammany was furious. They sent their emissaries from delegation to delegation looking for a coalition to stop Cleveland. "There was a battle royal in the New York delegation yesterday," the *Tribune* reported, "which while resulting in giving the Cleveland people the advantage, by no means settles the fight against the New York Governor."

Tammany's effort to recruit Tilden fizzled when he wired that he was not available under any circumstances; he was old, he said, and Cleveland was his man. Now Tammany considered Benjamin Franklin Butler, governor of Massachusetts. During the Civil War, Butler was known as "the Beast of New Orleans" for his heavy-handed rule as military commander.

He was also instrumental in the passage of the Civil Rights Act of 1875. So even though Butler had bolted from the Republicans, the Democrats distrusted him. The Anti-Monopoly Party, meeting in Chicago on May 14, already had nominated him as their presidential candidate. The National Party, or Greenbacks, had nominated him for the same post two weeks later in Indianapolis. He wanted regulation of corporate monopolies and tariff reduction to ease the existing price burden. He had not yet accepted the two nominations. With the Democratic nomination as well, he could win far better than Cleveland, Tammany argued.

On the second day, William Freeman Vilas of Wisconsin, another reformer, was elected the convention's permanent chair and again rallied the reform enthusiasm in his keynote speech. Now the convention turned to the long-awaited nomination Roll Call of the States. Delaware nominated its favorite son, Senator Thomas Francis Bayard. Thomas Andrews Hendricks, who had served as both senator and governor of Indiana and had been the vice presidential nominee under Tilden in 1876, believed he himself deserved the nomination. A party favorite, he rose to the opening of umbrellas and stomping of delegates. Hendricks feigned disinterest and nominated a stalking horse, former Indiana senator Joseph E. McDonald. But Hendricks used the occasion to expound on the state of the nation and thereby spotlight his own ideas and candidacy. Ohio nominated Governor Allen Granberry Thurman, a former congressman and senator, who had flirted with the Greenback heresy in the 1870s. Kentucky's John Griffin Carlisle, Speaker of the House of Representatives, also received a favorite son nomination.

Then Daniel N. Lockwood of Buffalo nominated Cleveland. He recalled marching in torchlight parades with the young Democrat when they were boys. "The world is moving and moving rapidly," Cleveland's friend exalted, "From the North and the South new men, men who have acted but little in politics, are coming to the front, and today there are hundreds of young men in this country, men who are to cast their first vote, men who are independent in politics, and they are looking to this convention, praying silently that there should be no mistake here." Then he told the hushed crowd how Cleveland had thrown the crooks out of Buffalo's government and was doing the same in Albany.

Chicago's own beloved mayor, the distinguished Carter Henry Harrison Sr., who was known to ride around town on a chestnut stallion as he tended to business, rose, to considerable local applause, to second the Cleveland nomination. Harrison had come to Chicago in 1855 from Kentucky, by way of Yale and a European tour, to make millions in the real estate boom. He showed dynamic leadership in rebuilding the city after the fire and was honest and caring. One of his election slogans was "A mayor who keeps his hands in his own pockets." His fellow citizens made him their congressman in 1874. But he returned home to run for mayor in 1879 and won despite charges from the papers that he was a communist. Indeed he was a friend of the working man and woman and treated everyone fairly. His "Live and Let Live" philosophy meant Chicago's wild frontier spirit still rode the streets day or night. Carter loved his city, and the city loved him. Now on the podium before a national forum, the mayor tried to unmask some of Grady's accusations, denouncing as slanderous ideas that the Catholic Church would try to defeat Cleveland or that Irish voters would desert him for Blaine.

The whole time Grady was on his feet, waving to get the attention of the chair. "Honest" John's minions who were planted throughout the convention floor and galleries, chanted "Grady, Grady, Grady!" He walked to the podium amid cheers and jeers, bowing gracefully toward both and began playing to the galleries with derogatory barbs toward the Republicans and Blaine. Then he did something no one had ever done before in convention history. "I should be glad to second Mr. Cleveland's nomination except that I know and believe I can show you," Grady hesitated and then shouted at the New York Clevelandites, "he cannot carry the state of New York." A chorus of boos and shouts of outrage ascended from the Cleveland contingent in all four quarters of the colossal hall. As Grady tried to explain himself, shouts to rule him out of order rose from the hall, while insults were hurled down from the galleries.

The chair pounded its gavel and ruled Grady was not speaking to the question, but New York State chairman Manning stood and magnanimously asked for the convention to let him finish. Grady then continued, referring to Mayor Harrison, "I am here to say to you that we do not claim, as suggested by the distinguished delegate from Illinois, that the Catholics

Cheering the nomination of Grover Cleveland at the 1884 Democratic National Convention.
Chicago Historical Society.

or the Irish are against Mr. Cleveland," Grady bellowed, as the convention sighed for a moment in relief. "We are here to say that the antimonopoly element of the state, and the laboring interests of the state, Catholic and Protestant, Irish, German, and American, every man who belongs to either of these great interests, is opposed to Grover Cleveland's nomination, and will be opposed to Grover Cleveland's election." This was more than Cleveland delegates could stand. They were on their feet screaming at the top of their lungs at the red-faced Tammany Hall boss. Then he completed his "seconding speech" by endorsing McDonald of Indiana.

Grady was quickly followed to the speaker's stand by another Tammany leader, Ireland-born Bourke Cockran, who launched into another anti-Cleveland harangue. He confided to delegates that he was "too warm a friend of [Cleveland] to desire his promotion to an office for which I do not believe he has the mental qualifications." He too rebuffed Harrison's suggestion that the mantle had fallen from Tilden to Cleveland, saying that "when the mantle . . . of a giant falls upon a dwarf, he is bound to be smothered." He seconded Thurman instead. New York del-

egate E. K. Apgar spoke on Cleveland's behalf, but the convention was in turmoil. Rather than continue, the chair dismissed the assembly in time for supper. The delegates were sweating and angry at Grady for ruining party unity. They swore under their breaths. The Clevelandites gained a toughened resolve to win and punish Tammany Hall.

On the convention's third day, July 10, tensions were high, and the mood was somber. Favorite sons, Ohio's Governor George Hoadly and Pennsylvania's Samuel Jackson Randall, former Speaker of the House, were nominated and seconded. As the nominating Roll Call of the States came to an end, Cleveland was seconded by Wisconsin's General Edward Stuyvesant Bragg, a Douglas Democrat. He brought the convention to life by castigating Tammany Hall and Grady for their performance. Cleveland was popular with voters, Congressman Bragg said, and his "name is upon their lips; his name is in their hearts . . . They love him, gentlemen, and they respect him, not only for himself, for his character, for his integrity and judgement, and iron will," Bragg hesitated and slowly ended his sentence pronouncing each word loudly, "but they love him most for the enemies he has made!" The convention concurred with loud shouts of glee aimed at the Tammany delegation.

Grady, red with anger, leaped to his feet, "Mr. Chairman, on behalf of his enemies I reciprocate that sentiment, and we are proud of the compliment." The entire convention erupted into conflict, men leaping to their seats, screaming angrily at one and other, and at Grady and Bragg. Clevelandites delighted in chanting, "They love him most for the enemies he has made, they love him most for the enemies he has made . . ." Finally Bragg continued: "Their study has been political chicane in the midnight conclaves." Movingly he concluded, "Our young men . . . have followed old leaders to death. They ask somebody to lead them to victory . . . Let our old war horses be retired with honor. Let the record of their achievements be recorded and pointed at with pride and pleasure; but our people say give us new life, give us new blood, give us something that has come to manhood and position since the war . . ." The Cleveland brigades applauded in deference. Then, since the platform was not ready yet, voting had to be delayed until that evening, and the convention recessed at midday.

The 1884 Democrats had a crowded platform to consider before the presidential voting began, but not one that differed much from the Republicans. One resolution called for majority rule for future conventions, instead of the current two-thirds rule. When the tide seemed to fall for the issue, the chairman suspended the vote and abruptly assigned it to committee. The Democratic platform charged Republicans with out-and-out corruption, of squandering millions on navy development, and of high tariffs that protected a few major industries but "impoverished" many others. Democrats in 1884 favored reduced tariffs "to promote healthy growth" of industries and wanted to tax luxury items the most, with a sliding downward scale. The party opposed "taxation known as 'Internal Revenue,' except to pay the war debt and pensions." Democrats backed "honest" money and were adamant about the rights of Americans abroad. They called for "honest civil service reform," free education by common schools, and, like the Republicans, did not "sanction the importation of foreign labor or the admission of servile races."

With its platform adopted, the presidential roll call began. Tammany demanded an adjournment but was refused. Cleveland immediately stormed to

a big lead, with 392 votes to Bayard's 170. Thurman attracted 88, Randall, 78, McDonald, 56, Carlisle, 27, Hoadly, 3. Hendricks received 1 vote, which he protested. Tilden also got 1. A call to adjourn was narrowly defeated 412 to 404. It was already getting late, well past one o'clock in the morning, and Manning noticed some of the older Cleveland delegates leaving. He suddenly feared that Cleveland would lose instead of gain strength on the second ballot and forsake momentum, so he moved for adjournment as well. The delegates reconsidered and departed until 10:00 A.M. Friday.

All night, Tammany Hall and other party leaders were on telephones and in hotel lobbies and bedrooms trying to make deals. They pulled out the last of their tricks. Richard J. Bright of Indiana, convention sergeant-of-arms and an anti-Cleveland man, controlled ticket authorization and distribution. "Honest" John supplied the cash to recruit hundreds of residents from nearby cheap hotels to sit in the galleries above the delegates and scream on cue. But one of the co-conspirators of "Honest" John's plan was a Cleveland spy who turned Manning out of bed. The New York chairman did the same to his advisers to plot a counterstrategy.

As soon as the convention resumed deliberations, part two of "Honest" John's plan unfolded. Illinois and Indiana made a bid to gather all the anti-Cleveland votes for Hendricks, the popular and imposing leader, hoping to trip a stampede. Indiana was a critical swing state that the Democrats had won with Tilden, perhaps important enough for a presidential nominee. The preplanned demonstration of Kelly's unfortunates broke out in the balconies. But Manning's men had already alerted all his allies to the ruse, and they simply let the paid spectators yell their lungs out. All the kindling in the city could not ignite Hendricks's fire. "Honest" John and Grady fell exhausted back into their seats along with the other Hendricks supporters, as the second ballot began. Cleveland forged further ahead with 475. Bayard held on to 151 1/2. Hendricks swelled to 123 1/2. The stampede failed. Thurman dropped back to 60.

Now, Pennsylvania, the second largest state in the Union, jumped onto the Cleveland bandwagon. In a moment, the North Carolina delegation switched to Cleveland. So did Virginia. Realizing that Cleveland was about to really stampede, Tammany Hall again moved for an adjournment, but failed. Cleveland's 683 second ballot votes overwhelmed Senator Bayard's 81 1/2 and Hendricks's 45 1/2. Cleveland had done it, and the convention erupted, chanting his name as his picture, under a ten-foot horseshoe of flowers, was hoisted on stage. The band played "For He's a Jolly Good Fellow." The chairman pounded on the podium until his gavel splintered. Outside the Exposition Building, thousands of spectators and Clevelandites who had been denied admission in the ticket scam were jubilant. Then the traditional cannon blast outside the building again set the convention into convulsions.

The cheering delegates had their man. Cleveland could rejuvenate the party. As they adjourned for dinner, Democrats were optimistic for the first time in years. They had polled a national majority in 1876 with Governor Tilden of New York and Hendricks. Now they would use the same strategy with Governor Cleveland of New York against the strongest candidate the Republicans could offer. But was Grady right? Could Cleveland win New York? The bull market ran wild the next day on the Chicago exchange. Republican investors concluded the young New York governor stood no chance against the popular elder statesman Blaine, who had all the big Eastern money behind him.

The final session of the 1884 Fourteenth Democratic National Convention reconvened Friday evening to celebrate a little more and pick a vice presidential candidate. Two Civil War generals, John C. Black of Ohio and Congressman William S. Rosecrans of California, were nominated. Black declined. Then Hendricks of Indiana was nominated by Pennsylvania. The chairman of the Indiana delegation protested on Hendricks's behalf and announced that the senator "is not and will not be a candidate for the vice presidency." He emphasized the final words haughtily. Within minutes, the convention unanimously drafted Hendricks, despite his protests. Again the band piped out "For He's a Jolly Good Fellow," and all sang along. Then the convention, mostly united, sang a verse of "Praise God from Whom All Blessings Flow." To bring the proceedings to an end, the standard-bearers for each delegation paraded out into the evening heat. With that the 1884 Democratic convention adjourned. "Grover Has It," shouted the *Daily Inter Ocean*. Now the great contest began, pitting the dashing and eloquent statesman against the stodgy and unproven governor.

Grover Cleveland's rise to national prominence had been mercurial. Just three years earlier, he had been a hard-working, though hardly wealthy, private attorney. His only political experience was as an assistant district attorney during the Civil War and three years as a sheriff after the war. But he had been a tough sheriff, personally hanging three convicts himself. When a delegation of Buffalo reformers asked him to run for mayor against an entrenched and corrupt machine, he accepted with no expectations of victory. He rode a hard-hitting, clean government campaign to an upset, then took personal control of the city's finances, supervising every penny spent, routing the spoilsmen, and protecting the public till.

Because he vetoed every boondoggle that came his way, Cleveland became known as the "veto mayor." His reputation spread statewide. In 1882, after just two years as Buffalo mayor, he was prompted to run for governor of New York as an upstate, independent Democrat, free of the strings of Tammany Hall. He won by almost two hundred thousand votes, an unheard-of margin. Once again he put his veto to work, as he did throughout his political career. This time he stood up to popular bills that reduced fares on New York City elevated trains to five cents and another that reduced the hours the elevated conductors had to work. Both were highly popular measures, but both violated previously negotiated contracts, so Cleveland vetoed them. Despite the uproar, the new governor stood his ground, something the stubborn Cleveland always did, gaining the respect of the public and enhancing his reputation for honesty.

Since Tilden was too old and Democrats had no real candidate for president, Cleveland's name had begun to surface as a potential choice. New York, along with Indiana, were key northern states. Win them, along with the South, and Democrats could win the White House, which is why the Democrats had selected a New Yorker for every presidential election since 1868. With Tilden, they actually won the 1876 popular vote, before Republicans snatched back the election.

But in both national and international matters, Cleveland was an inexperienced civilian. For the first time in years, neither candidate had been a Civil War general. Every Republican president after Lincoln had earned his general's rank in that conflict, but the war had been over for twenty years now. Most voters had other concerns, such as economic hard times, job losses, and reduced wages. On the other hand, Cleveland was a novice, a political newcomer. Still there was something exciting, even hopeful, about him and his pledge to clean up and renew government.

From the start of the campaign, Blaine was less than optimistic. He had not wanted the nomination in the first place and thought the mood of the country was wrong. But he was bound as the Republican's finest statesman to prevent the South from reversing all that his illustrious party predecessors had won and protected. Blaine's enemies went on the offensive in early summer, bringing up again the details of his railway-bribery-for-votes scandal a decade old. Newspapers such as the normally Republican-loyal *New York Times* blasted and distorted Blaine's record. Ministers and university presidents, such as Harvard's Charles William Eliot, spoke out against him.

All summer, the Republican mugwumps hit Blaine with charges of corruption and flawed character. They organized anti-Blaine clubs in the big cities of Boston, New York, and Philadelphia, and their legions were, as far as Blaine was concerned, dangerously swelling. They saluted Cleveland's virtues of honesty and efficiency. But when anti-Blaine clubs sent hundreds of delegates to the University Club in New York City for a national meeting on July 22, they were temporarily stopped in their tracks. Coming out of their first day meeting they were shocked to see the headlines of the Buffalo *Telegraph*: "A Terrible Tale: A Dark Chapter in a Public Man's History; The Pitiful Story of Maria Halpin and Governor Cleveland's Son!" The paper detailed Cleveland's "seduction" and scandalous sexual affair with a widow who bore him an illegitimate son.

The puritanical mugwumps were flabbergasted. Cleveland's election was clearly lost now, moaned Schurz and the others who had bolted the Republicans on the question of personal morality. Buffalo ministers confirmed the story and told mugwump minister Henry Beecher, "Cleveland's debaucheries continue to this hour!" It was too late to nominate someone else. For two days, most papers in the nation did not print the rumors; then the news spread like wildfire. In an editorial, the *Telegraph* preached, "The libertine is a foe of the home, and is therefore, in a certain sense, a traitor to the republic. Take it to yourselves brother! How would you feel about it if Maria Halpin were your sister? Take it to yourselves, fathers! What would you do about it if Maria Halpin were your daughter?"

Cleveland's conduct clearly affronted all proper values. The Boston *Journal* concurred: "We do not believe that the American people would elevate to the Presidency of the United States a betrayer of women, a man of shameless and profligate life. The failure to meet and disprove the charges will be a confession of guilt." Efforts to get Maria Halpin to exonerate Cleveland failed. Honesty was Cleveland's policy, so the candidate said little about the affair throughout the campaign. But Senator George G. Vest of Missouri defended him. "What of it? We did not enter our man into this race as a gelding."

Democrats counterpunched against the Cleveland scandal, which they suspected Jay Gould and Republicans had leaked. They falsely claimed that Blaine's oldest son, who had died at a tender age, was illegitimate. Blaine's men called Cleveland "a drunken sot," "the hangman of Buffalo," "a lecherous beast," "an obese nincompoop." Republicans chanted in parades as they marched, "Ma, Ma, Where's My Pa?" Cleveland confessed to friends that he wished he had never accepted the nomination, that he'd rather campaign in hell.

Indeed, Cleveland's personal characteristics were not the most virtuous. Before his election to governor, he frequented saloons and racetracks. Nor was he intellectually well-versed, or "deep." He lacked imagination and had no tact. He was often blunt and awkward when speaking to crowds. At 250 pounds, he was built like a "bull with a mustache." He sported a large muscular neck, thick chest, and well-fed stomach. But he was honest, did what he believed in, and didn't pull his punches. "Whatever you do, tell the truth," was his response to the sexual scandal that rocked his campaign.

In 1884 party affiliations were tenuous and changing under the charges and countercharges. Germans, who had been solidly with the Republicans because of their hatred of slavery, now saw the party in some states working with the Prohibitionists. In fact, the campaign of Ben Butler, presidential candidate of the Anti-Monopolists and Greenbackers, was getting hundreds of thousands of secret dollars from the Republicans who had unlimited Wall Street funds. Republican strategists also funded the Prohibition vote hoping it would hurt Democrats in key states by siphoning off worker and immigrant votes. Butler also tried to build bridges with Kelly and Grady at Tammany Hall to wreck Cleveland's chances in New York. Railroad and Wall Street tycoon Jay Gould, Blaine's chief financial backer and anti-Cleveland strategist, spread plenty of money around Tammany Hall, trying to pry out a defection that could cripple Cleveland.

But in late September, Tammany Hall, fearing Republicans more than the reform Democrats, began working to win New York for Cleveland. Actually, they were playing both sides of the fence, since "Honest" John never stopped working against Cleveland. In the end, the Prohibitionist votes turned against the Republicans, the party that had funded much of its campaign in New York, Kansas, Illinois, Indiana, Michigan, and Ohio. The Republican platform rebuff in Chicago also had fueled the Prohibitionists to work hard against Blaine.

Meanwhile, Irish Blaine Clubs sprang up in cities across the country, trying to capitalize on Blaine's anti-British/pro-Irish stance as Garfield's secretary of state and to draw Irish voters away from the Democrats. "Ireland would be free in thirty days, if Blaine were president," Irish voters were told. In addition to supplying any juicy tidbits they could find out about Cleveland's illicit romance, Republicans publicly pounded away at his critical lack of experience. But many forces were at work. As the September campaign heated up, Blaine took a beating. Democrat newspapers called him a "friend of the railroads," an "anti-Catholic, anti-immigrant Know-Nothing," and a "corrupt jobber."

Then Blaine's campaign was badly burned. Incriminating old evidence, the so-called Mulligan letters, which he had written about the railroad stock affair a decade before, came to light. One of his letters ended, "Kind regards to Mrs. Fisher. Sincerely, J. G. Blaine (Burn this letter.)" When the press got hold of the long-missing evidence, Blaine's position began to crumble. Blaine denied the new letters proved anything that he hadn't already made public. But during a huge pre-election campaign march for Cleveland down New York City's Fifth Avenue on the Saturday before the election, scores of men carried matches and sheets of paper endlessly chanting, "Burn this letter, burn this letter, Kind regards to Mrs. Fisher." Others shouted, "Blaine, Blaine, Continental Liar from the State of Maine."

In the final weeks of the campaign, Logan and even Grant trotted out the "Bloody Shirt" of the Civil War, but this time the anti-Democratic tactic had little sting. Grant's credibility was crippled by the May collapse of his Wall Street firm in deception and fraud, even though personally he seemed to be a victim as well. Blaine, sensing the situation was slipping away, broke all precedent and accepted speaking requests in a number of states, taking his campaign on the road to counter the calumnious charges against him. With the exceptions of Stephen Douglas in 1860, Horace Greeley in 1872, and Greenbacker John Weaver in 1880, no presidential candidate had actively campaigned on their own behalf. Blaine realized he had no choice. He was the Republican's greatest asset and most eloquent voice.

Beginning in late September, Blaine and his son Walker traveled from Maine to Massachusetts and then through New York, Pennsylvania, West Virginia, Ohio, Indiana, and, finally, Illinois, returning to New York City and Boston before election day. He made brilliant speeches in great meeting halls and from the rear of his railroad car. To a crowd at the rail station in Fort Wayne, Indiana, Blaine exhorted, "They believe they will surely get fifty-three electoral votes from sixteen southern states, and they expect, or they hope, they dream that they may secure New York and Indiana." The spellbound crowd roared back, "Never! Never!" Then with a familiar Republican theme, Blaine asked if they were willing to hand over their government to those who had fomented rebellion. "No! No! Never," the Hoosiers replied. "To give them control of the government would mean a change the like of which has not been known in modern times," Blaine said. His campaigning worked initially. Republicans won early state elections in Maine (September) and Ohio (October). Meanwhile, Cleveland accepted but a few speaking engagements in New Jersey and Connecticut.

All Blaine's heroics were to no avail. Back in New York, Blaine's old nemesis, Roscoe Conkling, was preparing to have the last laugh. When asked by Blaine's people to help with the campaign by delivering speeches, he refused, commenting, "No, thank you, I don't engage in criminal practice." Instead, Conkling put all his energies into electing Cleveland, freely giving advice and information to the mugwumps and Democrats. In his home district of Oneida, New York, strongly Republican by tradition, Conkling delivered Cleveland and the Democrats decisive votes that helped to carry New York State for the opposition.

Things got worse for Blaine. At a late October rally that denounced the "personal impurity" of Cleveland, a Republican Presbyterian minister railed against the "Rum, Romanism, and Rebellion" of the Democrats. Blaine failed to hear his remark or to rise in protest.

That Sunday morning the words appeared in tens of thousands of leaflets handed out by Democrats to Catholics as they exited from churches across the nation. That wasn't Blaine's final misstep down the stretch of the campaign, though. The coup de grace was an invitation to a dinner at New York City's exclusive Delmonico's restaurant on October 24, 1884. Blaine walked in expecting an intimate dinner, only to find it filled with America's "money kings," from Jay Gould to Levi Morton and Russell Sage. Republicans with the deepest pockets were there to raise funds for the final drive of the canvass. The fund-raiser backfired. On October 30 a *New York Daily World* cartoon depicted Blaine as "Belshazzar begging from the Money Kings." The image was reproduced in papers across the land and reinforced the idea that Blaine was a tool of the railroads.

On the day before the election, Blaine and his family traveled back to Augusta, Maine. The candidate went to bed early with instructions not to be awakened unless results were definitive. Cleveland voted in Buffalo and then traveled to the governor's mansion in Albany. By morning, November 5, 1884, the nation still did not know who was to be its new president. For ten days the New York election was under contention. Jay Gould was in the middle of the fray, using his Western Union Telegraph Company to send false results to the nation. Only when a mob of ten thousand gathered under his window yelling, "Hang Jay Gould," did he stop his devious actions and flee to his yacht in the Hudson River.

In the end, Cleveland won by just thirty thousand votes nationwide, out of more than nine million cast. The northern states of New Jersey, Connecticut, Delaware, and Indiana swung his way. In New York, Cleveland prevailed by only 1,149 votes out of 1,167,169. Six hundred voters, many of them in Conkling's district, stood between Blaine and his long-cherished goal of the White House. The electoral college vote was 219 to 182. Charges of fraud throughout New York State circulated for years, but Blaine himself humbly accepted the results, saying "by the narrowest of margins, we have lost . . . I have discussed the issues and consequences of that contest without reference to my own defeat, without the remotest reference to the gentleman who is elevated to the presidency. Toward him personally I have no cause for the slightest ill will; and with entire cordiality I may express the wish to him that his official career will prove gratifying to himself and beneficial to the country, and his administration may overcome the embarrassment which the peculiar source of its power imposes on it from the hour of its birth."

The political landscape had tilted. America was no longer Republican, it was Democratic. Grover Cleveland and his veto would be in the middle of the political fray for the next twelve years.

Benjamin Harrison
1888 Republican Presidential Nominee

Levi Parsons Morton
1888 Republican
Vice Presidential Nominee

Facts-at-a-Glance
★★★

Event:	Ninth Republican National Convention
Dates:	June 19–25, 1888
Building:	Civic Auditorium Building
Location:	Congress Street between Michigan and Wabash Avenues
Chicago Mayor:	John A. Roche, Republican
Candidates for Nomination:	Governor Russell Alexander Alger, Michigan; Senator William Boyd Allison, Iowa; Chauncey Mitchell Depew, New York; Mayor Edwin H. Fitler, Pennsylvania; Secretary of Treasury Walter Quintin Gresham, Indiana; former Senator Benjamin Harrison, Indiana; General Joseph Hawley, Connecticut; Governor Jeremiah M. Rusk, Wisconsin; Senator John Sherman, Ohio
Presidential Nominee:	Benjamin Harrison
Age at Nomination:	54
Number of Ballots:	8
Vice Presidential Nominee:	Levi Parsons Morton, New York
Number of Delegates:	831
Number Needed to Nominate:	A majority, 416
Largest Attendance:	8,550
Critical Issues:	Regaining the White House, retaining protectionist tariffs
Campaign Slogan:	"Protection and Sound Money—Harrison and Morton"
Convention Song:	"Marching through Georgia"

7
★★★

The 1888 Republican National Convention
Born for the Presidency

The Republicans were devastated by the election of 1884. Not only had they lost power for the first time in two decades to a political unknown, they lost with their best man, Blaine. Worse, Cleveland's idea of honest government and qualified civil service employees did not include Republicans. The Republican patronage army was dumped wholesale from federal offices and replaced with loyal Democrats. A party in confusion and without a leader, Republicans gathered in Chicago in late June 1888. But at least they were angry and resolved to be united. "Reform within the party, not without," as Benjamin Harrison of Indiana put it. Republicans had lost one of the closest presidential elections in U.S. history to date, many charged by fraud. They could win in 1888, they reasoned, if they could gain back lost territories, such as New York and Indiana, two pivotal states that turned the last contest Democratic.

Cleveland himself helped Republican spirits. He made a number of strategic mistakes in his first term by vetoing widely popular veteran pension bills. And the Democrats' current congressional proposal to drastically reduce tariffs gave Republicans the issue on which they wanted to run. So early on June 19, 1888, thousands of Republicans, many shaded from the intense sun by umbrellas and straw hats, stepped around giant blocks of granite and piles of dust to the ornate front doors of the new Civic Auditorium Building, site of the convention. Even in its unfinished state, the building was a marvelous facility. Its theater had the best acoustics in America. The Republican National Committee called the compact theater "unequalled." The only real drawback was that it offered half the capacity of the Interstate Industrial Exposition Building, which was to be torn down to make way for a new art institute in Lake Park, that had hosted the last two party conventions. The replacement was clearly a symbolic shift for the still rapidly expanding city. In the early days,

Chicago's primary commitment had been first and foremost to business and commerce. Now as it grew into a great metropolitan city, Chicago was beginning to open new cultural frontiers. But it was not giving up its devotion to commerce. Just two years earlier, a spectacularly lavish new Board of Trade had opened to rival Wall Street for commodities trading. In its legendary "pit," fortunes were won and lost with the change of the wind.

The Auditorium Building was a treasure, too. The citizens of Chicago had watched its construction with fascination since 1886 as it rose high above its neighbors. Designed by Dankmar Adler and Louis Sullivan, with contributions from a young Frank Lloyd Wright, the ten-story Auditorium was a $2 million marvel—part auditorium, part hotel, part office building—with a six-story tower that when finished brought the building to seventeen stories and would give spectators a panoramic view of their growing city and the vast lake beyond. Built of massive geometric forms, the tower would be the highest point in the city and a prime tourist attraction.

The entire structure, still under construction, was taken over in late June by Republicans from all over the land. The elaborate theater with seating for four thousand was packed from the floor to the multitier balconies. It was the world's largest opera house with an orchestra pit for 110 musicians. On the second largest stage in the world sat scores of dignitaries and party officials. Unlike earlier conventions, they had no problem being heard. A word from the stage could be clearly discerned in the boxes six stories high and half a block from the speaker. And since it was the first building in the world to be entirely wired for electric lighting, evening sessions were possible. What was even better for delegates used to the excruciating heat of summer conventions, the Auditorium was the world's first air-conditioned building. Huge fans pushed air down shafts over water and ice blocks before distribution into the auditorium. Outside, thousands scurried about in search of tickets, or stood in the searing Chicago heat waiting for the latest word-of-mouth report. Meanwhile, armies of campaign workers streamed into town ready to assist their candidates, whether Blaine, Sherman, Chauncey Depew, Governor Alger, Senator Allison, or General Harrison.

When the Ninth Republican National Convention was called to order that Tuesday, June 19, 1888, by B.F. Jones, chairman of the Republican National Party, no one had a firm idea whom the nominee might be. The sporting crowd down on Randolph Street where the gamblers gathered put two-to-one odds on Blaine, the 1884 nominee, who said he was retired.

The gavel used by the chairman to bang the proceedings to order came from the old oak tree in Jackson, Michigan, under which the first Republican slate was organized July 6, 1854. Also attached to the wooden mallet were pieces of "copper, wool, iron, salt and wood, the five industries that the party now in power would ruin . . ." said R. G. Horr, who presented the gavel. He urged the chairman to "pound the daylights out of it." The convention laughed heartily.

Chairman Jones stood before 831 delegates on the Auditorium's floor, and the thousands of spectators and special guests in the three tiers and special boxes. He spoke with great enthusiasm. "There is no doubt as to which side the majority of voters will fall, if each party be tried by its record . . . The two parties are diametrically opposed to each other. One favors progress, the other retrogression. Thanks to Mr. Cleveland and his Southern allies, the Democratic Party has thrown off the disguise in which it has heretofore fought its battles in the northern states, and has boldly declared for British free trade, and against American protection." The fervent applause the chairman received confirmed that this was to be the issue of the 1888 election: free trade or protection of American industries.

Judge John M. Thurston of Nebraska then took the gavel as temporary chair and addressed his legions for nearly twenty minutes, reflecting bitterly on the 1884 outcome. Thurston toasted the party's most recent "inspiration," noting "though James G. Blaine may not be our president, yet he remains our uncrowned king, wielding the baton of acknowledged leadership . . . honored and respected by all honest and loyal men." Indeed, much of Blaine's coalition from the 1884 convention remained intact in 1888, and many among them wanted to stampede the delegates with Blaine once more so he could claim the White House that had been denied him.

General John Charles Fremont, originally from Illinois and the first Republican nominee for president, was presented to the assembly. The "liberator of California" spoke briefly, thanking the admiring crowd for its graciousness before endorsing Republicans of 1888. But he urged the party to soon "charge itself with the solution of the questions of labor, which are now chief in importance today." Considerable applause followed his appeal.

Fremont's appearance was followed by the greatest of all the abolitionists, Frederick Douglass, who was in limited voice because of a speech he presented to an immense crowd the night before at the armory. He began:

> I hope this convention will make such a record in its proceedings as to put it entirely out of the power of the leaders of the Democratic Party and the . . . Mugwump Party, [at this there was laughter], to say that they see no difference between the Republican Party in respect to the class I represent . . . Democrats were faithful to the slave-holding class . . . They are faithful today to the solid South.

> I believe that the Republican Party will prove itself equally faithful to its friends, and those friends during the war were men with black faces. They were legs to your maimed; they were eyes to your blind; they were shelter to your shelterless sons when they escaped from the lines of the rebels . . . when your Star Spangled Banner, now glorious, was trailing in the dust, heavy with patriotic blood, you called upon the Negro, Abraham Lincoln called upon the Negro, [here Douglass was interrupted with wild applause], to reach out his iron arm and clutch with his steeled fingers your faltering banner, and they came, they came 200,000 strong.

The convention was up on its feet cheering earnestly.

> Let us remember these black men in the platform that you are about to promulgate, and let us remember these black men now stripped of their constitutional right to vote for the grand standard-bearer whom you will present to the country . . .

Douglass looked gravely at his audience as he admonished,

THE CITY OF CHICAGO.

SUPPLEMENT TO HARPER'S WEEKLY, JUNE 23, 1888.

Construction of the Auditorium building, site of the 1888 Republican National Convention.
Chicago Historical Society.

A government that can give liberty in its constitution ought to have power to protect liberty in its
administration.

Prolonged applause followed the elder statesman
as he took his seat with other guests of honor on the
giant stage.

The rest of the first day was devoted to the details
that burden every convention, assignments to committees so all parties were satisfied, filing reports
that had been under consideration, taking care of
ceremonial resolutions. The assembly retired early,
at 3:29 P.M., until noon of June 20.

On Wednesday, the second day, Morris M. Estee of
California was appointed permanent chairman.
Chicago mayor John A. Roche presented him a convention gavel symbolically made of gold and silver.
The rules committee belatedly made its report. The
fourteen rules it offered were "substantially those
adopted by the last national convention." A number
of delegates argued about various interpretations,
intended and otherwise, of the rules; minor amendments were offered but failed. The 1888 convention
did not want to prolong itself like the famed Garfield
convention of 1880, which lasted six days. Their work
quickly disposed of, the Republicans again adjourned
in early afternoon and scheduled an 8:00 P.M. session,
at a time when the city would begin to cool down.

The first order of business that night was a resolution by George Wellington of Maryland, sending
sympathies to Germany on the death of the emperor,
King Frederick. In the mood for resolutions, David
Dixon of Maryland offered up another, deploring the
loss of U.S. Grant, John A. Logan, and Chester Arthur,
"who so often led our armies to victory, and of the
Honorable Roscoe Conkling, the peerless statesman
and citizen of New York …" The chairman called for
all in favor to rise to their feet, and the entire assembly rose solemnly as one.

The Committee on Credentials was not ready, nor
was the Resolutions Committee, both of which had
been working for two days in the Palmer House and
Grand Pacific Hotels. So the crowd listened to more
old-time political oratory from Kentucky's William O.
Bradley, who fired up the assembly with a defrocking
of Democratic achievements: "We want to put this
Democratic Party out of power. It is a fraud and a
sham, it is a delusion and a snare. It never performed
a single promise that it made and the only history it

has is obstinate resistance to the grand measures
accomplished by the Republicans … Democracy is
now embarked on its perilous voyage. The old rotten
craft is top-heavy with state sovereignty and Grover
Cleveland. Its planks of civil service reform and tariff
are as rotten as the old ship itself."

The crowd wanted more. They called the names
of favored orators, McKinley, Ingersoll, Foraker, and
others. Finally, after not much urging, Joseph B.
Foraker, governor of Ohio, ascended to the podium
and delivered a windmill attack on the Democrats:

> We have come to formulate an expression of Republi-
> can principle and to nominate the next president of
> the United States … There is not an intelligent
> schoolboy in all the land who does not already know
> what our declarations will be … We believe … in a
> free ballot and a fair vote … We believe that the free
> trade message and tendencies of Grover Cleveland
> are fraught with harm to the highest and best inter-
> ests of our country … We believe in taking care of
> America, of American homes, American markets,
> American wages, American laborers, American inter-
> ests of every description.

His comments were met with a rousing ovation
throughout the auditorium. Then the convention fell
back into the dreary business of more delegate challenges before accepting the Majority Report on
Credentials.

The convention's third day, Thursday, June 21,
began with more national committee assignments.
The long-anticipated report of the Committee on
Resolutions, which had been working for two days at
the Union League Club, came next. As in 1884, the
draft was read with enthusiasm by Congressman
William McKinley of Ohio. This document differed
little in substance from that of 1884, but had rhetorical flair on key issues. After salutes to Republican
leaders from Lincoln to Blaine, McKinley reiterated
Republican principles found in liberty and sanctity
of the Constitution, of the value of the whole against
its parts.

Finally, the future president reached the heart
of his platform and the key campaign issue of 1888,
the tariff:

> We are uncompromisingly in favor of the American
> system of protection; we protest against its destruc-

tion as proposed by the President and his party. They serve the interests of Europe; we will support the interests of America . . .

McKinley continued:

> We declare our opposition to all combinations of capital organized in trusts or otherwise to control arbitrarily the conditions of trade among our citizens . . . and we recommend to Congress and the state legislatures in their respective jurisdictions such legislation as will prevent the execution of all schemes to oppress the people by undue charges on their supplies, or by unjust rates for the transportation of their products to market.

McKinley did not weary as he arrived to the question of public lands:

> We reaffirm the policy of appropriating the public lands of the United States to be homesteads for American citizens and settlers, not aliens, which the Republican Party established in 1862 against the persistent opposition of the Democrats in Congress.

And he demanded that the sixty million acres in "unearned lands" originally granted to the railroads should be accounted for by the Democrats. Statehood for Washington, North Dakota, and Montana also received support. One resolution continued the party's attack on the Mormons, "The political power of the Mormon Church in the Territories as exercised in the past is a menace to free institutions too dangerous to be longer suffered." The party called for a divorce of political power "from ecclesiastical power, and thus stamp out the attendant wickedness of polygamy."

The platform insisted on restoration of the one-cent stamp for one ounce of mail. The 1888 document did not make the same strategic mistake of 1884 by turning its back on Prohibition. Instead, "The Republican Party cordially sympathizes with all wise and well-directed efforts for the promotion of temperance and morality." Republicans also blasted Cleveland's foreign policy, which was "distinguished by its inefficiency and its cowardice." McKinley toughly denounced the mugwumps who deserted the party in 1884 and accused them of abandoning civil service reform, to which the Republicans again

pledged allegiance. McKinley, the party's young rising star, concluded with a flourish:

> In support of the principles herewith enunciated we invite the cooperation of patriotic men of all parties, and especially all working men, whose prosperity is threatened by the free trade policy of the present administration.

The document was unanimously adopted.

Then the long-anticipated Roll Call of the States for nominations began. The first name offered was that of the old Republican warhorse General Joseph Hawley of Connecticut. Then former Secretary of the Treasury Walter Quintin Gresham, from Illinois with Hoosier roots, was nominated by Chicagoan Leonard Swett, a close friend of Lincoln's. Swett recalled those glory days and then turned to his purpose: "We have assembled again to select a president for sixty million free people. Who most in character is the very essence of these people? Who, of all the names suggested, will draw support most largely from all classes? Who can best bring together and reunite our own broken party? . . . I suggest the name of Walter Q. Gresham of Indiana and Illinois."

Gresham appealed to independents like the mugwumps. Swett extolled the fifty-seven-year-old judge, who spent the first third of his life on a farm in Harrison County, Indiana. With the question of slavery hanging over the Republic, he had become a founder of the Republican Party in his county, served in the Indiana state legislature and he worked with the great war governor, Oliver P. Morton. "He served with Grant at Shiloh and Vicksburg, and was a distinguished figure with Sherman in his march upon Atlanta in 1864 . . ." becoming a general wounded in the fight of Leggett's Hill.

In peace, Gresham had served as a U.S. district judge under Grant and postmaster general and secretary of the treasury under Arthur. Swett argued that "under his leadership the campaign cry will be 'Live and Let Live.'" He concluded, "Judge Gresham is more like Abraham Lincoln than any other living man . . . Like Lincoln, Gresham . . . believes this exalted office should never be sought, and never declined."

Frank F. Davis of Minnesota seconded Gresham. Lynch of Mississippi added another second, as did McCall of Massachusetts. Gresham supporters paraded around the theater singing:

Oh we are the tin pail brigade
For Walter Q. Gresham arrayed
The hero who fights
For the homes and the rights
Of the men of the tin pail brigade.

Governor Albert G. Porter of Indiana rose to present the nomination of Indiana's favorite son, Benjamin Harrison, grandson of the ninth president of the United States, William Henry Harrison, "Old Tippecanoe." There were considerable hard feelings in the Gresham camp that Indiana would offer another contestant against the judge, even another distinguished Civil War general like the recently retired Senator Harrison. Porter, a close friend of Harrison's, began with a little local lore:

Mr. President and gentleman of the convention;
When in 1880, Roscoe Conkling visited Indiana to take part in the memorable campaign of that year, he was asked on every hand, "How will New York go at the presidential election?" "Tell me," replied the great orator, "how Indiana will go in October, and then I can tell you how New York will go in November." In October, Indiana's majority of nearly 7,000 for the Republican candidate for governor informed the country how she would go in November.

The argument pierced the consciousness of the convention. Porter was absolutely right. Indiana was a barometric swing state that the Republicans had to win back to oust Cleveland.

Republicans were ready to reclaim the presidency, Porter insisted. "Give General Benjamin Harrison your commission to lead them, and they will immediately fall into line and press forward with enthusiastic confidence to victory." Then he recounted Harrison's origins and character. He "came to Indiana in 1854 at the age of twenty-one. He came poor in purse, but rich in resolution. No one ever heard him make the first reference to his ancestors. Self-reliant, he mounted the back of prosperity without the aid of a stirrup . . . He received something from them, their talents, their integrity, their fitness for public trust . . ."

"Harrison," the delegates were told, "practiced law, and when war came, commissioned a regiment for Governor Morton and marched with Sherman to the Sea [as Brigadier General of the 70th Indiana]. In

Indiana, he had held public office, reporter of the decisions of the State Supreme Court and had been elected by the Indiana legislature as U.S. senator."

Porter paused, then described Harrison's "comprehensive grasp of mind, calm judgement, firm principle, unquailing courage, and pure character." And Porter pointed out:

We stand here today in the imperial city of the Northwest. The name of no family has ever been more identified with the Northwest than the family of General Benjamin Harrison. It is woven into the very fabric of the history of her people. I need only give a passing reference to sturdy Benjamin Harrison from whom he takes his name, a signer of the Declaration of Independence. He was the governor of Virginia when the possession of Virginia embraced the whole of the Northwest.

When the Northwest was formed by Congress into a territory, William Henry Harrison was, first, its secretary, and afterward its delegate to Congress . . . He held commissions as governor successively from Adams, Jefferson, and Madison . . . He negotiated treaties with the Indians, while governor, by which their title to seventy million acres of land was extinguished and the land was opened for settlement . . . He fought the Battle of Tippecanoe, and, defeating the plans of the great statesman and warrior Tecumseh, kept the portals of the West open . . .

Porter failed to mention that Benjamin Harrison's father, John Scott Harrison, had been a farmer and Whig congressman from Ohio. But since it was 12:45 P.M., and past meal time, the convention immediately adjourned until three o'clock in the afternoon, when more Harrison seconding speeches were made by E. H. Terrell of Texas and Jacob H. Gallinger of New Hampshire.

That afternoon Senator William Boyd Allison, Iowa's favorite son, was nominated by Mr. Hepburn. Allison was compared to Cleveland:

You would not find him sneering at the old veterans, nor heaping gratuitous insults upon them . . . You would not find him filling representative places of honor abroad with men who have no just conception of what this government is . . . You would not find him returning rebel flags, those honored trophies of grand victories, to rebel archives . . . You would not find him paltering about home rule in Ireland . . . But you would always find him true to country and the principles of our party. Wise in determining the better course, courageous in pursuing it, honest in the administration of public affairs, calm, deliberative, conservative, kind and honest.

Allison was seconded by Benjamin M. Bosworth of Rhode Island.

R. E. Fraser of Michigan then stood and addressed the crowd. "Michigan comes into the Republican convention for the first time in its history to ask of that convention a favor." He then entered the name of General Russell Alexander Alger, his governor. "I say to you, gentlemen of the convention, without fear of contradiction, there is no soldier in this nation that is better beloved by the rank and file of the Grand Army of the Republic than the man whose name I have mentioned." Fraser argued, "The businessmen of this nation have never had a candidate. I present to you a business man. This is to be a business man's campaign." And after half an hour, he ended with a quote from the widow of John Logan, who had been Alger's best friend: "A man who has proved true to his friends can be trusted by his country." Alger was seconded by Charles J. Noyes of Massachusetts.

Chauncey Mitchell Depew, president of the New York Central Railroad, was nominated by Senator Frank Hiscock. He contended that, unlike 1884, the New York Republican delegation was unified, and the vote of the Empire State would be greatly boosted by the nomination of its favorite son. G. G. Hartley of Minnesota seconded DePew. But the Knickerbocker didn't elicit much support from the convention floor.

Senator John Sherman, the proud, perennial candidate from Ohio, was nominated by D. H. Hastings of Pennsylvania, who launched into an immediate attack on the Cleveland administration:

The country is tired of shams, double-dealing, and mediocrity. We have seen a chief executive who proclaimed his belief that the president's office should be limited to a single term, eagerly clutching at the nomination for a second. His promised reforms of the civil service have resulted in the prostitution of his great office for the narrower partisan purposes.

Hastings continued:

He whom I nominate to you needs no introduction. His career, his character, his manhood and his illustrious achievements are a part of the nation's history . . . The people know him by heart . . . He stood by the side of Lincoln and the Army from the first days of Sumter until another Sherman marched from Atlanta to the sea, and peace came on golden wings.

Then he recounted Sherman's strong hand at the Treasury Department and how he stabilized the sound value of U. S. currency after the war. Governor Foraker of Ohio stood to second Sherman. The demonstration for Sherman was the largest by far, lasting half an hour. Sherman had chartered several train cars to Chicago and paid the way for hundreds of supporters. John Langston of Virginia and John C. Darcey of North Carolina added their seconds.

The night was growing old and the speeches had been long, but Charles Emory Smith of Pennsylvania bounded to the podium and nominated another favorite son, Edwin H. Fitler, mayor of Philadelphia. Governor Jeremiah M. Rusk of Wisconsin, who had been among the small group of original Garfield backers six months before the 1880 Chicago convention, was nominated by John C. Spooner of Wisconsin. A motion to adjourn was shouted down. Spooner, referring to the restlessness of the convention, commented that it was, "hard to attempt to wrestle with a cyclone." But he continued, "It is Jeremiah M. Rusk, the honored governor of Wisconsin [who] possesses what seems in these days to be considered by many a fundamental element of eligibility . . . he was born in the state of Ohio!" The convention laughed, but cries of "time" were scattered through the crowd. When Spooner stepped down from the podium an immediate motion came to adjourn.

On Friday, the fourth day of the 1888 Republican convention, the assembly came to order at 11:05 A.M. Delegates immediately began voting for their presidential nominees. Fourteen candidates, including many not formally nominated, attracted support. Exactly 416 votes were needed to win. California led the roll call with sixteen votes for James G. Blaine, the party's 1884 nominee. Immediately, a surprised convention broke into bedlam. Blaine had taken himself out of the 1888 race, though he remained a favorite in the hearts of many delegates. Could he be convinced to return? When at last order was restored, balloting continued. At the end of the first Roll Call of the States, John Sherman held the lead with 229 votes, a sound margin, but he still needed almost 200 more votes. Judge Gresham followed with 107; Depew, 99; Harrison, 85; Alger, 84; Allison, 72; Blaine, 35; Senator John James Ingalls of Kansas, 28; William Walter Phelps of New Jersey, 25; Rusk, 25; Fitler, 24; Hawley, 13; Robert Todd Lincoln, 3; and William McKinley, 2.

On the second ballot Sherman picked up twenty votes, increasing his lead to 249, while Alger jumped to 116. Gresham held steady. Harrison climbed to 91. At the end of three rounds of votes, Sherman fell back to 244, Gresham gained to 123, Alger was right behind him with 122, while Harrison added three to jump to 94. With little real movement in the totals, the convention adjourned at 1:59 P.M., until that evening.

When the delegates were again in their seats at 7:00 P.M. that Friday, Chauncey M. Depew was recognized by the chair and withdrew. Immediately after Depew's announcement, which changed the dynamics of the nominating process, Hastings of Pennsylvania stood and noted that "as the central point to be gained as the result of our action is unity and harmony," called for adjournment amid shouts of "No." By a 531 to 287 vote, the convention agreed and departed at 8:14 P.M. until the next morning. The managers of the remaining candidates scrambled to grab New York's seventy-two votes. Discussions lasted most of the night. The Harrison forces were in the middle of the fray. They had one advantage, Depew, the man the whole New York delegation respected, was "much impressed by General Harrison . . . a poor man with no corporate associations." Meanwhile, the telegraph line between the Grand Pacific Hotel and Harrison's Market Street law office in Indianapolis was heating up.

On the fifth day of the 1888 convention, Saturday, June 23, delegates convened at 10:08 A.M. after a wild night of caucuses and deal making. Senator Miller of New York presided over the session. Congressman McKinley of Ohio, mindful of the false charges that Garfield had betrayed Sherman in 1880, addressed the restless throng:

> Mr. President and gentleman of the convention: I am here as one of the chosen representatives of my state . . . to vote for John Sherman, and to use every worthy endeavor to accomplish his nomination . . . Some of the delegates in this convention have been pleased to give me their votes. I am not insensible of the honor which they would do me, or of the confidence which their action implies, but I cannot with honor longer remain silent . . . I do request, gentlemen of this convention, aye, I demand, that no delegate in this convention . . . cast a further ballot for me.

Senator Miller demanded quiet of all delegates while the fourth Roll Call of the States was tallied. Someone in the balcony shouted out "Harrison." The count proceeded with order until New York was reached. The entire convention held its breath, wondering what the powerhouse delegation would do. Mr. DePew, in a calm and exultant voice, answered, "Harrison 59, Blaine 8, Alger 4, Sherman 1." Sections of the balcony broke into cheers. Someone called for the New York delegation to be individually polled, with Harrison losing but a vote. Excitement was building.

When the fourth round was completed, Harrison jumped into second place, while Sherman slipped. The totals stood at Sherman, 235, Harrison, 216, Alger, 135, Gresham, 98, Allison, 88, Blaine, 42, McKinley, 11, Lincoln, 1, Foraker, 1, Frederick Douglass, 1. Harrison had picked up support across the map, but particularly in Massachusetts and from Rusk voters in Wisconsin. Harrison's men, organized for months, passed around a leaflet to delegates arguing that their candidate's support came from doubtful states needed for a Republican win. Meanwhile, Mark Hanna, the Ohio industrial and political boss, tried to make deals with Allison and Alger delegates to cinch it for Sherman, whose greatest support was in the Democratic states of the South.

The fifth ballot that rapidly followed showed Harrison closing the gap on Sherman, who had 224 to the Hoosier's 212. The swing votes were Alger, 143, Allison, 99, Gresham, 99, Blaine, 48, and McKinley, 14. Governor Foraker of Ohio called for a recess until 4:00 P.M., and the convention departed for lunch and some heavy bargaining. No sooner had they returned and the sergeant-at-arms demanded quiet of the gathering, than Mr. King of Maryland moved for adjournment until Monday. The assembly was visibly divided on the questions and amid cacophonous shouts of "No," "No," "Yes," "Yes," voted 492 to 320 to close down the convention for the Sabbath so party leaders and the various contingents could meet and hammer out a holy agreement that would not shatter party unity and make Cleveland's reelection certain.

On Sunday, Harrison's forces were active in their three rooms of the Grand Pacific Hotel, lining up support for Monday's vote. They had plenty of help. An estimated ten thousand well-trained Harrison supporters from nearby Indiana had descended on the city to cheer and aid the campaign by talking up the general. Pennsylvania was a key state, and Harrison's command was able to secure the support of Matt Quay, the Keystone State boss. But the Blaine votes were essential for Harrison, and on this issue, there was about to be a dramatic break.

The convention's sixth and final day, June 25, commenced with two letters from the railroads assuring delegates that their tickets would be good for one day after final adjournment. Then Mr. Boutelle of Maine was granted the floor to read a telegram from James G. Blaine, who was vacationing in Edinburgh at the Scottish castle of Andrew Carnegie: "I think I have the right to ask my friends to respect my wishes and refrain from voting for me," he tersely wrote. There was considerable confusion in the California delegation that supported Blaine as the sixth ballot was taken. Sherman slightly increased his lead to 244 against Harrison's 231. Blaine still received 40 votes, and McKinley fell back to 12.

On the seventh ballot that immediately followed, Harrison leaped into the lead for the first time, amid a growing sense of excitement and cheering, with 279 to Sherman's 230. Allison's support shifted to Harrison. Then finally, the eighth ballot saw Harrison break into an open lead as he headed down the stretch, with 544 votes, well above the 416 needed to nominate. Sherman fell back to 118, defeated for the third straight convention. Alger posted 100, Gresham, 59, Blaine, 5, and McKinley collected 4. The convention was in a state of confusion. Harrison had been nominated. They cheered and wondered what it really meant. The band burst into a rendition of "Hail to the Chief." The chairman declared, "Benjamin Harrison having received a majority of all the votes of this convention, shall his nomination be unanimous?" Governor Foraker of Ohio, answered for the convention, "The delegation from Ohio came here all Sherman men. They are now all Harrison men." He was interrupted by great applause. "It is easier for us to be so when we remember that General Harrison

had the good sense to be born in Ohio." The convention, now relieved, laughed once more.

Mr. Depew then spoke: "I knew when I came here that Ohio would carry away the prize." Again good-natured laughter resounded through the theater. "I was pretty willing to accede to it, because, in the experience of national elections, when an Ohio man is nominated he always wins." Speeches of congratulations and satisfaction continued until a vote came to make the nomination unanimous. The Harrison campaign against Cleveland had begun.

Harrison had won the nomination through his reputation for intelligence, eloquence, and his record as a lawyer and legislator. But he seemed born to the office with a natural nobility of character and mission. He was also aided by an aggressive behind-the-scenes campaign headed by Indiana attorney general Louis T. Michener and Hoosier lawyer Eugene Hay, who began organizing support months before the convention.

The convention quickly turned to the nomination for vice president. William O. Bradley of Kentucky, who had spellbound the gathering, was offered by the Kentucky delegation and seconded by several other delegates. Bradley was popular in Kentucky and had helped reduce a fifty thousand Democratic vote lead to five thousand in his own losing governor's race. Then the gathering adjourned until 6:00 P.M. to complete its business.

That evening more candidates were recommended for vice president. John W. Griggs of New Jersey nominated William Walter Phelps, a wealthy industrialist, former congressman, and Blaine's favorite among the group. Levi Parsons Morton of New York, the eventual nominee, was presented by Senator Miller of the Empire State. Morton, a banker who had been a congressman and four-term minister to France, received numerous seconds. Then William R. Moore of Tennessee was put forward, but withdrew his name. When the roll call was completed, Morton won on the first ballot with 592; Phelps had 119, Bradley, 103, Blanche Bruce of Mississippi, 11, and Walter S. Thompson, 1. The vote for Morton was then made unanimous. The delegates disbursed with, "Harrison/Morton—Protection and Sound Money," as their theme, seeking to knock Cleveland out of the White House.

General Harrison ran a traditional "front porch" campaign from his Delaware Street home in

Indianapolis. People in the tens of thousands came to listen to him speak during the months leading up to the November canvass. His speeches, which were widely admired for their insightfulness, were published in papers across the nation. He delivered more than eighty orations during the 1888 campaign to crowds numbering between a handful to fifty thousand. Harrison and Junior Harrison clubs were formed throughout the country, and their members marched through the streets chanting, "No, no, no free trade."

A quick biography of the candidate was written by General Lew Wallace of Crawfordsville, Indiana, author of the wildly popular *Ben-Hur*. National leaders, such as Blaine, upon his return to the United States, joined Harrison in Indianapolis before going out on the stump for him. Fremont also campaigned for him. John Wanamaker, the wealthy Philadelphia merchant, raised big money for the Republican war chest. The funds paid for an army of campaign orators who fanned out across the nation and for millions upon millions of campaign flyers.

Meanwhile Cleveland pursued his work in the White House and chose a new vice presidential candidate. Allen G. Thurman of Ohio replaced Hendricks, who had died. Cleveland refused to campaign actively because he thought it beneath the dignity of his office. He had given the nation an honest and conservative four years. He "administered" the government, he didn't try to shape it. He protected the taxpayer with his vetoes. He put two Southerners in his cabinet, breaking the post-Civil War taboo. Cleveland didn't warm much to the public side of being president. He preferred to work out of the limelight. He hated to make speeches, unlike Harrison, who relished each chance.

What was worse for him, Cleveland's term had witnessed continued economic hardship for many who were caught in the vice of deflation resulting from his sound money policies. Farmers were losing their land because they didn't have the available money to pay off their grain and transportation debts. Cleveland feared that if the federal government put more money into circulation, it would set off a depression. Instead, he called for lower tariffs, because that would lower the cost of goods. The

Mills Bill, designed to do just that, passed the House, but was defeated in the Senate.

In the 1888 contest Cleveland's backers also had to fight old battles, such as the accusation that he had paid someone else to take his place during the Civil War draft, a common practice at the time—the charge especially hurt him in comparison with General Harrison—and that he had vetoed veterans pensions. Cleveland was disturbed that his campaign was falling into disarray. In New York State, old divisions threatened to sink the sitting president. Tammany Hall had regrouped and its candidate for governor, David Bennett Hill, won the New York Democratic convention. But Cleveland and his admirers would not endorse him. New York's thirty-six electoral votes were in jeopardy. Things got worse for Cleveland when Tammany Hall and New York state Republican boss, Thomas Collier Platt, worked in secret to spring a "Harrison/Hill" ticket designed to wreck Cleveland in New York and hence tumble him from Washington.

It worked, in a way. On Tuesday, November 8, 1888, Harrison led the Republicans to a national victory, even though he lost the popular vote. Cleveland's total popular vote stood at 5,537,857. Harrison garnered 5,447,129. The Prohibition Party tallied 249,506, while the United Labor Party attracted just 2,818. But when it came to the electoral college, Harrison trounced Cleveland 233 to 168. As in 1876, the Democrats again won a popular victory but lost the White House.

Harrison's margin in the key states was small; in New York just fourteen thousand votes, but a turnaround from 1884. Harrison also won thin victories in Indiana, Illinois, Michigan, Ohio, and Pennsylvania. Cleveland's base was in the Democratic South. It was a bitter defeat for a sitting president, a win that Harrison graciously accepted. "Providence has given us a victory," he said upon learning the results. But Boss Matt Quay, who had raised millions of dollars for Harrison retorted, "He ought to know that Providence hadn't a damn thing to do with it." He noted that Harrison had no idea "how close a number of men were compelled to approach the gates of the penitentiary to make him president."

Grover Cleveland
1892 Democratic Presidential Nominee

Adlai Ewing Stevenson
1892 Democratic
Vice Presidential Nominee

Facts-at-a-Glance
★★★

Event:	Sixteenth Democratic National Convention
Dates:	June 21–23, 1892
Building:	The Wigwam
Location:	Lake Park, Michigan Avenue from Madison to Washington Streets
Chicago Mayor:	Hempstead Washburne, Republican
Candidates for Nomination:	Former President Stephen Grover Cleveland, New York; Senator David Bennett Hill, New York; Governor Horace Boies, Iowa; Senator Arthur Pue Gorman, Maryland; Senator John Griffin Carlisle, Kentucky; James Edwin Campbell, Ohio; Governor Robert Emory Pattison, Pennsylvania; William Eustis Russell, Massachusetts; Adlai Ewing Stevenson, Illinois; William Collins Whitney, New York
Presidential Nominee:	Stephen Grover Cleveland
Age at Nomination:	55
Number of Ballots:	1
Vice Presidential Nominee:	Adlai Ewing Stevenson
Number of Delegates:	910
Number Needed to Nominate:	Two-thirds, 607
Largest Attendance:	20,000
Critical Issues:	Regaining the White House, repealing the McKinley tariff, honest government, sound money
Campaign Slogan:	"Cleveland and Stevenson"
Campaign Song:	"Grover, Grover"

8
★★★

The 1892 Democratic National Convention
Cleveland's Comeback

Although intellectually talented and personally dignified, President Benjamin Harrison was not the favorite of the people that nominators of the 1888 convention had predicted. In fact, Harrison was a victim of his own success. He followed through on his promise to raise tariffs. Every import carried a duty. American cabbage, potatoes, fish, grain, and machinery were protected. But costs to consumers soared, and price gouging, an unintended consequence, became common. Harrison dedicated much of the tariff revenues to generous pensions for veterans, as promised, and pork barrel projects, as feared. The amount Harrison and Congress appropriated to pensions alone totaled an unheard of $1 billion for ten years.

The Republican Party regulars did not like Harrison for a simple reason—he ignored them. He alienated supporters and the big machine bosses who had helped to elect him by trying to enforce civil service standards. Asked if he was getting on the Harrison bandwagon, Republican Speaker of the House Thomas Brackett Reed quipped, "I never ride in an ice cart." However, Caroline Harrison kept the White House gay and cultured with frequent parties and was among the most active first ladies. President Harrison was devoted religiously and led morning prayers at the White House. He had an instinct for politeness, and his conduct was rigorously legalistic.

Harrison did post some significant accomplishments. During his term, Oklahoma was opened to settlers, while Idaho, Montana, North and South Dakota, Washington, and Wyoming were admitted as states. Chauncy Depew had been right, though. Harrison wasn't a "corporation man." After a bitter fight, Congress passed the Sherman Anti-Trust Act to stop the concentration of capital and power that resulted in monopolies. The Sherman Silver Purchase Act increased America's commitment to a bimetallic standard and stimulated economic growth although Populists argued that the amount of silver it authorized was much too small. Harrison's foreign policy was only slightly guided by James G. Blaine, his secretary of state. He made John Wannamaker, his campaign manager, postmaster general.

But bad publicity surrounded the first "Billion Dollar Congress." Worse was the economic hardships that the tariff imposed on families. The corrupt favoritism surrounding the McKinley Tariff Law of 1890 dearly cost Harrison in voter support. Rates were set by the various industrial business associations themselves. The public became so angry that the Democrats nearly swept the 1890 off-year elections, taking back the House, which went from a majority of Republicans to just eighty-eight Republican seats. Harrison's party still controlled the Senate, but the "silver senators" from the West held the balance of power. Even McKinley was defeated in Ohio in his reelection bid to the House. (He was elected Ohio governor in 1892.) A young but eloquent Democrat, William Jennings Bryan, a silver man, was sent to Congress from Nebraska in the 1890 Democratic nationwide landslide. The Republican Senate then passed a "free silver" bill, rejected by the Democratic House.

George F. Parker, publisher of the *Saturday Globe*, and Daniel S. Lamont, Cleveland's secretary (he would become secretary of war), sent the former president's speeches to newspapers around the nation. Without resources, Parker and Lamont ran the Cleveland renomination campaign out of a small, donated office in the back of a Manhattan printer's shop. Cleveland had no paid staff. The speeches made Republicans suspect he was running for the presidency again, but Tammany Hall and other New York politicians loyal to former governor, now Senator David Bennett Hill, declared Cleveland was a political corpse. Colonel Watterson, a Kentucky editor, flatly said, "The nomination of Cleveland would be an act of political suicide." In fact, the New

York bosses laughed, How can a man become president if his own state won't even nominate him?

Democrats flooded Chicago by the tens of thousands for the June 21, 1892, national convention. Chicago was now home to 1.2 million people and entering its golden age of architecture, music, learning, writing, and commerce. John D. Rockefeller had paid for the new University of Chicago, which was luring professors from prestigious Eastern colleges. The Art Institute of Chicago and the Chicago Symphony Orchestra, under the direction of Theodore Thomas, had just opened. Half a billion dollars in construction was changing the city's skyline.

The corner of State and Madison Streets was said to be the busiest in the world. A streetcar ran up and down State Street and new elevated trains had gone up in the business district, which they now called "The Loop," after the trolley line that had been there earlier. The Loop was filled with impressive department stores, corporate offices with large plate glass windows, banks, law firms, clubs, theaters, and eating establishments. South on Prairie Avenue and its "Millionaire's Row," Marshall Field had just built a new $250,000 house. Meanwhile, Potter Palmer constructed his Gothic castle on Lake Shore Drive. Delegates wandered over to the corner of LaSalle and Monroe Streets to gawk at the world's first steel skeleton skyscraper, the Home Insurance Building. But there was still plenty of squalor in the neighborhoods. Hull-House, started three years earlier by Jane Addams and Ellen Gates Starr, had inspired a citywide settlement house movement to help poor immigrants.

The Democracy was meeting in a specially erected, temporary convention hall again called the Wigwam, at Michigan Avenue between Washington and Madison Streets. The $35,000 convention hall was financed by Chicago private citizens at the urging of local Democrats, such as Potter Palmer, Judge John P. Altgeld, and former Mayor Carter H. Harrison Sr. It was built in just thirty days. But when the national committee refused to give complimentary tickets to the city council, members threatened to revoke its permit. The committee sent prizefight tickets instead. A construction fluke soon resolved the dispute.

The large, rectangular, two-story structure with a long, low, sloping roof featured a horseshoe amphitheater fifty rows deep. The speaker's stand stood under a decorated canopy on which was perched the sculpture of a giant American eagle. The speaker's rostrum was surrounded by seating for 300 reporters who gazed across the mass of 910 delegates and thousands of spectators. Hundreds of red, white, and blue streamers hung from the ceiling and pillars. Telegraph and telephone wires crisscrossed below the stage as the convention's highlights were sent almost simultaneously across the nation.

The Wigwam turned out to be larger by forty-five hundred seats than originally specified, which left a problem that Chicago's political machine was only happy to resolve. Fearing the worst, Tammany boss Richard Croker, who, like Bourke Cockran, was born in county Sligo, Ireland, demanded that the new seats be distributed to all the states. But "Bathhouse" John Coughlin, a first-term alderman from Chicago's notorious First Ward, flew into action with his own plan. He appointed his trusted precinct captains as sergeants-at-arms to make sure no one but invited guests—with tickets initialed by him—were seated in the new section C. Out-of-state delegations who showed up were hustled onto the sidewalk outside the Wigwam by "Bathhouse's boys." If they didn't like it, a police officer was called to haul them away. The end result was that all forty-five hundred seats went to Chicagoans who showed their enthusiasm for Cleveland. Tammany and Hill supporters were left to complain about the "mob methods" of the Chicago convention.

William Collins Whitney coordinated Cleveland's campaign from the Hotel Richelieu on South Michigan Avenue. He was a master negotiator who worked every delegation as it arrived in the city. Hundreds of dazzled pedestrians stopped to stare at the electric "Cleveland" sign outside the hotel. As the Democrats gathered, Whitney counted 601 delegates pledged to Cleveland. That was seven short of the nomination—a tough seven. The Hill Democrats again stood in Cleveland's way. This time Hill's populist "free silver" position was attracting support in the South and West. If they coalesced, they could block the former president from redeeming his office and defeat his gold policies.

Among the throng that pushed through the heavy rains to get to their seats that Tuesday morning marched several thousand New Yorkers. One thousand were from Tammany Hall, and all were sporting tall white hats. The only exception was Tammany chieftain Boss Croker, who wore an all-black straw hat. Croker, Thomas Gilroy, and Delancy Nicoll led the parade under the New York banner. As the delegates gathered, Lieutenant Governor William C. Sheehan of New York told the press "Cleveland is beaten."

The first session was called to order on Tuesday, June 21, 1892, by Calvin C. Brice of Ohio, national committee chairman. As in the past, the Democrats regulated their convention in accord with the parliamentary rules of the House of Representatives. Any state could impose the unit rule in voting. Nomination of the president required a two-thirds vote.

William C. Owen of Kentucky presided as temporary chairman. Committee assignments were made, and the delegates unanimously passed a resolution of sympathy for former Secretary of State James G. Blaine, who had fallen ill.

Outside the Wigwam a fierce rainstorm raged. As temporary president Owen was speaking, the roof of the hall suddenly sprang a leak. Rain rushed in on the Tammany delegation below. Ten days before the convention, a terrific rain and windstorm had swept over the city, lifting the building's roof and tossing it into the lake. Workmen had labored night and day to put on a new canvas roof before the convention. "Blue-Eyed Billie" Sheehan got a loud laugh when he sat undisturbed in his chair and simply opened his umbrella. The entire New York delegation followed their leader and popped up their black rain protectors. It was an odd sight, and perhaps proved true the adage about bad luck for those who open umbrellas inside. In hopes of better weather and in need of time to buy resistance to Cleveland, Tammany moved for adjournment, which was reasonably granted by their fellow delegates.

On the second day, William L. Wilson of West Virginia was selected permanent chair. With a zinc gavel (presented by miners who claimed they "need no protection"), Wilson hammered away at the Republicans, declaring, "Free government is self-government. There is no self-government where the people do not control their own elections and levy their own taxes."

Senator William Freeman Vilas of Wisconsin, who had served in Cleveland's first cabinet as postmaster general and secretary of the interior, read the 1892 platform:

> Representatives of the Democratic Party of the
> United States, . . . do reaffirm their allegiance to the
> principles of the party as formulated by Jefferson

and exemplified by the long and illustrious line of his successors in Democratic leadership, from Madison to Cleveland.

At the mention of Cleveland's name, the majority of delegates and spectators burst forth in wild cheers that lasted half an hour.

When Senator Vilas resumed, he outlined a platform condemning the "force bill" that would send federal troops to supervise southern elections and denounced the McKinley tariff. It also condemned the abuse and waste of tariff revenue, rejected the Sherman Silver Purchase Act as a stopgap, declared that "public office is a public trust," argued for a strong army and navy, recommended liberal support for public education, condemned Russian mistreatment of Jews and Lutherans, and declared support for Ireland.

The tariff plank was drafted by Cleveland. Another uproarious one-hour demonstration followed passage of the platform. A minority plank, offered by Lawrence T. Neal of Ohio, which denounced "Republican protection as a fraud and robbery of the American people for the benefit of the few," was adopted. Another Neal amendment that called for "free silver," meaning legalizing silver and a bimetallic standard, passed as well, despite Cleveland's opposition.

Though it was approaching midnight, the Roll Call of the States for nominees began. When Governor Leon Abbett of New Jersey ascended the rostrum, delegates wondered who the dark horse from the Garden State could be. Abbett, who made his reputation by imposing taxes on the powerful railroads, was about to do what New York's governor refused to do. Abbett placed the name of Grover Cleveland in nomination for his third run at the presidency. As Abbett began to charm the crowd, distant lightning and thunder heralded his announcement.

The governor then addressed a weary and delirious crowd, "I speak for the united Democracy of the state of New Jersey . . . we offer to the convention as a nominee . . . Grover Cleveland." Much of the floor and galleries were boisterous in support for Cleveland, cheering for fifteen minutes.

Abbett made his argument for Cleveland:

> The question has been asked, why is it that the
> masses of the party demand the nomination of

Grover Cleveland? Why is it that this man, who has no offices to distribute, no wealth to command, should have secured the spontaneous support of the great body of Democracy? Why is it, with all that has been urged against him, the people still cry, "Give us Cleveland?" . . . It is because he has crystallized into a living issue the great principle upon which this battle is to be fought out at the coming election. If he did not create tariff reform, he made it a presidential issue; he vitalized it.

Abbett concluded:

The Democracy of New Jersey, therefore, presents to this convention, in this, the people's year, their nominee, the nominee of the people, the plain, blunt, honest citizen, the idol of the Democratic masses, Grover Cleveland.

A blast of thunder and lightning shook the convention hall as Abbett finished. The Clevelandites took to the floor for three-quarters of an hour.

Then William C. De Witt of Brooklyn bounded to the podium to nominate Senator Hill. As he began to speak, the roof gave way again. Bourke Cockran called for adjournment. Proceedings were momentarily halted until the worst of the storm subsided. But the crowd urged De Witt on. He praised New York's "fertile valleys of the Hudson, the Mohawk, and the Genesee, and the opening up through the triple city, seated upon its bay." Then he warned the convention that Cleveland's nomination would drive New Yorkers into the Republican column, and the election would be lost. Further, he pointed out that Governor Hill had carried New York in 1888 while Cleveland lost it.

"The money power dominates the land and subordinates the sovereignty of the people," De Witt said. Then after a few more minutes of high oratory, De Witt finished: "It took just three hundred brave men to stop the Persians at the Pass of Thermopylae and rescue the immortal plains of Greece . . ." Three hundred delegates joining Hill could stop Cleveland, he declared.

Eight other names were submitted in the early morning hours. Governor Horace Boies, an anti-Prohibitionist; Senator Arthur Pue Gorman of Maryland, a protégé of Stephen A. Douglas and Cleveland's campaign manager in 1884; Senator John Griffin Carlisle of Kentucky, a gold man forced into

exile from his silver-converted state; James Edwin Campbell of Ohio; Governor Robert Emory Pattison of Pennsylvania; and William Eustis Russell of Massachusetts were recommended and seconded as the convention became more fatigued. Repeated efforts to adjourn were rejected.

Colonel John R. Fellows put Cleveland in his sights when he proclaimed that Hill was "a Democrat without a stain on his character." Clevelandites reacted angrily, screaming and hissing at Fellows. Then Tammany's Bourke Cockran, a former and future member of Congress and one of the most melodic and clever orators in convention history, took the podium to second Hill. It was nearly two in the morning. After unsuccessfully calling for adjournment, Cockran spoke persuasively for nearly an hour to the tottering delegates. "What is the excuse given for the course you are invited to take?" he inquired in his charming Irish brogue. "As I understand it, there are two excuses; one that we can get this mugwump vote. Now I warn this convention that . . . you cannot get one mugwump vote without driving away a hundred Democratic votes." He argued that only Hill could win New York. At 2:55 A.M., a big raindrop from the leaky roof struck Cockran on the bridge of his nose, and the New Yorker concluded his remarks. Unlike in 1884, Cockran avoided personal attacks on Cleveland.

Again adjournment was voted down. Not until 3:00 A.M. on June 23 did balloting for president begin. On the first ballot and with another lightning flash and crash of thunder, Grover Cleveland became the first man nominated for president three times by his party. With 607 required to nominate, the final vote tallied: Grover Cleveland, New York, 617 1/2; David B. Hill, New York, 114; Horace Boies, Iowa, 103; Arthur P. Gorman, Maryland, 36 1/2; Adlai E. Stevenson, Illinois, 16 2/3; John G. Carlisle, Kentucky, 14; William R. Morrison, Illinois, 3; James E. Campbell, Ohio, 2; William C. Whitney, (Cleveland's manager) New York, 1; William E. Russell, Massachusetts, 1; and Robert E. Pattison, Pennsylvania, 1. The convention was in turmoil amid a call to make the vote unanimous. Delegates madly rushed for their hotel beds.

Then Tammany's Bourke Cockran rose to add, "Mr. Chairman, . . . I deem it my duty to state to this convention that on the motion to make the nomination of Grover Cleveland unanimous, the vote of the state of New York, in full accord with the sentiment of the convention, was cast in the affirmative." Not until 4:40 A.M. did the convention at last adjourn.

At 2:55 P.M. June 23, when the delegates reconvened for their final session, they unanimously nominated Adlai Ewing Stevenson for vice president over Isaac P. Gray of Indiana, Michigan Chief Justice Allen B. Morse, and John Mitchell of Wisconsin. Stevenson had been assistant postmaster general in the first Cleveland administration. In tapping Stevenson, N. E. Worthington of Illinois, noted: "In this great city of Chicago, in this great commonwealth of Illinois bordering upon the lake and the Mississippi, in the center of this great republic, the Democracy caught the vibration of the groundswell" for Grover Cleveland. But for the vice presidency, Illinois had a candidate "so fully equipped by nature and education that it feels that it would be a political fault to fail to urge his name for nomination before you . . . a man that is known by every woman, child, and voter that ever licked a postage stamp, in every village and hamlet in the land. A big-bodied, big-hearted, big-brained man."

The Stevenson deal had been worked out in the Cleveland headquarters late that morning before delegates voted. One newspaper, the *Chicago Globe*, broke the story while three hundred national journalists waited on stage for the official vote. To the utter amazement of *Globe* editors, a temporary cub reporter, hired to comb the lobbies of the hotels for colorful sidebars, had phoned in from the lobby of the Hotel Richelieu the tip that it was to be "Cleveland and Stevenson."

The young reporter, in his first-ever assignment and totally bewildered by the enormity of presidential politics, was twenty-one-year-old Theodore Dreiser, who was a decade away from becoming America's most important and powerful novelist. In the hotel bar, a southern senator who had once been a green reporter in his youth took mercy on the lost and awkward Dreiser and directed him to the floor of Cleveland's headquarters where the greenhorn overheard a hall conversation confirming the deal for Stevenson. Later that morning the convention met and unanimously nominated Stevenson on the first ballot. Although not a natural reporter, Dreiser was kept on by the paper and encouraged "to write like Zola," which he did. Eight years later, he wrote the classic *Sister Carrie* and, much later, *An American Tragedy*.

In 1892 the Democrats met in a temporary convention hall, also called the Wigwam. Located at Michigan Avenue between Washington and Madison Streets, the $35,000 two-story structure was built in thirty days. Chicago Historical Society.

Amid more bursts of thunder, the 1892 convention adjourned, and the twenty thousand delegates and spectators broke into a campaign song scripted to a comic opera called *Wang*.

> Grover, Grover
> Four more years of Grover
> In we'll go
> Out they'll go
> Then we will be in the clover.

The song had a fine melody and would become popular across the nation, but it didn't offer much of a message.

On July 20 Cleveland broke with tradition and accepted his nomination in public. Another twenty thousand witnesses crammed into Madison Square Garden under a big electric sign, this time reading, "Cleveland and Stevenson." Tammany Hall and the Hill men did not show up. Cleveland boomed his response to the giant crowd:

> Mr. Chairman and gentlemen, the message you deliver from the National Democracy arouses within me emotions which would well be nigh overwhelming if I did not recognize here assembled the representatives of a great party who must share with me the responsibilities your mission invites.

Cleveland then denounced the McKinley tariff.

> Turning our eyes to the plain people of the land, we see them burdened as consumers with a tariff system that unjustly and relentlessly demands from them in the purchases of necessities and comforts of life, an amount scarcely met by the wages of hard and steady toil, while the exactions thus wrung from them build up and increase the fortunes of those whose benefit this injustice is perpetuated.

The crowd was enthusiastic about "Grover."

Harrison did not campaign in 1892. He stayed in the White House to tend to his wife, who was dying of tuberculosis. Cleveland, out of deference, did little campaigning either. He managed his own campaign and made occasional appearances. But when contacted by a club that wanted to use the name of his wife, he refused, "because the name now sacred in the home circle as wife and mother may well be spared . . ." Cleveland felt women had no role in politics, that it was beneath their dignity.

Despite their problems, Tammany Hall supported Cleveland this time, after a late summer meeting between the nominee, "Blue-Eyed Billie" Sheehan, Boss Croker, and other machine politicians. Whitney negotiated the delicate meeting. "I made no promises," Cleveland told the press. "My object was to meet political friends whom I desired to consult. The result has been quite satisfactory, and I think the prospects for Democratic success are good."

The campaign of 1892 drew a wild card in the form of the Farmers' Alliance or People's Party, better known as the Populists. In Omaha, on July 4, 1892, the Populists nominated Iowan James Baird Weaver for president, and James G. Field of Virginia for vice president. The People's Party, made up of farmers, city workers, break-away Republicans, Westerners, and Southerners, advocated "free silver" coinage at a sixteen-to-one ratio of value to gold to stimulate the economy and lighten the burden of debt on the masses of farmers and workers. They wanted popular elections for U.S. senators to replace their election by state legislatures, a federal income tax, and public ownership of monopolies, such as the railroads.

The Populists' "Omaha Platform" boldly proclaimed: "Corruption dominates the ballot box, the legislatures, the Congress, and touches even the ermine of the bench . . . The newspapers are largely subsidized or muzzled; public opinion silenced; business prostrated; our homes covered with mortgages; labor impoverished; and the land concentrated in the hands of the capitalists. The urban workmen are denied the right of organization for self-protection; imported pauperized labor bears down their wages; a hireling standing army, unrecognized by our laws, is established to shoot them down, and they are rapidly degenerating into European conditions. The fruits of the toil of millions are boldly stolen to build up colossal fortunes for a few, unprecedented in the history of mankind; and the possessors of these, in turn, despise the republic and endanger liberty. From the same prolific womb of governmental injustice we breed the two great classes of tramps and millionaires" (referring to Democrats and Republicans).

In November the Populists garnered 1,040,886 popular and 22 electoral votes. Political discontent was building throughout the nation. The

Republicans spent $6 million on the 1892 campaign, twice as much as four years earlier. On election day the oddsmakers favored Harrison. They were wrong. Cleveland won back his office in a mirror fashion of his 1888 loss. Thus, he became the first president with a split double term, as the twenty-second and the twenty-fourth president of the United States. Cleveland and Stevenson polled 5,556,918 votes to Harrison and Whitelaw Reid's 5,176,108 votes, winning by approximately 400,000 votes nationwide. The Prohibitionist Party claimed another 245,841 voters. Cleveland won the popular vote in three consecutive presidential elections. Tammany Hall, more loyal than given credit, fell in line. New York went for the former president—and president once more—by 44,475 votes. In the all-important electoral college, the former president posted 277 to Harrison's 145 and Weaver's 22 and claimed Illinois, California, and Wisconsin. Even Harrison's beloved Indiana turned against the old general.

Cleveland entered office on March 4, 1893, just in time to preside over the financial panic of 1893 that shook the nation to its economic roots. Corporations and banks were collapsing. The increasingly conservative Cleveland warned the public that, "While people should patriotically support their government, its functions do not include support of the people." Early in his term, Cleveland fought Congress to repeal the Silver Repurchase Act. Gold would restore American trust, he maintained. One critic called him a "360-pound tool of the plutocracy." (Actually, he weighed 250 pounds.) The depression worsened and, indeed, hung on during his entire term. The economic rubble it wrought manifested itself in Chicago's next gathering, the historic Democratic National Convention of 1896.

William Jennings Bryan
1896 Democratic Presidential Nominee

Arthur Sewall
1896 Democratic
Vice Presidential Nominee

Facts-at-a-Glance
★★★

Event:	Seventeenth Democratic National Convention
Dates:	July 7–11, 1896
Building:	The Chicago Coliseum
Location:	Sixty-Third Street between Harper and Blackstone Avenues
Chicago Mayor:	George Bell Swift, Republican
Candidates for Nomination:	Congressman Richard Parks Bland, Missouri; Governor Horace E. Boies, Iowa; former Congressman William Jennings Bryan, Nebraska; Senator Joseph Clay Stiles Blackburn, Kentucky; Governor Claude Matthews, Indiana; John R. McLean, Ohio; Senator David Bennett Hill, New York; former Governor Robert Emory Pattison, Pennsylvania; Governor Sylvester Pennoyer, Oregon; Governor William Eustis Russell, Massachusetts; Vice President Adlai Ewing Stevenson, Illinois; Senator Benjamin Ryan Tillman, South Carolina
Presidential Nominee:	William Jennings Bryan
Age at Nomination:	36
Number of Ballots:	5
Vice Presidential Nominee:	Arthur Sewall, Maine
Number of Delegates:	906
Number Needed to Nominate:	Chair ruling, two-thirds of those voting (744), 496
Largest Attendance:	25,000
Critical Issues:	Expansion of money supply, monometallic versus bimetallic money standard, or "Free Silver Coinage at 16 to 1" silver to gold valuation
Campaign Slogan:	"16 to 1"

9
★★★

The 1896 Democratic National Convention

A Cross of Gold

Certain years ring long in the song of American history. They are remembered for their impact on the nation, its politics, its patterns of thought, and its people's lives. They are remembered for the heroes they brought forth for the nation to idolize, for the principles they defended, and the battles they fought. Years like 1776, 1812, 1860, and 1865 all carry with them a special national characteristic that endures for generations, an identity that detaches them from mere numeric significance of chronology. Such a year was 1896. The election of 1896 marked a time when allegiances again shifted and parties radically redefined themselves, a time when millions of voters changed long-ingrained affiliations and voting habits based on core principles of their beliefs, a time when the nation's radical and conservative traditions once again clashed to define a new future. Once again the Democracy returned to Chicago.

Republicans had identified themselves with the struggles of everyday citizens, with the westward pioneers, the small farmers, the industrial workers, the oppressed slaves of the South, and the victims of human rights abuses throughout the world. But as the memory of the Civil War and its related issues faded from the political landscape, as the nation grew by the millions, as Republicans consolidated and cultivated their state and national power through successive victories, and as the party aligned itself with the industrial and financial powers that drove the expanding and contracting economy, the party of Lincoln gained a new identity.

It still championed the individual. But party insiders also developed complicated ties with special industrial interests, most often the large businesses and corporations that sprang up after the intersectional conflict was resolved. Republicans came to represent the viewpoint of the rich and the powerful more comfortably than that of the dispossessed of the land. The Republican fight for protective tariffs, a central

issue for the politics of the 1880s, was a clear response to the desires, wealth, and power of big business.

During the 1896 election, the Republican Party cemented those ties and completed its transformation from a party of moral outrage and political reform to one of protection for commercial enterprises and associated political power and wealth. Those who shared the vision of a United States guided by the interests of the new industrial corporations and the economic elites of business protection gravitated to the Republican Party of William McKinley. The transition was made easier by the political fact that Republicans had lost control of national power, twice, to Cleveland and the new urban Democrats. Republicans needed to redefine themselves to regain power. In 1896 they became the party of conservative Americanism, big business, law and order, and prosperity.

Likewise, from the time of Jefferson and Jackson, Democrats had represented the interests of farmers, particularly those in the South, and workers, such as the Irish in America's expanding cities. These constituencies remained loyal Democrats through the thick and thin of war and peace. By 1896 Democrats also appealed to the new urban professionals and others who were appalled by the graft of the Republican political machines in Washington and many states. Cleveland's twelve-year fight against the tariff was in defense of consumers, farmers, and workers, who saw prices soar and were hard-pressed to make ends meet. Yet by the time Cleveland entered his second term he was a "Wall Street lawyer," adamantly opposed to diluting the gold standard and the power of Eastern financial interests by inflating the money supply with readily available silver from Western mines. He saw the Democracy as a party of both workers and business, both protected through his policies of "sound" money and lower tariffs.

Thus 1896 was a watershed year in which a single political, economic, and social principle would cut through the two major parties. Republicans would now become the party of the gold standard, laissez faire business practice, and a law and order social policy aimed at protecting economic rights. The Democrats became the party of the working people, the dispossessed, and the common folk.

In the politics of 1896, support for gold was a declaration of allegiance to the eastern banks and the large corporate holdings they financed and the economic prosperity they promised. To declare for silver was to side with southern and western farmers and for working men and women whose standard of living was crushed under half a decade of the worst depression the United States had yet experienced. Silver as a political issue represented a dire cry for relief from insurmountable personal debt. As the 1896 election approached, the silver forces represented constituencies that were on the verge of open rebellion and violence.

On June 16, 1896, three weeks before the Democrats gathered in Chicago, Republicans in St. Louis rallied on the first ballot to nominate the fifty-three-year-old governor of Ohio, William McKinley, as their presidential nominee. Garrett A. Hobart of New Jersey was chosen for the second spot. McKinley, a Civil War major, was an appealing candidate and likable person— warm and simple, personally honest, patriotic, and religious. He was a good speaker—with a prepared text and after he had some time to think—but no orator. Voters trusted and respected him. For nearly a decade, he had been the party's chief advocate for the protective tariff. McKinley listened to his nomination on his telephone back home in Canton, where he would spend the campaign.

It was Democratic president Grover Cleveland who fought so staunchly for gold during his second term. At the 1888 convention Republicans had endorsed silver. But now the 1896 Republican platform trumpeted the gold standard. Although McKinley and his chief strategist, Ohio Republican Party boss and millionaire industrialist Marcus "Mark" Alonzo Hanna, were bimetallists, they in turn accepted the gold plank as a condition of faith for their party. McKinley believed, in the weeks before the Democratic convention, that he could campaign and win on the virtues of the tariff, something once synonymous with his name. It was a task he relished.

McKinley's support of the gold plank made Mark Hanna's job of fusing the policy interests of the big corporations to the financial interests of the Republican Party much easier. As the Democrats converged on Chicago, Republicans felt confident with McKinley as nominee and Hanna as his banker. They saw that the Democrats were divided, and now Grover Cleveland's enormous shadow no longer blotted out their Republican sun. McKinley would waltz to Washington, Republicans believed, down a golden Yellow Brick Road. The song he whistled, though, was of "protection and prosperity." McKinley sounded convincing when he promised American workers a "full dinner pail."

McKinley's was a sweet song to the ears of so many voters because of the deep and devastating depression that had haunted American life for four long years, the worst in U.S. history. Tens of thousands of small businesses remained shuttered, factories stood silent, farms foreclosed, and grain prices remained well below the cost of production. Nearly 25 percent of the industrial work force was unemployed. Many families lived on the verge of starvation, and thousands actually died of hunger. Two and a half million workers frantically looked for jobs. Bread lines snaked through the streets of every city in the land. Churches and charities were swamped and could not meet the demand of millions of mouths to feed several times each day.

Cleveland's cold response to pleas of governmental help made him appear to be a public pariah in and out of his own party. When Jacob Coxey of Ohio led an unemployed industrial army to Washington to ask Congress for a public works program and relief, the marchers were arrested for walking on the grass. Violence was becoming more common on the grange, where farmers burned their crops and killed their herds because they couldn't afford manipulated rail costs to ship them to market where they would lose even more money.

Just two years earlier, the streets of Chicago— where delegates now walked—had been a war zone. Railroad cars were burned, and angry armed men marched by torchlight in defiance of a Supreme Court order issuing a temporary injunction against strikers. President Cleveland ordered federal troops into the Pullman neighborhood on the South Side from Fort Sheridan north of the city to end the national railroad strike led by Eugene Victor Debs and the American Railway Union in support of Pullman Palace Car workers whose wages had been cut below subsistence.

Illinois Governor John Peter Altgeld, who had been elected in 1892 and had earned the condemnation and fear of the nation's business establishment for his pardon of the remaining Haymarket Square "conspirators," objected vociferously to Cleveland's response. For two weeks, battles raged on the avenues, boulevards, streets, and rail yards of the city. The strike was broken and Debs jailed. Yet the political situation looked even bleaker after the defeat.

Midterm elections of 1894 were disastrous for the Cleveland Democrats. Republicans reversed large majorities in both branches of Congress. Meanwhile, the independent Populist Party piled up nearly a million and a half votes with a "Free Silver campaign" that was sweeping the nation like a Nebraska broom. Whomever the next Democratic presidential nominee might be, he faced likely repudiation from voters. Forces were frantically organizing in preparation of the Democratic National Convention of 1896 to bring the silver issue to the forefront.

Over the previous few months before the convention, major battles between gold and silver delegates had been waged at state conventions across the land. Fearful that many silver delegates were being sent to Chicago by state voters, Cleveland and his allies tried to send competing gold delegations to the national conference to argue their case before the credentials committee. If the national committee could appoint the credentials committee, the gold forces could gain control of subsequent events. Silver supporters, concentrated in the West and South, were spreading like a hot summer grass fire across the prairie of the Midwest where the Grangers and Greenbacks had preceded them decades earlier. Democrats in the New England states, Michigan, Minnesota, and Wisconsin were all committed to gold and were ready to bolt if the silver supporters took control of the party.

Meeting in the oppressively hot Sherman House on July 4, three days before the 1896 Democratic convention opened, the silver leaders forged a steering committee composed of Governor Altgeld, Senator John W. Daniel of Virginia, Senator James K. Jones of Arkansas, Governor William Joel Stone of Missouri, and Senator David Turpie of Indiana. They sought to make sure that the Democratic National Committee, which was dominated by gold men, did not gain control of the convention through parliamentary mastery.

The 1896 Democratic Convention took place in the Chicago Coliseum, an iron and brick hall at Sixty-Third Street between Harper and Blackstone Avenues. This first Coliseum hall had been built on the edge of "The White City," as the 1893 Columbian Exposition was known. Mayor Carter Harrison had come out of retirement to preside over the five-month-long exposition. On October 28, 1893, toward the end of the great fair, Mayor Harrison addressed mayors from across the nation. After returning home, he was assassinated by a deranged job seeker. Then one night, soon after the Exposition closed, a southwesterly wind whipped flames through the fair's flimsy temporary buildings, reducing them to ash. "The White City" gave way to the gray city of Chicago winter, deep with joblessness, hunger, and vagrancy. Hundreds died of starvation during those long dark months of 1893–94 when Cleveland's depression reached its nadir, and strikes brought labor conflict to Chicago's streets.

The Chicago convention gave a national voice to the explosive silver movement that many farmers felt alone could save them from economic despair. Silver delegates swarmed into Chicago with a quixotic vision. They advocated "prosperity regained" for former debtors through a vastly expanded money supply, with easy credit that would assist all citizens to regain self-sufficiency and respect. Now, after a decade of sparring, the two forces, gold and silver, would finally clash in an epic conflict held in a majestic Oz by the great inland sea.

The Seventeenth Democratic National Convention convened on a sultry Tuesday, July 7, 1896. Just before noon the doors of the Chicago Coliseum were flung open. The convention was located south of the Democratic First Ward of Aldermen Michael "Hinky Dink" Kenna and "Bathhouse" John Coughlin, "vice lords of the Levee," Chicago's red-light district. "The Bath" showed his support for the "free silver movement" by naming his saloon and political watering hole The Silver Dollar, where everyone supported "16 to 1 . . . 16 shots of whiskey to 1 of water." During the winter months of the Cleveland depression, tens of thousands of out-of-work men avoided starvation by consuming the free sandwiches Coughlin, Kenna, and other saloon keepers handed out with a stein of brew.

A ragtag collection of 906 delegates, some from the Populist and Silver parties, gathered in a 125-by-80-foot area divided into five sections before a center stage. During the convention week, the Coliseum held as many as twenty-five thousand Democrats at one time. State delegations from Alabama to Wisconsin shared the space in alphabetical order, twisting across the aisles like a snake. American flags, banners, and portraits of party leaders hung from the rafters. Beyond the delegate space stretched hundreds of yards of floor seating for spectators, political operatives, dignitaries from the city, party officials, and all those diverse interests looking to gain a share of political power or spoils. Meanwhile, hundreds of reporters were situated at tables below the rostrum, and many now used a telephone and telegraph to report their impressions for the nation.

Thousands of curious Chicagoans, speaking a polyglot of European languages and with the accents of every state in the Union, came attired in a haberdasher's dream, wearing every style of hat in fashion. They walked south from the business district or rode the Illinois Central railroad to a nearby station, disembarking to follow the proceedings firsthand. The *Chicago Daily News* reported that "such crowds were never witnessed before at a National Convention." Hawkers sold drinks, fans, and umbrellas for protection from the sun, cabbage leaf cigars, and stale popcorn. Others peddled political badges and food. Here and there men winked and whispered that there was a saloon in the area. Most of the convention crowd crammed around the building, making passage by delegates difficult. The doorkeepers were not ready for such a crush. Twenty women fainted in the heat. Even the Illinois delegates led by Governor Altgeld were locked outside the giant building at one point by guards who feared opening the doors to the hordes.

Senator Richard Parks Bland of Missouri, known as "Silver Dick," was the leading silver advocate as the convention convened. The press predicted his victory by the third ballot. Bland badges were everywhere, and the Missouri delegates acted like Bland had already won. Governor Horace E. Boies of Iowa was another prominent candidate for nomination, as was ex-Republican Senator Henry Moore Teller of

Colorado, who had boldly walked out of the Republican Party that he had helped begin forty years earlier because it would not bend on its gold platform. His bimetallic plank was decisively defeated by an 818 to 105 count. Teller left the St. Louis convention with tears in his eyes and with thirty-three other Republicans at his side, including four senators.

Now the exiled silver Republicans joined hundreds of Populists, Prohibitionists, and Silver Party men in Chicago at a Democratic convention that welcomed them all. Prominent in the crowd was James B. Weaver, the 1892 Populist presidential nominee. His blessings were deemed important for the nomination, and his lack of support seriously hampered Governor Boies, as did the Iowa governor's opposition to Governor Altgeld during the Pullman Strike. Many thought this convention would be under the Illinois governor's control. Indeed, Altgeld expected to bend the outcome to his liking, and Bland was his man. "We have no second choice," the governor told the *Daily News.* "Bland will be nominated and supported by the Illinois delegation to the end."

Other silver horses mentioned for the party's highest honor included Kentucky's Joseph Blackburn, Governor Claude Matthews of Indiana, Vice President Adlai Stevenson, even Ben "Pitchfork" Tillman of South Carolina. Governor William Eustis Russell of Massachusetts and former Governor Robert Emory Pattison of Pennsylvania, gold men, were likely deadlock candidates. Though considered far too young to be nominated for president by party leaders, thirty-six-year-old, former two-term Congressman William Jennings Bryan of Nebraska attracted supporters in the form of "William Jennings Bryan" and "Nebraska 16 to 1" clubs. Bryan could become Nebraska's favorite son, even though Nebraska was a sparsely populated Republican state and his delegation had been displaced by the state's gold Democrats.

The 1896 convention was called to order at 12:30 P.M. by Democratic National Chairman William F. Harrity of Pennsylvania. Immediately, the first battle took place over the naming of temporary officers. Because the silver delegates demanded a silver keynote, they immediately upended tradition by challenging the designated temporary chairman.

The band played "Dixie" as the silver candidate, Senator John W. Daniel of Virginia, defeated the national committee's candidate, New York's David

Bennett Hill, for the position of temporary chairman, after a spirited three-hour debate, by a 556 to 349 vote. Hill was favored by the national committee even though he had been an anti-Cleveland, prosilver candidate in 1892 and had been nominated by Daniel. Daniel's victory was greeted with waves of enthusiastic endorsement among the silver delegates that lasted nearly half an hour. The early victory signaled that a strong silver contingent had made its way to Chicago from the state conventions. Senator Daniel, the Senate's leading orator, then hoarsely delivered a keynote address barely heard by distant delegates. His performance hurt his chances for a dark horse nomination.

On Wednesday, July 8, the convention heard from a number of speakers before getting down to business. Former Governor J. S. Hogg of Texas attacked the Republicans, telling delegates:

For over thirty years this party of promises has been telling the wageworker that the way for him to get rich and independent is for the government to first make the manufacturer rich; that by the process of protection wealth would flow into the corporate treasuries and be paid out in high wages. These people have to a great extent believed those promises, until they have found them to be shams, frauds, and farces. The quintescence of that farcical practice has been governmental protection of the wealthy, with the laborer left to protect himself.

Governor Altgeld added:

For a number of years there has existed in Europe and this country stagnation in trade, paralysis in industry, and a suspension of enterprise. We have seen the streets of our cities filled with idle men, with hungry women, with ragged children. The country today looks to the deliberations of this convention to promise some form of relief.

The governor, urged on by applause, continued:

During the decade which followed the Civil War we became the great debtor people of the earth. Everything from the government down to the sewing machine of the seamstress was mortgaged . . . The interest on this great indebtedness had to be paid each year out of the toil of our people . . .

The main battle between the gold and silver supporters was fought that Wednesday in the credentials committee, stacked by Daniel with silver allies, twenty-seven to sixteen. It faced two hard-fought delegate challenges in Michigan and Nebraska. John H. Atwood of Kansas chaired the committee. Some brief sparring took place in the afternoon, but then the convention adjourned and reassembled at 5:45 P.M. for a bitter, three-hour debate. Finally, the Nebraska silver delegates were seated.

Under the banner of the "William J. Bryan Club of Nebraska," the replacements defiantly marched down the aisle to shove aside the established Nebraska gold contingent that controlled the state party. Delegates shouted for a speech from Bryan himself, but he had not yet made his grand entry into the hall and strategically preferred to remain silent. His time would come. Then the silver men from the Fourth Congressional District were seated with the Michigan delegation. Another half-hour demonstration followed as the silver men sensed the power they were gaining within the national body.

California Senator Stephen M. White was elected the convention's permanent chairman and took the gavel from Daniel. But his "harmony" speech fell on deaf ears. When the Democratic gathering adjourned again until the morning of July 9, it was clear the silver forces held the majority of convention strength. But did they hold the two-thirds that Democratic convention rules required to nominate a candidate? William Collins Whitney, Cleveland's secretary of the navy, coordinated the strategy for the gold Democrats. Whitney, Senator David Bennett Hill, Governor William Sheehan of New York, and a host of other state party bosses and gold supporters called the "millionaire's contingent," had arrived on the New York Central with an army of men committed to thwarting the silver rush. They carried trunks full of cash to help their argument. Even now, Whitney did not think the silver side had yet won.

On Thursday, July 9, the convention's third and most decisive battle took place in the resolutions committee, headed by Senator James K. Jones of Arkansas, spilling over onto the floor when the planks were debated. Jones read the 1896 party platform to the Coliseum crowd. The Democrats called for greater regulation over corporations, monopolies, and trusts by the Interstate Commerce Commission. They denounced many of Cleveland's monetary policies, despite the fact he had been the only victorious Democratic president since the Civil War. They attacked the Supreme Court for declaring unconstitutional a new national 2 percent income tax law. They warned against dangerous court injunctions to break labor disputes, such as the Pullman Strike, objected to presidential third terms, proclaimed support of the Monroe Doctrine, and offered sympathy for Cuba's struggle for independence from Spain.

Most important, the Democratic platform committee's majority report called for free silver coinage. "The money plank" demanded "the free and unlimited coinage of both silver and gold at the present legal ratio of 16 to 1 without waiting for the aid or consent of any other nation. We demand that the standard silver dollar shall be full legal tender, equal to gold for all debts." When the money plank, which was written by William Jennings Bryan, was read to the convention, the silver-intoxicated crowd went wild, then demanded that it be read again so they could celebrate once more. One reporter said the scene was like "bringing a new mess of playthings into the violent wards of an insane asylum."

The minority report argued for the gold standard. It warned that the majority planks were "ill-considered and ambiguously phrased, while others were extreme and revolutionary," and that they would, "diminish the purchasing power of labor and inflict irreparable evil upon our nation's commerce and industry." The minority report reflected the position of the Cleveland Democrats that "free silver" was dangerous to the welfare of the nation and its property owners.

A classic debate, the real highlight of the convention, followed to resolve the party's formal position. Senator Ben "Pitchfork" Tillman of South Carolina led the defense of the majority report and its silver money plank. He argued bitterly against the gold camp. Waving a pitchfork, he denounced them for the economic plight of the South. "We have instead of a slave oligarchy, a money oligarchy," charged Tillman, which he called "Cleveland Republicanism." The gold men hissed and enraged him to irrational attacks. When Tillman finished, an embarrassed Senator Jones, seeing that Tillman had utterly failed to carry the silver argument, tried to soothe raw nerves and tone down the sectional divisions that he had agitated.

Then Senator Hill of New York, Senator Vilas of Wisconsin, and Governor Russell of Massachusetts, a rising star in the East who would not live past his fortieth year, rose to lead the minority dissenters. Hill was smooth and incisive. Silver supporters feared him and the possibility that he might still emerge as the nominee in a deadlocked convention. Hill made a complicated attack on silver, saying, "I tell you it is a question of economics, a question of business, a question of finance," not, he insisted, a question of politics. Hill also argued in support of the Supreme Court and its decision against the income tax. "Why was it wise to assail the Supreme Court of your country?" He continued his reasoned argument for fifty minutes.

Senator Vilas of Wisconsin followed. "The gold standard is now accused of responsibility for falling prices; but it is never credited when prices rise," he toyed. After Governor Russell made a final minority defense, it was time for the last majority defender of silver. Tillman had lost some of the silver force with his invective.

The silver forces needed to regain control of the controversy. At this moment, a handsome, slim, six-foot, thirty-six-year-old former two-term congressman from the Nebraska silver delegation that had been seated earlier in the convention by the credentials committee leaped to the speaker's stand two steps at a time. He wore a stylish black alpaca coat, Western boots, pants that bagged at the knees, and a white, string bowtie. The Nebraska delegation led deafening cheers and foot stomping that spread through the Coliseum. Amid the waving state banners and tossed hats, the crowd finally held its breath as the speaker stood for several minutes motionless, statuesque against the sea of waving handkerchiefs. The delegates and even the spectators sensed that they were about to be lashed by a verbal storm. Though few in the crowd had ever seen the Nebraskan before, his reputation had preceded him. Indeed, six years earlier in his very first speech on the floor of the House of Representatives, William Jennings Bryan had established his right to be called one of the greatest orators to pass through the halls of Congress, fairly ranked with Calhoun, Clay, and Lincoln.

Bryan appeared like a Democratic Apollo before them, his figure chiseled against the portraits of former presidents, his head tossed back, his hand upon the podium. "I thought I had never seen a handsomer man," said Chicago journalist Ray Stannard Baker, "Young, tall, powerfully built, clear-eyed, with a mane of black hair which he occasionally thrust back with his hand."

In 1896 the Democrats gathered at the Coliseum, Sixty-Third Street between Harper and Blackstone Avenues. The structure burned down on Christmas Eve 1897. Chicago Historical Society.

At this convention Bryan would join Roscoe Conkling and Robert Ingersoll in the hall of fame of great convention orators. His listeners consisted both of the merchants of gold who owned the nation and its properties, as well as the representatives of silver, the dispossessed who owned nothing but the mortgages on the properties that produced the great wealth of the land, the farms, and the factories. Though a lawyer of the highest quality, Bryan did not answer in kind the legalistic arguments of Hill and the gold men. Instead he elevated his political battle for silver to a moral and spiritual plane that would typify the campaigns he fought all his long life. His beautifully melodic voice resonated lute-like in the hearts of his sympathizers. He spoke "with intimacy of feeling," Baker recalled, "a fire of devoted emotion, an imparted sense of complete dedication to a sacred cause."

In his smooth and clarion voice that carried across the entire Coliseum as no previous speaker's had, Bryan began: "I come to speak to you in defense of a cause as holy as the cause of liberty," he paused to draw full effect, "the cause of humanity." A hush followed his argument.

> When this debate is concluded a motion will be made to lay upon the table the resolution offered in commendation of the administration and also the resolution in condemnation of the administration. I shall object to bringing this question down to the level of persons. The individual is but an atom; he is born, he acts, he dies, but principles are eternal; and this has been a contest of principle.

Bryan reviewed the history of the silver movement over the past year.

> We do not come as individuals. Why, as individuals we might have been glad to compliment the gentleman from New York, but we knew that the people for whom we speak would never be willing to put him in a position where he could thwart the will of the Democratic Party . . . We stand here representing people who are equals before the law . . . When you come and tell us that we shall disturb your business interests, we reply that you have disturbed our business interests by your action . . . The man who is employed for wages is as much a businessman as his employer . . . The merchant at the crossroads store is as much a businessman as the merchant of New York. The farmer who goes forth in the morning and

toils all day, begins in the spring and toils all summer, and by the application of brain and muscle to the natural resources of this country creates wealth, is as much a businessman as the man who goes upon the Board of Trade and bets upon the price of grain.

Bryan had half of the delegates in the Coliseum nodding with him as he continued.

> The miners who go a thousand feet into the earth . . . and bring forth . . . the precious metals to be poured in the channels of trade are as much businessmen as the few financial magnates who in a back room corner the money of the world.

Cheers now closed almost every sentence Bryan uttered.

Then Bryan launched into his assault.

> We come to speak for this broader class of businessmen. Ah, my friends, we say not one word against those who live upon the Atlantic coast . . . [But] we have petitioned and our petitions have been scorned. We have entreated and our entreaties have been disregarded. We have begged, and they have mocked when our calamity came. We beg no longer; we entreat no more; we petition no more. We defy them!

The silver supporters were on their feet shouting in approval.

> The gentleman from Wisconsin has said he fears a Robespierre. My friend, in this land of the free you need fear no tyrant who will spring up among the people. What we need is an Andrew Jackson to stand as Jackson stood, against the encroachments of aggregated wealth . . . They say . . . the government ought to go out of the banking business. I stand with Jefferson, rather than them, and tell them, as he did, that the issue of money is a function of the government, and that the banks should go out of the governing business.

Again howls of accord. Bryan later remembered that "The audience seemed to rise and sit down as one man . . . like a trained choir."

He went on.

> Now, my friends, let me come to the great paramount issue. If they ask us here why it is we say more

on the money question than on the tariff question, I reply that if protection has slain its thousands the gold standard has slain its tens of thousands.

The crowd was mesmerized. Even Hill, Russell, and Whitney were impressed by Bryan's delivery, though greatly disturbed at its effect.

You come to us and tell us that the great cities are in favor of the gold standard. I tell you that the great cities rest upon these broad and fertile prairies.

He swept his arm pointing across the hall, across the city, westward.

Burn down your cities and leave our farms, and your cities will spring up again as if by magic. But destroy our farms and the grass will grow in the streets of every city in this country . . .

Farmers began to weep as he spoke a truth they had always known but never uttered. Now Bryan spoke it for them and face-to-face with some of the very conspirators who they felt kept them in the bondage of collapsing prices. Bryan reached his passionate conclusion:

If they dare to come out and in the open defend the gold standard as a good thing, we shall fight them to the uttermost, having behind us the producing masses of the nation and the world. Having behind us the commercial interests and the laboring interests and all the toiling masses, we shall answer their demands for a gold standard by saying to them, "You shall not press down upon the brow of labor this crown of thorns."

Bryan touched his temples and extended his arms for several seconds, in a Christ-like gesture.

"You shall not crucify mankind upon a cross of gold."

The force of Bryan's last words electrified his audience first into stunned silence then into an ecstatic rapture that was deafening and chilling. This young man from Nebraska was the answer to their most earnest prayers, a leader who could unite all the silver forces. The floor broke into pandemonium as bands played, delegates marched, men cried, and the foot stomping spread like an earthquake through the immense hall. Immediately as Bryan descended from his perch, he was hoisted on the shoulders of delegates and paraded forward until the crowd running to greet him stopped the procession. Chicago poet Edgar Lee Masters, who was in the crowd, remembered, "They lifted this orator upon their shoulders and carried him as if he were a god." Then they deposited him on top of a chair where he stood receiving the handshakes of thousands of well-wishers and admirers. Reporters crowded in with questions. Others reached out simply to touch him. Some told him they would vote for his nomination. Bryan calmly responded to each request. The ovation lasted an hour. Bryan had won the day for the silver principle.

Governor Altgeld, who had months earlier told Bryan he was too young to lead the party, turned to Clarence Darrow, Edgar Lee Master's future law partner and Bryan's future adversary in the Scopes Monkey Trial a quarter of a century later, saying, "That is the greatest speech I ever listened to. I don't know, but its effect will nominate him." Josephus Daniels, a North Carolina editor, later remembered, "The fountains in the hearts of men were stirred. They believed that Bryan was a young David with his sling, who had come to slay the giants that oppressed the people and they felt a new day had come, with its new leader."

Stirred by Bryan's performance, the majority report was adopted 628 to 301 to more cheers and jabs of a convention still deeply divided. The East supplied most of the "no" votes. Had the presidential nomination been decided then and there, Bryan certainly would have won in a first round knockout. But in the delirium of his oration, in the truth of his accusations, in the righteousness of his crusade, and in the victory of the silver platform, his followers were glorifying and gladly adjourned until that evening. Back in his hotel, Baker found the young orator's room "literally crowded to the doors with excited followers . . . bronzed farmers and ranchmen . . . red-faced city politicians," with Bryan standing on his bed addressing them through a fog of smoke.

Delegations from the Alaskan Territory, Connecticut, Maine, Maryland, Massachusetts, New Hampshire, New Jersey, Pennsylvania, Rhode Island, South Dakota, and Vermont still swore by gold. Were they prepared to bargain or bolt? Could they block the man with the silver tongue with their own nominee? How could they stop this Democratic messiah, this social rebel, this economic anarchist? How could they protect their interests from the Populist revolution that was on the verge of capturing America's oldest political party?

On the evening of July 9, the Democratic delegates gathered again for the final fight. Since a two-thirds vote was necessary to secure the nomination, the silver forces were still not secure. A unity figure who secretly preferred gold might win in a stalemate. Ever since adjournment, the various camps had been in panic trying to win support for their candidates, while the popular sentiment cried out for Bryan. That night, while the camps struggled for votes, a newspaperman called McKinley in Canton, Ohio, to get his reaction to word that Bryan would win the nomination. McKinley simply answered, "That's rot," and hung up.

The convention was gaveled back to order at 8:26 P.M. Senator Jones moved for a Roll Call of the States for nominations for president. George G. Vest of Missouri led off by offering Congressman Richard Parks Bland of Missouri, explaining, "In this crisis of our country and party we must take no step backward in platform nor candidate . . . Twenty years ago the battle for silver was begun in the halls of Congress by a modest, unpretending, brave man, not an iridescent or meteoric statesman, but of the people and from the people, who has never faltered for an instant in the great struggle." Bland, the best organized of the comers, sparked a strong demonstration that lasted several minutes. David Overmeyer of Kansas and others, including J. R. Williams of Illinois, seconded him.

Then another seconder moved to the podium. But instead of speaking on behalf of Bland, Judge Henry T. Lewis of Georgia sent the convention into an uproar, exclaiming that "in behalf of the Democratic Party of the state of Georgia," he placed in nomination "a distinguished citizen whose very name is an earnest of success, whose public record will insure Democratic victory, whose public life and public record are loved and honored by the American people . . . I refer, fellow citizens, to William Jennings Bryan, of Nebraska."

The convention, for a moment confused, leaped to the occasion. Six delegations rushed forward with their banners, but no other states followed. A portrait of Bryan was lifted high. The cheering lasted for fifteen minutes, but the stampede for Bryan did not follow. Bland and Boies held their votes.

Bryan was seconded by T. K. Klutz of North Carolina, George F. Williams of Massachusetts, Thomas Kernan of Louisiana, and others. Bryan's

nomination was followed by that of Governor Claude Matthews of Indiana. Then the other names were put forward: Boies of Iowa, Blackburn of Kentucky, John R. McLean of Ohio, and Pennoyer of Oregon. Pattison of Pennsylvania was the only progold nominee. Governor William E. Russell of Massachusetts declined when his name was offered. New Jersey and New York declared they would not offer any candidate to run on the silver platform. General Bragg of Wisconsin touched off the cannon of party rebellion, vowing Wisconsin would not vote for any candidate who ran on the silver plank. When all the nominating speeches had been offered, it was already 12:55 A.M., so the convention adjourned until morning. But all night the negotiations continued as long as anyone would listen. William Jennings Bryan, always the man of principle, calmly turned down deals made in his name to get delegate votes. He had been far from a favorite when he reached Chicago. None of the powerhouses who controlled the convention supported, or even considered him, for the presidency. Certainly, he had a reputation for oratory and many admirers, but no solid constituency beyond those in his small state. Altgeld favored Bland. Most considered Bryan far too young and brash to seek such a high office.

But the young dynamo had lived an accelerated political life. He was born in downstate Salem, Illinois, in 1860, of Scotch-Irish decent and southern roots, the year Lincoln was elected. His father, Silas, was the local Douglas Democrat, respected but defeated in his run for Congress. Bryan grew up in a strict, religious home and was tutored by his mother and father. Among other topics, he was given oratory instruction and was on stage as early as age four. He carefully cultivated his skills through high school and at Jacksonville College in Illinois (where he once participated in a debate with Jane Addams, who was a student at Rockford Female Seminary).

In 1882 Bryan started at Union Law School on Dearborn Street, which was associated with Northwestern University and the old University of Chicago and worked for former Senator Lyman Trumbull. Trumbull admired Bryan's intellect and idealism and from him, Bryan learned how large corporations operated.

In 1888, after marrying his hometown sweetheart, Bryan relocated to Lincoln, Nebraska, where he thought he would have a better chance to start a law practice and a political career. He struck up immediate acquaintance with all the leading Nebraska Democrats and argued all sorts of cases in the growing court system, including some before the state's highest court. Soon his wife, Mary, became the first woman in the state to pass the bar. She joined her husband's legal practice and became his top political adviser.

Bryan could not help but notice that the problems facing farmers in Illinois were the same as those in Nebraska. As farm values fell, Bryan undertook to become the farmers' spokesman and advocate, seeking to make the Democratic Party of Nebraska a vehicle for solving the problems of the vanishing American farmer. Bryan spent the next two years barnstorming the state, speaking to crowds large and small on behalf of farmers and the national and state Democratic tickets. But in 1888 and 1889 the Democrats failed in Nebraska.

In 1889 he predicted to his wife that in the election of 1890 he would become only the second Democrat ever to represent Nebraska in Congress. She told him he was crazy. But William Jennings Bryan not only had one of the keenest political senses in American history but also was a great strategist capable of forging coalitions and personal connections, which is why Mary was only half incredulous when Bryan told her, a year before the Chicago convention, that he would be the 1896 presidential nominee. His magic carpet would be decorated with silver.

While Bryan wanted the nomination and had made strategic decisions to promote himself, he was the only candidate in Chicago without a major organization working on his behalf. Instead his friends spontaneously rose to promote his candidacy. Bryan personally welcomed their help and coordinated his efforts from his two flag-draped hotel rooms in the shabby Clifton House. Bryan was prophetically confident and calm about his chances. When asked by a Hearst newspaper reporter, on the second day of the convention prior to his "Cross of Gold" speech, whom he expected to win the nomination, he replied, off the record, "I am going to be nominated." The reporter thought Bryan had lost all reason and left shaking his head.

Balloting began on the morning of the convention's fourth day, July 10. The chair called for the Roll Call of the States. Emotions having settled after Bryan's speech, organization took over. Bland grabbed an immediate lead on the first ballot, based on his preconvention strength, with 235 votes. Bryan came from nowhere before the convention to rank second with 137, followed by the progold Pattison with 97,

Blackburn, 82, Boies, 67, McClean, 54, and Matthews, 37, with 43 not voting in protest. Stevenson, Teller, and Tillman also got votes. One vote was cast for Senator Hill. Many states fragmented their ballots despite the unit rule. Massachusetts announced eighteen delegates would not vote. New Jersey, New York, and Wisconsin refused to vote. As a result, getting the required two-thirds became more difficult.

On the second ballot, 160 delegates withheld their votes and some of the favorite sons faded. By the third ballot, Bland's strength had increased to 291. Bryan jumped to 219, while Pattison garnered 97. The 162 gold supporters still refused to vote. At this point the Illinois delegation was in a state of virtual rebellion against its leader, Governor Altgeld, who held out for Bland. White as death, Altgeld, who many believed would have been a Democratic nominee for president had he been born in the United States, led his delegation out of the hall to caucus.

Bryan made his breakthrough on the fourth ballot. With states such as Alabama, Colorado, and Kansas throwing their votes to him, the "Boy Orator of the Platte" moved up to 280 votes, while Bland slipped to 241. Pattison held at 97 and the eastern block of nonvoters leveled out at 161. Then Chairman White made a critical decision. He announced that based on an 1852 precedent the two-thirds required for nomination would be interpreted as two-thirds of those voting, rather than two-thirds of all 906 delegates. Now the state banners began to gather around the Nebraska flag.

As the fifth ballot commenced, Illinois reentered the hall and switched all its votes to Bryan. His bandwagon was picking up steam. Now Bland, Boies, Blackburn, and Matthews all stepped aside for the voice of the new Democracy, William Jennings Bryan, who swept to the nomination with 652. Pattison claimed 95, 8 went to Stevenson, 1 to Hill, 1 to Turpie, while 162 delegates cast no votes. Amid the wild cheers of silver men the vote was made unanimous among those who were voting. Then the convention recessed until evening.

Mary Bryan watched from the gallery as her husband was nominated to lead America's oldest political party. The nominee relaxed in his hotel room confident of the outcome. When a telegram reached him announcing victory, he dashed to the hotel barber for a quick shave and haircut. It was his last moment of peace until after the election. Soon he was engulfed by a sea of well-wishers, reporters, friends, and supporters, all wanting his opinion on something. Bryan immediately sent a telegram, "To the American People," announcing he would not seek a second term if elected so they could be assured he faced no temptation to corrupt his office.

The convention reconvened on the evening of July 10, but immediately recessed while discussions of the vice presidential spot could be debated in hotel rooms. When the assembly gathered again on the fifth and final day, July 11, it quickly selected a vice president to run with Bryan.

Arthur Sewall of Maine, a banker, shipbuilder, and railroad executive, won the prize to balance the ticket geographically and politically. He was a man of principle as well, with whom Bryan indicated he could work. The new Democracy had its silver ticket, Bryan/Sewall, and the gold delegates bolted. The party was split. When Senator Hill was asked if he would bolt, he replied, "I am still a Democrat, very still." The *Chicago Tribune* concluded: "Never has the Democratic Party been so torn to pieces as it is now." A new party had been born. But was it strong enough to win?

The 1896 campaign was a cavalcade of inspiring speeches and a mundane contest of money. Nor were the Democrats and Republicans alone in competition for endorsement of U.S. voters. That summer, the Prohibition Party also splintered into the Narrow-Gaugers whose platform focused solely on the temperance issue, and the Broad-Gaugers who wanted a wider platform to include promotion of women's suffrage, free silver, and antimonopoly action. The Narrow-Gaugers nominated Joshua Levering of Maryland and Hale Johnson of Illinois. The Broad-Gaugers offered Charles E. Bentley of Nebraska and James E. Southgate of North Carolina.

On July 22 the Populist and Silver parties also held simultaneous St. Louis conventions. After much soul-searching, fourteen hundred Populist delegates put forward the fusion candidacy of William Jennings Bryan, but nominated former Congressman Thomas Edward Watson of Georgia instead of Sewall for vice president.

Although many Populists feared their party would be absorbed by the Democrats, unity on the silver issue was paramount. It was now or never for "free silver." That same day, across town, the National Silver Party nominated both Bryan and Sewall. Bryan's men were actively involved in forging the historic electoral coalition of Democratic, Populist, and Silver parties. The fusion both drew and repelled votes. Bryan was also the nominee of nominal parties, such as the Single Taxers of Henry George, Edward Bellamy's Nationalists, and Reverend W. D. P. Bliss's Christian Socialists.

After a sentimental journey that took the nominee and Mary back to their childhood home of Salem, Illinois, and then across the prairie to Lincoln, Bryan began his whirlwind campaign. He traveled east by train, attracting attention and huge crowds, stopping repeatedly in towns large and small and even along the tracks where a few workers or families waited for him to pass. He startled McKinley when he stopped in Canton for a friendly chat.

Bryan followed Grover Cleveland's precedent and formally accepted his nomination on August 12 in Madison Square Garden, in the heart of the enemy's Wall Street bastion. The night was hot—nearly ninety degrees—and the crowd of twelve thousand was ready for Bryan's pyrotechnics. But this time, instead of passionate rhetoric, the boy orator read his letter of careful arguments for the silver position, as though he were trying to reach voters in the East who had been led to believe he was nothing but an anarchist foaming with fury.

His lackluster performance was a rare strategic error. Instead of the success they anticipated, many left the Garden unsatisfied, and New York papers blasted him anyway. Walter Hines Page wrote in the *Atlantic Monthly* that if Bryan were elected, "The paralysis of industry would be frightful . . . creating a panic that would produce such disastrous effects that the whole country would suffer a violent revulsion of opinion." The New York State party bosses boycotted his appearance. Whitney told the press he couldn't vote for a silver Democrat. Cleveland Democrats put their power to work trying to defeat Bryan so they could take back their political party.

On September 2 and 3, 7,900 gold Democrats, those who had withheld their votes from Bryan in Chicago and those who denounced the party's silver plank, reassembled under the banner of the National Democratic Party, holding their counterconvention in Indianapolis at Tomlinson Hall. Delegates from forty-one states nominated the seventy-nine-year-old Senator John McCauley Palmer of Illinois, a former Union general, and General Simon Bolivar Buchner, a former governor of Kentucky, who had fought for the Confederacy, as president and vice president. The rump party praised Cleveland and his policies on the tariff, "sound money," civil-service

William Jennings Bryan around 1890. Nebraska State Historical Society.

reform, and other old-line practices of the eastern Democrats.

McKinley ran a traditional "front porch" campaign from his home in Canton, Ohio, as Garfield had done sixteen years earlier. He gave speeches to visiting delegations and newsmen. By the end of the campaign, 750,000 carefully selected listeners had heard McKinley's calm but evasive approach to issues. He stood in stark contrast to Bryan's messianic style and revolutionary message. McKinley's patron, Republican strategist Mark Hanna, collected an estimated $16 million from industrial and financial concerns. Banks, railroads, and industries protected by the tariff all generously responded to Hanna's appeal for money to defeat Bryan. If Bryan didn't spook them, then the fear of his potential cabinet appointments of Altgeld, Tillman, and Debs did. The New York *Tribune* called Bryan "the wicked, rattlepated boy, posing in vapid vanity and mouthing resounding rottenness." He was, they insisted, a "willing puppet" who danced from "the blood-imbued hands of Altgeld, the anarchist, and Debs, the revolutionist, and other desperadoes of that stripe." Theodore Roosevelt called Silver Democrats— "dangerous men, a menace to the nation"—and expected to defeat them some day on the field of battle. He thought Bryan an "amiable and windy demagogue" whose platform consisted of a "preposterous farrago of sinister nonsense." (Evidently T. R. softened his view later when as a Republican president he enacted much of Bryan's progressive platform into law.)

Even without much cash, Bryan was a campaign cyclone. He traversed the nation in an eighteen-thousand-mile tour. Each day he delivered six to ten speeches to crowds of a few hundred to fifty thousand. Bryan accepted no money gifts in exchange for legislative favors later, including special railroad cars that were offered him. He always carried his own bags, booked his own train and hotel reservations, and did his own laundry. Like Lincoln and Blaine before him, Bryan became known as the "Great Commoner," or simply, the "Commoner," a name he later adopted for his newspaper.

In the tradition of Henry Clay and James G. Blaine, Bryan captivated crowds with his mastery of language, and scores of poor and desperate citizens who came to see him left with the feeling they had been touched by a moral crusader or a prophet. Wherever the "political evangelist" went, crowds appeared, whether in the cities or along the railroad tracks at night. Some observers concluded that the deeply religious William Jennings Bryan was the most revered man "since Christ."

At Labor Day ceremonies in Chicago, where forty thousand watched him lead a parade, the indefatigable candidate spoke to a throng at Sharpshooter's Park. Many in the vast crowd fainted from the heat. Here, Bryan's alliance with labor coalesced. J. R. Sovereign of the Knights of Labor endorsed the dynamic Democrat. Eugene Debs had supported him since the Chicago convention. Labor could see that Bryan sought to restore the democratic balance between individuals and large corporate entities that treated people like pawns, that he was leading the fight to break up the trusts, that he was fighting for popular elections of senators, and that he was a crusader for justice and democracy.

But Bryan was vilified by his enemies. Suddenly Republicans sensed Bryan's great strength and tried to brand him as an anarchist. Republican Senator Henry Cabot Lodge remarked, "They have set up an unknown stump orator as their candidate and they have filled their platform with all kinds of revolutionary and anarchistic doctrines. It is a very serious fight . . . and involves a great deal more than a money standard."

McKinley was portrayed as the upholder of law and order; Bryan as a threat to American civilization. Mark Hanna took a beating from cartoonists who depicted him clad in a dollar-bill suit, a plutocrat freely throwing around thousands at a time to buy votes. Republicans counterattacked by calling Bryan a radical, an American Napoleon out to destroy his nation, a demagogic "Popocrat" who would nationalize industry, a liar, a traitor, and an anarchist like Eugene Debs who endorsed him. Ministers compared the highly religious Bryan to the devil.

In mid-October the *New York Herald* predicted Bryan would take an electoral college victory with a 237, two-vote margin. To respond to Bryan's early fall surge, Hanna urged McKinley to take to the road. McKinley knew he was no match for Bryan as a speaker and had the good sense to refuse. In his stead, Republicans rolled out the best-financed campaign the nation had ever witnessed. Standard Oil alone donated $250,000 to the effort.

Tons of campaign literature tearing apart the silver position were mailed each week. Farmers in the critical Midwestern states, particularly farmers who found silver to be a sympathetic solution, were targeted by Hanna. Millions of dollars flowed into the active state party organizations and hundreds of speakers were hired to hit the stump for "sound money." Progold news stories were mailed to papers across the nation. Nor was the Hanna machine above using coercion in key states. Employees were threatened with job loss, farmers with instant foreclosure, and contracts carried a "Bryan clause" that invalidated them if Bryan won.

But McKinley did not shy away from the silver debate. Though he still emphasized the importance of the protective tariff to restart U.S. businesses racked by depression, he took on the silver issue as well. Bryan argued that it was a lack of money that caused lack of capital for investment. McKinley countered that there was enough money but that it had to be attracted back to investment by sound money and protective policies. While Bryan argued that the economy rested on the welfare of farmers, McKinley rebutted that industrial policies put money in consumer pockets so they could purchase farm goods. Low farm prices came ironically from the farmer's success in boosting production, not from the gold standard, McKinley explained. The tariff, not silver, was the only road to prosperity, he insisted. McKinley advertised himself to listeners as "the advance agent of prosperity."

Bryan stumped the East against the advice of the national committee. Then he stormed south, making fifteen speeches each day. As the crowds grew, so did the attacks against him. Bands of boisterous hangers-on, hired by Hanna, harassed him wherever he went. He raced through the East again, gaining popular support but no response from party bosses. His money ran out, yet still he journeyed on, through Tennessee and up the Mississippi Valley and into Michigan. Everywhere he was heralded and condemned; always he was spellbinding. As election day neared, Bryan traveled home to mobs of jubilant supporters. His friends seemed amazed that he was tranquil and hardly concerned with the impending vote.

The November 3, 1896, election settled the silver/gold battle, at least for the next four years. Bryan polled over a million votes more than President Cleveland had garnered four years earlier. The election was so hotly contended that voter turnout was the highest ever. But McKinley polled 7,107,822 popular votes to Bryan's 6,511,073. Palmer brought in 134,654 disloyal Democrats. Levering, the Narrow-Gauge

Prohibitionist, received 131,000, while the Broad-Gauger Bentley tallied only 14,000. Charles H. Matchett of the Socialist Labor Party based in New York City collected 36,000 votes. Bryan and Watson on the Populist ticket pulled another 222,000 votes. After the election, the Populists vanished from the American political horizon, along with their central issue of silver.

Bryan received results in his library on election night and retired at 11:00 P.M., convinced of his defeat. He had won twenty-six states to McKinley's twenty-one, but not one of them was an industrial state. In the electoral college, McKinley scored 271 to Bryan's 176, including 27 Populist votes. Many National Democrats abandoned their own candidate to vote for McKinley, lest Bryan win. Nearly one-third of McKinley's tally came from bolting gold Democrats. Populists and Republicans crossed over for Bryan. McKinley carried Democratic Delaware, Kentucky, Maryland, and West Virginia. He swept the critical farming midsection of Ohio, Indiana, Illinois, and Iowa.

Bryan won Western Republican states and the Democratic Southwest. Still, many firsthand observers asserted that Republicans and gold Democrats had simply stolen the election from Bryan in the key states of New York, Pennsylvania, and Indiana. Others testified about vote fraud in California, Kentucky, Maryland, Ohio, and Virginia. Altgeld, who also lost reelection, argued that 100,000 falsified votes stole the election in Illinois. But Bryan concluded without malice, "I have borne the sins of Grover Cleveland."

Bryan's candidacy had frightened too many voters. A deep strain of conservatism carried the day. Despite Bryan's heroic effort on behalf of a great social principle, voters chose to go with the dependable McKinley. They wanted economic gains, not moral direction and social experiments.

Still, Bryan's campaign was a magnificent journey, based on the concern and protection of common citizens, that pointed the Democratic Party down a path that Woodrow Wilson, Franklin Roosevelt, and Lyndon Johnson would later follow. In effect, William Jennings Bryan had founded the modern Democratic Party. His warnings about the dangers of concentrated wealth and power were not without truth. Within two decades, Bryan's calls for a progressive income tax would be enacted and upheld.

Republicans also won both houses of Congress, but the Senate was still prosilver. McKinley quickly passed the Nelson-Dingley tariff with 50 percent rates and launched the Spanish-American War to liberate Cuba. The biggest result of the war was the making of another Republican president, Theodore Roosevelt. Within a year, vast new quantities of gold were discovered in the Alaskan Klondike, in South Africa, and Australia, increasing the money supply and stimulating economic recovery.

In 1900 the United States, under McKinley's leadership, adopted a strict gold standard. That year, McKinley and Bryan would battle again, this time over the issue of American imperialism, but with the same outcome. McKinley was still president while William Jennings Bryan, without portfolio, remained the nation's second most influential leader.

Theodore Roosevelt
1904 Republican Presidential Nominee

Charles Warren Fairbanks
1904 Republican
Vice Presidential Nominee

Facts-at-a-Glance
★★★

Event:	Thirteenth Republican National Convention
Dates:	June 21–23, 1904
Building:	The Coliseum
Location:	1513 South Wabash Avenue
Chicago Mayor:	Carter Henry Harrison Jr., Democrat
Candidate for Nomination:	Theodore Roosevelt, New York
Presidential Nominee:	Theodore Roosevelt
Age at Nomination:	45
Number of Ballots:	1
Vice Presidential Nominee:	Charles Warren Fairbanks, Indiana
Number of Delegates:	994
Number Needed to Nominate:	A majority, 498
Largest Attendance:	14,000
Critical Issues:	Protective tariff, the gold standard, build up of merchant marine, maintenance of strong American navy, exclusion of Chinese labor, enforcement of civil service law, liberal administration of military veteran pension law, arbitration of international differences, protection of American citizens abroad, commercial policy toward China
Campaign Slogan:	"A Square Deal"
Convention Song:	"Yankee Doodle"

10
★★★

The 1904 Republican National Convention
A Rough Rider to the Rescue

When the Thirteenth Republican National Convention met in Chicago on June 21, 1904, President Theodore Roosevelt, former governor of the state of New York, "Rough Rider" hero of the Spanish-American War, and patrician descendent of New York aristocracy, was confident that he would receive his party's presidential nomination. He was the man of the hour—not only because he was the sitting president who in the wake of the national crisis following the assassination of President McKinley had risen to the moment, but because his youthful, colorful, brash, and sometimes eccentric personality mirrored the nation's concept of itself.

In Theodore Roosevelt, America found a handsome self-reflection. Despite his blue-blooded background, Roosevelt had a common touch and innate respect for plain American people. He would be a candidate with appeal to party stalwarts and the voting populace alike. The Chicago convention would provide his party the forum with which to further publicize the forty-five-year-old Roosevelt's political attractiveness, assuring continued Republican control of the national government. The party was rich with heroes, ranging from Abraham Lincoln to the late President McKinley. Their names would echo across the proceedings of the 1904 Chicago gathering many times, as household saints, gilding the political character of the party. But it was the new hero, Roosevelt, who would now be nominated in his own right to lead the nation.

President McKinley had not particularly wanted Theodore Roosevelt as his vice president. He had been convinced by party leaders, such as New York Republican boss Thomas Collier Platt, who wanted to get the excitable Roosevelt out of New York and keep him from a second term as governor where he had already instituted a corporate income tax. Nor had Roosevelt wanted the vice presidency. He knew it was a political graveyard. Yet when he discovered that Mark Hanna and McKinley himself didn't want

him and heard the cheers that his possible nomination inspired among everyday party members, Roosevelt fought for the post and won.

In fact, it was McKinley who was headed for the graveyard. On September 6, 1901, while visiting the Temple of Music of the Pan-American Exposition in Buffalo, New York, the popular second-term president was shot twice by anarchist Leon Czolgosz. McKinley, who began his service to the nation as a private in the Civil War, rose to a major in the army, served in Congress and as Ohio's governor, and finally was elected president, died eight days after being shot. Roosevelt, who had been on a camping trip in upstate New York, was immediately sworn in as the twenty-sixth president of the United States.

Under McKinley, and then Roosevelt, the United States had not only prospered but also assumed a dramatic international posture. The Spanish-American War stirred up resistance to U.S. "imperialism." Even Speaker of the House Thomas Brackett Reed was so disgusted by the war that he resigned from Congress. But ultimately, the war demonstrated that "America was at last a citizen of the world." The 1904 convention would reflect that international interest. Domestic affairs took second place. The convention celebrated a time in which Americans in general and Republicans in particular could glory in the stabilization that successive Republican administrations had secured for the nation.

Chicago Republicans began work in December 1903 to bring the convention to Chicago. Graeme Stewart, Republican national committeeman for Illinois and a partner with the Chicago Wholesale Grocery company W.M. Hoyt, headed the Illinois commission to obtain the convention. Chicago Republicans strategically established their headquarters at the Arlington Hotel in Washington, D.C. When the commission personally called on Roosevelt on December 10, 1903, the president eagerly welcomed his Illinois colleagues. To their entreaties of Chicago's ideal qualities, Roosevelt told them, "I would be a poor American if I were not a good Chicagoan."

So sure was the Republican National Committee that Chicago was a shoo-in for the convention that they booked hotel space before the vote was taken on the actual location. Samuel Raymond, the head of the Chicago committee, said the city would guarantee expenses. He also boasted of a new convention hall, the city's second Coliseum, with a normal seating capacity of twelve thousand. St. Louis, which was hosting the Louisiana Purchase Exhibition, and Pittsburgh also made bids. But it took only one ballot for Chicago to win the prize. Undaunted, St. Louis hosted the 1904 Democratic Convention.

The Illinois committee returned home victorious and ready for work, setting up political action and entertainment committees. Preparations of the new Coliseum on South Wabash Avenue began in May. (The old Coliseum on Sixty-Third Street burned down on Christmas Eve 1897.) The new Coliseum was built in 1900, in part with large stone blocks remaining from Libby Prison, which had inhabited the site. Libby Prison, a Southern stockade for Union officers, had been transported stone by stone from Richmond, Virginia, to Chicago and reconstructed from 1889 to 1899 by Alderman Charles F. Gunther as a Civil War museum. When the amusement business failed, the Coliseum took its place. The Republicans were the first to hold a convention in the mammoth hall.

Special opera chairs were installed with hat, cane, and umbrella racks for the delegates' use. Seats were set up directly in front of the speaker's stand. Behind the delegates sat the alternates and then the spectators. In addition to their four hundred reserved seats on the speaker's rostrum, the press had use of a telegraph room with two hundred operators. The Coliseum also boasted hospital rooms, police and fire headquarters, as well as a telephone exchange with twelve booths. Preparations were completed on June 19, two days before the convention was to open.

Chairman Raymond said of the facility, "It is the best hall in which a national convention has ever been held. Some people say that it is too small, but I predict that in the future, national conventions will be held nowhere else. They'll come because we have the best convention hall in the country." Seventy-five doorkeepers, all non-Chicagoans, were on hand to prevent Chicagoans from packing their friends inside. The committee had thought of everything.

Delegates and spectators to the Thirteenth Republican National Convention assembled at the doors of the Coliseum long before the hall was scheduled to open. When the eleven entrances were finally opened at 10:30 A.M, June 21, a fierce rush to gain admission to the huge building ensued.

From start to finish, the convention was controlled by Roosevelt. But the pale ghosts of the late President McKinley and his mentor Senator Mark Hanna of Ohio also haunted the hall. Roosevelt fans, however, made short work of them. Hanna, the powerful Republican "money god" who had guided McKinley's rise to power, was long a political rival of Roosevelt's. "I told William McKinley it was a mistake to nominate that wild man at Philadelphia," Hanna had said, "Now look, that damned cowboy is president of the United States." (Roosevelt had spent several years as a "cowboy" in the Dakotas after his first wife died.)

As president, Roosevelt initially followed McKinley's policies. But after a year of stability, he broke with Republican tradition and took on big business. First, he dusted off the Sherman Anti-Trust Act to go after the Northern Securities Company, a railroad trust of James J. Hill and Edward H. Harriman. Then he took on other new trusts, indicating the direction of his future administration. He also intervened in the bitter anthracite coal strike of 1902 on behalf of working families. The Eastern business interests shared Hanna's viewpoint, considering the aristocratic Roosevelt to be "a traitor to his class." They urged Hanna to run against the new president, but the Ohio senator died four months before the convention, relieving Roosevelt of any real rival for the nomination.

Hanna's death also denied the Republican Party its longtime chairman. Since no succeeding chairman had been chosen, out of respect for Hanna, the party began the convention without one. Senator Louis E. McComas of Maryland moved that Postmaster General Henry C. Payne of Wisconsin be appointed chairman. He was so appointed for the thirty minutes necessary to open the day's events. A huge illuminated portrait of Hanna was suspended just above the stage. The memorial tribute to the late senator was to have been the only image enshrined in the hall.

But when the doors of the Coliseum opened, many were amazed to see large lithographic portraits of Roosevelt affixed to shields, centered between the double American flags draped at alternating intervals on scores of columns. Roosevelt's people had been in the hall during the night and added the president's picture throughout to the sea of red, white, and blue, a visible indication of his tight grip upon the convention.

At 12:14 P.M. on June 21 Postmaster General Payne called the 994 delegates to order with a gavel mounted in gold. A prayer was then offered by the Reverend Timothy P. Frost of Evanston, Illinois. Following the sober invocation, convention secretary Elmer Dover read the Call for the Convention. Chairman Payne named former Secretary of War Elihu Root of New York as temporary chairman with unanimous approval. Before Root could take up the gavel, an air of expectancy stirred at the north end of the platform. A black-draped easel had been set in place, and six men stood at the edge of the platform. The cloth was pulled off the easel to reveal a painting of President Roosevelt. Delegates from New York stood up and cheered, and the convention followed.

When Elihu Root finally stepped to the speaker's stand, he began a one-hour, legalistic keynote speech:

The responsibility of government rests upon the Republican Party. The complicated machinery through which eighty million people of the United States govern themselves, answers to no single will. The composite government devised by the framers of the Constitution to meet the conditions of national life, more than a century ago, requires the willing cooperation of many minds . . . The president at Washington with his Cabinet, the 90 senators representing 45 sovereign states, the 386 representatives in Congress, are required to reach concurrent action upon a multitude of questions . . .

Within the past five years, more than thirty-six thousand bills have been introduced in Congress. Some method of selection must be followed.

In the next election, Root explained:

We shall ask the continued confidence of the people because the candidates whom we present are of proved competency and patriotism, fitted to fill the offices for which they are nominated, to the credit and honor of our country.

And of Roosevelt, Root said:

Our president has taken the whole people into his confidence. Incapable of deception, he has put aside concealment. . . . No people can maintain free government who do not in their hearts value the qualities which have made the present president of the United States conspicuous among the men of his time as a type of noble manhood. Come what may here, come what may in November, God grant that those qualities of brave, true manhood shall have honor throughout America, shall be held for an example in every home, and that the youth of generations to come may grow up to feel that it is better than wealth, or office, or power, to have the honesty, the purity, and the courage of Theodore Roosevelt.

Then, at the south end of the hall, a band played many popular national tunes, such as "Dixie," "My Old Kentucky Home," "Maryland," and others. Day one was a predictable, calm beginning for the Republicans. It did, however, offer some important moments in American political history. When the convention was called to order, four women sat in their places among the alternate delegates, marking the first time that women were chosen to represent their state at a national presidential convention. The four women had come from the West. One of the women, Emma C. Eldridge of Colorado Springs, Colorado, gained the right to vote at the convention because her principal delegate was absent. The other women alternates, Eva Le Fevre of Colorado, Susan West of Idaho, and Jennie B. Nelson of Utah, each represented states that had already adopted women's suffrage. During the convention, it was confidently expected that an effort would be made by the female politicians to incorporate a plank for women's suffrage in the national platform. But no such measure was added.

Headquarters for the Women's National Republican Association was opened at the Palmer House, just north of the Coliseum on Wabash Avenue. The most prominent women engaged in the national women's suffrage movement were there, including J. Ellen Foster, president of the association; Helen Yarick Bosswell, organization secretary; Mary Yost Wood; Elizabeth F. Pierce; and Mrs. George F. Lowell of Boston.

Local organizations of Chicago women lent their support. Catherine Waugh McCullough, author of the suffrage plank in the Democratic platform of Illinois, organized the work of the committee. Among those Chicagoans willing to serve was Jane Addams of Hull-House, the Chicago settlement house pioneer, who was a strong advocate of suffrage reform. All day long the club rooms of the Chicago Woman's Club, located in the Fine Arts Building on Michigan Avenue, were open to women delegates.

The convention's second day, Wednesday, June 22, began with much commotion. Crowds gathered early, the big rush coming at 11:00 A.M. Then, precisely on the stroke of noon, Senators Chauncey Depew and Thomas C. Platt of New York marched into the hall arm in arm, waving graciously to the crowd. At 12:15 P.M., the band played "with might and main," stirring renditions of "America" and "Yankee Doodle." Cheer after cheer erupted as the audience noise raised to fever pitch. Cries of "Roosevelt and Fairbanks" went up throughout the hall, but the delegates as a whole refused to take up the cheer. During the delay, one frustrated delegate from Maine stuck a picture of Roosevelt to his cane and attempted to stir up a little excitement. But he was unable to gather a stampede.

Temporary chairman Root called the day's business to order at 12:25 P.M. A prayer by the Reverend Thomas Cox, pastor of Saint Basil Roman Catholic Church, drifted out over the vast throng that packed the Coliseum. Delegates speculated that the New York delegation was getting ready to jump the gun on the nominations and force them to occur on day two. The Chicago papers were already reporting in their headlines that Roosevelt and Senator Fairbanks were to head the ticket and would do so by a unanimous vote. Committee reports and the routine business of the convention were rushed forward in order that they could get to the nominations quickly. A frenzy was brewing in the hall.

The powerful Speaker of the House Joseph Gurney Cannon of Danville, Illinois, was selected as permanent chairman. He walked down the aisle to the band accompaniment of "Columbia." Cannon countered a press charge that this convention had "no enthusiasm." "Uncle Joe," as the iron-fisted speaker was known, noted that, "In 1904, as in 1900, everybody has known for twelve months past who is to be our standard-bearer in this campaign. We are ready for business. I wonder if our friends, the enemy, would not be glad of a little of our kind of enthusiasm." Cannon then reminded his listeners,

"The Republican Party, born of the declaration that slavery is sectional and freedom national, achieved its first success in 1860 with Abraham Lincoln." That convention, only forty-four years earlier, was still fresh in the memory of some delegates. So too, was the war that ensued. Cannon tipped his hat to a veteran of the Civil War, General Osterhaus, who earlier had been introduced to the convention. "He helped to make it possible for us to have this convention," Cannon commended.

Cannon then pointed out the comparisons between 1860 and 1904. Decades of Republican government permitted him, he said, the opportunity to make wide economic analyses showing the enhanced opportunities for national success. The policy and leadership of the Republican Party preserved the Union, Cannon insisted. Under McKinley and Roosevelt, such preservation was still occurring, despite the "imported anarchy" that had taken McKinley's life. In a morale-boosting finale, Cannon catalogued the accomplishments that were the legacy of Republican policies. The pulse of the convention quickened at Cannon's fiery words. As the speaker concluded his address, the bells of nearby Saint James Church could be heard chiming two o'clock.

Senator Henry Cabot Lodge delivered the report from the Committee on Resolutions. The Boston patrician catalogued a tour de force of Republican initiatives with special focus on foreign issues. Special mention was given to Roosevelt's application of the Monroe Doctrine and the Panama Canal, which Roosevelt had engineered in a staged revolution to break Panama away from Colombia. The 1904 Republican platform supported an expansionist American foreign policy, reaffirmation of the protective tariff, and recommitment to the gold standard.

Upon completion of Lodge's report, the convention was read a telegram—a bold warning to the Moroccan government—that epitomized such policies. A U.S. citizen, Ion Perdicaris, had been abducted by a Moroccan bandit named Raisuli. Secretary of State John Milton Hay had sent a message to Consul General Samuel R. Gummer in Morocco, meant to reflect the U.S. government's belief that the Moroccans were not acting in good faith. The bulletin read simply: "We want either Perdicaris alive or Raisuli dead." Applause thundered through the Coliseum. A Republican "rough rider" rode to America's rescue.

The press claimed that these delegates "came to Chicago to vote for Roosevelt, not because they wished, but because they had to." While they could have chosen some other candidate, Speaker of the House Joseph Cannon or William Howard Taft, for example, Roosevelt's hold was far too strong. But in true Rooseveltian style, he sent no personal representative to the convention and was sincere in leaving delegates to their own devices. Theodore Roosevelt was not a man for mediators. What he desired, he proclaimed himself. His straightforward style was refreshing, an indication of a "new way of doing things." As *Harper's Weekly* pointed out, "Youth is Roosevelt's secret to power and popularity." The excitement of the convention rested with a wider and more subtle evolution at work in American politics in which the vision of the nation became more global. Theodore Roosevelt's international character was tailor-made for the age.

The final day of deliberation, Thursday, June 23, 1904, got under way at 10:30 A.M. The hall quickly filled to capacity. Even the gallery had standing room only. Chairman Cannon, wielding an oversized gavel he had been given the previous day, gave the table before him a great whack and declared the proceedings open. Then, unlatching a small leather casket, the Speaker of the House took out his own small wooden gavel. With this in hand, he advanced to the front and commanded silence. He was obeyed at once. Now it was time to nominate a president. Oscar R. Hundley of Alabama requested "the privilege and distinguished honor of yielding its place upon the call to the state of New York."

Former New York governor Frank S. Black rose to address the great body. "We are here to inaugurate a campaign which seems already to be nearly closed," Governor Black began. "So wisely have the people sowed and watched and tended, there seems little now to do but measure up the grain." After describing the president's achievements, Black concluded:

> Events sometimes select the strongest man, as lightning goes down the highest rod. And so it is with those events which for many months with unerring sight have led you to a single name which I am chosen only to pronounce: Gentlemen, I nominate for president of the United States the highest living type of the youth, the vigor and the promise of a great country and a great age, Theodore Roosevelt of New York.

As the band began to play, Chairman Cannon unfurled a tattered silk flag, which made its first appearance forty-four years earlier at the 1860 convention. First carried by the Missouri delegation, it was lifted above the platform when Lincoln was nominated. In frenzied fury, it was waved in Chicago once again. The deafening ovation continued as a crayon portrait of the president was carried by three men.

The flag was next given to a young man from Philadelphia, John H. Smythe Jr., who carried a megaphone. Grasping the flag tightly in his hand, he waved it as he shouted "Roosevelt, Roosevelt." At the same time, the Indiana delegation opened red, white, and blue umbrellas that bore the portraits of Roosevelt and Fairbanks. The commotion lasted for seven minutes, at which time Chairman Cannon began to wave the flag once more, revving the crowd into a further frenzy. When order had finally been restored, Cannon held the flag high and said, "It prophesied victory in 1860, its life has been baptized on many a battlefield since, and it is safe in the hands of President Roosevelt." Thence followed another burst of cheers.

Roosevelt's nomination was seconded by Indiana senator Albert Jeremiah Beveridge, George A. Knight of California, H.S. Edwards of Georgia, former Kentucky governor William O'Connell Bradley, Joseph B. Cotton of Minnesota, and Harry S. Cummings of Maryland. Then Franklin Murphy of New Jersey proposed that Roosevelt be chosen by acclamation, but his proposal was rejected. Yet when the roll was called, Roosevelt received all 994 delegate votes on the first ballot.

Without delay, the chairman preceded to call for the roll of states to nominate a vice president. Once more, Alabama yielded its place, this time to Iowa's J. P. Dolliver who nominated Senator Charles Warren Fairbanks of Indiana, a former railroad corporation lawyer and powerful state leader. He was seconded by Senator Chauncey Depew of New York. Three delegates made seconding speeches. Then Illinois withdrew the name of Robert W. Hitt. Missouri and Georgia withdrew their favorite son nominees to vote for Fairbanks. Depew proposed that Fairbanks be nominated by acclamation, and the measure was passed.

In a mood of celebration, the convention came to a close at 2:22 P.M., less than three hours after the session was called to order. "The people of this country trust the president as a statesman. They love him as a man," said Senator Albert Jeremiah Beveridge of Indiana, capturing the feeling of the hour. President Roosevelt received news of his unanimous nomination at the White House, surrounded by members of his family. The report was carried to him by telephone by the Associated Press, in advance of notification by the special telegraph wire that ran from the convention to the executive offices.

In St. Louis later that summer, Democrats nominated a political unknown and a Cleveland gold Democrat, Alton Brooks Parker, chief justice of the New York Court of Appeals. The party wanted to move away from the progressivism of William Jennings Bryan after his two defeats to McKinley. Henry Gassaway Davis, an eighty-year-old former senator from West Virginia, was nominated as vice president.

Republicans and Democrats disagreed significantly on international and domestic issues, particularly on how the United States should treat the Philippines, Cuba, and Puerto Rico in the wake of the Spanish-American War. Republicans adopted a con-

servative approach to the nation's new war "possessions," based on business investment and limited self-autonomy. Democrats were reluctant to maintain their colonial status. Domestically, Republicans rejected the popular election of U.S. senators, while Democrats favored a change to direct election. As usual, Republicans advocated protective tariffs and strong defense of American industry; Democrats rejected the tariff as a form of domestic tax on the American people, restricting fair competition, and causing monopolies to be formed at home. Roosevelt campaigned on his record, which he characterized as a Square Deal for the American people.

In November, following a campaign against opponents in both the Democratic and Socialist parties, Roosevelt handily won with 7,626,593 votes to Parker's 5,082,898. The Socialists, led by Eugene V. Debs, attracted 402,489 votes. With a powerful showing in the northern states, Roosevelt received 336 electoral votes while the South went to the Democrats with 140 electoral votes. Now Roosevelt would become an even bigger "trust buster" and enact much of the progressive agenda Bryan had advocated in 1896, to the distress of many in his own party.

William Howard Taft

1908 Republican Presidential Nominee

James Schoolcraft Sherman

1908 Republican
Vice Presidential Nominee

Facts-at-a-Glance
★★★

Event:	Fourteenth Republican National Convention
Dates:	June 16–19, 1908
Building:	The Coliseum
Location:	1513 South Wabash Avenue
Chicago Mayor:	Fred A. Busse, Republican
Candidates for Nomination:	Speaker of the House Joseph Gurney Cannon, Illinois; Vice President Charles Warren Fairbanks, Indiana; Senator Joseph Benson Foraker, Ohio; Governor Charles Evans Hughes, New York; Senator Philander Chase Knox, Pennsylvania; Senator Robert Marion LaFollette, Wisconsin; Secretary of War William Howard Taft, Ohio
Presidential Nominee:	William Howard Taft
Age at Nomination:	50
Number of Ballots:	1
Vice Presidential Nominee:	James Schoolcraft Sherman, New York
Number of Delegates:	980
Number Needed to Nominate:	A majority, 491
Largest Attendance:	14,000
Critical Issues:	Tariff revision, currency reform, control of trusts, railroad regulation, use of injunctions against strikers by the courts, preservation of natural resources and waterways, America's interests abroad
Campaign Slogan:	"Four More Years"
Popular Song:	"Shine on Harvest Moon"

II
★★★

The 1908 Republican National Convention
A Stand-In for Teddy

In 1908 Roosevelt took the high road. As a historical purist, the president found it inconceivable to run for a third term. Having occupied the White House for seven years since the assassination of President McKinley in 1901, Roosevelt believed another term was simply improper. On election night 1904 after his tremendous victory, he had even brashly pledged to the electorate that he would forego any third term. So despite his enormous popularity and the many who tried to talk him out of it, President Theodore Roosevelt was firm in his resolution not to stand for a second election.

Roosevelt's administration had been among the most progressive in the history of the nation, and one of the most energetic and flamboyant. T.R. did everything on a grand scale. He built the Panama Canal and the Roosevelt Dam, created national parks and expanded protected acreage from 43 million to 194 million, passed pure-food-and-drug legislation, busted big corporate trusts, and regulated the railroads. Few administrations could boast of his peacetime achievements. Roosevelt had a rigid conservative side as well, and he gladly signed the Immigration Act of 1903 with its provision for deporting anarchists like the one who had killed McKinley. He hated radicals and believed only by bold action against the abuses of capitalism could he preserve the American way of life.

Roosevelt was also an international jingoist, sending a U.S. Navy fleet around the world in a show of force and working to bolster the Hague tribunal as a way to maintain peace in Europe. He won a Nobel Peace Prize for mediating the 1905 Russo-Japanese War. Most of all, Teddy held himself up as a moral exemplar for the American republic. But his progressive agenda was not complete. Who, if not Teddy, could carry on?

Despite his decision not to run again, Roosevelt did, however, have every intention of handpicking his own successor. For that he looked to his Secretary of War William Howard Taft of Ohio, a man who had secured Roosevelt's most intimate political friendship. As a reward for Taft's faithfulness, when the Fourteenth Republican National Convention convened in Chicago from June 16–19, 1908, Roosevelt would direct the party to honor his request and pass the progressive torch onto Taft. Roosevelt would ask the convention for the same unbridled loyalty that had characterized Taft's own service as a party loyalist and patriot who had given up his judicial career to represent the United States in the newly acquired territory of the Philippines. It was a post that proved the testing of Taft's mettle.

Taft came from Cincinnati, was the son of a judge, and like his father, had studied at Yale where he finished second in his class and was elected class orator. After graduating from Cincinnati Law School, he took up legal practice. (But in one famous extralegal incident, the 250-pound lawyer thrashed the publisher of a newspaper for slandering his father in his unsuccessful gubernatorial race.) He then became an assistant prosecuting attorney and within two years was appointed by Governor Joseph Benson Foraker as judge of the superior court. Eventually, President McKinley appointed him as the first civil governor of the Philippine Islands. Then Roosevelt was elevated to the presidency. At least three times during his service as the Philippines governor-general, Roosevelt had offered Taft his lifelong prize of a Supreme Court appointment.

But three times Taft refused in order to carry out his responsibilities to the Filipino people and to create democratic institutions for that nation. His ultimate departure from the Philippines came when Roosevelt appointed Taft as secretary of war, a post from which he could continue to supervise Filipino affairs in Washington. The people of the Philippines had come to regard Taft as the personification of American justice. He would not let them down. As secretary of war, he could insure that there would be no deviation from the policy he had marked out in Manila.

Taft, the "combative altruist" whose hearty laugh and jolly humor made him a good friend as well, had proven his character in other ways that pleased Roosevelt. Taft had one of the great legal minds of his generation. He oversaw construction of the Panama Canal, and in his capacity as secretary of war managed the old Spanish colonies acquired by the United States following victory in the Spanish-American War. Roosevelt came to rely upon Taft as a trusted adviser on all significant matters in his administration.

Conversely, Taft's insider position at the Roosevelt White House gave him a presidential vision of the nation to which he brought his expansive international understanding. Taft seemed a perfect match for the presidency, a man with refined Republican sensibilities and enduring respect for the nation's greatness. Taft was a man after Roosevelt's own heart. The 1908 convention, it appeared, belonged to Roosevelt, and he would use it to anoint his friend, William Howard Taft, to assume command of his noble crusade.

By 1908 Chicago was the queen of convention cities for both the Democrats and Republicans, a city that made good on its promises to the national party organizations. Four years earlier, Chicago Republicans had pitched hard to entice the Republican National Committee (RNC) to bring the convention to town again. In 1908 it took a more relaxed approach. Fred W. Upham, chairman of the local 1908 committee that included Charles G. Dawes, a future vice president, and Samuel Insull, the traction and utilities magnate, insisted that Chicago send no group to Washington to campaign for the next meeting. Instead, Upham and Samuel B. Raymond, chairman of the local Chicago committee in 1904, sent a brief telegram to the national committee:

> Chicago wants the Convention. We offer the Coliseum with 14,000 seats, if required. We will pay all legitimate expenses of subcommittee pertaining to Convention. Cannot raise campaign fund now. We refer to Mr. Schneider, treasurer of the Convention fund in 1904. He knows what was done then and we will personally guarantee same amount.

The Chicago committee also sent the telegram to Frank O. Lowden, Illinois member of the RNC.

Chicago was awarded the convention even though other cities made presentations with checks in hand. Like Fred Upham, Chicago had learned the manners and style of boardroom negotiations. Upham also had a talent for fund-raising. For every $100 paid by convention subscribers, one ticket was made available and a dividend of 18 percent was paid out by the national committee at the convention's end.

A contract was quickly made with the Coliseum, and Arthur G. Brown, consulting architect for the Republican National Committee, began the supervision of the convention site. Arrangements within the Coliseum were to be different than in 1904. In 1908 the platform for speakers was located at the south end of the barrel-roofed center. When they finally arrived in Chicago, the Republican National Committee was entertained by Upham and the local committee with a special lunch at South Shore Country Club shortly before the convention opened. Chicago committee members furnished automobiles to drive the seventy-five members of the RNC and their guests to the club at Seventy-First Street and the lake. Upham's hospitality spilled over into the convention itself where he provided members of the national committee with elaborate luncheons in convention hall anterooms.

The Fourteenth Republican National Convention was called to order on Tuesday, June 16, 1908, at 12:25 P.M. As soon as the gavel, made from a log from old Fort Dearborn, came down, Harry S. New of Indiana, chairman of the Republican National Committee, greeted delegates saying, "The hour has arrived for the representatives of the Republican Party to meet . . . at the end of almost twelve consecutive years of the most brilliant administration in the history of the world." He then called forward several delegates who had been in attendance at the First Republican National Convention in 1856.

The Call for the Convention was read by John R. Malloy of Ohio. He recited recent accomplishments of the Republican administration both at home and abroad and set out the reasons President Theodore Roosevelt had chosen not to seek a third term. "Yet nothing has added so much to his just fame as his persistent and irrevocable refusal to break the unwritten law of the Republic by accepting a nomination for a third term. By this act of self-abnegation he places his name and fame in the secure keeping of history by the side of the immortal Washington." Malloy then set out the task of finding a worthy successor to the president, someone with "the patriotism and sagacity of a Lincoln, the tenacity of a Grant, the wisdom and moderation of a McKinley, and the courage of a Roosevelt."

Day two of the convention was called to order by temporary chairman Julius Caesar Barrows of Michigan. Senator Barrows had not been Roosevelt's first choice as temporary chair. His conservative Republican credentials appealed to that faction of the party who were determined to inflict damage upon Roosevelt and his policies. Roosevelt's first choice had been Senator Albert Beveridge of Indiana, but he was unacceptable to the conservative wing on the spurious grounds that he was from the same state as Vice President Fairbanks, who was a presidential contender. Barrows's presence as temporary chairman would give visibility to the strong sentiments of conservative leadership within the Republican Party. While the convention belonged to Roosevelt—that is, in his selection of a successor—in the days ahead the conservative faction within the party would hold tight reins on the shaping of the platform.

Rumors abounded that a split within the party was in the offing because of serious platform conflicts. The old guard had had enough of Roosevelt's progressivism. They wanted a party that stood for conservative Republican values of law and order. Trouble was in the air.

Senator Henry Cabot Lodge of Massachusetts, the personal choice of President Roosevelt, was elected permanent chairman. The keynote speech he delivered at the start of day two had been heavily edited by the president himself. The voice of Roosevelt rang the timbers through Lodge.

"I shall not delay or detain you with many words," Lodge assured his listeners. "Your resolutions will set forth the principles of the party and declare the policies upon which we shall ask for the support of the people . . . No political party in modern times can show such a record of achievement during the last fifty years as the Republican Party."

Lodge pointed out the clear distinctions between the Democrats and Republicans:

> Recall the cries which have sounded from the lips of these two parties during the last half century. On the one side "slavery; secession; repudiation of the public debt; fiat money; free trade; free silver; the overthrow of the courts; and government ownership." On the Republican side "Free soil; free men; the Union; the payment of debt; honest money; protection to American industry; the gold standard; the maintenance of law, of order, and of the courts, and the government; regulation of great corporations."

Lodge sketched Roosevelt's contribution to America's greatness, reinforcing for the delegates the seriousness of the times in which they lived.

> Under the lead of the president, the Republican Party has grappled with the new problems born of the new conditions. It has been no light task. Dangerous extremes threatened on either hand. On the one side were the radicals of reaction, who resisted any change at all; on the other side were the radicals of destruction, who wished to change everything. These two forms of radicalism are as far apart at the outset as the poles, but, when carried out, they lead alike to revolution. Between these two extremes the Republican president and Republican Congress were compelled to steer and while they advance steadily, soberly and effectively, they were obliged to repel the radical assaults on either hand.

Lodge then warned all assembled about the futility of any attempt to persuade Roosevelt to reconsider retirement.

> The president, who has led his party and the people of this great work, retires, by his own determination from his high office on the fourth of March next. His refusal of a renomination, dictated by the loftiest motives and by a noble loyalty to American traditions, is final and irrevocable. Any one who attempts to use his name as a candidate for the presidency impugns both his sincerity and his good faith, two of the president's greatest and most conspicuous qualities, upon which no shadow has ever been cast. That man is no friend to Theodore Roosevelt and does not cherish his name and fame, who now, from any motive, seeks to urge him as a candidate for the great office which he has finally declined.
>
> The president has refused what his countrymen would gladly have given him; he says what he means and means what he says, and his party and his country will respect his wishes as they honor his high character and great public service. But, although the president retires, he leaves his policies behind him. To those policies the Republican Party stands pledged. We must carry them out as we have begun,

regardless alike of the radicals of reaction and the radicals of revolution. We must hold fast to that which is good while we make the advances which the times demand.

The numbers men within the Republican Party were busy tabulating the solid votes for Taft. They knew, even on the second day, that he had the necessary strength for a first ballot win. But the deepening tension between party factions promised that despite the president's wishes, all would not go smoothly. Progressive Republicans were making their voice heard, above the louder noise of conservative rejection.

During the business of Wednesday, delegates were little surprised at the spectacle of marching clubs parading through the Coliseum, or the commotion raised by a glee club stretched in front of the Ohio delegation. In their half-hour songfest, they belted out the chorus "Billy Taft, Billy Taft, well, well for Billy Taft, of Ohio." But in an attempt to rev up the crowd to outdo the frenzy created four years earlier for Roosevelt, demonstrators failed miserably. Before the songsters could finish their half-hour set, the crowd yelled, "Enough, get out, go!" It was hard to pump enthusiasm for Taft into the crowd of party regulars. Lincoln J. Steffens, a reporter for the *Chicago Daily Journal*, reported a convention "frost" for Taft. What was really being demonstrated, he insisted, was the Republican organization upholding President Roosevelt's directive through good old-fashioned fear. All that day, the committee work dragged on, wearing away at everyone's patience. No one had the stamina to continue. John Franklin of New Jersey moved that the convention adjourn until the following morning. The fireworks would be saved for the next day's affairs.

Senator Lodge called the convention's third day, Thursday, June 18, 1908, to order at 10:00 A.M. sharp. From the outset it was brimming with energy and passion, a suitable tone for the day of presidential nomination. Senator Albert J. Hopkins of Illinois, chairman of the Committee on Resolutions, read the party platform. The document canonized Roosevelt into American political sainthood and articulated the issues that gave the 1908 Republicans their political identity.

In this greatest era of American advancement the Republican Party has reached its highest service under the leadership of Theodore Roosevelt. His administration is an epoch in American history. In no other period since national sovereignty was won under Washington, or preserved under Lincoln, has there been such mighty progress in those ideals of government which make for justice, equality, and fair dealing among men. The highest aspirations of the American people have found a voice.

Hopkins again reviewed the accomplishments of Roosevelt's presidency, then set forth for the assembled delegates the method by which the party would continue the progress begun under the Rough Rider. But the party's "pledge for the future" was essentially a conservative document with vague promises on various items, including:

tariff revision;
possible currency adjustments to prevent economic downturns;
creation of postal savings banks;
continued regulation of trusts and monopolies;
control of railroad rates and rebates that discriminate against small business;
promotion of the eight-hour day for wage earners;
possible control on writs of injunction against strikers by the federal courts;
a stand against state aid for the American farmer;
condemnation of the disenfranchisement of African Americans;
extension of conservation methods begun by Roosevelt;
protection of American citizens abroad;
extension of foreign commerce; and
greater use of the arbitration and the Hague treaties to prevent war.

The most contentious fight of the convention had taken place in the resolutions committee over the anti-injunction plank. For many delegates, the days had run together with secret meetings that lasted through the night at the Auditorium Hotel. Often, delegates were at the table until 5:30 A.M. Roosevelt and Taft insisted that the anti-injunction plank be included in the platform. Samuel Gompers of the American Federation of Labor was on hand to represent the position of American labor but was prevented from attending some of the meetings and was met with a hostile reaction from Lodge and other old guard Republicans.

J. W. Van Cleve, president of the National Manufacturers Association, strongly urged rejection of Roosevelt's plank. Van Cleve argued that if the measure was adopted by the Republicans, he would lead a move to the Democrats. With 200,000 manufacturers proposing to sit out the election, the stakes were high. A middle ground was sought by emphasizing that the Republicans believed that the courts should "protect life, liberty, and property," as well as become more moderate in the use of injunctions. In the end, it was Gompers and not Van Cleve who was sent packing to join the Democrats at their Denver convention.

A minority report, proposed by the Wisconsin delegation that contained recommendations advocating the direct election of United States senators (instead of election by state legislatures), regulation of campaign contributions, supervision of telegraph and telephone rates, establishment of a Department of Labor, and women's suffrage was rejected on a 917 to 63 vote amid decisive laughter.

Chairman Lodge then called for the nomination of presidential candidates. Henry Sherman Boutell of Illinois was first recognized to nominate the Speaker of the House and fellow Illini, Joseph Gurney Cannon. Boutell told delegates, "Nineteen times he has been elected to high office by the voters of a district that has no superior in the United States for intelligence and patriotism." Cannon's nomination was seconded by J.W. Fordney of Michigan.

Vice President Charles Warren Fairbanks was nominated for president by Governor J. Frank Hanly of Indiana. "With him the 'Square Deal' will be transferred from the forum of academic discussion to the field of accomplished fact. His spear will know no friend."

General Stewart L. Woodford of New York nominated Governor Charles Evans Hughes of New York. Woodford had been at the 1860 convention and saw Lincoln nominated. Hughes was the man, he told them, who could win the state of New York for the Republican Party. He delineated Hughes's record of fighting crime and big business in New York State as governor.

When Ohio was reached in the Roll Call of the States, Theodore E. Burton finally nominated Secretary of War William Howard Taft. It was 2:45 P.M. Burton first complimented the host city:

> It is especially appropriate that this gathering should
> be held in the marvelous city of Chicago, whence the
> steel bands of commerce reach out in every direc-
> tion, over plain and river and mountain, to almost

boundless distance, bringing the rich treasures of a continent to lay them at your feet. Here it was that the righteous uprising against slavery and Bourbonism, sprung from the nation's conscience, raised its first triumphant voice when Abraham Lincoln was nominated. And here, again, with notes of thunderous acclaim, enraptured throngs greeted the naming of Garfield, of Blaine, of Harrison, and of Roosevelt.

He was answered with waves of applause.

"Again, Ohio presents a candidate to the national Republican convention," he cried. Burton listed Taft's accomplishments and service to the nation. "No one has ever yet assumed the presidential chair who had received a more ideal preparation for the duties of that great office." George A. Knight of California seconded Taft's nomination.

A storm in Taft's favor went up from the crowd. As a band played, a Taft banner unfurled. Delegates stood on their chairs. A pair of pants from Texas was carried in and paraded through the hall. In a paraphrase of the psalm, a sign said, "As pants the heart for cooling streams, So Texas pants for Taft." The *Chicago Tribune* characterized the Texas salute as ridiculous and undignified, but illustrative. "Old men," it observed, "were as frisky as sophomores." At 3:05 P.M. a huge painting of Taft was carried through the hall. When calm was restored the nominations continued.

Senator Joseph B. Foraker, also of Ohio, was then nominated by C. R. McCoy. Foraker's nomination was seconded by W. O. Emory of Georgia, an African American who rose with pride to praise Foraker. His words were touched with historic references from the Greeks. Emory also raised the significant issue of race:

> Mr. Chairman, the battles of liberty have not yet all
> been fought out . . . the ballot box should be open to
> all whether white or black, rich or poor . . . We want a
> man who standing on the mountain top traces all the
> victorious steps of our party in the past . . . and looks
> forward prepared to meet the dangers to come.

Lieutenant Governor Robert S. Murphy of Pennsylvania nominated Philander Chase Knox of Tennessee, Roosevelt's conservative secretary of commerce and labor: "In the triumphs of the administration of Theodore Roosevelt, and they are many, no man has done more in contribution than this man, for upon his shoulders fell the success or failure of the policies that have made the present administration great." James Scarlet, also of Pennsylvania, seconded Knox's nomination.

The nominations were rounded out by Henry F. Cochems of Wisconsin, who recommended favorite son Senator Robert Marion LaFollette, a lightning rod for the progressive wing of the Republican Party and the wounded author of the minority report that had been so scornfully rejected by the convention. Cochems told his audience, "The successor to Theodore Roosevelt should be a man who is neither a rampant radical or a cowardly conservative, but a man strong to understand, fearless to execute, and just to conserve the honest rights of all." C. A. A. McGee, of Wisconsin, delivered LaFollette's seconding speech.

With the oratory silent now, Henry Cabot Lodge called for the first ballot for president. The Roll Call of the States began, continuing alphabetically until it reached New York, which requested that each member of its delegation be polled personally. South Carolina requested the same. But disputes aside, when the roll call was complete, 980 votes had been cast, and divided accordingly: Cannon, 58; Fairbanks, 40; Foraker, 16; Hughes, 67; Knox, 68; LaFollette, 25; Roosevelt, 3; and Taft, 702. Immediately, delegates clamored to make Taft's nomination unanimous, and their will was done.

Sitting in Section 63 of the giant Coliseum were Taft's brothers, Charles and Henry, along with his nineteen-year-old son Robert. Delegates squeezed their hands, and they were nearly carried off by well-wishers. Following the seven-and-a-half-hour drama of political maneuvering, C. W. Fulton moved that the convention adjourn at 5:25 P.M. It had been the longest day of the Fourteenth Republican National Convention. Speaker of the House Cannon quickly sent a telegram to Taft, in Hot Springs, Arkansas, unofficially informing him of the nomination.

The last day of the convention was its shortest day. Delegates were still exhausted from late-night caucuses. The full day on Thursday, with the fight over the platform and nomination of a candidate for president, had drained them. On day four, Friday, June 19, 1908, they would complete their business in less than one hour and forty-eight minutes. The matter at hand was the nomination of a vice presidential candidate.

The convention was called to order at 10:00 A.M. Henry Cabot Lodge then invited Rabbi Tobias Schanfarber of Chicago to deliver the invocation. Lodge

called for the presentation of candidates for vice president. Chase Osborn of Michigan moved that the vice presidential nominating speeches be limited to ten minutes and seconding speeches be limited to five minutes. The secretary proceeded to call the roll of states. When Delaware was summoned, it yielded its place to New York. Timothy Woodruff nominated six-term Congressman James Schoolcraft Sherman of New York. He was seconded by Speaker of the House Joseph Cannon of Illinois.

Lodge himself nominated Governor Curtis Guild of Massachusetts. Thomas N. McCarter of New Jersey nominated former Governor Franklin Murphy. The vote was a runaway. Vice President Fairbanks received 1 vote, Guild received 75, Murphy picked up 77, George Sheldon of Nebraska earned 10, while "Sunny Jim" Sherman received 816. A motion was quickly made to make the vote unanimous and endorsed to strong cheers.

Judson W. Lyons, of Georgia, made the motion to adjourn, and, at 11:48 A.M. the Fourteenth Republican National Convention came to a close. As the delegates left Chicago, many Republicans congratulated themselves on the organized and orderly fashion in which the allies of President Roosevelt had been able to shape and control the events of the convention. Yet while the dust settled, there were some issues that would not go away. The schism within the Republican ranks that seemed to be averted in Chicago would return to haunt the party. By 1912 both party regulars and Roosevelt himself regretted the president's decision not to seek a second elected term. The seeds for political and party furor had been planted and would be reaped in just four years. Teddy Roosevelt would return, reckless and angry, but unable to wield the power that had characterized his strength and ability in 1908. His Bull Moose days were yet to come.

In the immediate months that followed the Chicago convention, Taft battled Democratic nominee William Jennings Bryan on Bryan's third and final run for the White House. Because of Roosevelt, the Republicans shared Bryan's mantle of progressivism, and despite the Commoner's energetic fight for the direct election of U.S. senators, tariff reform, a graduated income tax, an end to U.S. imperialism, and rule of the people over big business, he had been outflanked by Roosevelt and his hand-picked successor. The nomination of Taft and Sherman turned out to be a winning combination in the November elections, garnering the White House four more years for the Republicans. Taft polled 7,677,788 votes to Bryan's 6,407,982. Socialist Eugene V. Debs attracted 420,890 votes. Taft would try to follow in Teddy's footprints, a task he soon learned was all but impossible.

William Howard Taft
1912 Republican Presidential Nominee

James Schoolcraft Sherman
1912 Republican
Vice Presidential Nominee

Facts-at-a-Glance
★★★

Event:	Fifteenth Republican National Convention
Dates:	June 18–22, 1912
Building:	The Coliseum
Location:	1513 South Wabash Avenue
Chicago Mayor:	Carter Henry Harrison Jr., Democrat
Candidates for Nomination:	Senator Robert Marion LaFollette Sr., Wisconsin; former President Theodore Roosevelt, New York; President William Howard Taft, Ohio
Presidential Nominee:	William Howard Taft
Age at Nomination:	55
Number of Ballots:	1
Vice Presidential Nominee:	James Schoolcraft Sherman, New York
Number of Delegates:	1,078
Number Needed to Nominate:	A majority, 540
Largest Attendance:	14,000
Critical Issues:	Taft versus Roosevelt, conservativism versus progressivism, a Roosevelt third term, honesty of delegate process, bias of convention decisions
Popular Song:	"Steamroller Bill"

12
★★★

The 1912 Republican National Convention

The Progressive Revolt

Teddy was back . . . back from Africa, back in politics, back in the presidential race, back in Chicago for the 1912 Fifteenth Republican National Convention. So was a contingent of his Rough Riders, who came dressed in full army uniform as either Roosevelt delegates or vocal spectators to see that their man won back his rightful place as president of the United States. Like Grant before him, the retired president, having installed his successor Taft safely in the White House, toured abroad while a fascinated American public read newspaper accounts of his every move. And again like Grant, he returned to the United States with his eye on regaining the presidency.

The political infighting between the party's old guard and Republican progressives that preceded the 1912 Republican National Convention was fierce. President Taft had slipped badly in popularity during his three years in office, despite a sometimes aggressive fight for progressive issues, such as the antitrust laws that were handed him by Roosevelt. His legislative record was impressive, even if his personal commitment to progressive issues was suspect. He had prosecuted the Standard Oil and American Tobacco Company trusts, promoted aggressive use of the Sherman Anti-Trust Act against monopolies, completed the Panama Canal without scandal, brought Arizona and New Mexico into statehood, reduced the tariff schedules, reorganized the army and navy, passed employer's compensation legislation, sent the income tax amendment to the states, enacted a corporate income tax, and opened China to U.S. trade. It was the kind of record that normally afforded an incumbent the right to seek reelection proudly, the kind of record that might normally afford victory in the general election.

Taft, however, a conservative at heart, seemed to alienate everyone along the way to his achievements: the workers who disliked tariff rates, the "insurgent" senators and progressive Republican and Democratic congressmen fighting for reform, and the farmers hurt by his trade deals. His biggest flaw was that he wasn't Roosevelt. As a loyal friend of Teddy's, Taft thought he was fundamentally following through on his pledge to push Roosevelt's agenda through Congress. But he had done it his way. He was, after all, the president of the United States.

Yet there was clear betrayal of the progressive cause in some of Taft's actions. He aligned himself with the most blatant conservative elements of Congress: the dictatorial Speaker of the House Joseph Cannon of Illinois, who had been in Congress since 1893 and had finally been stripped of his absolute power in the "Revolution of 1910," and Senator Nelson Wilmarth Aldrich of Rhode Island, who had been in the Senate since 1881 and was responsible for the Gold Standard Act of 1900. Both were in cahoots with the special interests. Taft also let corporations run rampant in some of the national parks against the protests of conservationists, who had been protected by Roosevelt. Further, he opposed new progressive initiatives, such as the national primary.

Upon his return to the U.S. in 1910, Roosevelt, still a vibrant man of fifty-two, felt excluded. Taft asked for advice, but Teddy didn't respond. One or two slights was all Roosevelt needed to precipitate a personal break with his former protégé. Still, they had been friends for years. They had gotten their first taste of Washington in minor posts with the Harrison administration. Taft and Roosevelt moved up together under McKinley. Taft was appointed solicitor general of the United States and judge of the Sixth Federal Circuit where he became the first judge to enforce the Sherman Anti-Trust Act. Then he was appointed head of the Philippines Commission, where he advocated for their self-government, education, and home ownership. Roosevelt became civil service commissioner, assistant secretary of the navy, agitated for war with Spain, then rose to national prominence leading his Rough Riders to liberate Cuba. When T.R. returned from Cuba, his popularity made him governor of New York, although by a small margin; his earlier reign as New York City police commissioner worked against him.

In 1900 McKinley reluctantly accepted Roosevelt as vice president. When McKinley was assassinated, Roosevelt ascended to the presidency. But when elected in 1904, he pledged not to seek a third term. Later Roosevelt appointed Taft as his secretary of war. After refusing the 1908 nomination and installing Taft as his successor, Roosevelt expressed high hopes for his close friend and even predicted greatness for him as president.

But Roosevelt had passed the progressive torch to a traditionalist who wanted to tread in the middle of the road. Republicans split along the old conservative/liberal fault line. Hence, Roosevelt became "greatly disappointed" in Taft; whether justifiably or conveniently, it was hard to say. He now considered the 300-pound president politically "weak" and "a flubdub with a streak of the second-rate and the common in him." T. R. concluded, "He is utterly hopeless."

"I don't know what I have done to offend Theodore," the baffled president wondered aloud as the hostility with his old friend grew serious. "Since he's come back he's scared me to my very soul." Roosevelt didn't need much provocation. He felt like an outsider, distant from Taft's policy making. Taft's alleged oversight in not totally and fully crediting Roosevelt for his election turned into a personal insult that became a yawning wound. Taft tried to appease T. R., but was rebuffed.

Despite the cooling of their friendship, Taft, at first, never believed Roosevelt would try to unseat him and destroy the slim Republican chances for holding onto the White House. Certainly he had done nothing drastic enough to merit political betrayal and destruction of the party, concluded Taft, who still called Teddy "Mr. President" on the few occasions they met. But Helen Herron Taft, who followed her husband's career and other political developments closely, urged him not to yield. "I suppose you will have to fight Mr. Roosevelt for the renomination. And if you get it, he will defeat you. But it can't be helped. If possible, you must not allow him to defeat you for renomination. It doesn't make much difference about the reelection."

Taft was wrong about how far the former president would go. Although Roosevelt repeatedly

declared in the months following his return to the U.S. that he was "not and shall not be a candidate for president," he was possessed by the drive to regain power, to make up for his mistake in not accepting a third term when it was his for the asking. Roosevelt was too proud and principled to act without a groundswell to urge him on. All across the nation he had followers who were writing and calling with advice, ready to spring into action on his behalf. The press constantly inquired and speculated on his next move. Finally, in early January 1912, Roosevelt modestly told them, "If at this particular crisis, with the particular problems ahead of us at this time, the people feel that I am the one man in sight to do the job, then I should regard myself as shirking a plain duty if I refused to do it."

Roosevelt may have been an ethical purist for the press, but in reality, he arranged for seven governors to draft a letter urging him to run to protect the progressive principles of his "Square Deal." On January 22, 1912, he told his friends, "I cannot decline the call." Finally, on February 24, Theodore Roosevelt again threw his hat in the ring after a speech in which he advocated giving voters the right of referendum to overthrow court decisions on constitutional issues. The idea was enough to turn old friends like Senators Elihu Root and Henry Cabot Lodge against him. They feared Roosevelt was now drunk on the lure of power. The newspaper cartoons lambasted T. R. for wanting the presidency "For Ever and Ever and Ever," whereas writer Henry Adams saw "nothing for him but the asylum."

Taft agreed. Without naming Teddy, the president told the New York Republican Club, "Such extremists are not progressives, they are politically emotionalists and neurotics." Roosevelt, in turn, argued that Taft was unelectable. T. R. called him his enemy, which led to an all-out political war whose battlefields were the state primaries and conventions leading to the titanic contest in the Chicago Coliseum. But a peculiar war it became. For starters, Taft became the first president to campaign for himself in the primaries.

Roosevelt not only turned on his old friend Taft, he sunk the sincere reform efforts of Robert Marion LaFollette of Wisconsin, who had long fought for progressive causes as governor and as an "insurgent" Republican senator. When Roosevelt feigned disinterest in challenging Taft, LaFollette, a humorless and intense man on a mission against the power barons, took up the progressive standard and rallied support. In October 1911 he organized the First National Progressive Republican Conference in Chicago, which in turn nominated him for president to fight Taft. Roosevelt cheered him on in *The Outlook*, a national magazine that T. R. edited after his return to the United States. Chicagoan Joseph Medill McCormick, publisher of the *Chicago Tribune*, helped finance the Progressives' run. At a crucial moment, Roosevelt turned his back on LaFollette and essentially drove him to a personal as well as political breakdown. Roosevelt supporters, like McCormick, deserted the senator as soon as their leader climbed on his campaign stallion.

Roosevelt agitated for all the Progressive planks: direct primaries to nominate candidates and convention delegates, regulation of business for the good of the common man and woman, control of corporations and monopolies, referendum, recall, initiative, and protection of natural resources. He declared, "Wealth should be the servant, not the master of the people." Voters loved him in the West and hated him in the East. But his former friends, including Elihu Root, wondered about his sincerity. "I have no doubt he thinks he believes what he says, but he doesn't. He has merely picked up certain popular ideas which were at hand as one might pick up a poker or a chair with which to strike." Henry Cabot Lodge remarked that Roosevelt's extremism had "turned Taft into a man of principle."

Taft took off the kid gloves and fought back against his former friend in a Boston speech. He tethered T.R. and offered his own defense, "I am here to reply to an old and true friend who has made many charges. I deny them all. I do not want to fight . . . Is he giving me a Square Deal?" he asked plaintively. Afterward the president sat alone in his railroad car and sobbed. Roosevelt was right. Taft was weak, humanly weak. And Roosevelt? Superhuman in his energy and drive and exhilaration and his private will to power, he was an American Nietzschean who would not weep for loss of an erstwhile fond friend. He stood alone, unflinching in the trenches of political battle with his banner blowing in a bitter wind—or so he presumed.

But Roosevelt the military man had made a tactical error. He had played coy too long. While he kept his friends and enemies waiting for his pronouncements, Taft was steadily gaining delegates, particularly in the southern "rotten boroughs," in state conventions, and boss-controlled venues where Republicans were never elected but held onto the spoils of federal power. The party did not apportion delegates according to real voting patterns. In fact, four years earlier, Roosevelt had blocked such an effort. Roosevelt's delay was a six-week margin between victory and defeat.

The boss-dominated states of New York, Connecticut, Rhode Island, Utah, Wyoming, and Colorado went against Roosevelt. Then the state conventions in the Midwest turned violent. In Missouri, the quadrennial event was dubbed the "Ball-Bat Convention," since both sides came out swinging and breaking bones. Two hundred Roosevelt men who were unseated took over the Oklahoma convention by force. One participant died in the chaos. Two rival conventions formed in Michigan, after the first broke up in scuffles. The Kentucky convention went for Taft. The selection was so patently biased in Indiana that the *Indianapolis Star*, a paper staunchly for Taft, denounced the results when Taft cornered without popular input nearly 400 of the 540 delegates needed to win. Senator Joseph M. Dixon of Montana, Roosevelt's campaign manager, charged Taft was "trying to steal the nomination."

In late winter, Roosevelt men moved in to challenge as many of the state conventions as possible, hoping to gain disputed seats at the Chicago convention. Nothing was spared in creating chaos and contention, including rump conventions and bribing delegates. With the flowing money of George W. Perkins, a partner of J. P. Morgan and director of U.S. Steel, Roosevelt's progressive campaign, ironically, was never financially hampered. Perkins and news magnate Frank Munsey dropped $1 million in six months, one of the more expensive tickets to Chicago.

Senator William Edgar Borah of Utah urged a national primary as a democratic way to pick delegates to the national convention. But Taft's advisers refused, saying it was unfair to change the rules of the game in the middle of play. Roosevelt stumbled in the early primaries, losing in North Dakota to LaFollette. In the April primaries, he finally scored popular victories. In 1904 Florida was the first state to enact the progressive idea of direct presidential primaries to break the control of party bosses on delegate selection for the national convention. Twelve other states had adopted the direct primary by 1912. Roosevelt built up big margins, first in Illinois on April 9, then in Pennsylvania, Nebraska, Kansas, and New Jersey.

The new Coliseum on South Wabash Avenue was erected in 1900, partly using large stone blocks from the Libby Prison, a southern stockade for Union officers that had been transported from Richmond, Virginia, to Chicago and reconstructed as a Civil War museum by Alderman Charles F. Gunther. Chicago Historical Society. Photo by William T. Barnum.

Roosevelt's most damaging win was in Ohio, President Taft's own home state, which gave thirty-seven of its forty delegates to the challenger and humiliated Taft. T. R. then took Oregon and California in delegate near-sweeps. At the end of Roosevelt's string of primary victories, the results were overwhelming. Teddy was still the thrill of Republicans by a popular vote of two to one. He garnered 1,157,397 votes to Taft's 761,716, with 351,043 for LaFollette. Roosevelt could claim outright 278 delegates of the 540 needed for nomination. T.R.'s electoral strength contrasted with Taft's solid block of machine delegates attached to his cause by patronage favors.

Roosevelt's train pulled into Chicago on June 15, 1912, filled with an entourage of advisers and his family, in advance of the June 18 convention. He proclaimed to the press that he felt "as fit as a bull moose," a label that became his 1912 moniker.

A huge crowd chanting, "We want Teddy, We want Teddy," greeted him and followed his auto to the Congress Hotel on Michigan Avenue where he set up his headquarters in a row of suites. His brain trust was already assembled in the Florentine Room. When the throng outside on Michigan Avenue refused to leave, Teddy strolled out onto the second floor balcony and exhorted, "It's a naked fight against theft, and the thieves will not win." His followers were ready to do whatever he commanded.

Roosevelt delegates stormed into Chicago looking for a fight. "Brute Force Feared at Convention," screamed the headlines of the *Chicago Daily News.* Meanwhile, Taft's commanders gathered at the Blackstone Hotel down the avenue from Roosevelt's headquarters. Root; "Uncle Joe" Cannon; conservative Congressman James Eli of Indiana; "Boss" Bill Barnes of New York, who was Roosevelt's arch-enemy; Senator Winthrop Murray Crane from Massachusetts; and Columbia University President Nicholas Murray Butler (who would win the Nobel Prize in 1931) all worried about how to hold the line against the colonel's onslaught. They agreed to "fight or ruin" Roosevelt. They were counting on the fifty-three Republican national committeemen, appointed four years earlier after the last Chicago convention by Taft, to pull the strings to seat disputed Taft delegates.

For T.R., all the effort, all the posturing, all the right involved in his cause now seemed cast upon the reefs of Republican conservativism. On Monday night, June 17, the eve of the convention, Teddy delivered his heroic call to arms. The Auditorium Theater, Chicago's second largest venue, was filled to its ornate ceiling with Roosevelt progressives. Was he not, after all, leader of their great crusade to free America from the grip of big money?

"Friends," T.R. told them, "here in Chicago at this time you have a great task before you. I wish you to realize deep in your hearts that you are not merely facing a crisis in the history of a party. You are facing a crisis in the history of a nation." The crowd responded with adulation, worshiping their leader and their cause, with waves of applause.

But it was the finale that drove his listeners wild:

> What happens to me is not of the slightest consequence. I am to be used, as in a doubtful battle any man is used, to his hurt or not, so long as he is useful and is then cast aside and left to die. I wish you to feel this. I mean it. And I shall need no sympathy when you are through with me . . . We fight in honorable fashion for the good of mankind, fearless of the future, unheeding of our individual fates, with unflinching hearts and undimmed eyes, we stand at Armageddon, and we battle for the Lord.

When the convention opened the next morning, Tuesday, June 18, 1912, six hundred police officers armed with billy clubs and five police ambulances surrounded the Coliseum. Police also guarded the stage to prevent the kind of turmoil that had engulfed many of the state meetings and to protect against the riots threatened by Roosevelt supporters. Eleven Red Cross stations were set up inside. The Coliseum, which had been painted a brilliant yellow to brighten spirits, was covered with banners and tri-colored shields, and flags waved from the arched ceiling. More than five hundred newspapermen

watched from the press box. Delegates and alternates were jammed together in the basin immediately in front of the stage. Beneath the stage railing, concealed under the bunting, were rolls of barbed wire. Outside, scalpers hawked spectator tickets for $100 each. They were in scarce supply among Roosevelt supporters. Sergeant-at-Arms William F. Stone of Maryland was overheard swearing "not a damned ticket for Roosevelt men."

Republican National Committee Chairman Victor Rosewater, a small, intense, and determined man, stood at the podium pounding his gavel, trying to tame the confusion. His slate of delegates had been defeated by Roosevelt in Nebraska, but he had pledged to act "impartially." Immediately after the national anthem and an opening prayer by Reverend James F. Callaghan, Roosevelt floor leader Governor Herbert Spencer Hadley of Missouri leaped to his feet, calling for recognition. Dressed in a knee-length, double-breasted coat, the dashing Hadley addressed the chair. "Mr. Chairman. I rise to a question of information, and that is whether or not the national committee has prepared a list of delegates and alternates claiming seats in this convention . . . ?" Hadley sought to replace the list of seventy-two key Taft delegates sanctioned by the national committee with Roosevelt supporters. "We cannot here in this convention close our ears to what the American people are saying today . . . The integrity of this roll has been challenged by fifteen members of the national committee whose signatures I have here in my pocket, who say that seventy-two names have been placed upon the roll of delegates, not honestly elected . . . You cannot settle a question of fundamental honesty, fair play, by disregarding it."

"Mr. Chairman," interjected former Congressman James Watson of Indiana, Taft's floor leader, "I make the point of order that no business of any character is in order until after the convention has been properly organized." The debate continued as Hadley outlined the long history of rulings at national conventions that supported his appeal. Watson contested all the way. Chairman Rosewater settled the issue: "We are here now simply as a mass meeting. We must appoint a temporary chairman for the purpose of organizing that mass meeting and converting it into a convention of delegates." He ruled Hadley's motion out of order.

Roosevelt's former secretary of war and of state and longtime supportive friend, Senator Elihu Root, was then nominated as the convention's temporary chairman. Root had worked for Roosevelt's nomination eight years earlier. Unfortunately for Roosevelt, the two men had fallen out over Roosevelt's attacks on Taft and his most recent extremism on judicial recall. In Chicago, Root was a Taft man. He would guide the president to renomination, if it were within his power, and his power was considerable.

Desperate now, the Roosevelt forces hoped to unite with many of the LaFollette contingent, without their leader, by trying to elect Governor Francis W. McGovern of Wisconsin as temporary chairman. But LaFollette, whose campaign had been torpedoed by Roosevelt, returned the "favor" and kept his troops in line. Meanwhile, Job E. Hedges of New York scolded the Roosevelt dissenters by quoting Roosevelt's own earlier statement: "Elihu Root . . . is the ablest man that has appeared in the public life of any country, in any position, in my time." The debate was raucous and at one point, the sergeant-at-arms rushed to the podium to announce, ". . . unless the speaker is treated with respect, those offending will be ordered removed from the building." But that didn't prevent Roosevelt supporters from yelling, "Liar, liar," at Senator William O'Connell Bradley, Kentucky's first Republican governor, as he spoke on behalf of Root.

In accordance with a precedent set at the 1884 convention, a roll call of individual delegates was taken to elect the temporary chairman. When William Flinn of Pennsylvania was called, he objected: "I say to you that you are raping your own roll . . . I protest. Steal! Thief! You are a pack of thieves; that is what you are . . . I challenge the vote."

Among those supporting McGovern was a rare woman delegate, Isabella W. Blaney of California, the lone woman on the convention floor. Illinois voted for McGovern, but Root won. The count of 558 to 501 in favor of Root was a defeat that put Roosevelt tantalizingly close to the nomination, lacking only fifty-seven votes. Everything depended upon the challenge of disputed delegates. Angry cries of protest accompanied Chairman Root as he walked across a long gangplank leading out above the delegates to the speaker's stand. The Coliseum was in bedlam. Crowds of Roosevelt backers headed for the exits shouting insults until nearly half of the seats were vacated. Root calmly addressed those who remained, starting his keynote with a trace of irony: "Gentlemen of the convention: Believe that I appre-

ciate this expression of confidence. I wish I were more competent for the service you require of me." He told the remaining Roosevelt dissidents, "Without organized parties, having qualities of coherence and loyalty, free popular government becomes a confused and continual conflict . . ."

Root avoided mentioning Roosevelt as he outlined Republican policies under Taft. He noted that,

The prosecution of the trusts and combinations in violation of the Sherman Act has proceeded with extraordinary vigor and success. The Standard Oil Company has been dissolved . . . The beef packers, the wholesale grocers, the lumber dealers, the wire makers, the glass window pool, the electric lamp combination, the bathtub trust, the shoe machinery trust, the foreign steamship pool, the sugar company, the steel corporation, the Harvester company, all have been made to feel the heavy hand of the law through suits or indictments against restraints and monopolies.

The opening disputes had taken almost 8 1/2 hours. But Root went into action and organized the convention, handing out committee assignments and preliminary rulings with the efficiency that had made him legendary. Hadley again tried to substitute his list of delegates for that of the national committee, but his question was deferred until morning. The first session adjourned at 7:43 P.M.

That night dissident delegates and counterstrategists jammed the Roosevelt headquarters at the Congress Hotel, trying to decide whether or not to bolt the convention. In the early hours, Governor Hadley convinced Roosevelt to stay and fight. On day two, the Coliseum was half empty as the gavel fell, before local Chicagoans from the outside crowd, many of them Roosevelt supporters, were given passes to take the empty seats. The morning's agenda, a three-hour debate over delegate seating, was divided between Hadley and Watson and their seconds. On the convention floor, Governor Hadley took up the T. R. fight for seventy-two delegates that Roosevelt had to have to win the nomination. It was a do-or-die battle, a last-ditch offensive against staggering odds. "I do not know whether a majority of this convention agrees with me upon the proposition that Theodore Roosevelt ought to be our candidate for president of the United States."

Hadley was here interrupted by riotous applause of local Chicagoans who backed T.R.:

> But there can be no difference upon the proposition in the mind of any intelligent man that his voice is today the greatest voice of the Western world. He can command the support of more people, and he can lead a larger number of American voters in a cause for which he fights than any other man who lives beneath the folds of the American flag.

Hadley warned that, "No candidate can go forth from this convention with the hope of success if the American people believe the nomination was given to him by the votes of delegates dishonestly seated here in this convention." The Missouri governor outlined his case for each delegation and then charged that the decision by the national committee to unseat the seventy-two "represents nothing less than naked theft, carried on with the sole and evil purpose of substituting the will of the bosses for the deliberately expressed judgement of the people of the United States."

Delegates from the various states took up their own defense on the floor. Then Watson replied, "Gentlemen, it is not easy to answer talk about mob law . . . My proposition is to send this whole question to a Committee of Credentials appointed by the convention." And in the end, the temporary chairman did just that.

Throughout the morning, the entire convention, enchanted by the style and passion of Hadley, gave him ovations. Then the delegates, weary of sitting on small kitchen chairs, set off in a spontaneous demonstration for Hadley that lasted half an hour. They chanted his name as if he ought to become their leader. Suddenly the demonstration turned to chants for Roosevelt, and again the demonstration gained steam.

When the crowd exhausted itself and fell back into its seats, only one person in the gallery still cheered for Roosevelt. The convention turned its eyes upward to a young woman in a pure white dress waving her handkerchief and a poster of her hero. Sensing the moment, the woman, Mrs. W. A. Davis of Chicago, began a pantomime speech, imploring the convention to nominate the former president. Then she threw kisses to the Roosevelt delegates below. Soon the hall was cheering her, lifting her on their

palms, passing her down the rows to the floor as she carried on her silent appeal. The crowd surged with whistles and howls and screams of delight only heard in America's wigwams. Forty-seven minutes later, the Roosevelt Woman in white was brought safely back to her throne in the gallery, and the convention returned wearily to its routine business.

Root ruled that the disputed Taft delegates could vote on all matters except the immediate challenge to their own delegations, thereby only momentarily diluting the Taft strength on any one issue. The Roosevelt supporters suddenly felt a political steamroller gaining speed, flattening their hopes. When the convention adjourned at 5:47 P.M., they stayed on, cheering the name of their leader, until Chicago police hurried them along. Root was still under police guard at the podium an hour after adjournment.

From the Florentine Room in the Congress Hotel, Roosevelt blasted that the convention had become, "a fraud as vulgar, as brazen, and as cynically open as any ever committed by the Tweed regime in New York forty years ago." Then in a moment of resignation, the Bull Moose conceded, "So far as I am concerned, I am through." His supporters roared back, "No, no." The colonel continued, "I went before the people, and I won. Let us find out whether the Republican Party is the party of the plain people or the party of the bosses." Then he instructed his followers, "If you are voted down, I hope you, the real and lawful majority of the convention, will organize as such, and you will do it if you have the courage and loyalty of your convictions."

The third day, June 20, James A. Hemenway of Indiana reported that the credentials committee, which he chaired, was still in nonstop session. Thus, the convention adjourned without any important action, still officially unorganized after days of bickering.

Back in Washington, President Taft played a relaxed round of golf with his son Robert, a student at Yale. On day four, the credentials report was still unfinished. Each delegate challenge was being fully debated, and the results challenged again by the Roosevelt forces. Finally, the bedraggled committee appeared, and cheers rose from all quarters. Root pounded the gavel to restore order. Someone yelled, "Play Ball." Everyone laughed. The Credentials Committee Majority Report and various state challenges embedded in the minority report took up the next

8 1/2 hours of heated debate. The upshot? After several days of disputes, Taft was the winner with all but nineteen of the disputed delegates. Meanwhile, skeptical Roosevelt delegates shouted out caustic references to the steamroller tactics of the majority. "Toot, Toot," shouted some. "Choo, choo," answered others. The sound of a steam engine, from delegates rubbing two pieces of sandpaper, filled the hall. The Hearst newspapers even parked a rented steamroller outside the Coliseum to mock the proceedings. The convention adjourned again at 7:38 P.M.

The Republican Party was a conservative bastion once more, as it had been in the days of McKinley. Could Roosevelt avoid the unavoidable defeat his followers faced? A compromise candidate might save the progressive cause and nudge enough delegates from Taft to coalesce a majority. The name of Progressive and Supreme Court Justice Charles Evans Hughes was circulated, but Hughes publicly refused to be considered.

Governor Hadley was another obvious choice. His brilliant leadership of the Roosevelt cause on the convention floor made it clear he had presidential possibilities. Was he another Garfield, to be chosen by the common will of the delegates when all he set out to do was promote the welfare of another man's candidacy? No. Roosevelt would not allow it. "I'll name the compromise candidate," Teddy defiantly roared. "He'll be me. I'll name the compromise platform. It will be our platform." Faced with certain defeat, Roosevelt forces now debated when to bolt. But someone broached a creative tactic to dramatize the Roosevelt presence without giving up their seats to Taft's alternate delegates. If Roosevelt delegates simply refused to vote, as the gold Democrats had done in 1896, their silence would scream out to the American public the injustice they felt they had suffered.

That night another plan was offered Roosevelt that could ultimately bring him the nomination. A group of thirty delegates from Michigan and a few other states bound to Taft on the first ballot, but fearing the destruction of their party, approached Oscar King Davis, the *New York Times* correspondent on leave to serve as T.R.'s publicity agent. If a few of them voted for a third candidate and a few Roosevelt delegates did the same, Taft could be blocked on the first ballot. Then they would be free to vote for Roosevelt as nominee on the second ballot. Davis was elated and rushed off to tell Roosevelt of the sudden opening to victory. The will of the people would be done after all.

But to Davis' shock, Roosevelt instantly replied, "No! No! No! I won't hear of it. I won't have it . . . You tell them that it is a crooked convention, and I won't touch it with a forty-rod pole. You tell them that the first thing they must do is purge the roll." The Michigan delegates were as stunned by T. R.'s response. Roosevelt had sacrificed victory to abstract and uncertain principle. He had surrendered the presidency that was miraculously within his reach. Later that same night another group of southern delegates made a similar offer. Again Roosevelt rebuffed them, this time demanding not just their vote for his nomination but their total allegiance to the progressive principles he was touting. Roosevelt would countenance no deal. His holy war would not compromise with this enemy. He let the nomination for which millions had labored on his behalf simply wash through his hands like the lapping waves of Lake Michigan.

After the majority and minority made their points about the credentials dispute—five days into the convention—the Taft position was endorsed by the remaining assembly. The convention was formally organized. Not until then was Root finally voted permanent chairman. Root recognized Henry J. Allen of Kansas who read a statement from Roosevelt.

The convention has now declined to purge the roll of the fraudulent delegates placed thereon by the defunct national committee, and the majority which thus endorsed fraud was made a majority only because it included the fraudulent delegates themselves, who sat as judges on one another's cases . . . I hope the men elected as Roosevelt delegates will now decline to vote on any matter before the convention. I do not release any delegate from his honorable obligation to vote for me if he votes at all, but under the actual conditions I hope that he will not vote at all.

A Taft delegate shouted back, "If a man does not know when he is dead, his friends ought to know . . ." Turmoil broke loose. Finally, Allen finished T.R.'s message:

Gentleman, you accuse us of being radical. Let me tell you that no radical in the ranks of radicalism ever did so radical a thing as come to a national convention of the great Republican Party and secure through fraud the nomination of a man whom they knew could not be elected.

Inside the "new" Coliseum, 1912. Chicago Historical Society.

At this late moment in the convention, Roosevelt's former vice president, Charles Warren Fairbanks, presented the Taft platform, a progressive-sounding document meant to draw Roosevelt sympathizers. It expressed concern about "the steadily increasing cost of living," called for "additional legislation . . . to prohibit corporations from contributing funds, directly or indirectly, to campaigns for the nomination or election of the president, the vice president, senators, and representatives in Congress," rejoiced "in the success of the distinctive Republican policy of the conservation of our national resources . . .," and called "upon the people to quicken their interest in public affairs, [and] to condemn and punish lynchings."

The document was endorsed by a 666 to 53 vote, with 343 abstaining and 21 not present. The convention then rejected a LaFollette-sponsored minority platform, called "the Wisconsin Idea." It cautioned that, "More dangerous even than the industrial trusts is that subtle, concentrated power exercised over money and credit, by what is ordinarily called the 'Money Trust.' It can make and unmake panics."

The moment of nominations arrived. Taft's name was offered by former Lieutenant Governor Warren Gamaliel Harding of Ohio, who told the convention, "You have heard much lately about the people's rule. Mr. Chairman and sirs, the people's rule is no new discovery to a sovereign American people. Nor is a demagogic employment of the term new to the world's hearing. Through such demagogic employment, centuries ago, republics tottered and fell, and republican liberties were lost in the sway of empires in their stead . . ." He argued that the people rule "with unwavering faith and increased confidence in that fine embodiment of honesty, that fearless executor of the law, that inspiring personification of courage, that matchless exemplar of justice, that glorious apostle of peace and amity, William Howard Taft."

The Roosevelt supporters had fun with Harding, tooting away. Chairman Root intervened. "I beg delegates who have announced their intention to sit mute in this assemblage, to preserve their self-respect for whatever cause the future has before them." The subsequent Taft demonstration lasted but a few minutes before he was seconded by John Wanamaker, Harrison's postmaster general, and Nicholas Murray Butler.

Michael B. Olbrich of Wisconsin nominated LaFollette. "Up the trunk of the legitimate industry in America, like some noisome parasitic tropic growth, the tightening coil of privilege has wound its way, extending itself into every branch of human endeavor, strangling industrial and commercial freedom, shutting out the light of hope from the sons of men, poisoning the very air of liberty."

The silent Roosevelt supporters did not even nominate their own candidate. As the Roll Call of the States began, so did hundreds of toots and hoots and whistles signaling the final path of the steamroller. When California was called, Chester H. Rowell replied, "Mr. Chairman, California declines to vote." When Illinois was summoned, Governor Charles S. Deneen answered, "It is impossible to get the exact vote of our state. I request that the roll of the Illinois delegation be called, with this preliminary statement: 'The great majority of our delegates feel that in view of the provisions of the primary law of our state, recently enacted, we have no power to cancel our instructions, and will vote for Roosevelt.'"

State after state delegation was individually polled. When Roosevelt delegates refused to vote, Root called on alternates, invariably Taft supporters, to answer the roll. Some Roosevelt delegates could not bear to let their great campaign go in the record books without a mark and cast votes for their man. Taft won the nomination with 561 votes to Roosevelt's 107. LaFollette had his revenge against Roosevelt and a meager 41 votes. Albert Baird Cummins of Iowa received 17 votes, and Charles Evans Hughes of New York 2 votes, while 344 abstained. For the first time in Republican convention history, no one moved to make the nomination unanimous.

The convention then hurriedly nominated James Schoolcraft Sherman, Taft's vice president, for a second term. ("Sunny Jim," as he was known, died before the November contest, and Taft left the spot open.) The assembly adjourned at 10:29 P.M.

The *Chicago Evening Post*, a Taft paper, concluded, ". . . that nomination was a tainted nomination. There was in it trickery and fraud. Stripped of its practical essentials, it was a nomination made by a minority instead of a majority. The miserable 21 votes above the nomination point which the steamroller drivers were able to muster fade instantly away under scrutiny . . ."

To many who had traveled all these months to find triumph, there was deep disappointment. But that same Saturday night, a rump convention convened at Orchestra Hall on Michigan Avenue. It was packed with disgruntled delegates who had bolted from the Republicans. Here Republican progressives, the foundation of a new party, bestowed on Roosevelt their mantle as presidential nominee. He provisionally accepted. One party had come to town, divided on a collision course. Now two parties departed. "The only question," commented the old and wise Chauncy DePew of New York, "is which corpse gets the flowers."

Chicago hadn't seen its last convention of the summer. On August 5, 1912, the Progressives, who had nominated Roosevelt at Orchestra Hall, again gathered to hold their own national convention at the Coliseum. The hall was bulging with intense delegates waving red bandannas and singing "The Battle Hymn of the Republic" and "Onward, Christian Soldiers." Theirs was the last of the great populist crusades before the Great War. In the tradition of the mugwumps, many were dissident Republicans like those who had bolted against Blaine in 1884. Back then, Roosevelt at his first convention had been a mugwump, but had not broken with the party and had reluctantly supported Blaine, much to the dismay of other mugwumps. Perhaps now he was making up for his transgression. Populists by the hundreds of every hue now joined the Progressive ranks.

Former Senator Albert Jeremiah Beveridge of Indiana presided over the great throng of independents and dissenters gathered under the Bull Moose Progressive banner. Delegates were mostly middle-class businessmen from small towns, editors, teachers, and prosperous farmers. On August 6, Roosevelt made his appearance before the new party, his new party. For the next fifty-two minutes his admirers released their pent-up political frustrations, screaming at the top of their lungs, leaping on to their chairs, throwing their fedoras into the humid air, howling for Teddy. The crowd then serenaded him with choruses such as, "Thy gleaming sword shall never rust, Roosevelt, Roosevelt!" Again the Exulted One spoke of Armageddon and the Lord and christened the cause for which they were to go forth and labor as the holiest of political battles.

On August 7, 1912, Theodore Roosevelt was formally knighted as the Progressive nominee. Jane Addams made his seconding speech. California governor Hiram Warren Johnson, with Roosevelt from the start of the campaign, became his Progressive running mate. Roosevelt called his new platform "A Contract with the People." It urged increased regulation of big business; popular initiative and referendum; popular recall of judicial decisions; greater taxes on inheritance and income; health insurance for all; laws to prevent "industrial accidents, occupational diseases, overwork, involuntary unemployment, and other injurious effects incident to modern industry"; workmen's compensation; child labor laws; a minimum wage; an eight-hour day; direct election of U.S. senators; and equal suffrage for women. Roosevelt may or may not have been consciously playing Don Quixote, but he had ventured forth into a quixotic campaign for "those not given fair play."

Woodrow Wilson, president of Princeton University, had been elected governor of New Jersey in the 1910 off-year elections. (That year Franklin Roosevelt, Teddy's distant cousin, was also elected as a Democratic member of the New York State senate.) On July 2, 1912, the Democratic convention in Baltimore avoided its own conservative/progressive split and under the tutelage of William Jennings Bryan nominated Wilson as its presidential standard bearer. Although Wilson was portrayed as a progressive, many Democrats had their doubts, seeing him more as a Hamiltonian than a Jeffersonian. In 1896 Wilson had opposed Bryan and the silver cause. He was suspected of being an Anglophile by others. His opposition to the enfranchisement of women sent thousands of them in states where they had the vote into the Progressive camp where they were welcome.

Roosevelt claimed Wilson would "beat Taft hands down" if T.R. simply dropped out of the race and waited to seek the 1916 Republican nomination. But he told the press, "I've got to run, because, while there's no chance of my success, the cause of liberal government would be advanced fifty years."

Neither Taft nor his cabinet members did much campaigning. Nonetheless, Roosevelt was relentless. He crisscrossed the nation by train giving hundreds of speeches in the tradition of Blaine and Bryan. That autumn, in Michigan, Illinois, Nebraska, Colorado, Wyoming, Utah, Washington, Oregon, and California, Roosevelt pounded his fist and kept his audiences roaring for "Teddy," for the "Bull Moose." Across the plains and through the South and back to New York, T.R. stormed, breaking Democrats and Republicans alike away from their parties. Then after a few days rest, he was back on the road. His energy seemed inexhaustible, his resolve unbreakable, his hopes of victory starting to awaken with the enthusiastic masses that greeted him wherever he went.

In Milwaukee, a stronghold of progressivism, he arrived for an October 14 speech to a hall full of small-business people and workers. In early evening the former president left his quarters at the Gilpatrick Hotel and boarded an open car, waving to his admirers. Suddenly a man broke from the crowd and fired one shot into Teddy's chest. Roosevelt jolted backwards into the rear seat like a stunned moose. The crowd grabbed the small man who had attempted to assassinate their beloved leader.

Then miraculously, Roosevelt was back on his feet, crying to them not to injure the man, but to bring him forth. T. R. did not know John Schrank, although he was avenging an alleged injury inflicted on him when Roosevelt served as New York City police commissioner. The young and puritanical Roosevelt had enforced a state law to shut all saloons on Sunday and made many enemies, among them Schrank. Schrank's bullet had burst through Teddy's coat and shirt, but its path was slowed by his spectacles' case and thickly folded speech. It bore into his flesh, doing no mortal damage. Only slightly delayed, Roosevelt commanded his driver to the hall where he proceeded to deliver his hour-and-a-half speech with a bullet lodged in his chest.

Afterward T. R. was taken to Emergency Hospital for treatment, before riding by train to Chicago's Mercy Hospital. The bullet had broken a rib and slept within an inch of his heart. It was too deeply embedded to remove. Every morning newspaper in the country carried T.R.'s exploit. Friend and foe alike praised his courage. He smiled, or at least gritted his teeth, throughout the entire ordeal, the headlines confirmed. Both Taft and Wilson sent personal notes, and Jane Addams visited him in his hospital room. Wilson offered to suspend his campaign, but T.R.

refused to halt his efforts. On October 21, Roosevelt traveled with his wife back to Oyster Bay, New York, to the family compound of Sagamore Hill, where Teddy enjoyed a fifty-fourth birthday party. Three days later he stood before an adoring Madison Square Garden Progressive Party rally that greeted him with a forty-one-minute standing ovation. There he characterized his quest as a campaign for the common citizen. "Our people work hard and faithfully . . ." he said. "But there must be bread for the work. There must be a time for play when the men and women are young. When they grow old there must be certainty of rest under conditions that are free from haunting poverty." The hearts of his listeners gladdened with agreement. Finally, he urged them onto victory.

On November 5, 1912, the United States again decided its future as a democratic nation. The split that T.R. had himself inflicted was too deep to overcome, and both the Republicans and Progressives went down like the *Titanic* that had sunk earlier that year. Wilson squeaked to victory between the old friends who had become enemies with 6,301,254 votes. Roosevelt placed second with 4,127,788. The sitting president finished last with 3,485,831. The electoral college vote was a lopsided 435 for Wilson, 88 for Roosevelt, and just 8 for Taft, who only carried Utah and Vermont. Taft and Roosevelt polled a million more votes than the new Democratic victor who would be minority president. Roosevelt positioned himself for 1916. Taft retired from public life until he was appointed chief justice of the Supreme Court by President Harding in 1921. It was the job that he had always aspired to and had told Roosevelt back in 1908 that he would prefer over the presidency.

Charles Evans Hughes
1916 Republican Presidential Nominee

Charles Warren Fairbanks
1916 Republican
Vice Presidential Nominee

Facts-at-a-Glance
★★★

Event:	Sixteenth Republican National Convention
Dates:	June 7–10, 1916
Building:	The Coliseum
Location:	1513 South Wabash Avenue
Chicago Mayor:	William Hale Thompson, Republican
Candidates for Nomination:	Martin Brumbaugh, Indiana; former Senator Theodore Elijah Burton, Ohio; Senator Albert Baird Cummins, Iowa; Coleman du Pont, Delaware; former Vice President Charles Warren Fairbanks, Indiana; Supreme Court Justice Charles Evans Hughes, New York; Senator Robert Marion LaFollette, Wisconsin; former President Theodore Roosevelt, New York; former Senator Elihu Root, New York; Laurence Y. Sherman, Illinois; Senator John Wingate Weeks, Massachusetts
Presidential Nominee:	Charles Evans Hughes
Age at Nomination:	54
Number of Ballots:	3
Vice Presidential Nominee:	Charles Warren Fairbanks
Number of Delegates:	986
Number Needed to Nominate:	A majority, 494
Largest Attendance:	14,000
Critical Issues:	Protection of U.S. rights, foreign relations, Mexico, Latin America, Philippines, right of expatriation, national defense, tariff protection, rural credits, rural free delivery, conservation, labor laws, women's suffrage
Popular Song:	"Beale Street Blues"

13
★★★

The 1916 Republican National Convention
Looking for a Progressive Regular

In the opening hours of the Republican National Convention of 1916, temporary chairman Senator Warren G. Harding of Ohio told the delegates: "We did not do very well in making for harmony the last time we met," which elicited laughter and applause. "We split over methods and preferred personalities."

Harding was referring to the 1912 stampede away from the Grand Old Party led by Rough Rider Theodore Roosevelt. The split still existed in 1916, as witnessed by the convening that same day of the splinter Progressive Party convention in Chicago's Auditorium Theater less than a mile north of the regular Republicans in the Coliseum. The Progressive delegates stayed at the Auditorium Hotel, the Republicans at the Congress, but the leaders of the two factions met at the Blackstone Hotel to exchange barbs.

The laughter and applause, no matter how hearty, that greeted Harding's keynote remarks was tinged with nervousness, because the paramount task of the Republican convention of regulars was to repair the schism of 1912 in order to present a united front to the Democrats. The Democratic presidential nominee, it was everywhere acknowledged, would be the incumbent President Woodrow Wilson, who "kept us out of war." His would be a strong candidacy.

Much as they might have wanted to return to the fold, the Progressive malcontents would never unite behind any regular of the old guard who had been significantly involved in William Howard Taft's 1912 steamroller that led to Roosevelt's defection. By the same token, regulars of the Republican Party would never unite behind any of the leaders of the Bull Moose Progressives. Thus, popular opinion held that regulars such as Elihu Root of New York and Henry Cabot Lodge of Massachusetts and Progressives such as Roosevelt and his 1912 running mate, California's Hiram Warren Johnson, were eliminated from consideration before the convention doors

opened. The convention looked for a compromise candidate who had not been involved in the 1912 intraparty fight between Taft and Roosevelt but who could command the respect of both camps.

The great majority of rank-and-file Republicans yearned for a return to the leadership of Teddy Roosevelt, but the old guard of the party was not likely to acquiesce. They desired a candidate who could make common cause with the Progressives but whose surname was any combination of letters except "Roosevelt," a man the bosses regarded as a turncoat. Before the convention, former President Taft declared, "Anyone but Roosevelt." T.R., on the other hand, was for "anyone but Taft or Root." The most eligible Republican, given these requirements, was Charles Evans Hughes, an associate justice of the U.S. Supreme Court.

Hughes, a lawyer, had not entered public life until his mid-forties. His only known interest outside of the law and his family was teaching Sunday school at New York's Fifth Avenue Baptist Church, known popularly as John D. Rockefeller's church. But in 1905 Hughes was asked to chair a committee investigating gas and electric utilities in New York City. The investigation revealed that the gas trust was ridiculously overcapitalized and that N.Y.C. gas was so heavily adulterated that its consumers' lives were at risk and that the city of New York paid three times as much for electric service as other customers. Remedial legislation was enacted by the city.

When the utilities investigation ended, Hughes was asked to serve as counsel to a joint committee of the New York State legislature investigating the insurance industry, an investigation of national importance. Hughes's questioning brought into sharp focus the tie between the insurance companies and politicians (Republican politicians), to the detriment of policyholders. It also led to a long list of recommendations for correction, much of which was enacted into law only because of Hughes's persistence. The era was one of reform as well as distrust of concentrated wealth, an era epitomized in the views and person of the nation's president at that time, Theodore Roosevelt. To the power brokers of the New York Republican convention of 1906, T.R. made it clear that he wanted Hughes nominated for governor, and so he was. In a bitterly fought campaign, Hughes defeated the powerful and unscrupulous Democratic candidate William Randolph Hearst, publisher of the *Chicago American*, among other giant papers.

An intelligent and prudent man, Hughes was a strong governor who effectively represented all of his constituents, including the lowliest wage earners, against a host of special interests always at work on the legislators in Albany. His methods were later, in 1911 and 1912, utilized by former governor Woodrow Wilson in New Jersey in Wilson's efforts at reform. As governor of New York, Hughes brought charges of gross negligence against the presidents of the boroughs of Manhattan, the Bronx, and Queens, removing them from office. He also helped to enact a substantial amount of progressive legislation. His record in two terms as governor gained him a national reputation, and in 1910 President Taft nominated him to the Supreme Court of the United States. He had been mentioned as a possible candidate for president in 1908, but T. R. squashed that possibility when he declared that "Hughes is not a man I care for."

In 1907 Hughes had declared his judicial philosophy. "We are under a Constitution," he said, "but the Constitution is what the judges say it is." In other words, Hughes understood that the Supreme Court wielded immense power. As much as possible, Hughes used his share of this power to extend federal sovereignty against that of the states, to define the rights of the individual, and to attempt to reconcile liberty with authority. The period between 1910 and 1916 was one in which the progressive movement—that is, efforts at social reform—grew to its greatest strength in the nation. Hughes's votes and the decisions he wrote as an associate justice extended federal authority, especially in the areas of inter- and intrastate commerce, and acknowledged the rights of labor and of the disadvantaged that had long been denied them.

In 1912, the year of the acrimonious battle between Taft and Roosevelt, Hughes's name was raised as a possible compromise presidential Republican candidate. Indeed, Taft went so far as to indicate his willingness to withdraw from the battle if Hughes were to be nominated. But Hughes rejected every overture from the party's managers, finally writing to Root at the convention itself. Paraphrasing General Sherman's famous comment, Root insisted that "even if nominated, I should decline."

In 1916 Hughes also steadfastly resisted all attempts to enlist him as a presidential candidate. "I am entirely out of politics," he wrote to a supporter. His wife, however, argued that if he were nominated, he had a duty to accept. Hughes himself was of two minds. He still devoutly believed that the court must be kept out of politics, but he also believed that Woodrow Wilson had not done what was necessary to prepare the United States for possible, perhaps inevitable, entry into the ongoing world war between Germany and the Central Powers and Britain and France and the Allied Powers.

The bosses of the Republican Party in 1916 would have preferred a mediocre candidate to the sharply intelligent Hughes, but they could not find one among the favorite sons who could capture the imagination of the voters. The political commentator Walter Lippmann described the bosses and their delegates as "the gathering together of distributed privileges, of tariff-protected manufacturers, business lawyers, and pillars of society from all over the Union. It was the quintessence of all that is commonplace, machine-made, complacent, and arbitrary in American life. To look at it and think of what needs to be done to civilize this nation was to be chilled with despair."

Of the Progressives, Lippmann spoke more kindly, if still despairingly: "The mass of the delegates there were the most warm-hearted crowd I have ever seen. But from the first it was evident where their hopelessness lay. . . . They trusted their leaders but their leaders never trusted them. . . . What happened was this: the men who controlled them tried to use the Progressives as a threat and a bluff to force Theodore Roosevelt on the Republicans."

On the first day of the two conventions, thousands of suffragettes paraded down Michigan Avenue, carrying a banner that read:

FOR THE SAFETY OF THE NATION LET THE
WOMEN HAVE THE VOTE. FOR THE HAND THAT
ROCKS THE CRADLE WILL NEVER ROCK THE BOAT.

Delegates at the Republican National Convention, 1916. Chicago Historical Society.

Their parade was literally rained upon, however, by an unseasonably chilly rain that might have been taken as an omen of what was to befall their cause. Although the suffragettes burst through the doors of the Coliseum, neither party's platform endorsed a constitutional amendment enfranchising women. Both the Progressive and the regular Republicans left the question of women's suffrage to the individual states.

When the regular convention adjourned after its first day of deliberations, Chicago mayor William Hale "Big Bill" Thompson's entertainment committee had one thousand automobiles waiting outside the Coliseum for use by badge-wearing delegates. Delegates, all 986 of them, were "invited to avail themselves thereof for the purpose of viewing the city or making any trips about the city which they would like to make."

The platforms of both the regular Republicans and the Progressives advocated preparedness (the Progressives' more eloquently), for the enforcement of American neutrality in the Great War, for a firm policy in Mexico (where Wilson had sent troops under the command of General "Black Jack" Persh-

ing), for a protective tariff, and for workers' compensation laws.

With their platform adopted the second day of the convention, the regular Republicans listened to an appeal from the Progressives asking for a joint conference. By voice vote the regulars accepted this invitation, and a committee of Progressives met with a committee of Republican regulars Thursday night. The conference agreed that the future welfare of the country depended upon the defeat of the Democrats, but the Progressives were adamant that Roosevelt was the only possible candidate for president. Hence, no agreement was reached.

On Friday the regular Republicans heard nominating speeches. After Hughes was nominated, applause was "enthusiastic and long continued," but by no means wild and unrestrained. The demonstration that followed after the Progressive convention nominated Roosevelt lasted almost forty minutes.

On the first ballot of the Republican convention, Hughes led with 253 1/2 votes. The runner-up, Senator John Wingate Weeks of Massachusetts, received 105 votes; Root, 103; and Roosevelt, 65. On the second ballot, Hughes's total leaped to 328 1/2 votes, while no other nominee exceeded 100 votes. As soon as the results were announced, an old guard party boss moved adjournment until the next morning. The motion passed. In a last-ditch attempt, party bosses tried unsuccessfully to find a favorite son candidate less able and more malleable than Hughes.

The joint conference of the regular Republicans and the Progressives met again Friday night but failed once more to reach agreement. The regulars proposed Hughes as a compromise candidate to the Progressives. The Progressives countered that it had to be Roosevelt or someone acceptable to T.R., but Roosevelt refused to accept Hughes until he knew the justice's views on the issues. Hughes refused to make his views known while he was a member of the Supreme Court, from which he would not resign until nominated. Hence, the joint conference reached another impasse.

At five o'clock the next morning, Saturday, a long telegram arrived at Progressive headquarters from Roosevelt. He stressed his fervent desire to see the two segments of the party reunited, and to this end he recommended his close personal friend Henry Cabot Lodge as the Progressive nominee. The Progressives were astonished. Lodge was an archconservative, hardly a man sympathetic to Progressive objectives. Thus, at 12:31 A.M. Saturday, by acclamation, the Progressives nominated Theodore Roosevelt as their presidential candidate, partly out of conviction, partly out of anger and spite. Two minutes later in the Coliseum, Charles Evans Hughes received 949 1/2 votes on the third ballot; his nomination by the regular Republicans was then declared unanimous. The ticket was balanced by the nomination of Charles W. Fairbanks of Indiana as vice president, who had been vice president in Roosevelt's second term. When Hughes was informed of his nomination, he sent a message to President Wilson:

> I hereby resign the office of Associate Justice of the Supreme Court of the United States.
> I am, sir, respectfully yours,
> Charles Evans Hughes.

With equal succinctness, the president responded:

> I am in receipt of your letter of resignation and feel constrained to yield to your desire. I therefore accept your resignation as Justice of the Supreme Court of the United States to take effect at once.
> Sincerely yours,
> Woodrow Wilson.

When Roosevelt was informed of the nomination, he replied that he would decline the nomination if Hughes could satisfy him on matters of policy. A few weeks later, T.R. met with Hughes and then withdrew. The Progressive Party was no more, nationally.

A week later the Democrats met in St. Louis and nominated Wilson for president by acclamation. As the chairman of the Democratic convention put it, "Without orphaning a single American child, without widowing a single American mother, without firing a single gun, without the shedding of a single drop of blood, Woodrow Wilson wrung from the most militant spirit that ever brooded over a battlefield an acknowledgment of American rights and an agreement to American demands."

Wilson campaigned on this accomplishment. "He Kept Us Out of War" was his theme. Early election returns showed Hughes sweeping the Northeast, except Ohio, and he went to sleep that night expecting to wake up as president. Wilson gloomily retired for the evening. But the West and South came in solidly Democratic. California put Wilson over the top. Wilson was reelected president by a majority of 9,129,606 votes to 8,538,211 for Hughes in the popular vote. The electoral college totals were closer, with 277 for Wilson and 254 for Hughes. Just a month after being sworn in for his second term, Wilson went before Congress and asked it to declare war on Germany "to make the world safe for democracy." He proclaimed, "We must fight for justice and right." Then he went back to the White House and wept.

Warren Gamaliel Harding
1920 Republican Presidential Nominee

Calvin Coolidge
1920 Republican
Vice Presidential Nominee

Facts-at-a-Glance
★★★

Event:	Seventeenth Republican National Convention
Dates:	June 8–12, 1920
Building:	The Coliseum
Location:	1513 South Wabash Avenue
Chicago Mayor:	William Hale Thompson, Republican
Candidates for Nomination:	Nicholas Murray Butler, New York; Governor John Calvin Coolidge, Massachusetts; Senator Warren Gamaliel Harding, Ohio; Herbert Clark Hoover, California; Senator Hiram Warren Johnson, California: Governor Frank Orren Lowden, Illinois; Senator Miles Poindexter, Washington; Senator Howard Sutherland, West Virginia; General Leonard Wood, New Hampshire
Presidential Nominee:	Warren Gamaliel Harding
Age at Nomination:	55
Number of Ballots:	10
Vice Presidential Nominee:	Calvin Coolidge, Massachusetts
Number of Delegates:	984
Number Needed to Nominate:	A majority, 493
Largest Attendance:	14,000
Critical Issue:	U. S. membership in the League of Nations
Campaign Slogan:	"Back to Normalcy"
Campaign Song:	"Harding, You're the Man for Us"

14
★★★

The 1920 Republican National Convention
Back to Normalcy

"The War to End All Wars" was over, and so was the fractured idealism that had led President Woodrow Wilson to propose a League of Nations to prevent future wars. Conservative Republican senators, such as Henry Cabot Lodge of Massachusetts had stirred the nation against the League and wanted to make it the central issue of the 1920 campaign. But the 1920 election signified more than just a treaty referendum. It represented a collective democratic decision about what the postwar American Republic would become and which party should lead it to renewed prosperity. The Democrats were still the party of Wilson, with all his triumphs and failures. The Republicans were no longer the progressive party of Hughes. Consumers were hit with spiraling inflation, and a great disillusionment overwhelmed postwar America. Voters wanted a party that could protect and promote the nation's new cultural freedom and industrial power.

The chief task of the 1920 Republican National Convention held in early June in a steamy Chicago was to decide the leadership question for the Grand Old Party. Three men led the fight for Republican leadership. Theodore Roosevelt, who again would have been a formidable and, perhaps, wiser candidate, had died a year and a half earlier. In his place aspired Major General Leonard Wood, Roosevelt's fifty-nine-year-old former Spanish-American War commander and close confidant, who became the front-running candidate. Wood was an archconservative and nationalist, with solid Eastern financial support. He preached continued military preparedness and practiced red-scare tactics that alienated progressive and moderate Republicans and those concerned about violations of constitutional rights.

Roosevelt's 1912 Progressive vice presidential partner, fifty-three-year old Senator Hiram Warren Johnson of California, also claimed the Bull Moose's legacy and was bolstered by a strong Progressive and Western Republican following. Like Lodge, he was "irrec-oncilable" against the League of Nations. Johnson had the financial backing of newspaper czar William Randolph Hearst and Chicago's larger-than-life mayor "Big Bill" Thompson, whose progressivism simply meant a wide-open town for gambling, spirits, and the new jazz that was taking over the African-American clubs on the South Side. Johnson brought delegates from eleven primaries to the convention, while Wood cornered many uncommitted delegations.

Also in the running for the Republican nomination was the highly respected, efficient, and charismatic governor of Illinois, Frank Orren Lowden, who had cut taxes while streamlining state services. Lowden was committed to social improvement and appealed to a wide range of traditional and progressive Republicans. He put his wife's Pullman Palace Car Company fortune to work seeking the nomination. He was also a pro-League of Nations Republican internationalist, but he had made a big mistake in turning his back on his local Chicago sponsor, "Big Bill," after the mayor helped to elect him.

Republican dark horses for 1920 included Senator Warren Gamaliel Harding of Ohio, who had done poorly in the Indiana primary and less well than expected in his home state of Ohio, where Wood challenged him. Harding was barely known outside the Midwest, and the press gave him little chance of victory. Herbert Clark Hoover, the young and energetic U.S. food administrator, had declared himself neither Democrat nor Republican until the California primary during the spring of 1920, which he then lost to Johnson. Hoover, who had actually won a few delegates to the San Francisco Democratic Convention, was supported by editorial writers around the nation as the best man for the job. Governor Calvin Coolidge of Massachusetts had come to recent prominence for breaking the Boston police strike. His campaign was launched as a lark, but he now found himself in full flight at the convention.

The majority of the candidates had tested the primary waters in a few of the twenty states where preconvention contests were held. Wood led the race coming into Chicago with 124 delegates to 112 for Johnson, 72 for Lowden, and 39 for Harding, with 493 needed to win. Most delegations arrived in Chicago officially uncommitted, but heavily courted. Wood and Lowden could afford to spend lavishly. Johnson could not. But both big spenders had been publicly reprimanded for their extravagances by a federal commission and criticized in the press. Johnson accumulated the greatest preconvention popular vote.

When the Seventeenth Republican National Convention convened in the Chicago Coliseum on Tuesday, June 8, 1920, it was the fifth consecutive quadrennial assembly in the party's adopted city. Chicago was growing in the postwar boom. Only a month earlier, Mayor Thompson had ridden in an open car with Charles H. Wacker up Michigan Avenue to cut the ribbon on the new bridge across the Chicago River to the North Side, still undeveloped by the towers of William Wrigley or the *Chicago Tribune*.

Once again during convention week, Chicago was caught in the midst of a late spring heat wave. Despite the soaring temperatures, tickets for the convention were being scalped for $300 each. The convention's permanent chairman, Senator Henry Cabot Lodge, gave a stirring eighty-minute keynote address, chastising the Wilson era. He boasted, "We have stopped Mr. Wilson's treaty." The delegates felt certain they could unseat the Democrats if they ran against Wilson's record of broken promises and autocratic style.

Among the delegates to the convention were twenty-seven women, even though the Nineteenth Amendment had yet to be ratified by all the states. Western and Midwestern states sent women delegates anyway; they were not challenged. During the week the convention also attracted some of the nation's top corporate leaders, including railroad magnate Cornelius Vanderbilt, steel potentate Elbert Gary, and oil baron Harry F. Sinclair. In the years to come, charges of money influence were circulated, without proof. But subsequent scandals such as Teapot Dome, which entangled Sinclair, gave credence to the accusations.

As usual, the first two days of the convention were consumed by meetings on credentials, the platform, and party organization. In the credentials committee,

General Wood lost many of his contested delegates. The events in revolutionary Russia were on the minds of members of the resolutions committee as they drafted the longest and most conservative party document in years. The Republican platform of 1920 began by declaring,

> The Republican Party, assembled in representative national convention, reaffirms its unyielding devotion to the Constitution of the United States, and to the guaranties of civil, political, and religious liberty therein contained. It will resist all attempts to overthrow the foundations of the government or to weaken the force of its controlling principles and ideals, whether these attempts be made in the form of international policy or domestic agitation.

Naturally, the platform attacked the Democratic record.

> For seven years the national government has been controlled by the Democratic Party. During that period a war of unparalleled magnitude has shaken the foundations of civilization, decimated the population of Europe, and left in its trail economic misery and suffering second only to the war itself. The outstanding features of the Democratic administration have been complete unpreparedness for war and complete unpreparedness for peace.

The words echoed General Wood's sentiments.

The key issue of the early proceedings was the platform plank on the League of Nations. Isolationists such as Idaho's Senator William E. Borah and Illinois's progressive Senator Joseph Medill McCormick threatened to bolt the convention if language in opposition to the League was not strong enough. The final plank was drafted by former Senator Elihu Root of New York, the party's sage statesmen, and was a work of intraparty appeasement between the internationalists and isolationists.

"The Republican Party stands for agreement among the nations to preserve the peace of the world," the plank stated. "We believe that such an international association must be based upon international justice and must provide methods which shall maintain the rule of public right by the development of law and the decision of impartial courts, and which shall secure instant and general international conference whenever peace shall be threatened."

Root later admitted that the plank, as written, "meant nothing except that it frankly did mean nothing, and we accepted it." On June 10, when the plank was finally read to the delegates by Indiana senator James E. Watson, chairman of the resolutions committee, they leaped to their feet, both sides cheering for the compromise. Roosevelt had been right. Root was the most brilliant of all Republicans of his generation.

Republicans also advocated a policy that gave farmers a greater voice on government commissions; promised a national inquiry on the coordination of rail, water, and motor transportation; sanctioned farm cooperatives; and recognized the value of collective bargaining as a means of promoting goodwill.

High taxation and inflation were major Republican complaints. The platform promised to lower the cost of living through credit and currency deflation. "The burden of taxation imposed upon the American people is staggering." But it could not promise lower taxes because, "The next Republican administration will inherit from its Democratic predecessor a floating indebtedness of over $3 billion, the prompt liquidation of which is demanded by sound financial consideration." Hence, the party advocated "the issuance of a simplified form of income return."

On the domestic social policy front, the Republican platform urged Congress "to consider the most effective means to end lynching in the country which continues to be a terrible blot on our American civilization." Further, the Republicans welcomed "women into full participation in the affairs of government and activities of the Republican Party. We earnestly hope that Republican legislatures in states which have not yet acted on the suffrage amendment will ratify the amendment, to the end that all of the women of the nation of voting age may participate in the election of 1920 which is so important to the welfare of our country." (Their plea was heard, and the Nineteenth Amendment went into effect on August 26, 1920.) On other gender issues, the platform urged that "the principle of equal pay for equal service should be applied throughout all branches of the federal government in which women are employed . . . We demand federal legislation to limit the hours of employment of women engaged in intensive industry, the product of which enters into interstate commerce." The platform was passed, with few objections, by voice acclamation.

A minority report from the Wisconsin delegation that kept alive Republican progressivism was read by Edwin J. Gross. It called for an end to compulsory military service and advocated bonuses for soldiers, elections for federal judges, and a constitutional amendment establishing initiative, referendum, and recall, so voters could have a say in decision making. Gross was mocked with hisses, catcalls, and laughter as he read the platform recommendations, before the report was defeated by a voice vote. His treatment showed how different the party of 1920 was from that of 1912, and led to a LaFollette Progressive race in 1924. Chicago's first African-American congressman, Oscar De Priest, introduced an amendment to the platform demanding federal legislation to prevent the deprivation of rights to southern blacks. It was declared void since it hadn't been referred to the resolutions committee.

By Friday, June 11, all the preliminary functions of the convention had been dispensed without too much rancor or division. Now it was time to inaugurate a new party leader. The Roll Call of the States began with great fanfare under a canopy of 1,751 American flags. The 984 delegates were ready for duty. Because twenty states had held direct presidential primaries, the early trends were predictable.

Kansas governor Allen's nomination of General Wood set off an exuberant, forty-two-minute demonstration of support in the blistering heat that nearly drained his backers. Another forty-six-minute outburst for Lowden followed the nominating speech of Congressman William A. Rodenberg. Charles Stetson Wheeler nominated Senator Johnson. Then Frank B. Willis, the former Ohio governor, nominated Harding. Willis gave the convention a chuckle with his closing line, delivered as he leaned confidentially over the podium as though whispering, "Say, boys, and girls too, why not name as the party's candidate . . . the man whose record is the platform of the party . . . , Warren G. Harding?" The Ohio senator's name sparked a ten-minute response.

Frederick Gillett, Speaker of the House of Representatives, offered Calvin Coolidge as the best choice because he was, "patient as Lincoln, silent as Grant, diplomatic as McKinley, with the political instinct of Roosevelt." President Nicholas Murray Butler of Columbia University, Governor Sproul of Pennsylvania, Senator Miles Poindexter of Washington, and Senator Howard Sutherland of West Virginia also had the honor of nomination.

Then, the long-awaited voting began. The temperatature on the Coliseum floor soared to 106 degrees.

To win, 493 votes were needed. General Wood with 287 1/2 and Governor Lowden with 211 1/2 took the lead, while Senator Johnson garnered 133 1/2 and Governor Sproul 84. Senator Harding placed sixth with 65 1/2. Wood's support hailed from the Northeast, Lowden's from the South, Johnson's from the West. The Midwest was divided. Thus, almost immediately, the convention was deadlocked. All day Friday, delegates haggled and argued in the oppressive heat with no effect. By the fourth ballot, Wood held 314 1/2, Lowden 289, Johnson 140 1/2, and Harding 61 1/2. At 7:00 P.M., Senator Reed Smoot of Utah, sensing the futility of going forward without negotiations between the candidate's representatives, called for an adjournment, and Chairman Lodge agreed.

All night, party insiders met and debated their options. Lowden's search for the needed support was encountering resistance, in part because of Mayor Thompson, who had revenge on his mind. He caroused through hotel lobbies and visited delegations on behalf of the city, and wherever he ventured with his boisterous entourage he had a bad word for Lowden. In "Big Bill's" mind, the governor had double-crossed him by denying patronage appointments, even though Thompson helped Lowden garner enough support in the city that virtually guaranteed a win. "His word's no good," "Big Bill" advised. "Nominate Lowden, and the Republicans'll lose Illinois." He took his story to Hearst who also feared Lowden might win and needed an edge for Johnson. Then he threw in the dynamite. Thompson told Hearst's *Chicago American* that he was resigning as an Illinois delegate-at-large over the "moral issue" of Lowden's excessive preconvention fund-raising and spending. The mayor's resignation made the headlines.

Meanwhile, Harding's brain trust was nestled in the Florentine Room of the Congress Hotel, T.R.'s old headquarters. During the first few days of the convention, the suite had been filled with delegates sampling the hospitality. Once the voting showed Harding behind, the crowds vanished. Harding had personally entertained visitors, but the effect of a hard week socializing, the long hours, and the scotch were taking its toll. The senator was stiff. Florence Kling DeWolfe Harding, the senator's wife, was telling the press that she didn't see why anyone wanted to be president.

As the evening wore down, a prediction of a late night compromise meeting made by Harding's savvy campaign manager Harry M. Daugherty four months earlier seemed to come miraculously true. Those involved denied it later. But others told of a "senatorial cabal" that met that night in the smoke-filled rooms 408 through 410 of the Blackstone Hotel—reserved by Colonel George Harvey, publisher of *Harvey's Weekly*—trying to break the logjam. Present were national party chairman Will Hays and Senators Brandegee of Connecticut, James Watson of Indiana, Reed Smoot of Utah, Medill McCormick, James Wadsworth and William Calder of New York, and Selden P. Spencer of Missouri, plus a few other delegates.

The freewheeling discussions on that hot and sticky evening ended in no formal agreement, the participants later claimed. Although they may have departed divided at 1:00 P.M., they all left with a good word for their colleague, Senator Warren Harding, as a compromise candidate, if Lowden and Wood failed to work out a deal. Meanwhile, Harding was not content to wait stoically in his room for his party's call. Disheveled and nervous, he stalked the halls of the Blackstone, stopping any politician he could find. Many were shocked to detect more than just a whiff of whiskey on his unshaven face. Then Senator Wadsworth bumped into Harding returning to his suite after midnight. They only exchanged a few words of encouragement, they later said. By 3:30 A.M. press rumors were circulating through the hotel corridors where the Republican delegates slept that Harding would be the man to carry the party banner.

On June 12, Saturday morning, the delegates gathered for the final time to select their 1920 nominee. On the convention's fifth ballot, Lowden took the lead with 303 votes, Wood dropped back to 299, Johnson at 133 1/2 fell 7, Harding rose to 78. It was clear that Lowden and Wood had failed to cut a deal. Neither would accept second place. By the seventh ballot, the convention began to feel a sudden movement. Harding gained 27 more votes to 105, while Lowden and Wood crawled forward neck and neck with 311 1/2 to 312. The convention was truly deadlocked. The only option was to look to the "best available candidate."

On the eighth ballot, delegates from Indiana, New York, Texas, and Wyoming turned to Harding, boosting his total to 133 1/2. As Lowden fell back to 307, and Wood tumbled to 299, the breeze in the old Coliseum was picking up. Lowden and Wood forces began to panic. They felt the momentum shift and frantically called for adjournment. Henry Cabot Lodge complied again, calling a three-hour recess until 4:00 P.M. that afternoon, over the objections of Harding's wily manager Harry Daugherty. In conference, Lowden's men again offered Wood the vice presidency. His representatives refused. Nor would Lowden accept the second slot. They were adamant, yet despondent.

Later that afternoon the convention reconvened for the last time. On the ninth ballot Connecticut switched from Lowden to Harding. Florida abandoned Wood for Harding. Kansas and Kentucky joined the swirling shift of votes, as did Louisiana. At the end of nine ballots, Harding tallied 374 1/2 to Wood's 249, Lowden's 121 1/2, and Johnson's 82. Now Wood and Lowden supporters demanded another recess, knowing they had lost their advantage. But Lodge was in no mood to delay the proceedings again. Pennsylvania endorsed the Ohio senator on the tenth ballot, and suddenly it was over.

Warren Harding had won another Ohio dark-horse Republican victory on the shores of Lake Michigan, just as Garfield had done so unexpectedly before him, but with greater ease thanks to a little help from his Senate friends. Harding now had 692 1/5, Wood had 156, Johnson had 80 4/5, and Lowden had just 11. Harding's reputation for reconciliation allowed him to emerge as a compromise candidate. Now the Ohio senator would take leadership of a party that had not held the White House in eight years. The nomination came at 6:05 P.M., eighteen hours after the "senatorial cabal" had broken up. "One of their own" was on the road to the White House. "Big Bill" was triumphant as well.

Though not widely known beyond Ohio, Harding was the ideal candidate for the 1920 Republicans. He represented everything respectable and wholesome in middle America. As a newspaper publisher who had struggled for success in Marion, Ohio, he typified the self-made businessman on Main Street, with good intentions, straight-arrow business ethics, and a nose for profit and politics. Harding was born in 1865, after the Civil War had ravaged the Union. He rose to national leadership after another war made the United States an uncertain world leader.

Harding brought to the White House race what he had learned in his boyhood farmhouse in Ohio. Harding's father was a doctor, his mother a midwife. They instilled in their first child the values of Christianity, home, and hard work. He excelled in baseball, loved animals, and worked odd jobs. He was hired at

a print shop and learned the trade: how to "stick type, feed press, make up forms, and wash rollers," skills he put to lifelong advantage as a publisher.

Harding graduated from a normal teacher's college in 1882, tried his hand as a one-room schoolmaster, and then bought the *Marion Star*, a failing weekly, for $300. He built the paper into the area's leading Republican voice and gained civic respectability and the chance to show leadership as well. He was an important member of the Chamber of Commerce and was invited to join the boards of the local banks. As an editor, he had written about the great questions of his day, and he became familiar with all the political leaders of Ohio.

Harding almost effortlessly launched his political career, because local politics was knowing people, listening to their thoughts, and helping them when they needed it, all activities that came naturally to the socially graceful publisher. In 1899 he was elected lieutenant governor, quickly gaining a reputation as a party reconciler. In 1914, as Europe plunged into World War I, Harding was rewarded for his years of party loyalty and congeniality, first with election to the Republican nomination for United States Senate in Ohio's first statewide primary, and then with a 100,000-vote general election victory over Progressive and Democratic candidates in the large Buckeye State.

But with Wilson Democrats in charge in Washington, Harding had little chance to make a legislative contribution. His first Senate term, which was scheduled to conclude with the 1920 election, was uneventful. He was Republican red, white, and blue, voting for business, but not necessarily the Wall Street variety. He opposed exorbitant taxes on business, but was not vindictive toward labor, which he respected. Unlike most Republican old guard senators, Harding opposed the Palmer Raids, which targeted the postwar remnants of a divided American political left. The witchhunts were un-American to Republican Harding, who valued individual freedom too much to buy into suppression of individual rights and liberty for political gains. Besides, few anarchists ever walked down his Main Street. Harding was neither progressive nor conservative, but kept to the middle of the road.

But Harding was an internationalist. His foreign-relations committee oversaw operations in the Philippines, left under U.S. "protection" by McKinley's war. Although Harding was among those to attack Wilson's

Republican National Convention, Chicago Coliseum, 1920. Chicago Historical Society.

League of Nations, he believed that the civilized world community could be self-regulated by commonly held laws. He even gained publicity when he questioned Wilson himself at committee hearings on the doomed treaty. Overall, Harding's vague and ambiguous rhetoric appeased both isolationists and internationalists. To voters, Harding seemed like a solid realist ready to clean up the wrecked idealism of Woodrow Wilson.

Actually, much of Harding's Senate term was spent in back room poker games at the home of Nicholas and Alice Longworth or at the Washington Country Club, swinging a wooden golf club. He was enjoying good bourbon on the rocks while the Doughboys were digging in gassed trenches on the Western Front. He was so preoccupied with the social whirl of Washington that he neglected to vote 43 percent of the time. The Hardings were at the center of Washington's social elite "Four Hundred" and shared dinner conversation with close influential friends, such as Edward B. and Evelyn Walsh

McLean, owners of the *Washington Post*. (His liaisons with mistresses didn't come to light until after his death.) Senator Harding had made a national ripple when he nominated President Taft in 1908 and was called upon to make the keynote address at the 1916 Chicago convention, but his political career, as the Democrats pointed out, hardly added up to an inspiring example of national leadership.

So how had Harding become the 1920 Republican nominee?

Harding's campaign for the nomination went into high gear on December 17, 1919, seven months before the Chicago convention. The run was guided by the candidate himself and Ohio political operative Harry Michael Daugherty, who was five years Harding's senior. Daugherty's own political career hit its zenith early and faded. He became a Harding booster in 1914, in part to keep himself afloat on the Republican riptides of the progressive/conservative struggle. When his political idol, Theodore Roosevelt, died in 1919, Daugherty could see the Progressive movement fading.

Daugherty was joined by Charles Hard, another Ohio newspaper publisher, and Harding's next-door neighbor and secretary, George B. Christian Jr. They saw an opening in the Roosevelt void and the need for someone with Harding's political skills to reconcile Progressives and regular Republicans, whose 1912 three-way split gave Wilson his prewar victory. The rift remained unhealed in 1916. But Harding had a more personally compelling reason to seek the White House. He simply had to keep moving. Local politics back in Ohio jeopardized his Senate seat. If he didn't push forward, his career would be over.

Entering the presidential race was a step that he took reluctantly. Like Garfield, he followed his political instinct, trusting himself to the hands of destiny and a small organization. Harding's wife resisted his moves toward the presidency with all her might, fearing some unknown force at work. While she was socially ambitious, she pleaded for Daugherty to leave her husband alone so he could tend to his Senate career. But, as Harding concluded, "there were political developments which necessitated entering the contest." Be that as it may, the one-term senator confessed, "The only thing I really worry about is that I might be nominated and elected. That is an awful thing to contemplate."

Later, Harding undertook a speaking tour in nearby states. After the Ohio split, Harding finished fourth in the Indiana primary, and his campaign fell into neglect. Then Daugherty made his fabled prediction: "I don't expect Senator Harding to be nominated on the first, second, or third ballot, but I think we can afford to take chances that about eleven minutes after two o'clock on Friday morning at the convention, when fifteen or twenty men, somewhat weary, are sitting around at table, some one of them will say, 'Who do we nominate?' At that decisive time the friends of Warren G. Harding can suggest him and afford to abide by the results." Daugherty seemed clairvoyant.

As the convention neared, the field narrowed to the clear favorites. Herbert Hoover was favored by some delegates, but most felt he didn't have the experience yet. Charles Evans Hughes had taken a beating by Wilson four years earlier. Henry Cabot Lodge had backers but was too acerbic and too old to win support. Coolidge had little popular charm. Harding was considered out of the running by the

press, bringing only a handful of delegates to the Chicago Republican wigwam. But once in Chicago, Harding, Daugherty, and his supporters buttonholed as many delegates as they could, and since they had carried on correspondence for months by mail, the delegates were happy to meet them in person.

Warren G. Harding was now the Chicago convention's clear choice. Florence Harding was in attendance in the Coliseum as her husband was elevated to distinction and felt the honor of the occasion as hundreds of well-wishers rushed forward to congratulate her. But she was simultaneously seized by another emotion. Later, she told a friend that one word had come to mind: tragedy. Like Daugherty, Florence Harding had a modicum of clairvoyance.

Meanwhile, the Ohio senator, much rested and restored to strength, was in a backstage room of the Coliseum with Columbia University president and dark-horse candidate Nicholas Murray Butler and Governor Frank Lowden, his close friends. When he heard the vote, he took their hands and asked for their help. Then Daugherty spirited him away to his hotel. Harding's assessment of his victory? "We drew to a pair of deuces and filled." In a more serious vein, Harding later remarked, "You see, it never pays to become bitter in political warfare."

After Harding's nomination, the Republican convention immediately moved to pick a vice presidential nominee. But word of the "senatorial cabal" and its alleged influence on the presidential nomination sparked conspiracy theories around town. Resentment was growing over a manipulated convention. Not satisfied with naming the top pick, the senators huddled in a small room under the Coliseum stage planning the nomination of Irvine L. Lenroot, their liberal Wisconsin Senate colleague, to balance the ticket. Minutes later on the convention floor, when Senator Joseph Medill McCormick rose to nominate Lenroot, he was suddenly confronted with delegates shouting the name of "Coolidge" over and over again. When McCormick finished, Wallace McCamant, an Oregon delegate, proceeded to nominate Coolidge, "the law and order man." "Silent Cal" won on the first ballot, 674 1/2 to Lenroot's 146 1/2. The convention, rebelling against "bossism," then unanimously endorsed the forty-eight-year-old Massachusetts governor on the recommendation of John G. Oglesby of Illinois.

Harding's Democratic opponent was fellow Ohioan, Governor James Middleton Cox. Democrats selected a young Franklin Delano Roosevelt, assistant secretary of the navy, as his vice presidential running mate. Cox had edged out A. Mitchell Palmer, the anti-red crusading attorney general, and Woodrow Wilson's son-in-law, Treasury Secretary William Gibbs McAdoo. The handsome McAdoo would have been the nominee if Wilson himself, who was too sick to fight for a third term, would have dropped out. But weak as he was from his recent stroke, Wilson yearned to be nominated by draft. His friends knew it would kill him. William Jennings Bryan came to the convention with 125 delegates, but his hopes of a stampede never materialized.

Cox won on the forty-fourth ballot. He was on the right side of Tammany, and for the first time in a long time, Tammany was on the right side of the convention. The power of big-city bosses was growing again in the Democratic Party. But Cox, who was prolabor and anti-Prohibition, was left to defend the Wilson legacy, one of disillusionment and unfulfilled promises. Americans wanted a change. Wilson had run on the promise to keep America out of war. Then he had promised the "War to End All Wars." He committed the country to a League of Nations that ran against America's long-held spirit of independence and new-found technical power. Wilson called the election of 1920 a "great and solemn referendum" on his international alliance. Cox concurred, but had little room in which to define himself.

In 1920 the Socialist Labor Party, decimated and divided after the war, nominated the popular and perennial Eugene V. Debs, who had stood up to presidents for his striking co-workers. Now Debs was convict number 9653, serving a ten-year term (in the Atlanta penitentiary) for sedition. His campaign literature showed him in a convict's striped uniform. Campaign buttons read, "Vote for Convict 9653." Meanwhile, the Farmer-Labor Party nominated Parley P. Christensen of Utah, a defense lawyer for the Industrial Workers of the World (IWW) who advocated "one big union" for all laboring men and women. The Prohibition Party nominated Aaron S. Watkins and David L. Colvin.

Harding ran the traditional Ohio Republican front-porch campaign, in the style of Garfield and McKinley. The campaign moved McKinley's old flagpole from his home in Canton to Harding's three-story Marion house with its sprawling porch and requisite swing to bless the strategy. Eventually, more than six hundred thousand visitors came to his door. Marion's hotels were bulging, and private homes filled up. Every visiting delegation got a photo of itself with the candidate to take back home to show and publish in their newspapers. Harding's July 22 acceptance speech in Marion's Garfield Park seemed more like a church service than a political rally. Gone were the strident wartime politics. Listeners were soothed with music and bathed with patriotic band tunes. Harding was, the *Chicago Tribune* announced, reasonable and mild. After all, his slogan "Back to Normalcy" evoked in voters a deep emotional yearning.

Harding sought the support of all the defeated candidates to present a united front in order to take back the White House. State Republican parties did their work as well. Will Hays, the brilliant young national chairman, and the veteran Daugherty coordinated strategies and resources. Hays devised a decentralized, national approach to fund-raising and expenditures. Republicans outspent Democrats by about $8 million to $1 million.

Ethnic voters, such as the new urban African Americans, were actively sought by the Harding camp. They gave him substantial support. The senior William L. Veeck, himself a master of publicity, brought his Chicago Cubs to Marion for an exhibition game to entertain the candidate. Harding, who loved baseball, appeared in newsreels coast to coast throwing pitches before he was relieved by Grover Cleveland Alexander. Harding won the nation's heart.

More than in any previous election, the image of the candidate became a dynamic contributor to the electoral outcome. Much of Harding's campaign was carefully choreographed by the Republican National Committee in close coordination with the Harding camp. Harding's image as a man of dignity, respectability, and mainstream values was conveyed to the nation through carefully edited newsreels and film shorts seen in the neighborhood theaters, heard on home radios, and published in the pages of favorite magazines. The press loved Harding because he made their job so easy. In short, Harding ran the first truly effective media campaign. Advertising executive Albert D. Lasker was hired to launch an aggressive mail blitz. Each week the Harding public relations machine sent out eight thousand publicity "bulletins" with a picture of Harding engaged in some activity or other. Hollywood stars, such as Ethel Barrymore and Lillian Gish, visited Harding in

Marion and were captured on camera. Al Jolson crooned, "Harding, You're the Man for Us."

Harding also had a staff of speechwriters, though he had a hand in the process himself. Several business and political operators advised him, too. Hays set up campaign offices in New York, Chicago, and San Francisco. Throughout the campaign, Harding urged a higher tariff to protect farmers, called for immigration restrictions, and endorsed good-faith collective bargaining to eliminate strikes. He also called for repeal of the excess profits tax laws and promised to protect the constitutional rights of African Americans, as well as appoint more blacks to federal offices. The latter position led to vicious attacks on Harding's character that gained credence among some voters, as a new wave of Ku Klux Klan activity affected both southern and northern politics. Harding had learned to simply ignore personal assaults, but his advisers feared the "foul eleventh-hour attack" would somehow wreck the victory train.

His vice presidential candidate, Calvin Coolidge, a weak public speaker, stayed home at Harding's request, tending to the government of Massachusetts. During the final weeks of the campaign he headed south for a week where he couldn't do any harm, since southern states were already heavily Democratic. He was expected to carry the Northeast for the ticket, nothing else. Meanwhile, Florence Harding hosted scores of delegations of women to meet her husband.

Harding was calm, confident, and conciliatory, with a sense of humility. He easily projected a gracious and gentlemanly manner to visitors on his front lawn and voters viewing newsreels across the land. He was a model citizen for Main Street America, capable, honest, gracious, simple, exhibiting all the right middle-class values of hard work, patriotism, and religious faith found in the small towns and municipalities of the Republic. He spoke in fine-sounding generalizations and did not attack Cox, because such a tactic was beneath his dignity and the dignity of the office he sought to fill. And he refused to "go to the White House over the broken body of Woodrow Wilson" and his League of Nations as his more militant "irreconcilable" advisers, such as Senator Lodge, harshly urged him.

Always dressed in meticulous country club suits, the handsome Harding looked presidential standing between the white Doric columns of his white front porch, addressing crowds quietly and without notes.

He was positive about America's future and sought to let the people and its businesses, rather than the government, determine the nation's course. "America's present need is not heroics, but healing," Harding urged, "not nostrums but normalcy, not revolution but restoration, . . . not surgery but serenity."

In the final weeks of the campaign, Harding consented to make a few appearances in Nebraska, Oklahoma, Indiana, Kentucky, Tennessee, and finally New York, before voting in Marion. Meanwhile, Cox campaigned from coast to coast as the champion of American progressivism, though the movement was shattered. Democrats tried to portray Harding as a "mediocre third-rater." Cox and Roosevelt attacked lavish Republican fund-raising and spending. Further, Cox charged Harding and the Republicans with being the puppets of the munitions makers, profiteers, and Germans, and argued that "every traitor in America" would vote for Harding. But Cox's campaign was seriously hampered by his need to defend Wilson, against whom there was still great bitterness among the American people. He also had to handle attacks on his divorce and his millionaire status. He was a vocal "wet" on the issue of Prohibition although the country was feeling "dry" at the moment. Sensing defeat, local candidates ran for shelter. By midfall Cox foresaw the outcome, but fought on, traveling twenty-two thousand miles in thirty-six states before coming home to Cincinnati to cast his ballot.

November 2, 1920, election day, saw a confident Harding out on the golf links. The candidate was relaxing; after all, it was his fifty-fifth birthday. A birthday party at dinner preceded the victory party that night. Harding turned in at 10:00 P.M., fully aware of the scope of his landslide and with the troubling knowledge that he would become the next president of the United States. His wife and guests celebrated until dawn.

Harding woke early to greet the well-wishers who carried him morning papers with the overwhelming results: Harding 16,181,289 votes; Cox, 9,141,750; and 941,289—nearly a million votes—for jailed socialist Eugene V. Debs. More than nine million first-time women voters flocked to the polls to swell the votes to an all-time high of more than twenty-six million. Women overwhelmingly favored Harding. With a thirty-seven-to-eleven-state sweep, Harding won the electoral college vote by 404 to 131, the largest Republican landslide to date. The *New York*

Post simply concluded, "The colossal protest was against Woodrow Wilson." Republicans also won 303 House and 59 Senate seats in a nationwide sweep.

Harding's cabinet included Charles Evans Hughes as secretary of state and John Wingate Weeks as secretary of war. Will Hays was rewarded with the postmaster general position. But as his wife so feared, Harding succumbed to the stress of the presidency, after less than two years in office, dying of a thrombosis or blood clot on August 23, 1923. After his death, the Teapot Dome scandal, in which oil from the navy was illegally leased, came to the forefront. Albert Fall, Harding's secretary of the interior, and his attorney general, Harry M. Daugherty, were tried. Daugherty was acquitted on charges of conspiracy and bribery. Fall was convicted of accepting bribes. Harding's reputation was tainted, perhaps through no fault of his own, yet he remained a gentleman of his times.

Herbert Clark Hoover
1932 Republican Presidential Nominee

Charles Curtis
1932 Republican
Vice Presidential Nominee

Facts-at-a-Glance
★★★

Event:	Twentieth Republican National Convention
Dates:	June 14–16, 1932
Building:	The Chicago Stadium
Location:	1800 West Madison Street
Chicago Mayor:	Anton Joseph Cermak, Democrat
Candidates for Nomination:	President Herbert Clark Hoover, California; former Senator Joseph I. France, Maryland
Presidential Nominee:	Herbert Clark Hoover
Age at Nomination:	58
Number of Ballots:	1
Vice Presidential Nominee:	Charles Curtis, Kansas
Number of Delegates:	1,158
Number Needed to Nominate:	A majority, 580
Largest Attendance:	21,000
Critical Issues:	Economic recovery from the Great Depression, Prohibition
Campaign Slogan:	"Speed Recovery"
Campaign Song:	"Onward, Christian Soldiers"

15
★★★

The 1932 Republican National Convention
The Temple of Doom

After a twelve-year hiatus, on June 14, 1932, the Twentieth Republican National Convention convened in Chicago, during one of the grimmest economic and political moments in U.S. history. The Great Depression was in its third year. Never had economic conditions been worse during an election. The situation was even more severe than the one that haunted the Grant or Cleveland administrations and brought half-crazed silver delegates to Chicago to nominate Bryan in 1896. Fear stalked the nation and strangled desperate cities. In the mind of the American public, Herbert Clark Hoover, the sitting president of the United States, bore much of the blame. Indecisive and with an antiquated philosophy of self-help, he had failed to act to save the country.

The Republican policies of Harding and Coolidge had ushered in the great speculative expansion of the 1920s that materially improved, mechanized, and standardized American life. In 1928 Hoover had been the candidate of prosperity. He built upon the work of his predecessors in his run against New York governor Al Smith. "We shall soon, with the help of God, be in sight of the day when poverty will be banished from the nation," Hoover prophesied. But even before the Wall Street collapse, U.S. industrial and farm workers were still far from comfortable. The average industrial worker earned just $1,500 a year, while farmers netted only $548 for twelve months of hard labor.

When the financial house of cards collapsed, voters were quick to pin the blame on the party in power. One in five workers lost their jobs. In 1932 the average American was worried. Exports were off 35 percent of the dismal 1931 levels. Farm foreclosures were running at 125 per 1,000 in the Central states, much higher in North Dakota and South Carolina. Many women in Chicago now earned just ten cents an hour. A new car cost $610, while a new house sold for $6,515. Eleven million people were out of work. Hoover's solution was simply to praise big business in hopes that it would recover and help the growing hordes of hungry Americans. The federal government could have no other role, Hoover argued. "Rugged individualism" was the answer. The American people must pick themselves up without government help.

But the times were extraordinary. Along the banks of the Chicago River, shantytowns dubbed "Hoovervilles" were crowded with urban refugees who scavenged through garbage looking for something to eat. Businesses and banks continued to fold while Hoover did nothing. What was worse in the eyes of many voters, Hoover blocked a $1.5 billion package for his own Reconstruction Finance Corporation to stabilize banks and business. He refused to approve other relief bills to alleviate the terrible social anguish felt by his destitute fellow citizens. He was also at war with a Democratic Congress.

Even as Republicans gathered in Chicago, Washington was under siege by twenty thousand jobless and homeless members of the Bonus Expeditionary Force, ex-veterans who had come to win further relief from Congress. Walter W. Waters, the thirty-four-year-old leader of the march, predicted fifty thousand more veterans would soon arrive. The Bonus City was threatened not only with military action to disperse its soldiers but also a pestilence of swarming flies. Eight men had already died from the ordeal of the march. Their welcome had worn thin. Hoover sent them back on the rails to starvation, with the help of the army.

Hoover was politically vulnerable in other ways as well. He may have been a great administrator before his White House days, but he proved to be a poor policymaker and leader. He had faltered on critical issues even before the Great Depression arrived. He had opened up the tariff for congressional negotiation, and the resulting Smoot-Hawley bill gouged consumers, brought a precipitous decline to trade, and protected monopolistic practices. Hoover's policy contributed to the depression.

Hoover's administration faced a constant series of storms. He failed to give farm relief to millions of family farmers. Instead he appointed a commission that recommended that farmers "try to prevent overproduction." He walked the middle ground on Prohibition while ignoring the national severity of the problem. Moreover, he turned his back on his own commission when it recommended a sound Prohibition policy. By 1931 the nation concluded that Hoover was a failure as president. His hollow optimism and cheery predictions made his offenses worse.

Democrats gained ground throughout the 1920s and even before the October 29, 1929, crash had attained a House majority and were vying for control of the Senate. One reason for the turning tide was that the nation was flooded with illegal liquor. Cities were in a state of war over the demon drink. The public had turned against Prohibition while Hoover still favored it.

Under these circumstances, even the ceremonial gaiety of Flag Day and the elaborate red, white, and blue flags and banners waving across the new Chicago Stadium on West Madison Street could not generate much optimism among the delegates gathered to renominate a faltering president. The Stadium, an art deco edifice that cost $7 million, was the largest indoor arena in the world. Completed in 1929, it filled a full city block, and the top of the building was decorated with a bas relief of Olympian athletes engaged in their events. Its acoustics were among the best in the nation; a person in the uppermost corner speaking in a whisper still could be heard from the center floor. It also featured the world's largest organ, the equivalent of 2,500 instruments.

The preconvention weather was cool and damp. Although the streetlights in the Loop were laced with party banners and symbols, Republicans felt as if they were attending a funeral. "Now is the time for all good men to come to the aid of their party," was the slogan. Some six hundred delegates and alternates cancelled hotel reservations.

Chicago's bid to bring the convention to town cost $150,000, raised, as H. L. Mencken, the *Baltimore Sun* columnist, noted, "by sweating the hotelkeepers of the convention city, with some assistance from the bootleggers and other purveyors of entertainment."

In addition, the city fathers organized a formal drive, hoping to keep Chicago afloat during hard times. The theory is that conventions always bring income and good publicity. In this case it was true. But Mencken had a different angle on national conventions:

> What really happens nine times out of ten, is that the city gets a black eye. Either the hotels gouge the visitors too ferociously, or the booze supply is insufficient, or the weather is too hot, or there is something else to complain of. The delegates and alternates go home complaining loudly, and so do the newspaper reporters, who commonly outnumber them, and the result is that the city suffers damage from which it is years recovering.

One thing Chicago did not lack in 1932 was a good supply of alcohol, even though most of the speakeasies shut down to increase the political pressure for repeal. Republican delegates enjoyed the speakeasy across from the Stadium on Madison Street and were admitted when they flashed their official convention badges. But they were barred from the Billy Goat Tavern, which stood next to the Twenty-Eighth Ward Regular Democratic Party headquarters across from the Stadium, by proprietor Gus Sianis. A sign in the window read "No Republicans Allowed."

The year 1932, like 1884, 1944, and 1952, was a double convention year for Chicago, and the city was grateful. For the Republicans, 1932 was a renomination convention for a sitting president, albeit one in big political trouble. Many of the delegates who came to Chicago were obliged to the federal government for their jobs and pledged to the administration. Hoover commanded party machinery like a field general. A rigid chain of decision making permitted no stragglers.

Potential rivals sensed the futility of a run and were resigned to Hoover and defeat. Republican progressive William E. Borah of Idaho, a dry, refused the favorite-son status of his state. A "draft Coolidge" movement faltered on the broken health of its hero. Only former Maryland senator Joseph I. France, a wet, took up the challenge against Hoover. He won a few primaries, but delegations of those states were not compelled to vote for him and indeed were organized by Hoover's managers to come to Chicago committed to the president.

The Republican National Committee selected Chicago because it liked the new Chicago Stadium and, most important, Illinois was a critical electoral state. Mayor Anton Cermak, a Democrat, guaranteed the personal safety of all delegates and visitors at the Stadium, in the streets and back at the hotels, during an era when one-third of the city's workers had been thrown out of their jobs and tens of thousands of jobless men and women roamed city streets. He was concerned about Chicago's image as a gangland graveyard, a portrayal that was riveting audiences across the country in films written by ex-Chicagoan Ben Hecht, such as *Scarface*, which was based vaguely on the persona of its most famous former resident, Alphonse Capone, now confined in the penitentiary for tax evasion.

Ultimately, Mayor Cermak was unable to protect even himself. He was assassinated in Miami on February 15, 1933, a year later, standing on a reviewing stand next to President Franklin D. Roosevelt. Most historians assume that the bullet missed FDR, its intended target. But Chicago mob insiders insisted there had been no mistake. Cermak was a reformer who had allegedly crossed Frank Nitti.

In the early afternoon of June 14, the sluggish Republican delegates were called to order by Senator Simeon D. Fess of Ohio, retiring chairman of the Republican National Committee. His weak voice was loudly amplified by speakers strategically located throughout the Stadium. The era of people who barely could be heard beyond the first few rows of delegates without a megaphone was over. A special telephone line also connected the White House to the activities backstage.

Women delegates and alternates participated as full partners. Congresswoman Ruth Hanna McCormick, the widow of Senator Joseph Medill McCormick, was prominent in the deliberations, as was Mrs. Ellis A. Yost, sister-in-law of legendary Michigan football coach Harris Yost, and Sarah Schuyler Butler, daughter of Columbia University president Nicholas Murray Butler.

Senator Lester J. Dickinson of Iowa was elected temporary chairman and praised Hoover richly in his keynote speech. Despite the new sound equipment, Dickinson, unused to the technology, sped through his lines so rapidly that his words sounded like static to his restless listeners. He attacked "zealots and demagogues, socialists and communists" whose radical solutions, he argued, threatened the nation even more than the current economic crisis. Dickinson portrayed Hoover as "patiently and persistently" attending to the "great task of restoring our normal economic balance."

The Stadium was only one-third full, attended, as it was, by lethargic delegates resigned to the inevitability of Hoover's nomination in June and likely defeat in November. In fact, as the convention opened, many delegates were huddled back at the Blackstone Hotel trying to work out a feasible Prohibition plank that would attract voters without further alienating the party's Bible Belt backers. As Dickinson continued his indecipherable defense of the Republican Party and its proud history, critiqued the Democrats in Congress, and praised the management skills of Hoover, more and more delegates hit the side exits. Exasperated by the exodus, Chairman Fess grabbed the microphone from Dickinson and called for order and respect for the speaker, to no avail. When Dickinson finally mentioned Hoover's name, he elicited only casual applause, lasting one minute and fifty-seven seconds, one of the shortest demonstrations in Republican convention history.

By the end of Dickinson's meandering keynote speech, the chair called for a recess. But the building was already deserted. The first session lasted less than two hours. As the delegates departed, the Stadium's monstrous organ mistakenly played "The Sidewalks of New York," the Democratic theme song for the 1928 Al Smith convention.

Embarrassed by the preceding day's events, broadcast by radio to voters from coast to coast, Republicans tried to put on a happier face during the next day of deliberations. On June 15 the first order of business was to elect Congressman Bertrand H. Snell of New York as permanent chairman. Snell took the gavel and launched into an animated party sermon calculated to wake up the delegates: "The Democrats have a minority complex which they simply cannot change. As a fault-finding, caviling minority, they are 100 percent perfect. As a driving, constructive majority they are a 100 percent failure. . . . This much must be stated to their credit: as long as they followed the leadership of the one man in America who has furnished leadership in this great crisis, Herbert Hoover, they functioned in splendid fashion."

This time when Hoover's name was praised by the speaker, a prearranged demonstration kicked off and lasted a full twelve minutes. The band played a rousing rendition of "Iowa," the president's birth-place, and "California, Here I Come," his residence before Washington. Instead of trying to defend Hoover as Dickinson had done, Snell further lambasted the Democrats and their historical shortcomings. He warned that conditions would deteriorate, if, by misfortune, they gained power. Only the Republicans could protect American voters. The audience seemed to catch some of Snell's spirit and gave renewed vigor to their tasks.

Challenges were few. The Hoover machine had carefully selected favorable delegates in almost all of the states. But a fight on the convention floor, at Hoover's request, revoked the credentials of South Carolina's Joe Tolbert, a national committeeman known as one of the South's worst Republican patronage kings. Hoover was left with a "lily-white" South Carolina delegation. The president had generally failed on his 1928 campaign promise to rid the government and the party of the most grievous patronage abuses. The state Republican parties acted as they had since the Grant era—hiring, firing, and purveying favors at the will and whim of the state party leadership. But in the national spotlight, the gesture of giving the boot to Tolbert allowed Hoover to show he still was committed to patronage reform.

The evening session of the second day was devoted to the 1932 Republican platform. The longest and one of the most conservative platforms in party history had Hoover's seal of approval. Most of it had been written by Hoover's secretary of treasury Ogden Mills. Dr. James Rudolph Garfield of Ohio, son of the late president and chair of the resolutions committee, intoned all thirty-seven planks of the 8,500 word document. His words echoed through the Stadium, which for the first time was full with Republican delegates, dignitaries, and operatives.

> We meet in a period of widespread distress and of an economic depression that has swept the world. The emergency is second only to that of a great war. The human suffering occasioned may well exceed that of a period of actual conflict.
>
> The solution?
>
> The people themselves, by their own courage, their own patient and resolute effort in the readjustments of their own affairs, can and will work out the cure. It is our task as a party, by leadership and a wise deter-

mination of policy, to assist that recovery . . . True to American traditions and principles of government, the administration has regarded the relief problem as one of State and local responsibility . . . There has been magnificent response and action to relieve distress by citizens, organizations, and agencies, public and private, throughout the country.

The platform then reiterated Hoover's current policies, boldly proclaiming, "We believe in the principle of high wages. We favor the principle of a shorter working week and shorter work day." In fact, millions of wages had been cut among those who held on to their jobs, and the work week had been eliminated for millions of others.

Republicans also endorsed collective bargaining, freedom of speech, and "rigid penal laws that will aid the states in stamping out the activities of gangsters, racketeers, and kidnappers," as well as a continuation of "the present relentless warfare against the illicit narcotic traffic and the spread of the curse of drug addiction among our people." The platform counseled "the wise use of all natural resources freed from monopolistic control . . . the conservation of oil," and pledged to "maintain equal opportunity and rights for Negro citizens."

Through most of the reading the delegates and spectators were fidgety and paid little attention. The convention did not particularly care what was in thirty-six of the platform planks. They cared about only one—the resolution on Prohibition.

A call for a mass meeting of drys in a North Side church a week before the convention drew only 187 devotees, while a similar rally of wets at the old Coliseum on South Wabash Avenue rallied 15,000. A wet-dry plank adopted by the platform committee majority after an all-night session on the morning of June 15 brought discontent on both sides. In the end, that plank, too, bore Hoover's mark. The president had let the bosses do their work to avoid being damaged by the fight. They had been loyal to his leanings.

> We . . . believe that the people should have an opportunity to pass upon a proposed amendment the provision of which, while retaining in the federal government power to preserve the gains already made . . . in dealing with the evils inherent in the liquor traffic, shall allow states to deal with the problem as their citizens may determine, but subject always to the power of the federal government to pro-

tect those states where Prohibition may exist and safeguard our citizens everywhere from the return of the saloon and attendant abuses.

Garfield adjusted his glasses and curled his white mustache as he read the compromise that allowed local preference without destroying the party in geographic factionalism, pitting East against West and South. Like Root's League of Nations plank twelve years before, it meant nothing in the real context, but it sounded good and seemed necessary for party unity. Then the debate began.

Whenever the dry majority speaker expressed an opinion, he was promptly met with jeers and boos from the Chicago wets who packed the galleries of the mammoth wigwam. Delegates from Illinois, Pennsylvania, Connecticut, New Jersey, New York, Vermont, Rhode Island, Michigan, Maine, and even Indiana led the razzing from the floor. Minority speakers opposed to Prohibition were heartily cheered, in turn, so much so, that the national radio audience became convinced the convention was stacked with wets. The advantage Hoover had won in committee was instantly drowned out by an opposite impression. Republicans saw a media conspiracy to discredit them.

The minority report was then read by Senator Hiram Bingham of Connecticut, who called the majority position a "sham plank." He recommended resubmission of the Eighteenth Amendment and direct repeal. "The time has come when the question must be met. I represent a group of states that desire repeal. All we ask is that you give the people a chance to come clear, and not give them a plank that no one can understand . . . We adopted the Eighteenth Amendment to win the war. Let us repeal it to win the depression." The gallery furiously chanted back, "We want repeal!"

Dr. Nicholas Murray Butler also advocated the minority side, criticizing the hypocrisy of the majority position. He was followed by Treasury Secretary Mills who argued with his fists thrust downward that the majority plank must be accepted. The long and heated debate, one of the most passionate in Republican convention history, lasted until the the early morning hours. In the end, the minority report was turned down 681 to 472. The halfway solution may have bought party unity, but it also brought public condemnation. The *Tribune* called the plank a "flagrant fraud." H.L. Mencken agreed. "I have seen many Conventions," he told *Baltimore Sun* readers, "but this one is the worst. It is both the stupidest and the most dishonest. . . . When the Roll was called this morning, at least 700 of the delegates in the hall were in favor of repeal. . . . But only 472 voted for the Butler amendment."

When delegates awoke from their shortened sleep and reconvened at noon on June 16, the third and final day of the convention, they faced their primary task, renomination of President Hoover. The Roll Call of the States began with Alabama, which immediately yielded to the state of California's Joseph "Plain Joe" Scott, a congressman whose rhetoric was anything but ordinary:

> Babylon and Nineveh and ancient Rome wallowed in the wealth of material prosperity, stood naked and unashamed in their perdition, and succumbed. But the human lampposts of Nero, the men, women, and children thrown to the lions at the Colosseum for a Roman holiday, gave us the artesian springs of Christianity that rule the world, while the splendors of Rome are almost forgotten memories.
>
> Why therefore be affrighted? Why stand frozen with fear and trembling like the slaves of old? Why not remember the inheritance which is ours, and stretch forth strong arms and stout hearts and be worthy of our patrimony? We have the illustrious example of such a spirit, the spirit of one who, through the last long grueling four years has stood at the helm as the captain of our ship of state, and has steered the vessel safely through fog and hurricane, and passed the terrors of the lee shore . . . This homespun American, Herbert Hoover.

Scott castigated the Democrats. "We deny the right of our political adversaries to arrogate to themselves the credit of placing human rights before property rights." After all, President Hoover had "taught us to strain our individual selves to the limit rather than cowardly to lie down under a paternal government because he knows that rewards come to those who bear the burden of the heat of the day." At the mention of the beleaguered president's name, a military band, joined by the Stadium's huge organ, broke into "Over There," the World War I classic, to remind delegates and the national listening audience of Hoover's heroic European relief missions. The Stadium audience joined on cue with a half-hour demonstration in favor of their president's renomination.

They were then further delighted by a sudden avalanche of red, white, and blue balloons with Hoover's name, cascading from the nets concealed near the ceiling. The stunt was one that conventions thereafter would make a regular part of their celebration. American flags were passed out to everyone on the floor, along with party noisemakers. Twenty-two minutes into the parade, the voice of President Hoover came across the Stadium's loudspeakers in a preplanned production. But because of technical problems it was blurred and inaudible. Finally, the organist played "Onward, Christian Soldiers," as delegates and guests stood at attention singing along. The entire proceeding was recorded with movie lights and cameras that would turn the scene into newsreel promotions to be shown in neighborhood movie houses across the land. California delegate Louis B. Mayer of Metro-Goldwyn-Mayer personally ran the slide projector that flashed ghostly images of Hoover against screens at each end of the Stadium. The organist played "Happy Days Are Here Again."

President Hoover did have one opponent. Lawritz Bernard Sandblast, an Oregon delegate, nominated former Senator Joseph I. France of Maryland, who had earlier delivered a strong repeal speech. But when the Oregon delegate began to speak, the public address system suddenly went dead. Skullduggery was suspected. Sandblast persisted. "This staunch Republican . . . occupies a unique position in our national life. At times he has been called too radical, at others, too conservative. He belongs neither to the right wing of greed nor to the left wing of license. He is as radical as the Declaration of Independence and the Constitution of the United States, and as conservative." Maryland delegates, steady for Hoover, booed.

Enraged that the microphones had failed, Dr. France himself charged the podium only to be intercepted by Chairman Snell. A hush fell over the Stadium crowd as they watched the struggle. When the presidential nominee failed to calm down, the chairman had him removed from the premises, after a rough struggle, by Chicago police officers who simply said his credentials were falsified. The convention broke into turmoil. Outside, France told reporters he wanted to remove his name from consideration and nominate Calvin Coolidge in his place. The Hoover managers, fearing an unexpected stampede for the former president, put their foot down. "This is a colossal piece of political racketeer-

ing," France told news hawks outside. "The nomination of this man Hoover is invalid."

Inside, Hoover was seconded by Roscoe Conkling Simmons, a local African-American politician named after the great Republican orator. Simmons told the delegates, with the sound system miraculously working again, that, "Not long ago I stood before the tomb of Lincoln. I sought a word from him for times that trouble and for the struggle that often almost overcomes me . . . He seemed to speak. He seemed to say . . . 'Go and speak to those who still gather in my name. Say that I dwell about the stout and burdened heart that now wears the nation upon it. Say to Hoover, if by chance you see him, that once I travelled the path now trod by him.'"

The drama of the convention was over. Now came the ratification. At the end of the first ballot, President Hoover was renominated with 1,126 1/2 votes to 4 for France, 4 1/2 for Coolidge, 1 for former Vice President Dawes, 13 for Senator John J. Blaine of Wisconsin, and 1 for former Senator James J. Wadsworth Jr. of New York. Hoover listened to the vote on his White House radio in the Lincoln study and was pleased. Things had gone as planned.

The vice presidential nomination had been in doubt when delegates reached Chicago. Twenty delegations, in the only show of independence from the White House, joined together trying to replace the ultradry and elderly vice president Charles Curtis with Coolidge's charismatic former vice president, and current ambassador to Great Britain, Charles Gates Dawes of Evanston, Illinois. But Dawes soon quashed the movement by refusing to let his name be used. Five others were nominated for the second spot in addition to Curtis. Former Massachusetts governor Alvin E. Fuller, World War I general John G. Harbord of New York, Hanford MacNider of Iowa, former commander of the American Legion J. Leonard Repogle of Florida, and Representative Bertrand Snell of New York were all presented to the convention for consideration. Snell, however, pleaded that no one cast a ballot for him.

On the first ballot, Fuller drew 57 votes, MacNider, 17 3/4, Repogle, 22 3/4, Dawes, 9 3/4, Snell, 55, Harbord, 161 3/4, General E. F. Martin of Pennsylvania, 1, Judge Kenyon of Iowa, 2, Senator Bingham, 1, Secretary Hurley, 25, Senator James Couzen, 2, and David Ingalls of Ohio, 2. Vice President Curtis was 19 1/2 shy of a majority, until Pennsylvania, at the

After a twelve-year hiatus, the Republicans returned to Chicago in 1932, during one of the grimmest economic periods in U.S. history. The Chicago Stadium, completed in 1929, was the largest indoor arena in the world at the time. Chicago Historical Society.

behest of Hoover's managers, switched its 75 votes from Martin to Curtis. Everett Sanders of Indiana was then elected chairman of the Republican National Committee and designated director of the Hoover reelection campaign.

Then, in accord with tradition, the nomination was made unanimous, and the delegates rapidly dispersed into the streets of Chicago where the hungry, homeless, and hopeless wandered by the tens of thousands. Incredibly, the real issues of the depression or economic recovery were barely debated. No delegates rose to protest the policies of an administration that had presided over the country's economic collapse and whose philosophy of laissez-faire individualism offered little hope of economic or social rejuvenation. No new dramatic program for recovery was unveiled by Hoover. A sense of apathy gripped the delegates and the nation.

One observer for *The Nation* concluded, "The sight of some hundreds of representatives, even Republican office holders, bawling for beer, while all about them is misery in the extreme, has virtually crushed what little faith I have left in American society. The wet circus might at least have been partly excused had the Convention in any substantial way recognized the need for action to meet the unemployment problem. But not a single voice was raised in behalf of the hungry millions."

Hoover sent a telegram to the convention.

I am deeply grateful . . . I shall labor as I have labored to meet the effects of the world-wide storm which has devastated us with trials and sufferings in but few [sic] of our history . . . Beyond platforms and measures lies that sacred realm of ideals, of hopes, of aspirations, those things of the spirit which make the greatness and the soul of the nation. These are our objectives and with unceasing effort, with courage, and faith in Almighty God, they will be obtained.

Hoover told the press he would campaign even less than during his 1928 run. "I have informed Republican leaders that except for a few major addresses expounding policies of the administration, I will not take part in the forthcoming campaign as my undivided attention must be given to the duties of my office." In November Hoover's judgment would be wrought. As the delegates scattered, the depression reached deeper toward some of its darkest days.

Franklin Delano Roosevelt
1932 Democratic Presidential Nominee

John Nance Garner
1932 Democratic
Vice Presidential Nominee

Facts-at-a-Glance
★★★

Event:	Twenty-Sixth Democratic National Convention
Dates:	June 27–July 2, 1932
Building:	The Chicago Stadium
Location:	1800 West Madison Street
Chicago Mayor:	Anton Joseph Cermak, Democrat
Candidates for Nomination:	Dr. Newton D. Baker, Ohio; Governor Harry Flood Byrd, Virginia; Speaker of the House John Nance Garner, Texas; Governor William H. Murray, Oklahoma; former Senator James Alexander Reed, Missouri; Governor Albert C. Ritchie, Maryland; Governor Franklin Delano Roosevelt, New York; former Governor Alfred Emanuel Smith, New York; Melvin Alvah Traylor, Illinois
Presidential Nominee:	Franklin Delano Roosevelt
Age at Nomination:	50
Number of Ballots:	4
Vice Presidential Nominee:	John Nance Garner
Number of Delegates:	1,154
Number Needed to Nominate:	Two-thirds, 770
Largest Attendance:	25,000
Critical Issues:	The Great Depression, Prohibition
Campaign Slogan:	"A New Deal for the American People"
Campaign Song:	"Happy Days Are Here Again"

16
★★★

The 1932 Democratic National Convention
Happy Days Are Here Again

The Republicans were still packing their bags when the Democrats eagerly moved into their Michigan Avenue hotels getting ready for the Twenty-Sixth Democratic National Convention, their first time in Chicago in thirty-six years. Once again, 1932 was a double convention year for Chicago. Unlike the Republican event, the fight for the 1932 Democratic nomination was stacking up to be a bitter classic between the old progressive and conservative wings of the Democracy.

The stakes were enormous. The winner, in all likelihood, would be elected president of the United States in November. The Democracy had its best chance in the generation since Wilson to regain national power. In 1928 Hoover had promised to abolish poverty. But four years later the depression plunged millions of Americans into economic distress and destitution. By 1930 the Democrats had swept to victory in the House of Representatives and cut the Republican Senate margin to just one vote. Only an economic miracle could save Hoover.

Franklin Delano Roosevelt, in his second two-year term as governor of New York, was the presumed front-runner for the 1932 garland, following in the tradition of other high profile New York governors. He represented the progressive Democratic tradition of Bryan and Wilson. Ever since Roosevelt's stunning gubernatorial election during the 1928 Republican landslide, observers both inside and out of the party knew Roosevelt was the man to watch. Roosevelt had won New York, albeit by a narrow margin of just 25,564 votes, while the Democratic presidential nominee Al Smith, Roosevelt's predecessor as governor and the man who personally pleaded for him to run, was defeated in his own home state that same year.

For four years Roosevelt's team quietly mapped a national strategy and rode the front-runner label to a long lead. He kept in constant touch with Democratic leaders throughout the nation. Roosevelt's personal secretary and political guru of twenty years, the diminutive and sickly Louis McHenry Howe, formerly a reporter with the *New York Herald,* guided the governor's presidential strategy. Along with James Aloysius Farley, the burly and gregarious chairman of the New York State Democratic Party, Howe had coordinated a national letter writing campaign from the "Friends of Roosevelt" headquarters at 331 Madison Avenue in New York City. They also encouraged "Roosevelt for President" clubs throughout the country.

Since 1930 Roosevelt had sent personal letters to 140,000 Democratic committeemen. Farley wrote hundreds of letters every day, made thousands of phone calls, and traveled thirty thousand miles by train on Roosevelt's behalf. The campaign also sent out half a million pictures of the governor and issue-oriented brochures to potential delegates. Much of the early preconvention campaign was bankrolled by financier Joseph P. Kennedy, father of the future president.

Roosevelt's front-runner status was further boosted by the new practice of public opinion polling. Five highly publicized national polls of past delegates and prominent citizens indicated Roosevelt to be the pacesetter. The New York governor gained the confidence of 478 delegates, compared to Smith's 73, with a scattered vote going to other hopefuls. Roosevelt even corralled the overwhelming majority of small businessmen in one of the polls. Newspapers picked up on the polling idea and conducted their own surveys only to confirm the governor's popularity.

Roosevelt's unofficial campaign parlayed those polls into political power as it organized supporters across the land, touting the "magic" of the Roosevelt name to Democrats and Republicans. Roosevelt was popular with "nine out of ten men in nine out of ten states," Representative Howard of Nebraska boasted with more than slight exaggeration in Washington.

Roosevelt was a shoo-in, his backers claimed. He'd win on the first ballot, Farley bragged.

Not if Smith could help it. The beloved and badly maligned Smith had been slow to throw his hat into the ring again. After the drubbing he received in 1928 at the hands of Herbert Hoover's rabidly anti-Catholic campaign, he had little taste for American presidential politics. Smith had been trounced in forty of the forty-eight states and attracted only 87 electoral votes to Hoover's 444. The bigotry of the campaign disgusted and convinced him that no Catholic could win in his lifetime. Worse, the Democracy deserted him in the South and West. Now his party was decimated. Smith grumbled, "I certainly do not expect ever to run for public office again. I've had all I can stand of it. I'll never lose my interest in public affairs but as far as running for office again, that's finished." Most Democrats reluctantly took their revered hero at his word and turned to Roosevelt, the new champion of the party.

But as the 1932 campaign approached, Smith's political instincts took over again. The old Brown Derby, as he was fondly called because of his familiar hat, still had many allies ready to fight at his side. After all, they reasoned, any Democrat would have been whipped in 1928 when times were good, but in 1932 no Democrat could avoid winning back the presidency after twelve years of Republican misrule from Harding to Hoover. And the charismatic Smith was the best Democrat they could offer to the country. The editorials predicted he could secure the nomination if he decided to run.

Many felt Smith could even edge out his gubernatorial successor and former friend, Franklin Roosevelt, who was making waves with his innovative efforts to relieve the distress caused by economic calamity. Roosevelt was a formidable opponent, even if he was, as some claimed, "wishy-washy." Roosevelt was an aristocrat who had gone to Harvard College and Columbia Law School. He was also a distant cousin of Teddy Roosevelt, but with his own charm and courage. He had enjoyed a successful career in the New York State senate, as assistant secretary of the navy under Wilson, and as vice presidential nominee with James Cox in 1920 before being stricken by polio the next year. After his partial and painful recovery, Roosevelt moved up to the Albany mansion. He had the personal presence of an Andrew Jackson and the progressive policy of a Woodrow Wilson. He

was admired by people of all strata and took interest in their concerns. He was a strange kind of underdog who fought for the underdog.

Although Roosevelt possessed modest wealth, in 1932 he was vying for the progressive leadership of the party of William Jennings Bryan. In his second term as governor, he had advocated depression relief, unemployment insurance, worker's compensation, old-age pensions, rural tax reform, labor legislation, and bank reform. He also lobbied for electricity for every home in the state through the development of St. Lawrence water power. He had called for government to help ordinary people in the towns and on the farms. As a result, he became the target of conservative Democrats and Wall Street barons.

But they were not alone in distrusting him. Liberal and radical reformers also accused Roosevelt of political opportunism and lack of integrity. Nor was he "dripping wet" like Smith. In 1930 he had advocated repeal of the Eighteenth Amendment, but with local options so individual communities could preserve the ban if so desired. Smith was for all-out repeal. Liberals suspected Roosevelt was simply experimenting with a national solution that would not offend the South and drive them away from the party as in 1928.

Smith, like Teddy Roosevelt before him, needed to separate himself from his hand-picked successor. He expressed disappointment at FDR's performance. He felt hurt and "ignored" by his former understudy. He even called him a "crackpot" for his strange ideas of government assistance. Smith, too, detected political expedience in the fast-dealing governor. Most of all, Smith resented FDR's snide remark to a mutual friend during the 1931 governor's conference at French Lick, Indiana, that Smith had been "a rotten governor." Yet Roosevelt was the man who had nominated Smith at the 1924 and 1928 conventions. He had received thunderous applause as he courageously walked across the platform in his braces to announce Smith's name. Now the two New Yorkers fell out. Party bosses and men of wealth who feared Roosevelt secretly encouraged Smith. Someone had to halt FDR's rise to power, had to stop his usurpation of government over private enterprise, had to block his crusade for public utilities. Smith had the trust of the gold Democrats.

Roosevelt was also having problems with Tammany Hall. Tammany was, in the words of *Time* magazine,

Democratic National Convention at the Chicago Stadium, 1800 West Madison Street, 1932.
Chicago Historical Society.

"First in war, first in peace, and first in the pockets of their countrymen." The critics charged that Franklin failed to fight Tammany graft in order to cultivate his presidential ambitions. Indeed, Roosevelt had not removed Tammany's favorite son, Mayor James J. Walker of New York City, on charges of corruption. An investigation by Judge Samuel Seabury, who himself had vice presidential ambitions, proved that Walker had pocketed hundreds of thousands of dollars in illegal kickbacks. Seabury sent Roosevelt a fifteen-count indictment on Walker, but it sat on the governor's desk. Walter Lippmann attacked Roosevelt's inaction, charging, "Governor Roosevelt has lost his moral freedom. He is so heavily mortgaged to Tammany that he must prove his independence of it . . . "

In fact, Roosevelt had fought and defeated Tammany years earlier in his first New York State senate term, and a certain defiance remained on both sides.

The charges of opportunism made Roosevelt appear to voters across the nation to be under Tammany control. Yet to move against Tammany Hall and its discredited mayor was to invite loss of New York state, its ninety-four delegates at the convention, and votes in the general election—a fatal historical failure for any candidate—and FDR knew it.

Roosevelt formally announced his candidacy on January 23, 1932. That same day six Alaskan Territory delegates pledged to him. But the *New York Herald Tribune* cast a black cloud over his candidacy, estimating that, "if Smith should actively and publicly oppose Roosevelt, Roosevelt would not have a chance in the world." Two weeks later, the Happy Warrior, as Smith was known, jumped in feet first. "I feel I owe it to the millions of men and women who supported me in 1928 to make my position clear. If the Democratic national convention should decide it wants me to lead, I will make the fight, but I will not make a preconvention campaign to secure the support of delegates."

Roosevelt took his case directly to the people in the primaries. During the spring of 1932, Roosevelt showed his strength by cornering delegates from state conventions in twelve of sixteen southern and border states as well as in Kentucky, Minnesota, and Washington. Warm Springs, Georgia, where he had opened his polio treatment center, was the New Yorker's second home. (The South had made him one of their own.) In 1932 seventeen states conducted primaries to select delegates. But Smith, who allowed his name to appear on the ballot despite his earlier declaration, scored quick victories in Connecticut, Massachusetts, New Jersey, and Rhode Island, which put the brakes on Roosevelt's runaway bandwagon. FDR even lost New York delegates to the Tammany forces in the state convention.

On April 7 Governor Roosevelt made his political position clear in a rousing defense of the "forgotten men of our economic infantry," the farmer, the businessman, the worker. A week later at a Washington, D.C., Jefferson Day dinner, Smith countered, "This is no time for demagogues. At a time like this when millions of men, women, and children are starving throughout the land, there is always a temptation to some men to stir up class prejudice . . . I will take off my coat and vest and fight to the end against any candidate who persists in any demagogic appeal to the masses of working people of this country to destroy themselves by setting class against class and rich against poor." Then he outlined his straight-thinking, commonsense platform. It was topped off by his call for repeal of the Eighteenth Amendment.

An appeal of poor against rich was indeed heard throughout the land, but not from Roosevelt. In May 1932 the Socialist Party nominated Norman Thomas of New York and James H. Mauer of Pennsylvania, and the Communist Party, meeting in Chicago on May 28, selected William Z. Foster and W. Ford, an African American, to carry forth their cause. A total of nineteen candidates from groups as diverse as the Jobless and the Farmer-Labor parties appeared on state ballots.

Roosevelt fought back against Smith, winning primaries in Georgia, Nebraska, Oregon, North and South Dakota, and Wisconsin. The Roosevelt boom was on. But Indiana committed to its favorite son, Colonel Paul Vories McNutt, candidate for governor.

And Speaker of the House John Nance Garner of Texas threw pepper into the mix by winning the California primary on May 3, gaining a total of ninety delegates. Some observers predicted Garner's victory was "a death blow" to Roosevelt.

By the time Smith rolled into Chicago, he was confident of victory, although he lacked a solid third of the delegates to insure a strategic stalemate. More objective observers didn't give Smith much of a chance. He was a sucker's bet. But as a veteran of every convention since 1908, Smith knew that he could deadlock the body if he could create a coalition of solid opposition. He approached the favorite-son states and lined up commitments for them to stay with their candidates until they broke the Roosevelt charge down the stretch. The front-runner was now the target, running for his life like a fox in the hunt.

Smith needed just one-third of the delegates—385 first ballot votes—to hold the line. The Happy Warrior personally courted Garner and other hopefuls. Tammany Hall's forty delegates, although officially uncommitted, started with Smith. Just to make sure they were with him, the candidate went fishing off Long Island with Tammany chieftain John Francis Curry and Brooklyn political boss John H. McCooey before accompanying them to the Midwest by rail. As a New York delegate-at-large, Smith was prepared to take control of his own destiny. Through his floor leadership, he could inspire the convention to turn to him at a critical moment. He believed that they would embrace him as the one to save the party from progressive folly and the nation from economic despair. He would ride the popular issue of Prohibition repeal to the White House. Smith set his calculations on the most remote but powerful phenomenom of an American political convention, the stampede.

Smith's campaign was building up speed as it pulled into Chicago. A week before the convention, twenty-five powerful Scripps-Howard papers across the nation ran front-page editorials with the blazing headline, "Give Us Alfred E. Smith." The papers argued that

> Herbert Hoover and Franklin Roosevelt possess in common one dominating trait. Faced in a pinch with political consequences, they yield. Between the two, it's a toss up . . . The nomination of Roosevelt is possible but not certain. Between Roosevelt and the White House there now stands a man endowed in

the very highest degree with those qualities which both Hoover and Roosevelt lack and which the country so sorely needs. That man is Alfred E. Smith. . . . As Roosevelt generalizes, Smith is specific. Roosevelt loves to delay, Smith loves action. Irresolution is ingrained in one; boldness in the other . . . In Franklin Roosevelt we have another Hoover . . . The election of either Hoover or Roosevelt would be a blow from which the nation would not recover in a generation . . . The times call for courage and action. We have those qualities in Smith.

Roosevelt supporters redoubled their efforts at lining up delegates, of making offers to uncommitted delegates one by one, of finding out the political price, of cutting the deal like Manhattan street merchants. Even before they arrived in Chicago, each Roosevelt delegate received a specially prepared phonograph record through the mail from the New York governor. "My dear friend," the voice resonated with typical Roosevelt grace and verve, "I wish it lay in my power to talk with you face to face on the eve of one of the most critical conventions that our party has ever held . . . I appreciate the high honor . . . I am a progressive in deed as well as in word in the truest and most Democratic sense. We are in a safe majority . . . if we stand together . . . I hope that history will point to your wise action at Chicago . . . I shall welcome any suggestions you may have to make and I hope to see you in person very soon. Please accept my assurance that you will always have the gratitude and friendship of Franklin D. Roosevelt."

Roosevelt supporter or not, all delegates also received a mail pamphlet entitled "Roosevelt or Smith?" written by Manhattan attorney Hamilton A. Long. Using New York newspaper editorials, it showed delegates what the "home folks" really thought of the two candidates. The piece implicated Roosevelt in a number of Tammany scandals and complained that he had failed to remove Mayor Jimmy Walker for gross financial violations. It exorbitantly praised Smith and his career as the state's governor.

Smith's strategy of bringing all the non-Roosevelt delegates into a solid block seemed to be working. The headlines were heralding the fight, and Roosevelt had stirred enough uncertainty about his experimental policies that Smith felt he himself would win. "Roosevelt can't be elected," Smith supporters told Chicago newshawks.

When the Republicans finally vanished from Chicago unnoticed, more and more Democrats moved into their hotel rooms, confident that Chicago was but a stop on the road to the White House. "We'll put on a show that will make the Republican shindig look like child's play," boasted Democratic national secretary Jouett Shouse, a candidate for the convention's permanent chair.

A week before the gavel fell, Farley, Roosevelt's campaign manager, left New York City by rail, confidently predicting the governor would receive 691 votes on the first ballot. Then a round of rapid delegate switches to latch onto the governor's bandwagon would result in 770 votes before the first roll call was completed. As for the general election, Farley forecast, "Governor Roosevelt stands a better chance in more states than any of the other names brought forward . . . I now predict that when nominated he will have no less than 345 votes (266 needed) when the electoral college assembles. This would still leave a very large majority without the votes of New York, which I am convinced we will secure, and it also does not include the highly probable states of Illinois and Ohio."

But when "Big Jim" Farley got to Chicago and spent some time with delegates, he counted just 563 committed delegate votes, 15 short of a majority and 207 shy of the required two-thirds—770—required for nomination. The New York and Pennsylvania delegations were holding out for the best bargain. Texas and California were with Garner.

Along with Farley and Bronx boss Edward J. Flynn, Louis Howe coordinated the convention campaign, bringing their own telephone operators to protect the private line to Albany. Howe also had an army of spies working for him, reporting news from opposition camps. By convention eve, Farley, ensconced in Room 1702, the presidential suite of the Congress Hotel, was waving the vice presidency around for the right person with the right number of votes to solidify FDR's coronation.

Smith called those calculations "Farley's fairy stories." His supporters used rougher terms, calling Roosevelt "the corkscrew candidate" and a "feather duster." The atmosphere was caustic and intense. Mayor Frank Hague of Jersey City argued, "Governor Roosevelt, if nominated, has no chance of winning in November. He cannot carry a single state east of the Mississippi . . . why consider the one man who is weakest in the eyes of the rank and file?" Shouse added, "We have Roosevelt licked now."

Other hopefuls rolled into Chicago. Four-term Maryland governor Albert C. Ritchie, a vehement crusader against Prohibition, controlled sixteen votes. Ritchie warned that unemployment was "the strongest challenge to our social order and the strongest argument in favor of communism." Melvin Alvah Traylor, who had risen from barefoot poverty in Kentucky to the presidency of the First National Bank of Chicago, was favored by the Chicago contingent. Former senator James Alexander Reed of Missouri controlled his state's thirty-six delegates. William H. "Alfalfa Bill" Murray of Oklahoma brought thirty-three delegates and an appetizing slogan with him, "Bread, Butter, Bacon, and Beans." His down-home appearance belied a broad classical education. Harry Flood Byrd, brother of Arctic explorer Admiral Richard E. Byrd, represented Virginia's twenty-four votes, though he was favorable to Roosevelt. Governor George White of Ohio arrived with fifty-two votes. But the real favorite of the Eastern financial establishment was Newton D. Baker of Cleveland. Baker, Ohio's "little great man," had been Wilson's secretary of war, and was a vocal advocate for the League of Nations.

James Hamilton Lewis of Illinois, who had started as a longshoreman and was known for his wild, bushy sideburns, held fifty-eight delegate votes. Garner boosters waved signs reading "No Doles But Jobs—Garner." The speaker had the strong and visible support of the sixty-nine-year-old elder party statesman William Gibbs McAdoo, who harbored some lingering desire for the nomination, if his first choice Garner couldn't win it. Those who could not side with Roosevelt or Smith gravitated to Garner, the "Democratic Old Hickory," who disliked Smith. Farley had been working on Garner's camp since it arrived in town, hoping to swing support. Garner himself was ambivalent about becoming president. After visiting Hoover in the White House, he commented, "I always thought of the White House as a prison, but I never noticed until today how much the shiny latch on the executive office door looks like the handle on a casket."

Back in Albany, Roosevelt talked by a private telephone to every delegate Farley could round up and bring into his suites. The governor also casually joked with reporters about the hot weather that was gripping Chicago. Would he go to Chicago? the press

wanted to know. Well, he didn't know about that, he bantered, all the while keeping track of every development in the Chicago wigwam. Smith was equally buoyant, playing golf every day while his men worked the arriving delegations from the train stations to their hotel rooms. When the press asked the former governor if he was heading a "stop Roosevelt" campaign, he indignantly replied, "I'm combating a 'Stop Smith' movement that began a year and a half ago." And who was his second choice? they wanted to know. "I'm for myself alone," he insisted.

Mayor Anton Cermak of Chicago was also a Smith supporter and had considerable influence with the Illinois delegation. Farley supplied the biggest preconvention-week scoop when he announced that Senator "Ham" Lewis, Illinois's favorite son, would release all his fifty-eight votes. His announcement proved to be a blunder. Instead, the Illinois delegation swung to favorite son Traylor. Lewis was stuck in Washington, as was Garner.

But the polished and politically sophisticated Roosevelt suddenly faltered on the eve of the convention. Smith, the inheritor of the conservative Cleveland tradition, saw an unexpected opening in Roosevelt's bid to scrap the two-thirds rule for nomination and hoped to stalemate the convention. Others saw possible disaster for the Democrats if the party again split along the progressive/conservative lines of Bryan and the gold Democrats, or even like Roosevelt's cousin Teddy and Taft, who made way for Franklin's own political hero, Woodrow Wilson.

With all the players in place, the first big fight, perhaps the critical fight of the convention, took place the day before delegates started official proceedings. It was the contest that threatened Roosevelt's nomination. Though having lined up an impressive collection of preconvention pledges, the New York governor did not have the two-thirds vote required for the nomination. Fearing Smith's deadlock strategy might work, Roosevelt and his brain trust of clever and resourceful advisers secretly worked to overturn the two-thirds nomination rule and replace it with a democratic majority for nomination, like the Republicans used.

The two-thirds rule was a Democratic relic left over from the first Democratic convention in 1832. Andrew Jackson instituted it to ensure the South would never be railroaded by the party it had created into a nomination it didn't like. The rule was veto power for the South. The two-thirds requirement had denied James Beauchamp "Champ" Clark the nomination in 1912 and made it possible for William Jennings Bryan to swing the party to Wilson. Essentially, the rule had also defeated Wilson's son-in-law Bill McAdoo of California and Al Smith and deadlocked the 1924 convention in Madison Square Garden for seventeen long and frustrating days before John W. Davis and William Jennings Bryan's brother, Charles, then governor of Nebraska, emerged as the party's presidential and vice presidential nominees on the 103rd ballot, only to be defeated by Coolidge.

Roosevelt's effort to overturn the rule was providing an occasion to rally the Smith troops, particularly southern delegates. Yet Roosevelt was confident that he had those 578 votes in his pocket, enough to pull off the coup. Surprisingly, much of the momentum for change came from some southerners themselves. Governor Huey "Kingfish" Long of Louisiana was for the change, as was Senator Cordell Hull of Tennessee, a vice presidential aspirant. Publisher William Randolph Hearst also drummed up sound and fury against the two-thirds rule in his powerful string of nationwide newspapers, which had endorsed Speaker of the House Garner for the nomination back in February without much persuasion. But Hearst hated internationalists like Roosevelt and Baker and backed away.

By the morning of the convention, the plan was blowing up in Roosevelt's face as southerners and westerners defected right and left. The story in the press rallied anti-Roosevelt forces for a final stand against the magnetic leader. Smith protested, "The spirit of American fair play will not tolerate any eleventh hour, unsportsmanlike attempt to change the rule after the game has started. This radical change sounds like a cry for the life preserver." Senator Carter Glass of Virginia, the party's oldest and most distinguished member, complained that under the circumstances, Roosevelt's nomination would be "damaged goods" that resulted from a "gambler's trick."

Roosevelt panicked. His power and prestige were on the line. On Monday morning, just hours before delegates were called to order in the Chicago Stadium, the governor telegraphed Farley from Albany and ordered him to back away. "I have been giving much thought to the subject of adopting a majority nominating rule instead of the two-thirds rule," the telegram read. "I have always believed that the two-thirds rule should no longer be adopted. It is undemocratic. Nevertheless, it is true that the issue was not raised until after the delegates to the convention had been selected, and I decline to permit either myself or any of my friends to be open to the accusation of poor sportsmanship or to the use of methods which could be called, even falsely, those of a steamroller. I am accordingly asking my friends in Chicago to cease their activities to secure the adoption of the majority nominating rule." (In 1936 the rule would be cast aside.) Roosevelt was gracious in retreat. Subsequently, Smith's coalition claimed its first victory.

The convention was gaveled to order at noon, June 27, 1932, by retiring Democratic National Committee chairman John J. Raskob. Buntings and flags were flying, courtesy of the Republicans, who had simply left their decorations behind when they were done. After a long invocation by Salvation Army commander Evangeline Booth, Mayor Cermak greeted the crowd. Then the key struggle of the day took place to name a temporary chairman. Senator Alben W. Barkley of Kentucky, a Roosevelt supporter and future vice president, won that round. Although he was a dry, he had dropped his favorite-son candidacy in exchange for Roosevelt's support for the convention post. Barkley launched into a two-and-one-half-hour keynote address to both the convention and the country over nationwide radio. Dressed in his gentlemanly southern white suit, the witty Barkley vilified Hoover's era. "Stocks were manipulated, bonds were manipulated, prices pyramided then split up, then distributed among innocent people under the influence of the opiate of fabulous financial hopes built up by the most gigantic of official ballyhooing ever witnessed in the annals of American history."

Barkley then woke the convention up. "Two weeks ago in this place, the Republican Party promulgated what it called a plank on the Eighteenth Amendment. It is not a plank. It is a promiscuous agglomeration of scrap lumber." The delegates gyrated for forty-five minutes at Barkley's call for repeal. The stadium organ and band played an up-tempo version of "How Dry I Am." During the remainder of his speech delegates wandered about the hall, gabbing and trying to get a beat on the nomination horserace. Six African-American delegates, the first ever elected to a Democratic convention, were in the crowd. With just two-thirds of the gallery filled, the overall applause was polite but not overpowering. Meanwhile, Roosevelt's organization was at work everywhere on the convention floor. Howe and Farley

Delegates at the Democratic convention, Chicago Stadium, June 27, 1932.
Chicago Historical Society. Photo by Kaufmann and Fabry.

were consumed with delivering personal messages, reporting back to Albany on every detail of the latest deals. Then the convention adjourned midafternoon so delegates could board special city buses for a tour of "A Century of Progress" world's fair grounds on the lakefront. The fair would run from 1933 to 1934.

The convention's next big battle was scheduled for the second day. The credentials committee, which was controlled by the national committee, recommended unseating Huey Long's Louisiana contingent and another Roosevelt group from Minnesota. Smith supporters had bolted the regular Minnesota state convention and formed a rump body. Roosevelt delegates in Chicago were ready and turned back the challenge by 100 votes. The early Smith victories were proving useless in front of Roosevelt's show of force on crucial power issues.

After seating the delegations, attention turned to the contest for permanent chair. Fearing that party secretary Shouse's gavel would be used against him as he tried to assemble his two-thirds vote, Roosevelt had earlier switched his allegiance to Senator Thomas J. Walsh of Montana, who held the same post at the 1924 Madison Square Garden convention.

Smith chastised Roosevelt for his betrayal and told delegates, "There is a principle at stake, the principle of keeping your word." But Walsh took a 100-vote victory to the podium and then delivered the party's message to the tune of "Happy Days Are Here Again."

The Montana senator pounded the lectern. "The theory that national well-being is to be looked for by giving free rein to the captains of industry and magnates in the field of finance, and accommodating government to their desires, has come through the logic of events to a tragic refutation. If confirmation of the folly of that notion of how best to subserve the commonwealth were needed, it is furnished by revelations concerning the appropriation of huge sums of corporate profits by managing directors as bonuses, the peddling by great banking houses of questionable foreign securities running into the billions, and by disclosures touching stock-jobbing and kindred practices on the exchanges by those on the inside in corporate management." He was preaching to the choir. By the end of the convention's second day, Roosevelt was in full control. Yet "Roosevelt himself is anything but popular," wrote H.L. Mencken, "either in the Convention or outside. I can recall no candidate of like importance who ever had so few fanatics whooping for him . . . The small band of Garner men from Texas is making at least ten times as much noise . . . the whole Roosevelt fight is being carried on in a curiously stealthy and pianissimo manner."

The resolutions committee had been at work in the Rose Room of the Congress Hotel on the platform since June 22, but on Wednesday afternoon, June 29, when it came time to present the platform to the stadium crowd, the committee was still not ready. In the meantime, the convention was entertained with popular music, and comedy renditions by Amos 'n Andy and Will Rogers. When show time ended and the resolutions committee continued to work, the convention adjourned until Wednesday evening.

Much of the Democracy's fifteen-hundred-word platform, the shortest in party history, was written before the convention at Roosevelt's direction by A. Mitchell Palmer, Woodrow Wilson's red-busting attorney general. Roosevelt wanted to focus on emergency economic measures. But he persuaded the committee majority to retreat from a plank calling for bank deposit guarantees. FDR told a former governor of Nebraska, Keith Neville, "These bankers in New York think I'm a communist now, so let's leave the plank out of the platform. I'll take care of it later."

Delegates reassembled in the Stadium on the third night. Security was so tight that when Mayor Cermak showed up without a ticket, an usher refused to let him in. "But I'm the mayor," Cermak complained. "Yeah, and I'm the governor," the usher replied. Cermak eventually was identified.

Nebraska Senator Gilbert Hitchcock, chair of the resolutions committee, read the document to a packed house and attentive radio audience.

In this time of unprecedented economic and social distress, the Democratic Party declares its conviction that the chief causes of this condition were the disastrous policies pursued by our government since the World War, of economic isolation, fostering of the merger of competitive businesses into monopolies, and encouraging the indefensible expansion and contraction of credit for private profit at the expense of the public.

Those who were responsible for these policies have abandoned the ideals on which the war was won and thrown away the fruits of victory, thus

rejecting the greatest opportunity in history to bring peace, prosperity, and happiness to our people and the world. They have ruined our foreign trade, destroyed the values of our commodities and products, crippled our banking system, robbed millions of our people of their life savings, and thrown millions more out of work, produced widespread poverty, and brought the government to a state of financial distress unprecedented in time of peace.

The only hope for improving present conditions, restoring employment, affording permanent relief to people, and bringing the nation back to the proud position of domestic happiness and of financial, industrial, agricultural, and commercial leadership in the world lies in a drastic change in economic governmental policies. We believe that a party platform is a covenant with the people to be faithfully kept by the party when entrusted with power, and that the people are entitled to know in plain words the terms of the contract to which they are asked to subscribe.

We advocate an immediate and drastic reduction of governmental expenditures by abolishing useless commissions and offices, consolidating departments and bureaus, and eliminating extravagance to accomplish a saving of not less than 25 percent in the cost of the federal government. And we call upon the Democratic Party in the states to make a zealous effort to achieve a proportionate result. We favor maintenance of the national credit by a federal budget annually balanced on the basis of accurate executive estimates within revenues, raised by a system of taxation levied on the principle of ability to pay.

The platform also called for a competitive tariff, the extension of federal credit to the states to provide unemployment relief, expansion of federal programs with a public interest, a substantial reduction in the hours of labor, better financing of farm mortgages through recognized farm bank agencies at low rates of interest, credits for the redemption of farms and homes sold under foreclosure, extension and development of the farm cooperative movement, enforcement of antitrust laws to prevent monopoly, and regulation of banks.

Finally, Senator Hitchcock reached the section that most interested the stacked gallery. Palmer's original platform draft contained a moderately wet plank calling for the Eighteenth Amendment to be resubmitted to voters, a position not very different from that adopted by Republicans earlier that month. It was modeled on Roosevelt's New York State position that allowed local options and was particularly designed to appease the dry South and West. But that did not pacify the majority in the resolutions committee or on the convention floor.

Chicago cheered and hooted for repeal. But Senator Cordell Hull was booed by the galleries at every sentence in his defense of a moderate minority dry plank. Knowing he couldn't control the tide, Farley released Roosevelt delegates to vote their conscience. Then Smith took to the speaker's stand and fanned the fires, hoping the repeal fervor would light a flame to his campaign. This was the moment for which he had been waiting, hoping like Bryan had on the free silver plank, to sweep the convention with his eloquence. The crowd roared, "Who do we want? We want Smith. What do we want? We want beer." The Smith demonstration lasted ten minutes. Smith answered Hull's argument that the Democracy shouldn't advocate constitutional amendments. "What about the income tax, Senator, didn't we as a party declare for that? What about the direct election of United States senators [referring to the Seventeenth Amendment]? Did we not as a party declare in favor of that?"

In reference to Roosevelt, Smith proclaimed, "If there is anything in the world today that people dislike, its a dodger. That time has thoroughly passed when you can carry water on both shoulders, when you can be wet when you are among wets and dry when you are among drys." The delegates loved him and cheered roundly. The raucous debate lasted until midnight, when repeal was at last endorsed by a massive 934 3/4 to 213 3/4 vote. The Democracy had given American voters a real wet/dry choice. Delegates went mad when Hitchcock read the final plank to the gathering. Repeal of the Eighteenth Amendment in 1932 was the hottest issue to hit the Democratic Party since free silver in 1896.

On Thursday, June 30, the fourth day, the convention dispensed with other minority planks, but endorsed one by Eleanor Roosevelt's New York friend, Caroline O'Day, promoting human welfare work. "The next order of business is the calling for nominations for president of the United States," ordered Chairman Walsh.

Nominating speeches lasted for ten hours, into the early hours of July 1. Alabama yielded to New York's John E. Mack, one-time New York supreme court justice and the man who had nominated FDR for his first state office. He urged Roosevelt's nomination in an uninspiring discourse. Tammany and the entire New York delegation refused to rise to the explosive demonstration that greeted their governor's name. But the rest of the delegates yelled their lungs out for forty-five minutes. Senator Tom Connally of Texas nominated Garner. Will Rogers paraded around the stadium floor with the Oklahoma standard in support, while the Texas band belted out "The Eyes of Texas Are Upon You."

But Al Smith's name raised the longest, loudest, and wildest roar. Governor Joseph B. Ely of Massachusetts shouted, "Give us a man who dares! . . . There is a man who sits among us who is a modern Andrew Jackson. You know who he is . . ."

At 3:00 A.M., after the arduous process of nominations was completed, most delegates wanted to adjourn to get some sleep. The Stadium was half-empty, with people sprawled out on empty chairs trying for a moment of rest. Both Farley and Howe were beyond the point of physical and mental exhaustion. Farley issued orders while lying down on a cot in a small room off the gallery. In Albany, Roosevelt, in shirtsleeves, tensely sat with one ear to the radio, the other to the phone line connected to Howe. Roosevelt ordered Farley to push forward. He was mindful of the mistake Seward forces had made in 1860 when they confidently came to Chicago to nominate the New York Republican senator, then casually recessed thinking victory was theirs, and awoke the next morning to be outflanked by Chicago politicians who brought Lincoln the prize.

So at 4:28 A.M. the first ballot began and slowly proceeded with challenge after challenge to delegation votes that required individual polling. The most dramatic moment developed when the name of Mayor Walker was called out in a poll of the New York delegation. Walker was awakened from his snooze to defy the fates and vote against the man who held his future in his hands, "I desire that my vote be cast for Alfred E. Smith," he loudly declared. Yet despite Tammany's opposition, Roosevelt surged to a big lead with 666 1/4, but stood 104 votes short of his two-thirds goal. Smith attracted 201 3/4 votes, Garner, 90

1/4, and other favorite sons held their state votes alone. Baker, the dark horse feared by Roosevelt and Smith alike, totaled only 8 1/2 votes.

However, Farley's prediction that the extra 100 votes would jump onto the Roosevelt bandwagon for a first ballot victory proved false. Only two other first ballot front-runners in party history had failed to eventually secure the two-thirds: Martin Van Buren and Champ Clark. But Farley was now sick with worry and feared the lead would disintegrate. He begged Mayor Cermak to bring Illinois aboard the Roosevelt train, but Tony refused. "Had he jumped on our bandwagon then," Farley later reminisced, "he would not have been in Miami a few months later seeking political favors, only to stop an assassin's wild bullet aimed at Roosevelt." Farley added that Illinois would have also gained a vice president. California, Indiana, and Ohio also refused to budge.

The second ballot began immediately. Roosevelt gained 11 1/2 votes to 677 3/4, while Smith slipped by 7 1/2 votes to 194 1/4. Kansas City boss Tom Pendergast tossed six votes Roosevelt's way. Oklahoma's votes switched to honor comedian Will Rogers. California held to Garner, and Mayor Cermak retained 40 1/4 votes for Chicagoan Traylor. Now it was Roosevelt who wanted to adjourn, but the Smith forces, sensing weakness, demanded a third ballot. It was already dawn.

This time Farley averted disaster by holding the restless Mississippi delegation to its Roosevelt pledge and added a few votes he had cleverly held back to prevent slippage. At 9:15 A.M., when exhausted delegates broke until evening, Roosevelt had risen to 682 3/4. Smith had fallen back to 190 1/4, Garner posted 101 1/4. The "stop Roosevelt" campaign had lasted longer than most had anticipated. Smith had not lost—his strategy was working—but neither had Roosevelt faded.

The delegates spilled into the morning light, drenched in sweat and wrung of any energy. Most went straight to their hotel beds. Roosevelt forces, however, went back to work, desperately seeking delegate switches, knowing that to fail on the fourth ballot meant a dead end for their candidate. Howe and Farley turned all their efforts on Texas. Arthur F. Mullen of Nebraska, a Roosevelt floor leader, had been negotiating with Senator Thomas Connally of Texas at a hot dog stand just outside the Stadium

doors to clear the way for a deal. Then Farley and Sam Rayburn, Garner's manager, huddled at the Congress Hotel presidential suite and began bartering. Farley was weary at heart, fearing the Roosevelt battle was already lost and that delegates who had pledged to be with him early were now looking for an alternative. He knew that Roosevelt was not the second choice of many delegates. The phone was ringing off the hook. Unread cables were pouring in.

Then on the afternoon of July 1, Garner, who was still locked in congressional battle with President Hoover and did not want to deadlock the convention as he had done in 1924, called his friend Sam Rayburn and told him to end his candidacy. Rayburn reported that California was ready to switch to Roosevelt, but the forty-six Lone Star delegates wanted Garner to do no worse than the vice presidency. Garner replied, "All right, Sam, release my delegates, and see what you can do. Hell, I'll do anything to see the Democrats win one more national election."

Before heading back to the Stadium, Farley checked in with the Tammany forces huddled at the Blackstone to inform them that Roosevelt would win on the next ballot. They refused to believe him. Hague had just assured them that they had the votes to stop Roosevelt. The Smith forces were unaware of Garner's deal, but heard rumors that McAdoo was talking with Farley. Smith's floor leaders had won some delegates of their own from the Mississippi delegation and were ready as the convention reconvened on the evening of July 1, at 9:00 P.M., the fifth day and seventh session. Chairman Walsh arrived a few minutes late. His limousine had run out of gas, and he had to hitch a ride on a Chicago police motorcycle to make it at all. He suspected his chauffeur was on the take.

Smith was confident of victory. But when the fourth ballot reached California, William Gibbs McAdoo asked to address the Stadium. Sensing the switch, the gallery controlled by Mayor Cermak began booing and hissing, so McAdoo could barely be heard when he announced, "California came here to nominate a president. She did not come here to deadlock this convention or to engage in another disastrous contest like that of 1924." The boos lasted thirty minutes before Mayor Cermak was called to the podium to calm his troops. "Let me appeal to my friends in the galleries. The Democratic National

Committee was kind enough to come to our city with this great, wonderful convention. You are their host. Please act like their host. Please, I appeal to you, allow this great gathering to go home with nothing but pleasant memories of our city."

McAdoo resumed. "I want to thank the galleries for the compliment they have paid me. The convention wants to know, for the guidance of future Democratic conventions, whether or not this is the kind of hospitality Chicago accords its guests?" A few boos echoed his query. Then McAdoo switched all forty-four California votes to Roosevelt. It was sweet payback for Smith's refusal to give him the nomination that was within his reach in 1924. Farley watched, jubilant though exhausted, then charged onto the platform to slap the former treasury secretary on the back. The convention floor was lukewarm in its cheers, but drowned out the spectators above who now recognized their battle was lost and grew silent. Roosevelt, at his radio in Albany sighed, "Good old McAdoo!"

Illinois, Indiana, and Maryland immediately jumped on the Roosevelt bandwagon. Cermak was angry at Chicago Democratic Party boss Pat Nash for instructing him to hold his position too long and losing all political leverage. Texas padded the 945-vote fourth ballot victory, while Smith held at 190 1/2 votes. An enraged Smith charged out of the hall and didn't stop until he reached New York City on the Twentieth Century Limited. The bitterness of the fight was more than evident when Smith forces refused to release their delegates to make Roosevelt's nomination unanimous. Traylor came in with 3, Baker with 5 1/2, and James M. Cox, the party's 1920 nominee, with 1 vote. Farley used his private line to become the first to congratulate Franklin Delano Roosevelt, the official nominee of the 1932 Democracy. Garner wired Roosevelt from his room in the Washington Hotel in the nation's capitol, "Your nomination means your election." But journalists, like H.L. Mencken, weren't so sure. "Here was a great party convention, after almost a week of cruel labor, nominating the weakest candidate before it." The local bookies gave Hoover five-to-one odds over Roosevelt.

The next day, on July 2, John Nance Garner was nominated for vice president to join Roosevelt on the ticket. General Matthew A. Tinley of Iowa was his only opponent. After the first ballot, Garner was nominated by acclamation while the band played "Turkey in the Straw." Then a stream of speakers congratulated the party, the candidates, and Chicago for another great convention. The band played "For He's a Jolly Good Fellow."

Meanwhile, Roosevelt flew through turbulent skies in a trimotor airplane to Chicago to make an unprecedented appearance before the Democracy. He was the first candidate to use the new mode of transportation in a campaign and the first to address a presidential nominating convention. Late that afternoon a crowd of fifteen thousand mobbed Municipal Airport on the city's Southwest Side, craning their necks and watching for the governor's plane to break through the clouds. When at last FDR landed, Farley greeted him. "Great work, Jim," the nominee told his manager. Mayor Cermak offered his hand. "Mr. Mayor, I am glad to be welcomed by you, my old friend," Roosevelt grinned. Then he was whisked away by a city limousine to the Stadium.

As the car sped north through the city's neighborhoods, Roosevelt looked over the speech he had brought along. His alter ego Howe, sitting beside him, had another speech ready for him. Roosevelt glanced over it on his ride to the Stadium. As the nominee hobbled to the podium, dressed in a blue sack suit with his wife, Eleanor, at his side, the band again played "Happy Days Are Here Again." The crowd was electric with excitement. At 6:00 p.m., Roosevelt delivered Howe's first page before reverting to his own version. A national audience listened.

"Chairman Walsh, my friends of the Democratic national convention of 1932," the new nominee began in a voice filled with optimism. "I appreciate your willingness after these six arduous days to remain here, for I know well the sleepless hours which you and I have had." The Stadium rolled with laughter. "I regret that I am late, but I have no control over the winds of heaven and could only be thankful for my navy training."

He continued.

The appearance before the national convention of its nominee for president, to be formally notified of his selection, is unprecedented and unusual, but these are unprecedented and unusual times. I have started out on the tasks that lie ahead by breaking the absurd traditions that the candidate should remain in professed ignorance of what has happened until he is formally notified of that event many weeks later. My friends, may this be the symbol of my intention to be honest and to avoid all hypocrisy or sham, to avoid all silly shutting of the eyes to the truth in this campaign. You have nominated me and I know it, and I am here to thank you for the honor.

The crowd rose in appreciative applause. After giving homage to the progressive spirit of Woodrow Wilson, Roosevelt went on.

I have many things on which I want to make my position clear at the earliest possible moment in this campaign. That admirable document, the platform which you have adopted, is clear. I accept it 100 percent. And you can accept my pledge that I will leave no doubt or ambiguity on where I stand on any question of moment in this campaign. As we enter this new battle, let us keep always present with some of the ideals of the party: The fact that the Democratic Party by tradition and by continuing logic of history, past and present, is the bearer of liberalism and of progress and at the same time of safety to our institutions.

There are two ways of viewing the government's duty in matters affecting economic and social life. The first sees to it that a favored few are helped and hopes that some of their prosperity will leak through, sift through, to labor, to the farmer, to the small businessman. That theory belongs to the party of Toryism, and I had hoped that the Tories left this country in 1776.

The convention laughed once more.

But it is not and never will be the theory of the Democratic Party. This is no time for fear, for reaction, or for timidity. Here and now I invite those nominal Republicans who find that their conscience cannot be squared with the groping and the failure of their party leaders to join hands with us; here and now, in equal measure, I warn those nominal Democrats who squint at the future with faces turned toward the past, and who feel no responsibility to the demands of the new time, that they are out of step with their party.

The convention cheered while Smith's backers glared back.

Yes, the people of this country want a genuine choice this year, not a choice between two names for the same reactionary doctrine. Ours must be a party of liberal thought, of planned action, of enlightened international outlook, and of the greatest good to the greatest number of our citizens.

The cheers of the Roosevelt delegates were the loudest on this count.

Now it is inevitable, and the choice is that of the times, it is inevitable that the main issue of this campaign should revolve about the clear fact of our economic condition, a depression so deep that it is without precedent in modern history. It will not do merely to state, as do Republican leaders to explain their broken promises of continued inaction, that the depression is worldwide. That was not their explanation of the apparent prosperity of 1928. The people will not forget the claim made by them then that prosperity was only a domestic product manufactured by a Republican president and a Republican Congress. If they claim paternity for one, they cannot deny paternity for the other.

Roosevelt then criticized Hoover's policies and commended the convention on its call for repeal of Prohibition, before returning "to this dry subject of finance" and the problems of unemployment. He suggested that one million men alone could be employed in activities of reforestation of America's abandoned lands to combat soil erosion and "timber famine." He laid out his plans to aid farmers, the 50 million people who made up nearly half of America's population, through planned production to avoid surpluses that drove prices down. "We are going to make the voters understand this year that this nation is not merely a nation of independence, but it is, if we are to survive, bound to be a nation of interdependence, town and city, and North and South, East and West. That is our goal."

The crowd hung on his every word. He gently, patiently, and intelligently explained his vision to a nation in desperate need of a candle in the darkness.

My program, of which I can only touch on these points, is based upon this simple moral principle; the welfare and the soundness of a nation depends first upon what the great mass of the people wish and need; and second, whether or not they are getting it. And what do the American people want more than anything else? … work; with all its moral and spiritual values that go with it; and with work, a reasonable measure of security, security for themselves and for their wives and children.

Then Roosevelt confidently arrived at his conclusion.

Out of every crisis, every tribulation, every disaster, mankind rises with some share of greater knowledge, of higher decency, of purer purpose. Today we all have come through a period of loose thinking, descending morals, an era of selfishness, among individual men and women and among nations. Blame not government alone for this. Blame ourselves in equal share. Let us be frank in acknowledgment of the truth that many amongst us have made obeisance to Mammon, that the profits of speculation, the easy road without toil, have lured us from the old barricades.

To return to the higher standards we must abandon the false prophets and seek new leaders of our own choosing … On the farms, in the large metropolitan areas, in the small cities, and in the villages, millions of our citizens cherish the hope that the old standards of living and of thought have not gone forever. Those millions cannot and shall not hope in vain. I pledge you, I pledge myself, to a New Deal for the American people. Let us all here assembled constitute ourselves prophets of a new order of competence and of courage. This is more than a political campaign; it is a call to arms. Give me your help, not to win votes alone, but to win in this crusade to restore America to its own people.

He had spoken for forty-seven minutes. To those millions in their homes listening to Roosevelt's words by radio, it seemed that a storm exploded within the Stadium. The convention floor and the galleries erupted in stupendous ovation for the new leader of the Democracy, who in a single speech had redirected the hopes and destiny of the nation. Roosevelt stood waving at the mass of his supporters, leaning on the arm of his son James. Now the United States would lean on him.

Ironically, as the economic cataclysm worsened, Hoover's rating slowly improved. But it wasn't enough. On election day, the nation showed it had been listening to Franklin Roosevelt, who polled 22,815,539 votes to Hoover's 15,759,930, almost opposite the 1928 results. Roosevelt swept all but six states, racking up an electoral college total of 472 to 59. Democrats won 59 Senate and 313 House seats. It was a Roosevelt landslide. After the 1932 election, the Democrats became America's majority party.

Franklin Delano Roosevelt
1940 Democratic Presidential Nominee

Henry Agard Wallace
1940 Democratic
Vice Presidential Nominee

Facts-at-a-Glance
★★★

Event:	Twenty-Eighth Democratic National Convention
Dates:	July 15–18, 1940
Building:	The Chicago Stadium
Location:	1800 West Madison Street
Chicago Mayor:	Edward Joseph Kelly, Democrat
Candidates for Nomination:	Postmaster General James Aloysius Farley, New York; Vice President John Nance Garner, Texas; Secretary of State Cordell Hull, Tennessee; President Franklin Delano Roosevelt, New York; Senator Millard E. Tydings, Maryland
Presidential Nominee:	Franklin Delano Roosevelt
Age at Nomination:	58
Number of Ballots:	1
Vice Presidential Nominee:	Henry Agard Wallace, Iowa
Number of Delegates:	1,100
Number Needed to Nominate:	A majority, 551
Largest Attendance:	25,000
Critical Issues:	War in Europe, a third term, vice presidential selection
Campaign Slogan:	"Win Votes with Facts"
Campaign Song:	"Hail to the Chief"

17
★★★

The 1940 Democratic National Convention

A Voice from the Sewer

The winds of war had already roared through most of Europe when the Democrats gathered in Chicago on July 15, 1940, for their Twenty-Eighth National Convention. The United States, however, was still at peace and had just struggled through the "Roosevelt recession," a downturn that began in late 1937. The average U.S. income was still $1,725. A new car cost $850, a new house sold for $3,925. Although the storm clouds raging over the rest of the world cast their shadow all the way to Chicago, the convention equally focused on domestic concerns.

In 1940 Franklin Delano Roosevelt had been president for almost eight years, and he was inclined to defer to the two-term precedent set by George Washington. He was tired and longed for the solitude of his Hyde Park estate overlooking the Hudson River. But the advance of Hitler's troops created an extraordinary situation. Who would guide the nation in such perilous times, Democrats wondered, if not FDR?

Several big-city Democratic bosses wanted Roosevelt to run again, Chicago mayor Ed Kelly chief among them. Kelly first approached Roosevelt about running for a third term in the summer of 1939. At a White House meeting, Roosevelt told Kelly, "We ought to be thinking about somebody to carry on what we've started. You know, President Jackson electrified the country with his liberalism and financial program. But once he was out of office, the country went right back to where it had been." Roosevelt worried that conservative Democrats might capture the party again and reverse the social progress of the New Deal, or that the Republicans might make a comeback with the popular and dynamic Wall Street lawyer Wendell Willkie or Thomas Dewey.

Kelly took the opportunity to inform Roosevelt that he had a candidate in mind. "You have?" Roosevelt asked. "Yes," Kelly replied. "Franklin D. Roosevelt." The president snorted and told Kelly to forget it. "Why should we?" Kelly persisted. "Well to begin

with," Roosevelt sighed, "this is what George Washington had to say about . . ." At which point Kelly, in true Chicago fashion, interrupted with, "George Washington wouldn't make a good precinct captain these days." Kelly left with the matter unresolved.

Roosevelt and Kelly were an unlikely pair. The president was the scion of a famous political family steeped in Protestant, monied Knickerbocker society. Kelly was a large, redheaded Irish Catholic from Chicago's working-class Bridgeport neighborhood. He was smart and handsome and had spent thirty-nine years with the Chicago Sanitary District before becoming mayor in 1933. Yet political self-interest and a genuine affinity for one another made them friends and allies. Roosevelt's New Deal policies had provided Kelly with money he desperately needed to keep Chicago and his political machine functioning during the depths of the depression. In return, Kelly and Cook County Democratic Party chairman Pat Nash had built the machine into a force powerful enough to carry Illinois for the president. Personally, Roosevelt thought enough of Kelly to allow him into his inner circle, and Kelly thought Roosevelt was "one of the greatest Americans of all time."

Later that year Kelly met with Roosevelt again and had another go at him, but the president remained adamant. He insisted that they could find someone else in the party who was qualified. "Listen, Mr. President," Kelly said, "if we did find another man and he replaced you in the White House, and a war came on, you'd never rest in retirement. Your successor would be new and green, and he wouldn't have the support you have in Congress. He'd make mistakes, big and little ones. And you, Mr. President, you'd find yourself lying awake in bed at night, gnashing your teeth, wishing you were back on the job." The next day, top Roosevelt aide Harry Hopkins telephoned Kelly. "Ed," he said, "what in the name of God did you tell the boss? He's a changed man. I think he's going to be a candidate."

Kelly had successfully planted the seed, but bringing a third term for Roosevelt to fruition would be a difficult task. Many people, including powerful Democrats, were opposed to a third term on principle. Postmaster General Jim Farley, who also served as chairman of the Democratic National Committee since 1932, was among them. He thought a third term was bad for the party because it frustrated the normal growth of party leaders and bad for the country because it diminished political interest among young people. Besides, he had his eyes on the nomination, though he knew his chances were slim.

Kelly did not share Roosevelt's ambivalence. He had no doubt who the next president of the United States should be, and he went back to Chicago to make sure it would be Roosevelt. The first step was to bring the Democratic National Convention to Chicago, where, according to the mayor, reluctant delegates could be "pressurized" into supporting FDR. His strategy dated back to the days of Lincoln and the first Wigwam. Farley wanted the convention in Philadelphia, where the Republicans would also meet that summer. Jack Kelly, that city's Democratic boss, put together a $150,000 bid. The situation looked bleak when the Democratic National Committee convened in February 1940 to decide the site. Dealt a weak hand, Ed Kelly and Pat Nash, Kelly's righthand man, bluffed. Kelly told the committee that Chicago would match the $150,000 offer, although he neglected to inform them that he had yet to raise a dime.

Next, Kelly and Nash, the two old ward heelers, went to work on the committee members, exploiting old rivalries here while playing to party loyalties there. At one point during the somewhat stormy meeting, old Pat Nash shook his finger at Chairman Farley and cried, "You're not going to steal this convention for Philadelphia, Jim." Kelly shouted as if Farley were the interloper. He told the delegates that the president wanted Chicago because he had considered the city a good omen for the party since the 1932 convention that first nominated him. The bluff and bluster paid off, and the committee awarded Chicago the 1940 Democratic National Convention by a single vote.

Although he left the door open, Roosevelt remained noncommittal about a third run. On the one hand, he was keenly aware of the two-term precedent and was weary after eight hard years of leading the United States through the Great Depres-

sion. On the other hand, the Nazis were racing toward Paris, and the rapidly deteriorating international scene highlighted the fact that no other candidate could match Roosevelt's stature. He also feared the Republican isolationists in Congress would somehow gain control, leaving the United States ill-prepared for the moment if war came. Most members of the Democracy waited for FDR, their leader, to lead. His coy and indecisive attitude was creating an unpleasant tension in party ranks and, some feared, would unsettle the convention, perhaps transform it into a runaway convention like the one that nominated Wilson in 1912 or Bryan in 1896. Many conservative Democrats resented the president's imperial airs. If he wanted the nomination, they would give it to him. If not, they would find someone else as they always had—Farley, Vice President Garner, former Indiana governor Paul Vories McNutt, or Senator James Byrnes of South Carolina, FDR's confident. But FDR should declare, most thought.

Farley arrived in Chicago as the president's most formidable foe. The affable, bald, rotund, fifty-two-year-old New Yorker had run Roosevelt's two previous presidential campaigns. Roosevelt had even appointed him postmaster general. Two weeks earlier, the pair had met at Roosevelt's Hyde Park estate. During a tense conversation, Farley let the president know that he would not back down. On principle, he had to fight him on the third term. Farley would resign from the cabinet and have his own name entered into nomination. Roosevelt was not outwardly upset and expressed his hope that their long friendship would not be adversely affected as a consequence. But their remarkable political partnership that had twice won the presidency and saved an economically distressed nation did end.

Roosevelt turned the convention strategy over to Harry Hopkins, the WPA boss now serving as secretary of commerce. Hopkins, who had never been involved with a national convention before, set up operations in the Blackstone Hotel with a direct phone line to the president in Hyde Park, while Farley set up his headquarters at the Stevens Hotel on Michigan Avenue (later known as the Conrad Hilton.)

The convention convened on Monday, July 15, 1940, at the Chicago Stadium, 1800 West Madison Street, a little over a mile west of Kelly's city hall. "Roosevelt for President" signs were planted in the yard of every building within three blocks of the Stadium. Although it was only twelve years old, the

"Madhouse on Madison Street," as the arena became known, had already seen its share of spectacles, from six-day bicycle races to an indoor National Football League game. This convention would prove, though, to be one of the more memorable events ever held inside the Stadium.

When the proceedings began, Roosevelt still had made no official announcement, but seemed eager for a draft. Lacking any direction, the convention opened on a somber and desultory note. The mood was that of a giant party at which the guest of honor had failed to show. The situation was politically dangerous for Roosevelt.

The convention was gaveled to order by Farley, the national chairman. Archbishop Samuel Stritch led the opening prayer. Then Kelly welcomed delegates, giving them keys to the city with tickets to ball games, theaters, golf courses, and restaurants. Kelly explained that,

> Chicago is a happy town today. We are proud and we have the right to be. Chicago, the city of militant liberals, the melting pot of American democracy, the crossroads of the country's commerce and culture, comes into its own once more. Chicago's welcome is your kind of welcome. We are a plain people. We take our democracy straight. Our understanding of our fellow men, and our intense loyalty to the things democracy means, are a part of our living traditions. Yes, we are the city of broad shoulders. We have come up the hard way. Our citizens still respond to the call of the shirtsleeve brigade to safeguard and build even stronger our moral arsenals and our spiritual barricades. Our struggle has always been to keep ourselves free of selfishness and reaction . . . We Chicagoans are known to be "Stand-uppers" from start to finish.

Kelly hoped to stampede the convention for Roosevelt from the outset by offering an unabashed endorsement of the president.

> The human family of democracy everywhere will be forever grateful, or forever saddened, by the final verdict of this convention . . . We are praying and hoping that a man who can keep the White House as the lighthouse of humanity will accept the crushing load the next four years are sure to bring. That is why I am praying that this great Democratic convention . . . will stand and put forward and confirm again . . .

the kind of man that mankind needs: our beloved president, Franklin D. Roosevelt.

In the absence of any word from Roosevelt himself, however, Kelly's draft effort fell flat.

Next Farley took the podium and was given a rousing reception:

> Ladies and gentlemen of the convention. As I stand here facing the representatives of democracy, I am overwhelmed by a flood of recollections. It was here eight years ago we met in the midst of a great emergency with a mission to save America . . . We reached here through a lane of idle factories; farm products were rotting on the farms and in the market places; the great banks of this city were struggling to head off the menace of financial panic as were the banks in every other city, town, and hamlet of the country. The riot of unbridled speculation had brought its day of reckoning. Nobody knew what tomorrow would bring forth. We did our job then, and I am sure we will do it today.

Farley then reviewed the accomplishments of the New Deal and the new threat menacing the world. He finished without ever mentioning FDR by name, but again he was cheered wildly.

The next morning, the *Chicago Daily Tribune* commented, "Unless the Roosevelt leaders succeed in evoking a greater display of enthusiasm for the renomination of the President in the subsequent sessions than materialized on the first day he might decide not to run . . ." In fact, Roosevelt did not intend to run unless he received an overwhelming show of support from the convention. He refused to either attend the assembly or to ask the delegates to vote for him. Roosevelt wanted to be nominated spontaneously, partly because he felt he deserved to be and partly because he knew it would help in the general election if he didn't appear too eager for a third term. Days before the Chicago meeting, Roosevelt had told Kelly and a few others of his plan to send a message to the convention. They argued against it, but Roosevelt remained firm. Kelly was worried.

No one knew the president's plans. Rumors circulated throughout the city. The presidential suite at the Congress Hotel was under reserve in case Roosevelt suddenly decided to come to Chicago. It was the same one he had used back in 1932. If he wanted a historic third term, he certainly would make an appearance, many folks argued. Kelly told reporters the odds were 100 to 1 against his appearance. Finally, on the evening of the second day, Senator Alben W. Barkley, permanent chair of the convention, finished his keynote speech by reading Roosevelt's statement to the body:

> Tonight, at the specific request and authorization of the president, I am making this simple fact clear to the convention. The president has never had, and has not today, any desire or purpose to continue in the office of president, to be a candidate for that office, or to be nominated by the convention for that office. He wishes in all earnestness and sincerity to make it clear that all the delegates to this convention are free to vote for any candidate. That is the message I bear to you from the president of the United States.

Upon hearing the news, the delegates sat in stunned silence, sweating in the heat, not knowing what to do. Of course, there was still room for a draft. Roosevelt hadn't been as forceful as General William Tecumseh Sherman's legendary statement of 1884: "If nominated, I will not run. If elected, I will not serve." Suddenly, a deep voice broke the silence. "No! No! No! We want Roosevelt, we want Roosevelt," it said, reverberating throughout the big barn. "We want Roosevelt. The party wants Roosevelt. The world wants Roosevelt." Over and over again, for forty-five minutes, the chant went on. Hundreds of delegates and spectators joined in, catching the cadence and the spirit.

Unbeknownst to them, the source of this wellspring of support was neither divine providence nor a spontaneous burst of party loyalty. It was electronic, the amplified voice of Thomas D. Garry, Chicago's potbellied superintendent of sewers and a delegate from the Seventh Congressional District. Kelly, forewarned of Roosevelt's letter, suspected it might harm the president's chances for renomination and open the way for Farley. To be on the safe side, he outfitted a tiny electrician's room in the basement of the Stadium with a microphone hooked into the public address system, which was supposed to be controlled only from the rostrum. All the other microphones were cut off. Kelly stationed Garry at the microphone in case the delegates needed a little coaxing. "I was ready, and so were the others who

wanted a third term." Kelly later said, "We could not take a chance on a lull, for fear Roosevelt's message would be damaging."

Like-minded delegations took up the chant. "Alabama wants Roosevelt," Garry boomed through the loudspeakers to the surprise of Alabama. "Jersey City wants Roosevelt!" the voice roared, and New Jersey boss Frank Hague wheeled around in his delegation and yelled, "Who said that?" And so it went, with delegations chiming in when Garry did not chime in for them. The organist was supposed to play "God Bless America," but Kelly persuaded him to strike up a livelier popular song entitled "Franklin D. Roosevelt Jones." Finally, after midnight, the convention recessed with the Roosevelt draft echoing in their sleepy minds.

On Wednesday night, Robert F. Wagner of New York read a long platform to the convention, mostly written by Hopkins in Washington. "The world is undergoing violent change," began Wagner. "Humanity, uneasy in this machine age, is demanding a sense of security and dignity based on human values." The document outlined the broad achievements of the administration over the previous seven years. Delegates were told: "We must strengthen democracy against aggression . . . by strengthening our economic efficiency." It outlined goals for farmers, workers, and businessmen; laid out a strategy for increased electric power, and for dealing with unemployment, health, youth, and education; called for slum removal and low-rent housing, economic and social advances for African Americans; and promised to keep America out of war, "except in case of attack."

Next came the nominations. Senator Lister Hill of Alabama nominated Roosevelt, "In the name of the people of the state of Alabama, in the name of the people of the whole United States, and in furtherance of the cause of freedom and law and justice, in a world gripped with chaos." A twenty-two-minute demonstration ensued. Virginia's aging and sickly Senator Carter Glass nominated Farley, "An incomparable Democrat who has managed the affairs of the Democratic Party for seven years in a way that no other man within my recollection of forty years of public service has ever done." A five-minute demonstration followed.

Less than thirty-six hours after Kelly had bamboozled the convention, on July 18 at 2:00 A.M., the delegates renominated Roosevelt as their candidate for president with 946 13/30 votes to 72 9/10 for second-place finisher Farley. Vice President Garner, who had become hostile to the New Deal, attracted just 61 votes, Senator Millard E. Tydings, 9 1/2, and Cordell Hull, 5 2/3. Roosevelt had broken the two-term tradition with a little help from his friends.

Meanwhile, Roosevelt's choice for vice president, Henry Agard Wallace of Iowa was stirring up lots of controversy. At least eight candidates were lining up for the position. For one thing, Wallace had been a Republican. (His father had been secretary of agriculture under Harding.) He also seemed aloof, an idealist. Even so, Roosevelt trusted him and hoped to win the Midwest with his help. The convention delegates, still upset with Roosevelt's cat-and-mouse game about the presidency, were angry and showed a mind of their own. Hopkins was worried. Roosevelt himself did not plan to attend the convention, as he had in 1932. Instead, he convinced his wife Eleanor to go to Chicago to make a short speech to calm the delegates. She would become the first First Lady to address such a political gathering.

Frank O'Connor of Iowa placed Wallace's name before the body. "For eight years, he sat beside the president and I know, as I think you do, he has been a trusted adviser of the president, not alone in matters of agriculture, but in the broader field of national and international action." There was a chorus of boos. Eleanor Roosevelt reached down and took the hand of Mrs. Wallace, who was sitting beside her. Shocked by the verbal assault hurled against her husband, she strained to hold back her tears. Several of the vice presidential nominees, including former Indiana governor Paul V. McNutt, withdrew their names after they were nominated.

Roosevelt awaited the results in Hyde Park, staying close to his radio with a group of advisers. As the nominations were made, the atmosphere in the wigwam turned bitter. Wallace was vigorously booed and hissed by the Kelly-controlled galleries and denounced in speeches on the floor. Roosevelt became furious. He drafted an announcement to be sent to Chicago should Wallace lose. He would withdraw and show them. Before the voting for vice president began, Eleanor Roosevelt stood, to a rousing ovation:

> First of all, I think I want to say a word to our national chairman, James A. Farley.

Her friend's name evoked strong applause.

> For many years I have worked under Jim Farley and with Jim Farley, and I think nobody could appreciate more what he has done for the party, what he has given in work and loyalty, and I want to give him here my thanks and devotion.

She was cheered. Then she turned to the topic of her husband.

> I know and you know that any man who is in an office of great responsibility today faces a heavier responsibility perhaps than any man has ever faced before in this country . . . You cannot treat it as you would treat an ordinary nomination in an ordinary time. We people in the United States have got to realize today that we face now a grave and serious situation.
>
> Therefore, this year the candidate who is the President of the United States cannot make a campaign in the usual sense of the word. He must be on his job. So each and every one of you who give him this responsibility in giving it to him assume for yourselves a very grave responsibility because you will make the campaign . . . This is a time when it is the United States that we fight for, the domestic policies that we have established as a party that we must believe in, that we must carry forward, and in the world we have a position of great responsibility. We cannot tell from day to day what may come. This is no ordinary time, no time for thinking about anything except what we can best do for the country as a whole . . .

The First Lady finished to rousing cheers. Her appeal worked. The delegates had second thoughts about rebuffing the wishes of their leader in these extraordinary times. In the balloting that followed, Wallace won 626 votes to 329 for his closest rival, Speaker of the House William B. Bankhead of Alabama.

Then, at 12:25 A.M., Friday, July 19, a relieved president gave his acceptance speech to the gathering by a special hookup from Hyde Park:

> It is with a very full heart that I speak tonight because I find myself, as almost everyone does sooner or later in his lifetime, in a conflict between a deep personal desire for retirement on the one hand, and that quiet, invisible thing called "conscience" on the other.

Then he outlined the pressing world situation that forced him to reconsider.

It is my obvious duty to maintain to my utmost the influence of this mighty nation in our effort to prevent the spread of war . . .

He also thanked them for honoring his choice of Wallace.

His firsthand knowledge of the problems of government in every sphere of life and in every single part of the nation, and indeed the whole world, qualifies him without reservation. His practical idealism will be a great service to me individually and the nation as a whole.

FDR added his personal thanks to Farley, "my old friend." He then outlined the world situation and concluded with the options before the nation.

We face one of the great choices of history. It is not alone a choice of government of the people versus dictatorship. It is not alone a choice between freedom and slavery. It is not alone a choice between moving forward and falling back. It is all of these rolled into one. It is the continuance of civilization as we know it versus the ultimate destruction of all that we have held dear, religion versus godlessness, the ideal of justice against the practice of force, moral decency versus the firing squad, courage to speak out and to act versus the false lullaby of appeasement. But it has been well said that a selfish and greedy people cannot be free. The American people must decide whether these things are worth making sacrifices of money, energy, and of self.

The delegates were weary, yet satisfied that they had picked the right man. The Twenty-Eighth Democratic National Convention adjourned, and delegates flooded Madison Street in search of cabs back to their hotels.

Within days, Kelly's trick became famous. Garry, who mugged for photographers from newspapers and magazines across the country, became known to posterity as the "Voice from the Sewer." "It was a job right up my alley," Garry laughed, adding that, "Outside of my wife, my hobby is Mayor Kelly and Pat Nash. They're the greatest human beings in the world." Afterward, Hopkins wired Kelly: "Dear Ed, you did more to swing it than anybody else." Roosevelt also wrote, "I want to send you this letter to tell you of my real appreciation for your loyalty. You know, of course, that I consider you one of the arch-conspirators in the placing of this millstone around my neck, even though I appreciate the motives which impelled you!"

On November 5, 1940, Franklin Delano Roosevelt defeated Republican candidate Wendell Willkie to become the first man elected to serve three terms as president. One year later, the Japanese attacked Pearl Harbor, drawing the United States into World War II. It seems inconceivable that Roosevelt almost left office in 1940. It is difficult to imagine anyone else declaring war on Japan after the "infamy" of Pearl Harbor or plotting the defeat of the Nazis with Churchill and Stalin. The phrase "led the United States through the depression and World War II" has become so synonymous with Roosevelt that it is as if there was never any doubt about his leadership. But for Mayor Ed Kelly and his "Voice from the Sewer," Tom Garry, the course of history might have been altered.

Thomas Edmund Dewey
1944 Republican Presidential Nominee

John William Bricker
1944 Republican
Vice Presidential Nominee

Facts-at-a-Glance
★★★

Event:	Twenty-Third Republican National Convention
Dates:	June 26–28, 1944
Building:	The Chicago Stadium
Location:	1800 West Madison Avenue
Chicago Mayor:	Edward Joseph Kelly, Democrat
Candidates for Nomination:	Governor John William Bricker, Ohio; Governor Thomas Edmund Dewey, New York; General Douglas MacArthur, Arkansas; former Governor Harold Edward Stassen, Minnesota; Governor Earl Warren, California; Wendell Lewis Willkie, Indiana
Presidential Nominee:	Thomas Edmund Dewey
Age at Nomination:	42
Number of Ballots:	1
Vice Presidential Nominee:	John William Bricker
Number of Delegates:	1,057
Number Needed to Nominate:	A majority, 529
Largest Attendance:	25,000
Critical Issues:	New Deal inefficiencies, postwar peace, U.S. communist influence, no fourth term, no "one-man" rule
Campaign Slogan:	"Win with Dewey"
Campaign Song:	"What Do We Do on a Dew, Dew, Dewey Day?"

18
★★★

The 1944 Republican National Convention
Prosecuting the President

As delegates gathered in Chicago for the Twenty-Third Republican National Convention on June 26, 1944, the United States was still engaged in the most destructive war in human history, a war that not only threatened the nation's future, but the fortunes of the entire world. The fate of millions of human beings rested on the steady and faithful execution of promises by the armed forces of the United States of America.

Fortunately, in Europe, the Nazi blitzkrieg had recently been blunted. German Panzers and S.S. divisions were finally on the run under a combined Allied assault led by the Soviet Union in the East and U.S. and British forces from the West. In the Pacific, U.S. troops were fiercely fighting from island to island, moving inevitably toward Japan. Finally, an end was in sight, but the sacrifices to get there had been horrifying. On both fronts, tens of thousands of young G.I.'s from every hometown in the land had died and were dying on foreign soil. The American people knew full well that the presidential election of 1944 was among the most important in the nation's history.

Not since 1864 had U.S. voters been afforded the chance to endorse or reject a sitting president while the nation was at war. Some Republicans feared Roosevelt might suspend wartime elections and rule by fiat. But barring that, the Republican Party was determined to offer voters an attractive choice, a man who would reverse the alleged damage of Roosevelt's "communist" New Deal, someone to give America, "Youth instead of decadence, vigor instead of cynicism, integrity instead of double dealing," as Governor Dwight Griswold of Nebraska, who nominated Thomas Edmund Dewey, put it.

The Chicago that Republicans visited in 1944 was forging ahead, building and rebuilding itself, its steel, electronics, aircraft factories, and scores of other industries working around the clock for the war effort. To get people to work efficiently, Chicago had opened its first subway that year. As was often the case during Chicago national conventions, the city was caught in the grip of another early summer heat wave that sent temperatures outside the Chicago Stadium over the 100 degree mark, while it hit 105 on the convention floor. (The situation was so extreme that one Kansas delegate died from heatstroke during the week.) Unlike most conventions, the Stadium was virtually devoid of the elaborate decorations and banners that mark the typical quadrennial event. Wartime sacrifices and scarcities dictated that the party display modest restraint to the American people who had been asked to do the same. The bland look fit how most delegates felt about the task before them.

Roosevelt was a war president, and unless the hostilities miraculously ended, Republican chances were remote. Thus, the convention mood was further restrained not only by the oppressive temperatures but also by the lack of expectation that America would switch commanders in the heat of battle. Even so, Republican strategists thought the party had a fighting chance with a fighting candidate, if they could hammer away at Roosevelt's failure on domestic issues and the uncertainty of victory abroad. They would also try to link him with the domestic communists who advocated a "united front" with the Soviet Union. Unlike 1940, U.S. communists now supported Roosevelt. "Why are the communists so strongly for Roosevelt?" Republicans asked. The president had even pardoned their leader, Earl Browder, after conviction for falsifying his passport. They wondered, Could Roosevelt and Stalin be trusted?

Because of the military situation, Roosevelt was equally in danger of losing millions of absentee votes from servicemen and women in the field. Given the chance, most would probably vote for their commander-in-chief, but that chance was remote and states, such as New York, under the leadership of its new Republican governor Thomas Dewey who was thinking ahead to November 1944, had passed

absentee voting rules that made it even more difficult. Republican strategists also figured that a swing
of the ten million independent voters who supported Roosevelt in 1940 to their candidate in 1944
would bring upsets in such key industrial states as
New York or Illinois and tilt the electoral college.
Besides, Republicans had scored significant gains in
the 1942 off-year election and now held more than
half of the governorships. Still, most of the delegates
seemed bored or just bothered by the heat, anxious
to stay in their air-conditioned hotels back on the
lakefront or have a good time with their fellow convention travelers.

Their task seemed clear-cut. They had come to
nominate Governor Thomas E. Dewey, the first presidential candidate born in the twentieth century.
They knew it. Dewey knew it. Roosevelt knew it. And
the nation knew it. For the first time in presidential
convention history, the drama over the party nominee in a nonrenomination race had been eliminated
in the months preceding the gathering. Dewey, who
a year earlier had declared he was not a candidate,
had nevertheless defeated all contenders and stood
ready to lead his party. As ambitious as Dewey may
have or have not been, Republican voters had
turned to him.

It was his turn. This was 1944. That hadn't been the
case four years earlier at the Philadelphia convention.
Wendell Lewis Willkie, the charismatic former Democrat who had fought Roosevelt over the Tennessee
Valley Authority, stampeded the 1940 Republican
convention, snatching the prize from Dewey, the former racket-busting U. S. attorney. Coming into the
fray, Dewey thought he had the nomination all sewed
up. So did everyone else. But the delegates became
delirious over Willkie, who was president of the Commonwealth and Southern Corporation, one of the
nation's largest electric companies.

Willkie was a civil libertarian from Indiana who
became a prosperous Wall Street lawyer. During the
depths of the Great Depression, he was suddenly
compelled to take over the broken power company
when its stock value had collapsed. By 1940 he had
rebuilt the company into one of the most successful
in the nation and spread the use of electricity to
homes throughout the country. Willkie was a national
hero. Thousands of Willkie volunteers pressured the
delegates to "Win with Willkie." Indeed, Americans
loved Willkie, a rumbling, dynamic speaker. The candidate rode a convertible through the main street of

his hometown of Elwood, Indiana, to deliver his
acceptance speech, ecstatically extending his arms to
the mob of admirers on a hot Indiana afternoon,
wildly loving every minute of it. His picture was on the
cover of national magazines. Republicans couldn't
help but admire and trust the handsome, enthusiastic, and endearing Willkie, especially next to Dewey,
the hard and cold little man with a mustache who was
in such a hurry to achieve power. Willkie lost to FDR
after a spirited race that took him across the nation on
a barnstorming speaking tour.

In the intervening four years, Willkie, "conscience
of the Republican Party," proved to be an intellectual
leader as well. Since childhood he had read widely.
He wrote a million-selling book, *One World*, which
painted a noble and hopeful role for the U.S. after
the war. Willkie would create peace through international cooperation of all nations. He appealed to the
old progressive and international wings of the
Republican Party that hadn't been heard from since
the days of Theodore Roosevelt and Charles Evans
Hughes. But Willkie was hated by the Tafts and
McCormicks of the party, the isolationists who had
inherited their perspectives from the post–World
War I "irreconcilables." The "irreconcilables" had
sunk the League of Nations.

A year before the 1944 contest, Willkie was the
favorite for renomination in Chicago. But he made
the tactical error of identifying four hundred delegates who were pledged to support him. Dewey went
to work to defeat or convert them. Without office and
organization, Willkie was no match for Dewey. The
New York governor's managers systematically fielded
delegates from coast to coast, moving against
Willkie's supporters whenever possible in a "Sink
Willkie" movement, hence alienating independents
who were needed in November. Dewey's machine
also challenged old-line Republicans, beating them
for the right to come to the convention. Many of the
old-timers who made it to the city's West Side wigwam that summer felt uncomfortable around the
Dewey supporters. "If you've been a Republican for
more than five years, you're unwanted here," some of
them complained.

Willkie won the 1944 New Hampshire primary,
then entered the Wisconsin race confident he could
tap into the state's progressive tradition, even though
he had lost the state four years before. An electrifying
speaker, Willkie delivered forty speeches and traveled fifteen hundred miles across the Dairy State.

Instead of the victory that would bring him triumphantly to Chicago, he was decisively beaten on
April 4, by the Wisconsin isolationist Republicans
who had historically rejected the internationalist
arguments of Roosevelt and Wilson. Wisconsin delegates overwhelmingly chose Dewey. Like the party
nationally, Wisconsin Republicans were divided. The
bitterness and cynicism of the war had deflated their
progressive illusions. Willkie, campaigning in
Omaha, Nebraska, immediately withdrew from the
race. He had hoped lightning might strike twice.
Although he still was held in great regard throughout
the nation and the world, his short and spectacular
political career was over.

Willkie wasn't Dewey's only potential opponent.
General Douglas MacArthur, commander of U.S.
Army forces in the Far East and an ultraconservative
enemy of the New Deal, had tacitly let others organize on his behalf while he fought a war a half a
hemisphere away. But MacArthur's private correspondence with a Republican congressman was
leaked. The general denied any interest whatsoever in
politics until the war was won. Expectations in the
party were that the general would return in 1948.

In 1938, at age thirty, Harold E. Stassen was
elected governor by Minnesota voters, then twice
reelected before entering the army. He, too, was a
boy wonder of the party and had served as Willkie's
successful floor leader at the 1940 convention. Like
Willkie, he was an internationalist. But in his *New
York Times* review of *One World,* Stassen took Willkie
to task for underrating the evils of communism and
being highly critical of colonialism. Like Warren
Harding before him, Stassen hoped for a deadlock
between Dewey and Willkie that would bring his
name to the fore at the convention.

Another potential rival for Dewey was California
governor Earl Warren. The popular chief executive of
the Sunshine State was elected in 1942 as a liberal
Republican capable of drawing Democratic support.
He had already established himself as a tax cutter,
who through increased governmental efficiency, had
expanded state services. His imposing frame and
magnetic personality loomed large before the convention. Indeed, Warren was scheduled to address
the body as its temporary chairman.

John William Bricker was as charismatic to voters
in his home state of Ohio, as he was effective as its
governor. Like Lincoln and Garfield, Bricker even had
been born in a log cabin. A self-made man, he had

worked his way through Ohio State University. With
the nickname "Honest John," he seemed destined to
political involvement. Just fifty years old, Bricker had
served as Ohio's governor since 1938 and won party
acclaim by slashing the state's budget. Unlike Dewey,
Bricker was warm and outgoing. Like Robert Taft and
the *Chicago Tribune*'s dominating Colonel Robert
Rutherford McCormick, Bricker was extremely conservative and an isolationist in the anti-League of
Nations tradition. He wanted no part of postwar
internationalism and the "One Worldism" of fellow
Republican Willkie. The added intangible on Bricker's
side was the tradition of Ohio presidential nominees.

Even before delegates gathered in Chicago, most
Republicans agreed, Thomas E. Dewey deserved the
nomination. At age forty-two he was the real "boy
prodigy" of the party and had proven himself an
incorruptible public servant. His reputation as a
crime buster was well-known across the land. His
prosecution of Lucky Luciano, Dixie Davis, and
Judge Kunstler had made him a hero of the matinee
newsreels. Dewey's grandfather cofounded the
Republican Party in the state of Wisconsin. In 1942
Thomas Dewey was elected the first Republican governor of New York in two decades. Sitting in the governor's chair, he amply demonstrated his
administrative skills. Dewey was an efficient administrator and relentless budget cutter, even when it
meant budget reductions for overcrowded schools.

After U.S. entry into the war, Dewey revised his
extreme isolationist rhetoric and modified his bitter
critique of New Deal social benefits. But his dedication to big business never faltered, and he worked to
relax the restrictions that hampered the New York
business community. He passed bills handed to him
by the Chamber of Commerce, including one that
took away the right of legal action against corporations by their minority shareholders. He sided with
the powerful Dairymen's League and the insurance
agencies against worker's compensation reform.
Additionally, critics charged, he ran the most rigid
party apparatus since Senators Tom Platt and Roscoe
Conkling. The state legislature found Dewey dictatorial and hostile, while the press disliked and dogged
him. His greatest credibility problem was that he,
only two years into his term, had promised New York
voters he would be their governor for four years.
Dewey clearly was still a young man in a big hurry.

Nor was Dewey particularly liked by the party regulars. Cold, rigid, power-intoxicated, and a New

Yorker to boot, he generated considerable mistrust among the GOP's old guard. Even though he was an avid "anti-One Worlder," Dewey, in the opinion of Ohio senator Robert Alphonso Taft, was captive of "too much of the New York viewpoint." But Taft conceded that Dewey "was a very able fellow, even if difficult to get along with." The two men represented two at-odds wings of the party, Main Street versus Manhattan (even though Dewey was originally from Owosso, Michigan).

However, Republicans across the U.S. felt Dewey would take on the Democrats like the relentless prosecutor who had nailed Murder Inc., (the New York mob). They expected him to break up the "alphabet soup" of New Deal agencies. With his eye on the presidency, Dewey built a political machine of dedicated workers. Despite denials that he was a candidate, Dewey piled up delegates. His covert campaign was managed by Herbert Brownell, a corporate lawyer who had run his gubernatorial race; J. Russel Sprague, a Republican national committeeman; and Edwin F. Jaeckle, the New York State Republican chairman. They negotiated with party bosses from the forty-eight states in their Roosevelt Hotel headquarters in New York City. In addition to his Wisconsin victory over Willkie, Dewey attracted an amazing 156,000 write-in votes in the Pennsylvania primary. A Gallup poll, released on the eve of the convention, gave Dewey 65 percent of Republican support.

The Chicago convention was called to order at 10:00 A.M. on Monday, June 26, by Harrison E. Spangler of Iowa, chairman of the Republican National Committee. The national anthem was sung by Naomi Cook of the Chicago Light Opera Company and an invocation was delivered by Reverend John W. Holland, of the Little Brown Church of the Air on WLS radio. The convention itself was broadcast to a nation of radio listeners. Then delegates were welcomed by Illinois's Republican governor Dwight H. Green, who made a pitch, to hearty applause, for contributions to the $5 million goal of the Fifth War Loan Drive.

Governor Green, taking aim at President Roosevelt, warned, "The most serious threat to our liberties is the assumption by a small group that it possesses a monopoly on wisdom, goodwill, and social justice; a group that seeks to exercise arbitrary power over the legislative and judicial departments of government by its concentration in a domineering bureaucracy; that challenges the motives of those who differ with it on public issues; that appeals to the prejudices of the underprivileged and unthinking."

The governor completed his welcome while an Illinois delegate waved the state banner. Other states responded in kind. The Stadium's big pipe organ broke into a rendition of "God Bless America." When the delegates finally fell silent, Mrs. Clyde Bradley Corbin, chief of the Young Republicans, introduced the winner of its national essay contest winner on the noble topic of "Why the Republican Party Should Win." First prize went to Army Private First Class, Harry Reasoner of Minneapolis for his effort, "A First Voter Looks at the Republican Party." The crowd enthusiastically greeted the young army writer, not knowing that they were launching a national writing career for the man who one day would cover future conventions as a national television news anchor.

Unopposed, Governor Earl Warren of California was then elected as the convention's temporary chairman. The rest of the morning session was devoted to organizing various committees, before recessing until the evening. It took Chairman Spangler nearly ten minutes of gavel banging to quiet the evening crowd that had been singing popular songs with the opera company and house organ until 9:00 P.M.

Temporary Chairman Earl Warren then ascended the speaker's stand to make his keynote address. He advanced the patriotic theme of the night. "What is our job?" he inquired of the throng. "Ask any American. Ask the anxious American mother and father. Ask the anxious wives and sweethearts of our fighting men. Ask our fighting men themselves. They will tell you what our job is. They will give you the keynote for this convention . . . To get our boys home again, victorious and with all speed. To open the door for all Americans; to open it, not just to jobs, but to opportunity! To make and guard the peace so wisely and so well that this time will be the last time that American homes are called to give their sons and daughters to the agony and tragedy of war."

Warren continued for nearly an hour, touting a new kind of Republican vision for postwar harmony, domestic and foreign, and attacking the New Deal along the way.

> We believe the New Deal is leading us away from representative government . . . We believe the New Deal is destroying the two-party system. The New Deal is no longer the Democratic Party. It is an incongruous clique within that party. It retains its power by

Thomas E. Dewey, "boy prodigy," was the 1944 Republican convention choice to unseat FDR.
Chicago Historical Society.

patronizing and holding together incompatible groups. It talks of idealism and seeks its votes from the most corrupt political machines in the country.

He was constantly interrupted by cheers.

The leaders of its inner circle are not representatives of the people. They are personal agents of one man. Their appointments to public office are not made on the basis of efficiency or public approval, but on the basis of their loyalty to the clique only.

By the time Warren finished, the delegates were drained, though it was only 10:30 P.M.

Although delegates convened again at 10:30 A.M. on Tuesday, they spent an hour in the growing heat simply singing songs like "Home on the Range," "Dixie," "I've Been Working on the Railroad," and "Pass the Ammunition" with Frank Bennett and his Singers because committee reports were not yet

ready. Meanwhile, the temporary chairman brought the meeting's attention to two empty seats with a wreath denoting the absence of delegates from the Philippine Islands, under Japanese occupation.

The delegates came to attention when they heard from Colonel Carlos P. Romulo, aide-de-camp to General MacArthur. His presence was the general's only hope to stampede the convention.

Somewhere in the Southwest Pacific today is a man, an American, who first raised the banner of flaming courage over the fields of the Argonne; a man, this American, whose name was later sanctified because of his great leadership and heroism in leading the martyrs on the field at Bataan and at Corregidor; a man who, if he gets your support, yes your military support, if he gets the planes, ships, and material, will win today, not tomorrow. This man whose every act stands for courage and gives hope for victory, the great soldier, General Douglas MacArthur . . .

The delegates approved. The colonel ended:

> For my buddies, I, acting as their mouthpiece, ask
> you; For God's sake don't let them down! Don't let
> them down!

His plea resonated through the hall and across the radio wires of the nation, and many listeners shivered.

After another recess, the remainder of the morning session was spent in hearing organizational and committee reports. After a late afternoon recess, the party representatives rallied again to hear the report of the Committee on Resolutions, headed by Senator Robert A. Taft of Ohio. Six subcommittees, "with a full representation of ladies," had done most of the work in drafting a document. Senator Taft listlessly read the five thousand-word platform to the faithful congregation withering in the heat. It was a patriotic compromise meant to hold the center of a party split between internationalists like Willkie and isolationists like Taft. But Willkie, who had managed to get a copy of the document, had already released it to the press on June 26, condemning its international planks as inadequate.

War and peace were the first concerns.

> We declare our relentless aim to win the war against
> all our enemies . . . We shall seek to achieve such
> aims through organized international cooperation
> and not by joining a World State.

As for domestic policy, the 1944 Republicans declared,

> We shall devote ourselves to reestablishing liberty at
> home. We shall adopt a program to put men to work in
> peace industry as promptly as possible and with spe-
> cial attention to those who have made sacrifices by
> serving in the armed forces. We shall take government
> out of competition with private industry and termi-
> nate rationing, price fixing, and all other emergency
> powers. We shall promote the fullest stable employ-
> ment through private enterprise.

On taxation, the GOP promised,

> As soon as the war ends the present rates of taxation
> on individual incomes, on corporations, and on con-
> sumption would be reduced as fast as is consistent
> with the payment of the normal expenditures of gov-
> ernment in the postwar period. We reject the theory
> of restoring prosperity through government spend-
> ing and deficit financing.

What of women in the postwar economy? The 1944 Republicans favored "submission by Congress to the states of an amendment to the Constitution providing for equal rights for men and women. We favor job opportunities in the postwar world open to men and women alike without discrimination in rate of pay because of sex."

On the issue of racial and religious intolerance, the party piously declared, "We unreservedly condemn the injection into American life of appeals to racial or religious prejudice . . ."

Uncharacteristically, the 1944 Republican platform did not generate minority reports and was adopted with unanimous consent, despite Willkie's warning. Here, a potential fight between the party's governors and the Taft isolationists was averted. Days later, the press would condemn the platform as nothing but contradictory statements trying to appeal to every spectrum of the party. Dewey angrily defended his party's document.

After the Republican faithful finished congratulating themselves on common principles, Alf Landon, the 1936 Republican presidential nominee, was escorted to the stage and honored. He in turn presented the convention's permanent chair, Joseph W. Martin, Jr., of Massachusetts, who denounced the New Deal "bureaucrats" and warned "the day of reckoning is at hand."

On Tuesday night at 8:00 P.M. few seats could be found in the Stadium despite the unrelenting humidity. The evening's highlight was to be an address by a Republican with even more service than Landon, former President Herbert Hoover, who, the permanent chairman assured the delegates, "will be better appreciated as time passes on." Hoover was escorted to the podium as the entire hall loudly sang "The Battle Hymn of the Republic."

"We meet at a difficult time for a political convention," the former president began. "Millions of sons of both Republicans and Democrats are fighting and dying side by side for the freedom of mankind. But it is the part of freedom for which they are dying that we should carry on at home. Nothing could be a greater shock to freedom than for us to suspend the national election . . ." He gave greater credence to the unreasonable fear: "Tonight I propose to speak to you upon some larger forces which are contending in this world convulsion and the direction our country should take if freedom of men is to be preserved."

Hoover then outlined the nation's "170-year struggle for freedom" and the "degeneration of freedom in the United States" under Roosevelt. Hoover's solution was "a world in which freedom can live." The former president, a Dewey backer, argued that it was time for "a new generation" of leaders to take the reins of the Republican Party, that freedom was "the job of youth." He concluded his philippic by advising Republican youth,

> You have a great material heritage. You are receiving millions of farms and homes built by your forbearers. There have been prepared for you magnificent cities, great shops, and industries. But you have even a greater heritage. That is a heritage of religious faith, of morals, and of liberty. There is no problem which confronts the nation that you cannot solve within this framework.

When Hoover finished, "The Battle Hymn of the Republic," by now the convention's anthem, played as the crowd cheered their former leader.

Then party activist Clare Booth Luce addressed the gathering. The wife of *Time* magazine publisher Henry Robinson Luce delivered a patriotic zinger that proved she had a voice of her own. Luce detailed the military situation across the globe. She cynically wondered, "if this war might not have been averted . . . these are bitter questions . . . We Republican men and women are here to build a greater America not only for ourselves but for the millions of triumphant G.I. Joes who are fighting their way home to us." The crowd seconded her themes then spilled into the sultry streets and headed back to the lakefront in search of a breeze of any kind.

The convention was running like a Swiss clock. Potential problems had been minimized with Dewey emulating Hoover's convention control tactics. Wendell Willkie, for example, was prevented from speaking to the delegates. Dewey's handlers feared that he would again sweep to sudden victory, so powerful was this "barefoot Wall Street lawyer." On Wednesday morning, June 28, the Call of the Roll of States began.

Young Dwight Griswold, governor of Nebraska, was given the honor of nominating Dewey.

We are here to restore the presidency of the United States to the American people. We are here to bring Washington, D.C., back into the union . . . For that job we have the means and we have the man . . . As governor of New York State, what a job he has done. When he took over state government it was loaded down with the bureaucratic growth of twenty years. It was cluttered up with political hacks who after so long a time thought they had a vested interest in their jobs . . . The government of New York was revitalized until once more it is the effective servant of the people.

> In naming this man we are not merely choosing a candidate: we are choosing a nominee who cannot fail to win . . . I give to you as the nominee of the Republican Party, the spokesman of the future, Thomas E. Dewey.

Preprinted signs from New York reading "Dewey Will Win" and "Dewey, The People's Choice" waved like prairie grass in the summer wind. Dewey's mother, Annie, looked down with pride from the dignitaries' box in the stands. The Dewey demonstration lasted just seven minutes.

It was already 11:51 P.M., when Governor Bricker ascended the podium while the band struck up a chorus of "Beautiful Ohio," to withdraw his name.

> Mindful as I am to the devotion to the cause which I have tried to represent, of the many that are gathered here, I understand as you do, the overwhelming desire of this convention to nominate a great, a grand, a vigorous fighting young American, the noble, the dramatic, and appealing governor of the great State of New York, Thomas E. Dewey.

Bricker's loyalists were heartbroken.

Senator Joseph H. Ball of Minnesota, sensing the obvious, withdrew Commander Stassen's name. Illinois' Everett Dirksen, who had himself campaigned in twenty-seven states before the convention met, next spoke.

> This is indeed a happy and felicitous moment for me. I come here to help along the cause of Republicanism, which is true Americanism, and to volunteer the service of whatever talents I may possess to the great Republican ticket you have indicated your

desire to have, consisting of the wonderfully successful governor of New York.

Dewey was seconded by Governor Leverett
Saltonstall of Massachusetts, Congressman Leonard
W. Hall of New York, Patrick B. Prescott of Illinois,
and Rose Mayes of Idaho. Now Dewey's name stood
alone atop the party. Without ever openly campaigning for the post, Thomas E. Dewey received nearly
unanimous acclaim from his fellow Republicans. On
the first ballot, Dewey received 1,056 votes. The lone
holdout was Grant Ritter, a Beloit, Wisconsin, dairy
farmer who refused to budge from his support for
General MacArthur, shouting "I am a man, not a jellyfish." His intransigence didn't deter the convention, which let loose a genuinely enthusiastic
response. A band pitched in with "What Do We Do
on a Dew, Dew, Dewey Day?" Then they adjourned.

Dewey wanted Earl Warren to be his vice presidential partner, but arrogantly failed to consult the
future Supreme Court justice before the convention.
When he was finally approached, after Dewey won
the nomination, Warren refused, leery of taking the
second spot, particularly since he expected Roosevelt to win. Besides, Warren was not a rich man
and was worried about how he could support a
young family in Washington where the social scene
required a more lavish lifestyle than he lived in California. Neither was he willing to take a $5,000 pay cut
or play second fiddle. When he saw his nomination
for president was impossible, Warren instructed California's delegates to join the Dewey bandwagon.

Then Warren took a dig at Dewey by saying that
he was unavailable since he had promised to give
Californians a full four years. With Warren out of the
picture, delegates adopted Dewey's backup recom-
mendation and unanimously endorsed "Honest
John" Bricker as their vice presidential nominee. As a
Midwesterner and isolationist, Bricker balanced the
New Yorker's ticket.

Like Grant Ritter, Dewey was no jellyfish either.
He was about to wage a prosecutorial campaign
against Roosevelt that matched his reputation,
charging FDR with everything from coddling up to
communists, international and domestic, to assert-
ing in private that Roosevelt knew about the Pearl
Harbor invasion before it occurred and did nothing
to prevent it so he could join Britain in the war
against Hitler. He hammered away at the inefficiency

of the New Deal and the war itself for which Roosevelt had created 156 government agencies.

Meanwhile, Dewey and a private party of thirteen
followed the flight pattern Roosevelt had taken from
Albany to Chicago in 1932. Dewey left the governor's
mansion that afternoon as soon as he heard the
nomination on his radio. That evening he became
the first Republican nominee to directly address the
convention with an acceptance speech, again following the precedent of his opponent, Roosevelt. On
board the plane, the confident Empire State governor appeared immaculate, cool, and collected,
despite the heat wave. He sported a brand new suit
he had ordered from New York City a week earlier in
preparation for his "coronation." He rehearsed an
acceptance speech he had prepared for days. He was
ready to campaign against Roosevelt with the same
fervor and aggressiveness with which he had
indicted Legs Diamond ten years before.

A thunderstorm deluged Chicago, breaking the
intensity of the heat, just before Dewey landed in his
small plane. Inside the Stadium, twenty-five thousand Republicans listened to stump speeches as they
waited for the nominee to appear. Then just after
9:00 P.M. the lights dimmed and a spotlight caught
their determined leader as he emerged on stage. An
immense roar rocked the Stadium. Dewey bowed
and waved to every corner of the ocean of admirers.
Again the cheers hit a crescendo as Governor Bricker
and Dewey's wife, Frances, joined the nominee
before taking seats to listen to the man they had
selected to beat Roosevelt. The audience did not
know he was standing on a box to appear taller.

> I am profoundly moved by the trust you have placed
> in me. I deeply feel the responsibility which goes
> with your nomination for president of the United
> States at this grave hour of our nation's history . . .
> To Americans of every party I pledge a campaign
> dedicated to one end above all others, that this
> nation under God may continue in the years ahead
> a free nation of free men.

After discussing the military situation and his
resolve to quickly win the war, Dewey turned to his
Democratic opponent. "Does anyone suggest that
the present national administration is giving either
efficient or competent government?" Shouts of "No,
No," answered the animated candidate. "We have

not heard that claim made, even by its most fanatical supporters." The delegates laughed. "No, all they tell us is that in its young days it did some good things." More laughter. "That we freely grant, but it has grown old in office. It has become tired and quarrelsome. It seems that the great men who founded this nation really knew what they were talking about when they said that three terms were too many."

Applause answered Dewey again and again as he reached his conclusion.

It is the New Deal which tells us that America has lost its capacity to grow. We shall never build a better world by listening to those counsels of defeat . . . True, we now pass through dark and troubled times. Scarcely a home escapes the touch of dread and anxiety and grief. Yet in this hour the American spirit rises, faith returns, faith in our God, faith in our fellow man, faith in the land our fathers died to win, faith in the future, limitless and bright, of this, our country. In the name of that faith we shall carry our cause in the coming months to the American people.

The delegates and spectators reveled in his twenty-six minute acceptance speech. Here was a Republican who just might stop Roosevelt. Then, as promptly as he had appeared, Dewey disappeared again, whisked by his handlers back to the Stevens Hotel where he was mobbed by several thousand supporters. He waded through the ardent crowd shaking hands and exchanging words of gratitude. The next morning he bantered with a press corps of more than one hundred and dashed off to meetings with state delegations to discuss strategy. He also appointed Herbert Brownell as the new chairman of the Republican National Committee and Warner Schroder of Illinois, recommended by Colonel McCormick, as one of the four new vice chairmen. Then he flew back to Albany to launch his relentless attack against America's commander-in-chief.

Franklin Delano Roosevelt
1944 Democratic Presidential Nominee

Harry S Truman
1944 Democratic
Vice Presidential Nominee

Facts-at-a-Glance
★★★

Event:	Twenty-Ninth Democratic National Convention
Dates:	July 19–21, 1944
Building:	The Chicago Stadium
Location:	1800 West Madison Avenue
Chicago Mayor:	Edward Joseph Kelly, Democrat
Candidate for Renomination:	Franklin Delano Roosevelt, New York
Presidential Nominee:	Franklin Delano Roosevelt
Age at Nomination:	62
Number of Ballots:	1
Vice Presidential Nominee:	Senator Harry S Truman, Missouri
Number of Delegates:	1,176
Number Needed to Nominate:	A majority, 589
Largest Attendance:	40,000
Critical Issues:	Victory in Europe and Japan, an international approach to peace, civil rights
Campaign Slogan:	"Walk, Do Not Gallop to the Polls"
Campaign Song:	"Hail to the Chief"

19
★★★

The 1944 Democratic National Convention
Finishing the Job

The 1942 midterm elections exposed broad discontent with Roosevelt's New Deal. In 1932 when Roosevelt was first elected, nine million U.S. workers were unemployed. In 1942, despite the war effort, some ten million were still without jobs. By 1944 war rationing and inflation along with higher taxes were taking their toll. The threat of strikes increased in industry after industry. As a result, Republicans made big gains in the House of Representatives, leaving Democrats with just a nine-vote margin of control. In the Senate, the Democratic edge was a comfortable fifty-eight to thirty-seven. Still, the New Deal hung on because of one man.

Roosevelt devoted most of his energies in 1944 to the war effort. He traveled to meet troops on both fronts. When he was in Washington, he consulted with visiting world leaders. His efforts were rewarded domestically with renewed support at the polls. The president hinted at his intention to seek an unprecedented fourth term during his 1944 State of the Union Address on January 11, the eleventh he had delivered, though in the following months he refused to clearly declare his candidacy. He preferred to be courted again by the party's various constituencies. Besides, the polls showed big defections to the Republicans in November if Roosevelt was not the candidate. No other Democrat approached his stature. He had effectively derailed any potential spoilers along the way.

According to his aide James MacGregor Burns, Roosevelt's 1944 State of the Union speech was "the most radical in his life." The president called for new war taxes, price controls on food, and a national service law to prevent further wartime strikes. He also outlined his postwar domestic goals. "We cannot be content, no matter how high our standard of living might be," he inveighed, "if some fraction of our people, whether it be one-third or one-fifth or one-tenth, is ill-fed, ill-clothed, and insecure." He then called for

an economic bill of rights for all Americans, which included the right to a job that paid enough to provide for a family, the right for farmers to secure a livable price for their produce, the right of business people to trade without unfair competition, the right of a decent home for every family, the right to adequate medical care for all, the right to protection from economic fears of old age and sickness, and the right to a good education. The ideals of the New Deal were not dead. Roosevelt knew what kind of America he wanted to build after the war ended.

One June 6, 1944, the Allies stormed the beaches of Normandy, and the war tides shifted. That summer again brought dual conventions to Chicago. A month after the Dewey Republicans left town, Democrats streamed into the Windy City to renew their support for FDR. Only a week earlier, the president formally announced in a letter to national chairman Robert E. Hannegan of Missouri that he would be "a good soldier" and "reluctantly" accept his party's desire to renominate him for a fourth term. The decision was his. The opposition that had materialized against a third term was muted by the reality of world conflict. Roosevelt was waging war on behalf of the people of America and the world. There was no reason to doubt his leadership now when it shone the brightest since the early New Deal.

The convention opened on July 19 in the same building the Republicans used to anoint Dewey. But this time the Stadium was jammed. Mayor Edward J. Kelly welcomed delegates.

We're a city of neighborhoods, neighbors numbering almost four million persons who trace their ancestry to almost every nation on the globe; neighbors who, despite the fact that they speak sixty-two different dialects and stem from more than thirty different nationalities, have learned that only through united effort, through cooperation, working together, can their city expand and develop. In Chicago, labor and industry enjoy the most harmonious relations of any place in the world.

Then Kelly turned to the issues at hand.

I cannot help but compare the position of our nation in the world today with that of four years ago, when I had the privilege, as now, of opening the historic convention of that year . . . Four years ago Denmark and Norway had been invaded. Belgium and Holland were overrun. France had crumbled and her leaders were forced to sign an infamous pact of peace. Four years ago we were a nation still at peace, but it was a precarious peace that eventually would have destroyed us and added America to Hitler's then fast-growing list of slave nations . . . The whole world knows now that the tide of battle and world events has shifted in favor of the democracies under our farsighted and courageous leader, Franklin D. Roosevelt.

Illinois senator Scott Lucas added his greetings and argued, "This is the hour when America deserves the best. This is why the solemn verdict of a free and independent people will reelect for a fourth term the Honorable Franklin D. Roosevelt. Illinois was for Roosevelt in 1932. Illinois was for Roosevelt in 1936. Illinois was for Roosevelt in 1940. And Illinois will be for Roosevelt in 1944."

William L. Dawson, a veteran of World War I and Chicago's powerful African-American congressman, added his salutations.

In the midst of a terrible global war, we are called upon to present again to the American people candidates and principles to determine the fate of the civilized world. Today American citizens of every race and color and creed, American citizens from every section of our vast country, fight and die that our nation might live . . . The knowledge and experience gained by Democratic leaders in performing their duties of public affairs are a vital, valuable asset, too precious in these perilous times to be sacrificed on the altar of local or selfish or racial or sectional differences. Let us today, Democrats of America, join hands and hearts, concerning ourselves primarily with the great task of advancing and preserving Democracy in our nation and assuring lasting peace to a war-torn world.

Robert Kerr, governor of Oklahoma, served as temporary chairman and delivered a stirring keynote. "Our aim is complete and speedy victory. Our goal is a just and abiding peace. Our promise to a world at peace is responsibility and cooperation." Disputes in the rules committee led to revamping how delegates were apportioned to the states, based upon the number of Democratic voters, hence giving greater strength at future conventions to the South. The move was a payback for southern support during the 1936 convention in scrapping the two-thirds vote needed for nominating a presidential candidate. The Texas delegate dispute between two competing groups was solved on the convention floor by seating both delegations.

The Democratic platform of 1944 was a short one of just over one thousand words, mostly praising administration accomplishments, standing "on its record in peace and war." It argued for a strong postwar international organization to protect peace. Like the Republicans' platform, it endorsed the idea of a Jewish state in Palestine. But the convention was split on the historic issue of civil rights, a cause for which Eleanor Roosevelt had fought hard over the past decade. The northern and western wings of the party stood against the white supremacist South. The majority prevailed, declaring, "We believe that racial and religious minorities have the right to live, develop, and vote equally with all citizens, and share the rights that are guaranteed by our Constitution. Congress should exert its full constitutional powers to protect those rights."

On women's rights, the 1944 Democrats, like the Republicans, favored, "legislation assuring equal pay for equal work, regardless of sex. We recommend to Congress a constitutional amendment on equal rights for women." The delegates also voted for "federal aid to education administered by the states without interference by the federal government."

On the convention's second day, Senator Samuel D. Jackson of Fort Wayne, Indiana, was elected permanent chairman. "We meet in the firm belief that mankind is not doomed to a perpetual fear that each generation must send its millions to meet death in order to preserve liberty." That night the body turned to its main order of business, the renomination of the nation's commander-in-chief. Kentucky Senator Alben W. Barkley presented the president: "I come to the fulfillment of this assignment not simply as a Democrat, but as an American, seeking to promote the welfare of my country and the enduring happiness of her people." After reviewing Roosevelt's twelve years of accomplishments, Barkley concluded, "I present to this convention for the office of president of these United States the name of one who is endowed with the intellectual boldness of Thomas Jefferson, the indomitable courage of Andrew Jackson, the faith and patience of Abraham Lincoln, the rugged integrity of Grover Cleveland, and the scholarly vision of Woodrow Wilson, Franklin Delano Roosevelt." For the next half hour delegates devotedly demonstrated their support.

Vice President Henry A. Wallace heralded Roosevelt, "Not as vice president, as the chairman has indicated, but as chairman of the Iowa delegation, I am deeply honored to second the nomination of the greatest living American . . . The strength of the Democratic Party has always been the people, plain people like so many of those here in this convention" (here he was interrupted with cheers), "ordinary folks, farmers, workers, and businessmen along Main Street. Jefferson, Jackson, and Woodrow Wilson knew the power of the plain people. All three laid down the thesis that the Democratic Party can win only if and when it is the liberal party. Now we have come to the most extraordinary election in the history of our country. Three times the Democratic Party has been led to victory by the greatest liberal in the history of the U.S.

"President Roosevelt has long known that the Democratic Party, in order to survive, must serve men first and dollars second." Again wild cheers. Wallace concluded, ". . . in the cause of liberalism, and with a prayer for prompt victory in this war, permanent peace, and full employment, I give you Franklin D. Roosevelt."

The president was overwhelmingly renominated, although the vote was far from unanimous. Roosevelt swept to victory with 1,086 votes. But eighty-seven dissenting votes were cast for the budget-conscious Virginia senator Harry Flood Byrd, and one symbolic vote from the New York delegation went to former party chairman James A. Farley, who had challenged Roosevelt over a third term four years earlier and quit the New Deal.

That evening the convention listened as Helen Gahagan Douglas of California broadened Wallace's description of the party and mocked the Republi-

cans. "The Democratic Party is the true conservative party. We have conserved hope and ambition in the hearts of our people." She too was cheered. "We have conserved the skills of their hands. We have husbanded our national resources. We have saved millions of homes and farms from foreclosure and conserved the family stake in democracy." More cheers rang out. "We have rescued banks and trust companies, insured crops and people's savings. We have built schools. We have checked the flooding rivers and turned them into power. We have begun a program to free men and women from the nagging fear of unemployment, sickness, accident, and the dread of insecure old age." The convention whooped and hollered.

"We have turned a once-desolated, flood-ravished, poverty-stricken valley . . . into what is now a happy and productive place to live, the Tennessee River Valley. We have replanted the forest, refertilized the soil. Ours is the conservative party. We have guarded children, protected them by labor laws, planned school lunch programs, provided clinics. Ours is the party that has created laws which give dignity and protection to the valiant working men and women of this country. Ours is the party that has made the individual aware of the need of his participation in a true democracy. We are the conservative party. We have conserved the people's faith in a people's government, a democracy . . . And because we are the conservative party, we reject the hazy Republican dream that this country can get along with its government dismantled, its housing programs destroyed . . . They have no contact with the people or with the realities of their needs and wants." By the time she had finished, the convention was on its feet cheering her every utterance.

When order was at last restored, President Roosevelt delivered his fourth and final acceptance speech by radio from the San Diego Naval Base. He was on his way to Pearl Harbor.

I have already indicated to you why I accept the nomination you have offered me in spite of my desire to retire to the quiet of private life. It seems wholly likely that within the next four years our armed forces and those of our allies will have gained a complete victory over Germany and Japan sooner or later, and that the world will be at peace under a system, we hope, that will prevent a new World War.

(That very day, a continent away, Hitler narrowly escaped death in a bomb plot by some of his own military officers.)

In the last three elections, the people of the United States have transcended party affiliation. Not only Democrats but also forward-looking Republicans, and millions of independent voters have turned to progressive leadership, a leadership which has sought consistently and with fair success to advance the average American citizen who had been so forgotten during the period after the last war. I am confident that they will . . . look to that same kind of liberalism to build our economy for the future. I am sure that you will understand me when I say that my decision expressed to you formally tonight is based solely on a sense of obligation to serve if called upon to do so by the people of the United States.

Roosevelt then surveyed human history and the slow awakening of humanity to its own global existence.

The isolationists and the ostriches who plagued our thinking before Pearl Harbor are becoming slowly extinct. The people of America now know that all nations of the world, large and small, will have to play their appropriate part in keeping the peace by force, and in deciding peacefully the disputes which might lead to war. We all know how truly the world has become one . . . Some day soon, we will be able to fly to any other part of the world within twenty-four hours. Oceans will no longer figure as greatly in our physical defense as they have in the past. For our own safety and for our economic good, therefore, if for no other reason, we must take a leading part in the maintenance of peace and in the increase of trade among all nations of the world.

And that is why your government for many, many months has been laying plans and studying the problems of the near future. . . . preparing itself to act so that the people of the United States may not suffer hardships after the war, may continue constantly to improve its standards and join with other nations in doing the same.

Then the president turned to the war itself.

What is the job before us in 1944? To win the war, to win it fast, to win it overpoweringly . . . The people of the United States will decide this fall whether they wish to turn over this 1944 job, this worldwide job, to inexperienced or immature hands, to those who opposed Lend-Lease and international cooperation against the forces of aggression and tyranny, until they could read the polls of popular sentiment; or whether they wish to leave it to those who saw the danger from abroad, who met it head-on, and who have now seized the offensive and carried the war to its present stages of success, to those who have by international conferences and united actions have begun to build that kind of common understanding and cooperative experience which will be so necessary in the world to come.

When Roosevelt finished his radio address, the convention broke into hysterics as though he were standing in front of them, cheering the man who would win the war for America.

The only real drama in the Democratic wigwam was over who would be Roosevelt's vice president. By the time it was over, pundits were calling the Chicago assembly "a vice presidential convention." Henry Agard Wallace, the administration's idealistic liberal voice, wanted to retain the second spot, but opposition to the agriculturalist among big-city party bosses was strong. The South particularly objected to Wallace and his advocacy of unions and civil rights. But Wallace had loyal support of his own throughout the party, including the president's wife and organized labor. Roosevelt feared losing Wallace supporters if he replaced him. But party chairman Robert E. Hannegan and Edward J. Flynn of the Bronx, tried to convince Roosevelt that he faced a floor fight in Chicago over Wallace that could split the party wide open and possibly give Dewey the election in November.

But if not Wallace, who would Roosevelt select? The issue was a serious one since those around the president could see that his health was not robust. A week before the delegates gathered at the West Side wigwam, Roosevelt conferred with political bosses, including Mayor Ed Kelly of Chicago, in the White House and considered a little-known conservative senator from Missouri, Harry S Truman. All FDR's advisers agreed that Truman was the man who could least hurt Roosevelt's reelection hopes. Truman was unaware of the developments, although his name had been bandied about along with James Francis Byrnes and Senator Alben Barkley as possible replacements.

But Truman did not know Roosevelt well and had criticized wasteful practices in the war effort.

Meanwhile, Wallace was informed that Roosevelt was willing to let him go if need be. However, when meeting face to face, Roosevelt could not bring himself to dismiss his vice president and friend. Wallace argued that polls showed his popularity at more than 60 percent, much higher than any other Democrat in the nation except Roosevelt himself. Roosevelt denied he wanted a change and instead talked about a "really progressive" fourth term. Wallace offered to step aside if the president so desired, but managed to get a letter of endorsement, which Roosevelt sent to Senator Samuel Jackson of Indiana, the convention's permanent chairman, who read it to the delegates.

"The easiest way of putting it is this," the president explained: "I have been associated with Henry Wallace during his past four years as vice president, for eight years earlier while he was secretary of agriculture, and well before that. I like him and respect him, and he is my personal friend. For these reasons I would personally vote for his renomination if I were a delegate to the convention." Cheers arose among the many Wallace admirers. "At the same time," the president's note continued, "I do not wish to appear in any way as dictating to the convention. Obviously the convention must do the deciding . . ." Four years earlier, Roosevelt almost threatened to step down if the convention failed to declare for Wallace. Delegates could see the difference in 1944.

But Wallace, who was headquartered at the Sherman Hotel, had lined up labor support, particularly from the CIO and brought his fight to the wigwam. He appeared on the convention floor on the evening of the first day. Wallace was cheered for fifteen minutes

In July 1944 the Democrats convened to nominate Franklin Delano Roosevelt to an unprecedented fourth term as president. Chicago Historical Society.

by the delegates and spectators who saw him as champion of their progressive causes. And when he seconded Roosevelt's nomination the next day, shouts of "We Want Wallace" choked the stadium.

Former senator and supreme court justice James F. Byrnes of South Carolina, another close friend, was sometimes called Roosevelt's assistant president. He also sought Roosevelt's support. FDR confided to Byrnes that forces were mobilizing against Wallace and that he would probably fail in his bid for renomination. The president told him, "You're the best qualified man in the whole outfit, and you must not get out of the race. If you stay in, I'm sure you'll win it." But Byrnes had little credibility with labor or the National Association for the Advancement of Colored People and saw the forces aligning against him. Then someone leaked information that Byrnes had shed his native-born Catholicism for Episcopalism. Finally, after coming to Chicago, he stepped aside "in deference to the president's wishes." But he felt slighted by Roosevelt's ambiguous behavior.

Rumors swirled across the convention floor. Who did Roosevelt want? Wallace, who was wildly popular with most of the delegates, touted his letter of endorsement from the president. Some insiders said that party chairman Hannegan was carrying a second letter endorsing someone else. Speculation centered on the liberal Supreme Court associate justice William Orville Douglas, who operatives, such as Ed Kelly, thought would be the worst choice. Others named a quiet party loyalist, Missouri senator Truman. Wallace forces, under the floor management of Florida's junior senator, Claude Pepper, moved from delegation to delegation insisting their man was the only candidate Roosevelt had endorsed. Besides, Truman was a pawn of the Kansas City machine of Tom Pendergast, Wallace supporters argued, and therefore would not get labor votes.

But as soon as Roosevelt secured the nomination, Hannegan made public the second letter favoring Douglas or Truman. He had gotten the note when the president's train, on its way to California, secretly stopped on a side track in the Chicago railyards. Hannegan was later charged with altering the note's message by putting Truman's name above that of Douglas, reversing the president's preference. Big city bosses like Mayor Ed Kelly of Chicago and Ed Flynn of the Bronx went into action against Wallace while the southern delegations now had all the ammunition against the vice president that they

needed to win. Still, Truman had to be convinced. He had been working the delegates in favor of Byrnes and had agreed to place his Senate colleague's name in nomination before Byrnes withdrew.

Truman confided to the Missouri delegation that he was happy in the Senate and did not want to become vice president. When Truman was called to Hannegan's Blackstone suite, number 708–709, he was informed that Roosevelt wanted him. But he still declined. Roosevelt was on the phone with Hannegan who called Truman "the contrariest Missouri mule I've ever dealt with." Then Roosevelt told Hannegan to tell Truman, "If he wants to break up the Democratic Party in the middle of a war, that's his responsibility." Truman went along with the decision.

Delegates were caught in the middle of Roosevelt's vacillations; the floor fight was bitter. The situation was volatile for party unity as well. On Thursday night, July 20, the Stadium was packed to the rafters. Mayor Kelly had given away fifteen thousand extra tickets and the balcony, the floor, and the aisles were clogged with people. Wallace had stacked it as well. After the president's address, pressure began to mount to charge ahead with the vice presidential nominations. "We want Wallace, we want Wallace" filled the chamber. Hannegan began to panic, fearing Truman would lose if the vote was taken then. He looked for Mayor Kelly to help. The mayor then sprang into action. Kelly threw open the Stadium door, end even more people poured into the sweltering barn. Meanwhile, Claude Pepper rushed toward the podium, trying to get the attention of the chair so he could move that vice presidential nominations begin. But before he could get Senator Jackson to recognize him, Mayor Kelly convinced his fire marshall to declare the entire Stadium, with its forty thousand screaming delegates and spectators, to be a fire hazard. The meeting was abruptly adjourned before Pepper reached the podium, and Wallace's nomination was deferred.

The next night Chicago police and the Andy Frain ushers, acting on Mayor Kelly's orders, screened out thousands of Wallace supporters who again sought to pack the galleries as Willkie had done in 1940 to gain the Republican nomination. Frain himself made sure those who got in were scattered through the huge barn. Jack Brickhouse, who was broadcasting the convention for WGN radio, spotted what was happening. "Some of them were so far apart they had to signal each other with flashlights," he reported. Meanwhile Kelly brought in patronage workers to scream for Truman.

Senator Bennett Clark of Missouri nominated Truman.

> I propose to present . . . a man whose name, as Roscoe Conkling once said, rests not alone on things which are written or things said, but upon the arduous greatness of things done. I propose a man whose name is a household word in the United States by reason of his services in connection with the war as head of the great committee of the United States Senate that bears his name. I propose to present the name of a man, a lifelong liberal Democrat by inheritance as well as by conviction . . . the name of a man who is a superb soldier, and I can testify to that because I served in the same outfit with him . . . on behalf of the State of Missouri, I have the honor of presenting . . . the name of my colleague and friend, my old comrade in the army, the Honorable Harry S Truman.

His name evoked strong support, particularly in the galleries.

Then Judge Richard F. Mitchell of Iowa nominated Wallace.

> The Democratic Party does not give the vice presidency as a consolation prize. It has already given to the nation a vice president who sees clearly his role as a leader and a man of action. He did not sit idly by and let his commander-in-chief carry the whole burden of the war forced upon us by treacherous foes. No! Instead he became the special messenger of the president, taking the American way of life to the homes of our great allies, to the Russians, to the Chinese, to our neighbors of the southern continent.

The judge further argued, "Henry Wallace is a man who believes in the system of free enterprise at a time when that system is challenged all over the world. We have in him a staunch defender. But by the system of free enterprise, he does not mean the freedom of the powerful to dominate or crowd out their weaker brothers." The line drew heavy applause from labor. "He does not mean that the accumulation of wealth should be allowed to curb the enterprising spirit of those who are not so fortunate. He knows that in our complex, modern civilization, we need vigilance in order to maintain our freedom." He concluded, "I am giving you a man . . . who is the choice of the people by every

poll taken . . . Henry A. Wallace of Iowa." The demonstration following was one of the wildest of the week.

Senator John H. Bankhead of Alabama, Senator Joseph C. O'Mahoney of Wyoming, Senator Scott Lucas of Illinois, former Governor Paul V. McNutt of Indiana, Senator Alben W. Barkley of Kentucky, Michigan Supreme Court Justice Frank Murphy, Governor Joseph Melville Broughton of North Carolina, Governor Robert S. Kerr of Oklahoma, Governor Prentice Cooper of Tennessee, and Senator Elbert D. Thomas of Utah were all nominated as well for the second spot.

Wallace took the first ballot lead over Truman, 429 1/2 to 319 1/2 with 589 needed to win the nomination. The ten favorite sons split the rest. On the second ballot, Roosevelt's influence came to the fore as Kelly and other party leaders instructed state delegations how to vote. Truman surged to victory behind the big-city boss pressure. Even though labor supporters screamed in protest, the CIO forces of Sidney Hillman were pushed aside. Truman, the "Missouri Compromise," would be vice president of the United States. The next day, Wallace left town on a train from the LaSalle Street Station, alone and feeling betrayed.

Dewey was painted into a corner before the campaign even began. The advance of Allied troops made criticism of Roosevelt's war effort impossible. At the same time, it was evident that victory would not be achieved until after November, and most voters were reluctant to abandon their commander-in-chief while the battle raged. Instead, Dewey and his surrogates hinted at the president's poor health and the possibility that he could not finish his term. A bronchial infection had caused Roosevelt to lose fifteen pounds in the spring before the convention. He looked sick and drawn throughout the summer of his fourth presidential campaign. He fit the profile Dewey drew of an administration of "tired old men."

During the summer months Roosevelt and his friends lightly laughed at Dewey—he was five-feet eight-inches tall—who had "thrown his diaper into the ring" and spent nights "pacing up and down, under his bed." But the fiery Republican could not be taken lightly. By the end of summer, a Gallup poll showed Dewey running even with Roosevelt. The president complained that Dewey had taken after him like he was a common crook. Dewey charged the president with perpetuating the depression, sending the U.S. into deep debt, violating the

Constitution, and turning American democracy into one-man rule at a time when the nation was fighting totalitarianism around the world. Despite these charges, some old-line Republicans still accused Dewey of being too close to Roosevelt on domestic issues, guilty of "me-too-ism."

Roosevelt had his own machine in states across the country and the accumulated power of incumbency. Labor was with him, despite the defection of John L. Lewis of the United Mine Workers, who was seething over Roosevelt's anti-strike legislation. Sidney Hillman directed the PAC (Political Action Committee) of the CIO, spending hundreds of thousands of dollars in support of Roosevelt and sending scores of organizers to factories across the land to get out the Roosevelt vote. But Dewey made Hillman himself an issue in the campaign. When the *New York Times* reported that Roosevelt had told subordinates working on the vice presidential selection, "to clear everything with Sidney," the quote became a taunting refrain among Republicans who hoped to imply that Roosevelt was controlled by unseen Jewish influences.

With Dewey's approval, the phrase, "clear everything with Sidney," was repeated thousands of times by Republican publicists. Despite condemnation from leading newspapers, the tactic was not withdrawn. By the end of the election, the Republican strategy had been reduced to attacks on the "Hillman/Browder Axis," further implying a communist conspiracy. Unfortunately for Dewey, the approach clearly smacked of fascism, and the American people knew it. Dewey was practicing the strong-armed tactics of tin-horn dictators.

Twenty-four Republican governors and congressmen, including Dirksen of Illinois, were sent speeches that Dewey's managers demanded be delivered verbatim. Governor Green of Illinois, Baldwin of Connecticut, and Earl Warren simply refused to spout the party line, much to the campaign's displeasure. Wherever he went, Dewey conveyed a sense of rigidity that permeated his campaign. Spontaneous events were impossible, because every stop, every speech, every action was calculated to the second. Dewey was obsessed with orderliness.

Despite early blunders, Dewey caught fire, traveling by train from coast to coast, delivering rapid-fire speeches to growing crowds. "This is a campaign against an administration which was conceived in defeatism, which failed for eight straight years to restore our democratic economy, which has been the most wasteful, extravagant, and incompetent administration in the history of the nation, and, worst of all, which has lost faith in the American people," Dewey shouted. Now people listened to his theme, "It's Time for a Change."

Both Roosevelt and Dewey competed for Wendell Willkie's support, but the great "One Worlder" played coy until October when he suddenly died of an infection and heart problems, casting a shadow over the campaign. Finally, in the last six weeks of the race, Roosevelt was spurred to action. The negative slogan of a commander-in-chief, "Don't change horses in midstream," was not enough to stem the Dewey momentum. Instead of attacking Dewey, whom he ignored, Roosevelt simply took on Herbert Hoover again, linking Dewey to his predecessor's policies, warning that Republicans could again bring the downfall of the economy. He went on a speaking tour and talked to voters over the radio. He easily projected the personal warmth and charm that had so reassured his fellow citizens during the darkest hours of the Great Depression. Roosevelt told voters that he "got quite a laugh" at the Republican platform calling for progressive labor legislation, after they had fought so hard against it.

And of course he injected his special brand of humor and ridicule. At the end of one broadcast, he told listeners that he really didn't mind all the Republican mudslinging against him personally, but he did take exception with their attacks on his "little dog Fala." The president had been falsely accused of sending a battleship to bring home the Scotch terrier from the Pacific Aleutian Islands. The public loved it and felt Dewey was petty and cold-hearted. (The dog trick was a maneuver that vice presidential nominee Richard Nixon successfully duplicated in his famous 1952 "Checkers Speech.")

By the end of October the Gallup poll showed the two candidates neck and neck. Democrats urged their voters to "Walk, Do not Gallop, to the Polls." Late in October, after a speech at Ebbets Field for Senator Robert Wagner of New York, Roosevelt even rode through New York City in a convertible during a torrential rainstorm to show voters he was not "a tired old man." Two million New Yorkers cheered him along his four-borough parade. A week later, he told tens of thousands of Chicagoans packed into Soldier Field that he would implement his "Economic Bill of Rights" as soon as the U.S. won the war.

During the campaign's final week, defections hit the Republicans. Minnesota senator Joseph H. Ball, who had nominated Stassen, endorsed Roosevelt because he didn't believe Dewey was spouting anything but rhetoric on the vital international issues. On election eve, after "the meanest campaign" of his life, Roosevelt delivered an elegant radio prayer to the nation, asking "Almighty God" for protection for American troops and to "make the whole people of this land equal to our high trust, reverent in the use of freedom . . . Make us ill content with the inequalities of opportunity which still prevail among us."

On November 7, 1944, while the president relaxed at his Hyde Park, New York, estate, it was the same old story for the Republicans. Dewey drew twenty-two million votes to Roosevelt's twenty-five million yet failed to match Willkie's totals of four years earlier. Roosevelt controlled the large cities and industrial states, Dewey won in the small towns and the countryside. But in the electoral college, it was another Roosevelt landslide, 432 to 99. Once again, the Democrats retained their majority status, and the celebrations were satisfying. No one knew, of course, that just five months later, on April 12, 1945, Franklin Delano Roosevelt would die suddenly of a massive brain hemorrhage. His vice president, Harry S Truman, selected in the Chicago wigwam, was left to win the war and battle Dewey once again three and a half years later. One could speculate about the fate of the world had it not been for one Chicago fire marshall.

Dwight David Eisenhower
1952 Republican Presidential Nominee

Richard Milhous Nixon
1952 Republican
Vice Presidential Nominee

Facts-at-a-Glance
★★★

Event:	Twenty-Fifth Republican National Convention
Dates:	July 6–11, 1952
Building:	The Stockyards International Amphitheatre
Location:	4300 South Halsted Street
Chicago Mayor:	Martin H. Kennelly, Democrat
Candidates for Nomination:	General Dwight David Eisenhower, Kansas; General Douglas MacArthur, Arkansas; Governor Theodore McKeldin, Maryland; former Governor Harold Edward Stassen, Minnesota; Senator Robert Alphonso Taft, Ohio; Governor Earl Warren, California
Presidential Nominee:	Dwight David Eisenhower
Age at Nomination:	61
Number of Ballots:	1
Vice Presidential Nominee:	Richard Milhous Nixon, California
Number of Delegates:	1,206
Number Needed to Nominate:	A majority, 604
Largest Attendance:	16,000
Critical Issues:	Credentials of disputed delegates, internationalism versus isolationism, conservative wing of GOP versus liberal wing
Campaign Slogan:	"We Like Ike"
Popular Song:	"The Sunshine of Your Smile"

20
★★★

The 1952 Republican National Convention

A House Divided

Five-star General Dwight David Eisenhower, the world's greatest living soldier, had been supreme commander of Allied forces in their victory over Nazi Germany in World War II. Courted by both the Democratic and Republican parties to be their presidential candidate in 1948, the general told his would-be supporters, "My decision to remove myself completely from the political scene is definite and positive." When Thomas E. Dewey, the Republican presidential candidate in 1948, managed through towering overconfidence to lose to incumbent Harry S Truman, however, Eisenhower's prospects were altered, and he began to look cautiously toward the 1952 race. America was feeling good and growing. But a shadow darkened the horizon with the H-bomb. America needed a hero, and it wasn't ready to disarm just because the Nazis had been vanquished.

After World War II ended, "Ike," as he was familiarly known, had written a best-selling book about his wartime experiences, then put in several lackluster years as president of Columbia University. The kindest judgment of his term at Columbia was that he was not a bad president because he was no president at all. In 1950, still a five-star general of the army, Eisenhower was ordered by President Truman to assume the post of supreme commander of the North Atlantic Treaty Organization. From NATO headquarters in Europe early in 1952, Eisenhower issued a statement of his political intentions: "Under no circumstances will I ask for relief from this assignment in order to seek nomination for political office, and I shall not participate in activities of others who may have such an intention with respect to me."

This statement was for public consumption. Privately, the general had been participating in political activities for some time, and his participation intensified as the Republican national convention drew nearer. At the prompting of his many wealthy friends in business, financial, and legal circles—and his own

ambition—he had determined to become a full-fledged candidate for the Republican nomination for president.

His chief rival for the nomination was Senator Robert A. Taft of Ohio, "Mr. Republican," leader of the Grand Old Party's Midwest conservative wing, who had officially announced his own candidacy in October 1951. The son of William Howard Taft, twenty-seventh president of the United States, Taft was a graduate of Yale University and Harvard Law School. He was a bitter foe of the Democrats' New Deal and Fair Deal and, unlike Dewey, the leader of the GOP's Eastern, liberal wing, Taft advocated a complete break from Democratic domestic and foreign policies.

Taft's chief interest was in domestic policy, where he favored less government spending, less bureaucracy, less economic planning, and fewer restraints on business. On these matters, Eisenhower's views and Taft's were similar. Both men were also concerned that labor unions were abusing their power. Eisenhower looked with favor on Taft's tough anti-labor bill, the Taft-Hartley Act.

In foreign policy the two men were at opposite ends of the spectrum. Taft did not believe the United States should seek to impose American democratic institutions on other countries nor should it commit the country's resources abroad. He believed there were limits to American power. In 1949, for example, he opposed the North Atlantic Treaty (which fathered NATO). For his views on foreign policy, Taft was branded by many as an isolationist. Eisenhower, on the other hand, because of his service abroad in World War II and with NATO and his backing by the Eastern wing of the GOP, was considered an internationalist in foreign affairs.

In late June 1950 North Korea sent its troops into South Korea. President Truman responded by coming to the aid of South Korea with U.S. troops, but he did so without first obtaining the consent of the Congress. Truman's unauthorized "police action" greatly angered Taft and other conservative Republicans. In late 1950 Chinese forces joined those of North Korea and as their combined armies began to roll southward, many Americans became disturbed about the encroachments of communism not only in Korea but also throughout the world and, perhaps, at home. Capitalizing on the country's unease, Senator Joseph McCarthy of Wisconsin made headlines and gained strong support nationally, especially among conservative Republicans, with repeated charges of "twenty years of treason" by the Democrats and his attacks on "communists in the state department" and finally on General George C. Marshall, Eisenhower's wartime commander and former secretary of state and of defense. As secretary of state, Marshall devised and administered the Marshall Plan, which brought economic relief to war-ravaged Europe.

Taft endorsed McCarthy's strident, largely unsubstantiated charges. Eisenhower made no public statements on this issue or on President Truman's recall for insubordination of General Douglas MacArthur from command in Korea in April 1951. MacArthur had been Eisenhower's peacetime commanding officer. Taft heatedly denounced MacArthur's recall, claiming that it proved that the Democrats did not want to win the war in Korea. Beginning in 1951 the Taft organization worked assiduously to line up delegates to the 1952 convention. By February 1952 it had 450 delegates pledged to Taft with another 70 or so likely. Eisenhower's volunteer clubs throughout the country had secured him about the same number of delegates, leaving roughly 300 unpledged. It would take 604 votes to win the nomination.

Eisenhower's backers became insistent that he return to the states to campaign for the support of these 300 delegates and to put to rest the many ugly rumors Taft's supporters were circulating about Eisenhower's personal life and about his wife, Mamie. After issuing his annual report, Eisenhower resigned from his NATO assignment, and on June 1 he and Mamie returned to the United States.

The strategy of the Republican image-makers was to present him as a simple country boy, an image the five-star general, national hero, and worldwide celebrity was still able, with the aid of his boyish, winning grin, to project. On June 2 Eisenhower returned to his hometown of Abilene, Kansas, and

spoke to the crowd: "I ask you this one question: If each of us in his own mind would dwell more upon those simple virtues, integrity, courage, self-confidence, an unshakable belief in the Bible, would not some of these problems tend to simplify themselves? . . . I think it is possible that a contemplation, a study, a belief in those simple virtues would help us mightily." Two nights later he gave his first nationally televised political speech and more or less repeated the same simple counsel.

In the next few weeks, from headquarters in Denver (chosen so he could disassociate himself in the public's mind from the Eastern wing of the GOP), Ike campaigned throughout the Midwest, Texas, and New York. Although rejecting Taft's isolationist stance on foreign affairs, he embraced his rival's domestic views, sometimes even positioning himself farther right than Taft himself. Ike opposed socialized medicine, wage and price controls, and called for "sound fiscal practices and integrity in government." He also strongly supported the United Nations and opposed the Taft-MacArthur proposals for a military victory in Korea.

But as the summer wore on, Taft accumulated more than five hundred pledged delegates to Ike's four hundred. Ike's managers, from the Eastern, Dewey wing of the party, realized early they would still have to wrest sixty or seventy of Taft's delegates from him and for their own candidate. They disputed seventeen delegates from Georgia, thirteen from Louisiana, and thirty-eight from Texas. Subsidized by Texas oil barons, Eisenhower's supporters went to work in the Lone Star state, and on May 3 thousands of Democrats in 185 Texas precinct conventions crossed over to vote as Republicans to endorse Eisenhower as their candidate. At the state convention at Mineral Wells on May 27, however, the state chairman (a Taft supporter) ruled that the Eisenhower delegates were not truly Republicans and, thus, excluded them. He ruled that only Taft supporters were qualified to attend the national convention in Chicago.

Ike's managers reacted with appropriate shock and outrage to what they called a "steal" and sent their candidate out to portray a morally offended man. "The rustlers stole the Texas birthright instead of Texas steers," Ike declared in a Dallas speech. On a campaign tour of the Great Plains he denounced corrupt political practices and politicians who "stirred people up." He also dismissed the "scary talk about Russia." If all Americans pulled together, he said, Russia was no more to be feared "than there is to fear polliwogs swimming down a muddy creek."

In his campaign speeches, Taft depicted Eisenhower as a "me-too" front man for the Dewey-led, liberal, internationalist, Eastern wing of the party. As for the disputed delegates from Texas, Louisiana, and Georgia, Taft knew that he controlled the Republican National Committee, which would play an important role in seating delegates, and he knew that his campaign had momentum going for it.

Former president Herbert Hoover, a Taft supporter, offered Ike's campaign manager, Senator Henry Cabot Lodge Jr. of Massachusetts, a compromise in which Hoover and two other "eminent persons" would mediate the delegate dispute. Lodge disdainfully rejected Hoover's offer, remarking loftily that, "It is never right to compromise with dishonesty." Lodge then put forth what he called the "Fair Play Amendment," an amendment to Republican rules that would deny the national committee the right to seat delegates on a temporary basis. If the Taft-controlled national committee were divested of this right, the Taft delegates from Texas, Louisiana, and Georgia might not be seated even temporarily and therefore could not join the other Taft delegates on the floor to vote themselves permanent seats. Such a rule would have allowed Teddy Roosevelt to win against Taft's father in 1912. But if the full convention endorsed the Fair Play Amendment, then Ike's delegates, together with delegates pledged to various favorite sons, who also wanted to thwart Taft, would have a majority. Instructed to flash his seldom publicly displayed but nevertheless famous temper, Eisenhower angrily proclaimed he would "roar out across the country for a clean, decent convention. The American people deserve it."

Meanwhile, Dewey controlled New York's delegation, which leaned toward the Fair Play Amendment. Harold Stassen, the former governor of Minnesota and quadrennial seeker of the GOP presidential nomination, promised that delegates pledged to him would vote for Fair Play. Ike's forces also needed the pivotal votes of California's large delegation. California's favorite son, Governor Earl Warren, opposing Taft's politics, was hoping for a deadlock between Taft and Eisenhower that would secure himself the candidacy. Thus, a month before the convention Senator Lodge approached California's junior senator, Richard M. Nixon (who was pledged to Warren), and hinted that

Nixon was being seriously considered for the vice presidential slot on Eisenhower's ticket. In New York, Dewey also repeated this likelihood to the thirty-nine-year-old Nixon, who as a member of the House Committee on Un-American Activities had crafted an impeccable record of red-baiting anticommunism.

Dazzled by the vice presidential carrot that had been dangled before him, Nixon indignantly denounced the "Texas grab." Then, privately, on the train from California to the convention in Chicago, he worked on the California delegates individually with threats and promises. In Chicago, in a stormy state caucus, Nixon wrested control of the California delegation from Warren's people. (From that time forward Warren supporters equated the name "Nixon" with "treachery.")

Just before the convention officially opened on July 6, Taft had 530 delegates pledged to his candidacy (including 72 contested); Eisenhower had 427 (21 contested); Warren, 76; and Stassen, 25. Twenty were scattered among other candidates, including MacArthur, and 118 remained uncommitted.

General MacArthur was to be the keynote speaker, and Hoover and McCarthy would give major addresses. The chair, Joe Martin of Massachusetts, was a Taft supporter. Taft was optimistic about his prospects. To indicate his good faith, he offered a compromise: He would split the Texas delegation with Eisenhower—16 to Ike, 22 for himself—which would mean 8 less than he already had.

"Gee, that sounds good," Eisenhower said when told of Taft's offer. "That's swell." But his campaign manager, Lodge, immediately recognized the trap and rejected the compromise. As he patiently explained to the general, Taft's offer, if accepted, would deprive Ike of the high moral ground of charging that delegates had been stolen by Taft. Worse, acceptance would give Taft enough strength to win on the credentials challenges of other delegates. As tactfully as he could, Lodge told Eisenhower that he had been naive and foolish and asked him to refrain in the future from commenting on political maneuvering.

On July 5, 1952, Eisenhower arrived in Chicago and established his headquarters in the Blackstone Hotel. In two adjoining suites he met state delegations—first in one suite with one delegation, then to the other with another delegation—back and forth, almost nonstop. His pitch was the same to all: What happened to him as an individual was of no consequence; what

General Douglas MacArthur delivers the keynote speech at the Republican National Convention at the Stockyards International Amphitheatre, 1952. Chicago Historical Society.

was of "paramount importance" was the principle of Fair Play. Mamie was at his side, smiling.

The 1952 Republican presidential convention was the first national political convention to be televised live gavel to gavel. As the convention opened, a seemingly detached Eisenhower remained in his air-conditioned Blackstone suites. In the Stockyards International Amphitheatre, originally built in 1934, temperatures reached 100 degrees. The "Temple of Agriculture," as the amphitheatre was originally called, had cost $8 million and replaced an original building that had burned down. Ike had his own furnished suite there, but most of Eisenhower's time was spent reminiscing in the Blackstone with his four brothers about the good old days growing up in Abilene. Occasionally he watched the television screen—Herbert Hoover delivering his reverently received speech; Douglas MacArthur giving a long-winded, bombastic, and right-wing keynote address.

Dewey, who always seemed to be caught by the television cameras smiling toothily beneath his mustache, ostensibly divided the party by ordering the New York delegation to boycott MacArthur's address.

Five hundred and thirty-two Taft supporters marched into the Amphitheatre on opening day, July 6, singing "Onward, Christian Soldiers," as if walking arm in arm into battle. Joseph McCarthy was introduced as "Wisconsin's fighting marine," who had been attacked for "exposing the traitors in our government," which touched off a wild, adulatory demonstration. "Tail Gunner" Joe, as he was sometimes called, claimed he had survived fourteen bombing missions during the war. By 1947 that number had risen to seventeen, by 1951, thirty-two. He also claimed to have won a purple heart. He hadn't. (However, in 1943 he did meet and befriend a young navy lieutenant named John Kennedy, who had just returned to active duty after the sinking of PT-109.)

Eisenhower had by now learned enough to know that, if he wanted to win, he could and should leave everything to his managers, who acted as the peacetime equivalent of his wartime staff. Broad strategical moves were dictated by Dewey to Lodge; to Sherman Adams, governor of New Hampshire; to Herbert Brownell, a New York City lawyer; and to retired general Lucius Clay, now chairman of Continental Can. It appeared to many that Eisenhower was little more than a figurehead, that he did the bidding of his more powerfully-willed backers and their designates unquestioningly. During the convention, at least, the general did little to dispel this growing impression.

By the time the issue of the disputed delegates came before the convention as a whole, the national public began to think of the delegates' dispute in black-and-white terms: Taft and his supporters, in trying to "steal" the nomination, were defying the will of the people with an immoral act. Although the majority of the delegates to the convention were old guard Republicans who supported Taft, they shuddered at the possibility of giving even the appearance of condoning such tactics. By a vote of 658 to 548 the delegates rejected an amendment proposed by Taft forces to allow contested delegates to vote on all credentials challenges except their own. Then they passed the Fair Play Amendment by voice vote. (In 1912 Teddy Roosevelt had failed on both fronts and lost the nomination.) Eisenhower's managers then won on the Georgia challenge 607 to 531. The Louisiana and Texas challenges were settled in Ike's favor without a vote. The momentum no longer belonged to Taft.

Before the Fair Play vote, Taft needed about seventy votes beyond those already pledged to him to gain the nomination. Afterward, he needed 120. Harry Truman remarked with a smile after the 658-548 vote, "I am afraid that my favorite candidate is going to be beaten."

Maryland's twenty-four votes, pledged to favorite son Governor Theodore McKeldin, were released, with Eisenhower getting sixteen. The governor was selected to give Ike's nomination speech on national television. On the second and third days of the convention Eisenhower's managers secured majorities in the previously uncommitted delegations of Pennsylvania and Michigan. Taft lost thirteen New York delegates when Dewey reminded the thirteen that he had a "long memory." On the convention floor bitter words were spoken by the outflanked old guard. Dewey was attacked as the mastermind behind Ike's campaign and characterized as "the most cold-blooded, ruthless, selfish political boss in the United States today."

During the televised debates on the contested delegates, Senator Everett Dirksen of Illinois leaned over the podium and pointed an accusing finger at Dewey, who was seated with the New York delegation. Dirksen observed that the GOP "had a habit of winning conventions and losing elections." He charged Dewey with taking the GOP "down the path to defeat." Dewey's adherents loudly booed Dirksen. Taft delegates loudly booed Dewey. Fist fights broke out on the floor. A national television audience of one million Americans watched the televised convention and had its first taste of American political violence. The thirty-five hundred television, radio, and print journalists were there to relay every detail.

On the morning of Friday, July 11, at the end of the first ballot, Eisenhower was nine votes short of victory, with 595. Taft had 500; Warren, 81; Stassen, 20; and MacArthur, 10. The ever-hopeful Harold Stassen detected the possibility of a Taft-Eisenhower deadlock in this vote and thus a chance for himself. But the chair of the Minnesota delegation, Senator Edward Thaw, forestalled him. When Thaw raised his arm and was recognized by the chair, he shifted Stassen's nineteen Minnesota votes to Eisenhower. Dwight Eisenhower was now officially the party's nominee. Taft's legions had lost, but 281 of them (212 from the Midwest) refused to make Eisenhower's nomination unanimous. Finally, Taft's campaign manager, Senator John Bricker of Ohio, told them they must.

The selection of a vice presidential candidate offered the Eisenhower camp an opportunity to heal the deep split in the Grand Old Party by choosing someone from the old guard: Taft himself, perhaps, or Taft's recommendation, Dirksen. They didn't take it. Dewey and Brownell suggested Nixon as a running mate, and Ike, who barely knew Nixon, shrugged his assent.

Senator McCarthy met with the general the next day. McCarthy had called Eisenhower's wartime commanding officer, General George C. Marshall, part of "a conspiracy so immense, an infamy so black, as to dwarf any in the history of man." Marshall would, McCarthy charged, "sell his grandmother for any advantage." Eisenhower continued to say nothing in rebuttal to these libels, causing many liberals and moderates who supported him, as well as his former military comrades-in-arms to wonder what ailed America's most famous war hero. Emerging from Eisenhower's rooms at the Blackstone, McCarthy was asked if he was pleased with the ticket. He responded, "I think Dick Nixon will make a fine vice president."

The party's platform, accepted by a voice vote of the convention, was essentially a conservative, right-wing document, but it managed by its vagueness and ambiguities to avoid antagonizing the GOP's liberal (and victorious) wing. Its weakest section was on civil rights. Reserving to "each state to order and control its own domestic institutions" and proving its "good faith" by promising "federal action toward the elimination of lynching," the party essentially wrote off the African-American vote that had been courted and won by the New Deal two decades earlier.

Because he did not want to further alienate the old guard, Eisenhower largely accepted the party's platform as it stood but he did insist that it include an endorsement of NATO. He avoided the issue of foreign policy altogether in his acceptance speech. "I know something of the solemn responsibility of leading a crusade," he told the convention (his book about his World War II experiences had been titled *Crusade in Europe*). "I accept your summons. I will lead this crusade." Nixon's acceptance speech was notable for its fulsome praise of Taft.

Eisenhower began his "ad agency" campaign six weeks later with a whistle-stop train swing through the South. His speeches were dull, however; he read them badly, and they were poorly received. A front-page editorial of the Scripps-Howard newspapers proclaimed that "Ike is running like a dry creek."

On September 12 Ike met with Taft for breakfast in Morningside Heights, New York. Taft brought along a statement he had composed dismissing differences between his own and Eisenhower's foreign policy stands as matters of "degree" only and stating that the real issue was "liberty against creeping socialism." Eisenhower approved the statement, and it was given to reporters. Only then did Taft begin to urge his many supporters, who had been holding back, to work for Ike.

Nixon had been conducting a slam-bang assault on the Democrats, promising his audiences that Ike's "crusade" would rid Washington of crooks and communists. On September 18 the *New York Post*'s front-page headline read:

SECRET RICH MEN'S TRUST FUND KEEPS NIXON IN STYLE FAR BEYOND HIS SALARY

The charge was that Nixon had accepted an $18,000 "slush fund" from wealthy California oilmen, bankers, and businessmen.

Eisenhower's managers panicked. Almost all, except Dewey, advised the candidate to drop Nixon from the ticket. The old guard of the party, however, demanded that Eisenhower stand by his running mate. For three days Eisenhower refused to phone Nixon. When he finally did he advised him to explain the fund on television; then, Ike said, depending on the public's response, he would decide whether or not he should continue as his vice presidential candidate. "There comes a time in matters like this," Nixon responded, "when you've either got to [expletive deleted] or get off the pot." There was a long silence. No one had ever talked to Dwight Eisenhower like that. Ike never forgave it.

On September 23 Nixon appeared on national television before the largest audience to that date ever assembled on living room couches. He mentioned his wife's "Republican cloth coat." ("Pat doesn't have a mink coat.") He declared that, no matter what, he was not returning one gift his family had received: a little cocker spaniel, Checkers, that his daughters loved. (After all, a dog had worked for FDR in his "Fala" speech.) Public response was overwhelmingly supportive, at least among Republicans. The next night Eisenhower met Nixon's plane when it landed in Wheeling, West Virginia, put his arm around his running mate, and said, "You're my boy!"

Eisenhower's critics within and outside the party were still concerned about his silence on Senator McCarthy's attacks on General George C. Marshall. Ike was scheduled to give an address in Milwaukee, and he asked his speechwriters to prepare a paragraph praising Marshall, a tribute he could deliver, he said, "right in McCarthy's back yard."

The old guard in Wisconsin learned of the intended rebuke and pressured Ike's managers to have it removed from the speech. Copies of the address had been distributed to reporters, however, and when Eisenhower began to speak in Milwaukee on October 3, as McCarthy stood behind him on the platform, they waited expectantly for Ike to praise Marshall "as a man and as a soldier, . . . dedicated with singular selflessness and the profoundest patriotism to the service of America" and to counter charges of disloyalty as "a sobering lesson in the way freedom must not defend itself." Eisenhower's resolve melted at the podium, however. He did not read the controversial paragraph praising Marshall and condemning McCarthy's slurs. When he was finished, McCarthy reached over several chairs and vigorously shook the candidate's hand.

The reaction was swift. The Democrats, of course, vilified Ike, but so did many of the country's newspapers that supported him. Many of his Republican followers were gravely disappointed. Senator Wayne Morse of Oregon resigned his membership in the GOP because of "reactionaries running a captive general for president." The editorial cartoonist Herbert L. Block depicted a leering, black-jowled McCarthy standing in a pool of filth and holding a sign reading: "ANYTHING TO WIN."

Much of the advertising for Ike's final stretch consisted of a saturation blitz of television and radio spots during the last three weeks of the campaign, including forty-nine key counties in twelve states.

Typical of the breadth of discussion in these "Eisenhower Answers America" spots was this exchange:

Average citizen: "Mr. Eisenhower, What about the high cost of living?"

Eisenhower: "My wife, Mamie, worries about the same thing. I tell her it's our job to change that on November 4."

Despite the Nixon slush fund uproar and the botched McCarthy rebuke, Eisenhower had a commanding lead over his Democratic rival as election day neared. But his managers remembered only too well that Dewey had appeared to hold an insurmountable lead over Truman in 1948. Thus, on October 24, eleven days before the election, Ike made a promise that he and his managers hoped would drive the last nail into his opponent's coffin. If elected, Ike promised he would concentrate on ending the Korean War. "That job," he said, "requires a personal trip to Korea . . . I shall go to Korea."

Photographs of Dwight D. Eisenhower, presidential nominee of the 1952 Republican National Convention, adorn the main entrance to the Conrad Hilton, 720 South Michigan Avenue.
Chicago Historical Society. Photo by J. Sherwin Murphy.

Adlai Ewing Stevenson II
1952 Democratic Presidential Nominee

John Sparkman
1952 Democratic
Vice Presidential Nominee

Facts-at-a-Glance
★★★

Event:	Thirty-First Democratic National Convention
Dates:	July 21–26, 1952
Building:	The Stockyards International Amphitheatre
Location:	4300 South Halsted Street
Chicago Mayor:	Martin H. Kennelly, Democrat
Candidates for Nomination:	Vice President Alben William Barkley, Kentucky; Governor Paul A. Dever, Massachusetts; William Averell Harriman, New York; Senator Hubert Horatio Humphrey, Minnesota; Senator Estes Kefauver, Tennessee; Senator Robert Kerr, Oklahoma; Senator Richard Brevard Russell, Georgia; G. Mennen Williams, Michigan; Senator James William Fulbright, Arkansas; Governor Adlai Ewing Stevenson II, Illinois
Presidential Nominee:	Adlai Ewing Stevenson II
Age at Nomination:	52
Number of Ballots:	3
Vice Presidential Nominee:	Senator John Sparkman, Alabama
Number of Delegates:	1,230
Number Needed to Nominate:	A majority, 616
Largest Attendance:	15,000
Critical Issues:	Party loyalty, seating of southern delegates, civil rights, Tidelands oil
Campaign Slogan:	"Madly for Adlai"

21
★★★

The 1952 Democratic National Convention
To Be or Not to Be

Harry S Truman did not officially take himself out of consideration for the 1952 presidential race until March 29, 1952. But as early as January he had told Governor Adlai Ewing Stevenson II of Illinois he would not run again. The stalemate in Korea between U.S. and communist forces and a series of minor scandals in government had tarnished his administration, and it seemed fairly clear he would not be able to repeat his miracle victory of 1948.

The first Democrat to declare himself a candidate was Estes Kefauver, the forty-eight-year-old junior senator from Tennessee, who did so the day after Truman and Stevenson met in Washington. Kefauver was a foe of Democrat Kenneth McKellar of his own state and had overturned the corrupt Edward Hull "Boss" Crump machine in Memphis. Kefauver was considered a renegade by many in his own party. He had come to prominence nationally through daily television exposure during coverage of the special Senate Crime Investigating Committee. The committee had, however, uncovered links between organized crime and big-city Democratic politicians, and Kefauver's leadership in the investigations rendered him further suspect to many powerful, more regular Democrats.

A few weeks after Kefauver announced his candidacy, William Averell Harriman of New York and Senators Robert Kerr of Oklahoma and Richard B. Russell of Georgia announced their availability.

Harriman, a progressive multimillionaire, was Truman's national security director and had been ambassador to the Soviet Union for both Roosevelt and Truman, as well as secretary of commerce. He had a strong grounding in foreign affairs, but his liberal views on civil rights made him an implausible national candidate in 1952.

Senator Kerr had been governor of his state and had delivered the keynote address at the 1944 national convention. He was a millionaire partner in the oil firm of Kerr-McKee and had used the Congress to advance the fortunes of his firm, so much so that he was often referred to as the "Senator from Kerr-McKee." He was a supporter of most of Truman's policies, but the president did not return the favor.

Senator Russell staunchly opposed Truman's Fair Deal policies. As chairman of the Armed Services Committee he was a powerful presence in the Senate and had blocked much of Truman's Fair Deal legislation. He had, however, remained loyal to the party four years before when the Dixiecrats bolted. His chances for the nomination were slim, and his candidacy furthered the cause of southern segregation.

At their January meeting President Truman had asked Adlai Stevenson to run and said he would back him if he did. Stevenson replied that he was deeply moved, greatly honored, and profoundly grateful, but he was only interested in running for a second term as governor of Illinois. Later, Stevenson told his friends that he had "made a hash of the meeting."

Despite his professed unwillingness to make the race, a boom for Stevenson, fueled by feature stories about him in national magazines, quickly built in the country. Kefauver, meanwhile, was steadily winning state primaries, campaigning with great energy, indefatigably shaking hands, and criticizing Truman's seeming slowness in searching out corruption in government. The symbol of his folksy campaign was his Daniel Boone coonskin cap. His criticism of the administration further antagonized party leaders.

Before announcing his withdrawal in late March 1952, Truman met with Stevenson again, and once more Stevenson told him he did not wish to run. (He had to be persuaded into running for governor, too.) Truman selected Adlai Stevenson as his candidate of choice precisely because of Stevenson's excellent record as governor of Illinois. Grandson of Adlai E. Stevenson, vice president in Cleveland's second administration in the 1890s, the twentieth-century Stevenson had cleaned up Republican corruption in Illinois while at the same time proving he could work with big city Democratic pols, such as Jacob Arvey of Cook County.

Born in 1900, Stevenson had graduated from Princeton in 1922. He flunked out of Harvard Law School, then worked as a journalist in the Bloomington, Illinois, family newspaper. In 1926 he received his law degree from Northwestern Law School and began to practice in Chicago, living on the Gold Coast and pursuing an active social life with other Ivy Leaguers and North Shore socialites. In 1928 he married Ellen Borden, ten years younger than him. Their marriage produced three sons.

From 1933 through 1937 Stevenson worked as a lawyer for various New Deal agencies in Washington, D.C., and then returned to law practice in Chicago. In July 1941 he was appointed personal assistant to Secretary of the Navy Frank Knox (owner of the *Chicago Daily News*) and served him until Knox's death in 1944. Stevenson then attempted to buy control of the *Daily News*, was unsuccessful, and returned to government service in 1945 as special assistant to Secretary of State Edward R. Stettinius Jr. He advocated U.S. participation in the newly formed United Nations, traveled widely, and returned to Chicago, where in 1948 he was persuaded to run for governor. He won by the largest plurality in Illinois history. Stevenson's chief liability was his marital status—in 1949 his wife filed divorce proceedings.

Yet after his March meeting with Truman, Stevenson fulfilled a number of speaking engagements throughout the country. Many organizations, all unauthorized by him, were formed to draft him as the nominee. He wrote to a friend that he'd "held off the political leaders … about so long as I can." The plan, he said, was to say "nothing more about my availability so that I can get out of it if it's Ike and go if it's Taft." He prayed it would be Ike, and Ike it was. Stevenson for the umpteenth time publicly stated his disinclination to run. Asked by a supporter what he would do if he were drafted, he responded wearily, "Guess I'd have to shoot myself."

On the eve of the Democratic convention, Kefauver had locked in 257 1/2 delegates; Russell, 161 1/2; Harriman, 112 1/2; Kerr, 45 1/2; and Stevenson, the favorite among party leaders, 41 1/2. Truman controlled the votes of about 400 delegates. It took 616 to win the nomination.

Exasperated by Stevenson's refusals, the president settled on Alben W. Barkley of Kentucky, his vice president, as the man to unify the party, since nei-

ther Russell, Kerr, Harriman, nor Kefauver were likely to win. In hopes of bolstering his chances, Vice President Barkley gave a breakfast on July 21, the opening day of the convention, for sixteen labor union leaders to enlist their support. Partly because they considered him, at seventy-one, too old for the office, but also because they anticipated that Kerr and Russell might unite behind him and in combination wield excessive power in the party, the labor leaders rebuffed Barkley, who was thus obliged to withdraw from the race almost before he entered it.

July 21 may have been a dark day for Barkley, but it was a bright and shining day for Stevenson. As governor of the host state he gave the welcoming address. *Life* magazine had just run a long story on the governor and a copy of the issue, with Stevenson's photo on its cover, was on every delegate's chair when the Amphitheatre's doors opened.

Six minutes of spontaneous demonstration greeted Stevenson's appearance on the rostrum. Midwesterners, he said, "want no shackles on the mind or the spirit, no rigid patterns of thought, and no iron conformity. We want only the faith and the conviction that triumph in free and fair contest."

He continued:

As a Democrat perhaps you will permit me to remind you that until four years ago the people of Illinois had chosen but three Democratic governors in a hundred years. One was John Peter Altgeld, whom the great Illinois poet, Vachel Lindsay, called "the Eagle Forgotten." He was an immigrant. One was Edward F. Dunne, whose parents came from the old sod of Ireland, and last was Henry Horner, but one generation removed from Germany. John Peter Altgeld, my friends, was a Protestant, Governor Dunne was a Catholic, Henry Horner was a Jew. And that, my friends, is the American story, written by the Democratic party here on the prairies of Illinois.

Reviewing the New Deal and Fair Deal era that had begun in 1932 in Chicago with the nomination of Franklin D. Roosevelt (a convention Stevenson had watched from the gallery), he referred to the present era and the Republican convention that had ended the week before:

But our Republican friends have said that it was all a miserable failure. For almost a week pompous phrases marched over this landscape in search of an idea, and the only idea they found was that the two great decades of progress in peace, and of victory in war, and of bold leadership in this anxious hour, were the misbegotten spawn of bungling, of corruption, of socialism, of mismanagement, of waste and of worse. They captured, they tied and they dragged that ragged idea here into this hall and they furiously beat it to death for a solid week.

After listening to this everlasting procession of epithets about our misdeeds I was even surprised the next morning when the mail was delivered on time . . . But we Democrats were by no means the only victims here. First, they slaughtered each other and then they went after us. And the same vocabulary was good for both exercises, which was a great convenience. Perhaps the proximity of the stockyards accounts for the carnage.

He said of the GOP platform:

I have a notion that the voters are going to respond in November to those Republican promises the way a certain young lady responded to the proposal of a young farmer friend of hers. He said, "Marry me and I'll paint the house and the barn inside and out. I'll put in electricity, I'll buy a brand new stove and refrigerator. Will you marry me?" And she said, "Honey, let's leave it this way: you do all those things, and then ask me again."

Near the end of his fourteen-minute address he said,

Who leads us is less important than what leads us, what convictions, what courage, what faith, win or lose. A man doesn't save a country or a civilization, but a militant party wedded to a principle can.

He ended with an implicit rebuke of the conduct of the recently concluded Republican convention:

And let us remember that we are not meeting here alone. All the world is watching and listening to what we say, what we do and how we behave. So let us give them a demonstration of democracy in action at its best, our manners good, our proceedings orderly and dignified, and, above all, let us make our decisions openly, fairly, not by the processes of synthetic excitement or mass hysteria. Let us make them as these solemn times demand, by

earnest thought and prayerful deliberation. And thus can the people's party reassure the people and vindicate and strengthen the forces of democracy throughout the world.

There was wild and continuing applause, and chants of "We want Stevenson!" filled the hall. The ovation did not cease until he left the rostrum. When order was restored, a resolution was approved requiring delegates to sign a loyalty pledge. This was a sectional battle that began with a challenge to the seating of the seventy delegates from Texas and Mississippi. Those who signed it promised thereby to support the convention's nominees, as some had not four years before. In 1948 southern Democrats, led by Governor Strom Thurmond of South Carolina, had bolted and formed a third party, the Dixiecrats, to protest Truman's civil-rights program. Delegates from Louisiana, South Carolina, and Virginia had refused to sign the pledge. Senator Harry Byrd of Virginia had said, "We're just going to sit here, and maybe they'll have to throw us out."

On Thursday evening a floor fight developed over the seating of the Virginia delegation. Maryland introduced a resolution that Virginia delegates be seated, which was opposed by the Kefauver and Harriman forces, who hoped to deflate the draft-Stevenson movement. The resolution was finally passed 650 1/2 to 518. The delegates from Louisiana and South Carolina were also seated. Most observers felt that these actions virtually assured Stevenson's nomination. So did Stevenson himself, apparently, because he began to rewrite an acceptance speech he had already drafted. That afternoon he had placed a courtesy phone call to the president and asked him if it "would embarrass" him if he, Stevenson, "allowed his name to be placed in nomination." Truman later recalled that "I replied with . . . some rather vigorous words and concluded by saying to Stevenson, 'I have been trying since January to get you to say that. Why should it embarrass me?'"

On the afternoon of the fifth day of the convention the first ballots for the presidential nomination were cast. Kefauver received 340 on the first ballot; Stevenson, 273; Russell, 268; Harriman, 123 1/2; and Kerr, 65, with the rest going to a scattering of others, mostly favorite sons. On the second ballot, Kefauver's total increased to 362 1/2, Stevenson's to 324 1/2. At 6:15 P.M., the convention recessed for dinner.

The Illinois delegation at the 1952 Democratic National Convention. Richard J. Daley
(*lower left*), who would be elected mayor of Chicago a few years later, offers his advice.
Chicago Historical Society.

President Truman called Harriman and asked him to withdraw. Harriman not only agreed but also released the large New York delegation to Stevenson. Governor Dever of Massachusetts also withdrew and released his delegates to Stevenson. On the third ballot Stevenson received 613 votes, 3 votes shy of the majority needed. Utah switched its votes to Stevenson, and Kefauver and Russell did the same. (Kefauver had tried to release his delegates earlier but Chairman Sam Rayburn of Texas, a "regular" Democrat, would not recognize him.) Early in the morning of Saturday, July 26, Stevenson became the Democratic presidential nominee for 1952. By that time, though, most of the television audience had retired for the evening.

After a lengthy delay, there was finally a long, loud roar that grew in intensity as the president of the United States mounted the Amphitheatre rostrum with Stevenson beside him. The president gave the delegates one of his patented "Give 'Em Hell Harry" speeches and then presented the candidate.

When the shouts and cheers and swelling organ music at last fell silent, at 2:00 A.M., Stevenson began to speak, "I accept your nomination," he said, "and your program . . . None of you, my friends, can wholly appreciate what is in my heart. I can only hope you will understand my words. They will be few."

Then he delivered his formal acceptance speech, the second of two classic, inspirational addresses he delivered that week:

> When the tumult and the shouting die, when the bands are gone and the lights are dimmed, there is the stark reality of responsibility in an hour of history haunted with those gaunt, grim specters of strife, dissension and materialism at home, and ruthless, inscrutable and hostile power abroad.
>
> The ordeal of the twentieth century, the bloodiest, most turbulent era of the Christian age, is far from over. Sacrifice, patience, understanding and implacable purpose may be our lot for years to come. Let's face it! Let's talk sense to the American people! Let's tell them the truth, that there are no gains without pains, that we are now on the eve of great decisions, not easy decisions, like resistance when you're attacked, but a long, patient, costly struggle which alone can assure triumph over the great enemies of man—war, poverty, and tyranny—and the assaults upon human dignity which are the most grievous consequences of each. . . .

> Better we lose the election than mislead the people; and better we lose than misgovern the people. Help me to do the job in this autumn of conflict and of campaign; help me to do the job in these years of darkness, doubt, and of crisis which stretch beyond the horizon of tonight's happy vision, and we will justify our glorious past and the loyalty of silent millions who look to us for compassion, for understanding, and for honest purpose. Thus we will serve our great tradition greatly.

After the speech, Stevenson met in a small room behind the podium with Truman; Frank McKinney, chairman of the Democratic National Committee; and Sam Rayburn, Speaker of the House and convention chairman. They agreed that Senator John Sparkman of Alabama was the logical choice for vice president. Thus, at the Saturday morning session Sparkman was nominated. Though Sparkman was a relative moderate by southern standards, his record on civil rights was not acceptable to northern progressives. Fifty African-American delegates, including Congressman Adam Clayton Powell of New York, bolted. "They cram a candidate down our throat," Powell said, "but they can't make us vote for him."

The party platform advocated repeal of the Taft-Hartley labor law, supported and praised New Deal and Fair Deal policies, and promised their continuation and extension at home and abroad. The plank on civil rights used all the correct phraseology, but it was indecisive and weak on specifics, reflecting the struggle between northern and southern party interests. Civil rights in 1952 was not as divisive an issue as it had been four years before.

In campaigning, Stevenson had the ticklish task of distancing himself from the administration while at the same time supporting Truman and enlisting his active support. On the whole, he managed to do this, although in August, in response to a letter, he announced that he could clean up the "mess in Washington," and he did briefly incur Truman's wrath.

Reminiscent of Lincoln, Stevenson established his campaign headquarters in Springfield (he was still governor of Illinois). His advisers and speechwriters were liberal, many of them from Americans for Democratic Action. Although they included many brilliant historians, journalists, and editors, Stevenson extensively reworked the speeches they drafted for him, rewriting and revising them up to the very moment of their delivery.

On domestic issues, Stevenson departed from Truman slightly on civil rights. The president was his party's leading advocate of rights for African Americans, but Stevenson remained more moderate than Truman. Still, he was able to win Adam Clayton Powell and other black defectors back to the party. His stand on civil rights did not endear him to southern Democrats, nor did his position on the Tidelands oil issue. When the Supreme Court ruled that these submerged oil lands off the shores of California, Louisiana, and Texas were public domain, Congress had adopted a joint resolution transferring ownership to the states. President Truman vetoed this resolution. On the other hand, Dwight Eisenhower sided with Congress, a position that undoubtedly pleased the giant oil corporations that stood to reap immense profits from such legislation.

Against intense political pressure, Stevenson came out unequivocally for federal retention of title to the offshore oil. As a result of his stand on Tidelands and his position on civil rights, both Texas and Louisiana Democratic parties endorsed Eisenhower and Nixon. Similarly, Virginia's Senator Byrd supported Eisenhower as well as Truman's former Secretary of State James F. Byrnes of South Carolina. Richard Russell declined to campaign for the Democratic ticket. Many other conservative Democrats in the South moved toward voting for the Grand Old Party.

There was yet another significant difference between the candidates: the general believed a presidential campaign should be a straight-faced performance—there was no room for humor in an Eisenhower speech. Stevenson thought otherwise. Stevenson laced his speeches with such asides as, "Whenever the Republicans talk of cutting taxes first and discussing the national security second, they remind me of a very tired rich man who said to his chauffeur, 'Drive off the cliff, James, I want to commit suicide.' " On another occasion, remarking on his opponent's christening of his campaign as the "Great Crusade," Stevenson said, "The general has dedicated himself so many times he must feel like the cornerstone of a public building."

The Republicans viewed such attempts at levity as flippant, undignified, and unworthy of a presidential candidate. So, too, perhaps, did some Democrats. Stevenson's response was that "to be surrounded by the Republican old guard night and day would be a melancholy fate . . . and I can understand why it is no laughing matter for the general."

On August 27 Stevenson appeared before the American Legion Convention in New York City. Two days earlier Eisenhower had addressed that body, praising the Legion "for its unending, effective efforts to uproot subversion . . . [and] communism from wherever it finds it in our country." Some believed that the general might take the opportunity to defend his old wartime chief, General George C. Marshall, who had been viciously attacked as a traitor by GOP senators McCarthy and Jenner, among others. He did not.

In his own address to the Legionnaires, an unsympathetic audience, Stevenson remarked:

> There are men among us who use "patriotism" as a club for attacking other Americans . . . What can we say for the man who proclaims himself a patriot, and then for political or personal reasons attacks the patriotism of faithful public servants? I give you, as a shocking example, the attacks which have been made on the loyalty and the motives of our great wartime Chief of Staff General Marshall. To me this is the type of patriotism which is, in Dr. Johnson's phrase, "the last refuge of scoundrels."

Stevenson campaigned courageously, eloquently, and effectively, defending Truman's domestic and foreign policies and attacking Eisenhower's alliance with the Republican old guard, his "surrender at Morningside Heights" to Taft, and a Republican foreign policy that wanted to roll back communism by force of arms throughout the world without becoming involved. Arrayed against him, however, was every mass circulation magazine in the country, more than 90 percent of the nation's daily newspapers, and the bottomless pockets of the GOP treasury, which were able to buy vastly more space and time in the media for their candidate than the Democrats.

Perhaps even more telling was the mood of the country. What the citizens of the United States desperately wanted in 1952 was exactly what Dwight Eisenhower's advisers suggested the general give them: a hero who would solve all of their problems without effort or thought or sacrifice on their part.

Seven years after the climactic end of World War II, many of the veterans had started families and lived relatively comfortable, neat-lawned lives barbecuing on the patio (the latest craze), in nearly all-white, lower-middle-class suburbs. What they feared most was disorder and disruption. They were scoutmasters, Little League coaches, Elks, Lions, Rotarians, PTA members, community boosters. Their wives thought as they thought. They were satisfied with a limited number of choices so long as they did not have to wrestle with tough and uncomfortable situations or issues. They wanted simple solutions, simply put. They did not want to have to make hard decisions. They wanted to feel good about their lives and themselves and their families.

Most of them did not want to hear Stevenson's message. He posed tough questions. Though he came from a sheltered patrician background himself, Stevenson told them something they no longer wanted to acknowledge: that the world was complicated and a dangerous place.

In the last months of the campaign, Thomas E. Dewey and John Foster Dulles promised that Eisenhower's election would virtually guarantee peace in Korea. On October 24, when the general told the country, "I shall go to Korea," there was never any further doubt he would be victorious in his great crusade.

A week later, speaking in New York, Stevenson declared: "There is no greater cruelty, in my judgment, than the raising of false hopes, no greater arrogance than playing politics with peace and war. Rather than exploit human hopes and fears, rather than provide glib solutions and false assurances, I would gladly lose this presidential election."

On November 2 he did, by 6,509,364 votes in the greatest turnout of voters in American history. Still, 47 percent of the poor in the country did not vote, compared to 24 percent middle-class and 14 percent high-income voters. The "other," non-suburban America made its presence felt by its absence at the polls. Eisenhower received 33,824,351 votes or 55.4 percent of the two-party vote: Stevenson, 27,314,987 votes or 44.4 percent. His was still the second largest Democratic vote in American history. The electoral college count was quite decisive: 442 for Eisenhower, 89 for Stevenson. Dwight Eisenhower overwhelmingly was the people's choice to be the thirty-fourth president of the United States.

Adlai Ewing Stevenson II
1956 Democratic Presidential Nominee

Estes Kefauver
1956 Democratic
Vice Presidential Nominee

Facts-at-a-Glance
★★★

Event:	Thirty-Second Democratic National Convention
Dates:	August 13–17, 1956
Building:	The Stockyards International Amphitheatre
Location:	4300 South Halsted Street
Chicago Mayor:	Richard Joseph Daley, Democrat
Candidates for Nomination:	Governor William Averell Harriman, New York; Senator Lyndon Baines Johnson, Texas; Senator Estes Kefauver, Tennessee; Governor Adlai Ewing Stevenson II, Illinois
Presidential Nominee:	Adlai Ewing Stevenson II
Age at Nomination:	56
Number of Ballots:	1
Vice Presidential Nominee:	Estes Kefauver, Tennessee
Number of Delegates:	1,372
Number Needed to Nominate:	A majority, 687
Largest Attendance:	15,000
Critical Issues:	Civil rights, desegregation of schools
Campaign Slogan:	"Stevenson/Kefauver"
Popular Song:	"Heartbreak Hotel"

22
★★★

The 1956 Democratic National Convention
Don Quixote

After being defeated for the presidency in 1952 by Dwight Eisenhower, Governor Adlai Stevenson gave a concession speech in Springfield, calling up the memory of a fellow Illinoisan, Abraham Lincoln: "They asked him how he felt once after an unsuccessful election. He said he felt like the little boy who had stubbed his toe in the dark. He said that he was too old to cry but it hurt too much to laugh."

The defeated governor also appeared at a Gridiron Club dinner in Washington, D.C., shortly after the election, where the speakers were expected to exercise their wit: "The general was so far ahead," he told his audience, "we never saw him. I was happy to hear that I had even placed second." He reiterated his faith in the American people. "As to their wisdom," he went on, "well, Coca Cola still outsells champagne."

As warily as the boy who had stubbed his toe once, Stevenson tested the waters for a second candidacy in 1956. He spent the first year after his defeat giving speeches to help pay off his party's $800,000 campaign deficit. In February 1953 he gave an address at a Jackson Day dinner in New York and criticized the Eisenhower administration's foreign policy and its domination by big business: "The New Dealers have all left Washington," he said, "to make way for the car dealers." Then he made a plea for respect for individual freedoms. "Only a government which fights for civil liberties and equal rights for its own people can stand for freedom in the world," he said. This was during the heyday of the McCarthy-led Red Scare hysteria. Many observers worried that the senator from Wisconsin was leading the country toward fascism. President Eisenhower remained above the outcry over McCarthy's methods and other extremists in the Republican Party.

In March 1953 Stevenson left on a five-month world tour that took him to thirty countries in Asia, the Middle East, and Europe. He was merely the titular leader of the Democratic Party in the United States, a position of prestige only, but abroad his power was thought to be great. He was greeted by enthusiastic crowds wherever he went, meeting with heads of state and other leading figures. On his return he gave three lectures at Harvard that indicated he still believed that containment of communism should be the chief priority of American foreign policy. (The lectures were later published in book form as *Call to Greatness*.)

In an article in *Look* magazine, Stevenson complained that "McCarthyism had done America more harm in eight months than Soviet propaganda had done in eight years." Twelve months later, in a speech on March 6 at a Democratic fund-raiser in Miami, he continued his theme, stating, "A group of political plungers has persuaded the president that McCarthyism is the best Republican formula for political success." Not so, he declared. "A political party divided against itself, half McCarthy and half Eisenhower, cannot produce national unity, cannot govern with confidence and purpose."

In early 1955 Stevenson established a law practice in Chicago, dividing his time between the firm and his Libertyville farm north of Chicago. The firm prospered, numbering among its clients Radio Corporation of America, Reynolds Metals, and Illinois Bell. At a strategy meeting in Libertyville the first week of August 1955 attended by his aides and supporters, he made the decision to run again. Stevenson was not indecisive, as his opponents charged. When he had all the facts and information he wanted, he made a firm decision. Neither, strangely, given the grace of his prose arguments, was he an intellectual, as some disparagingly claimed. A close friend noted that he rarely finished books.

Not long after he decided to run again, on August 12, a delegation of twenty Democratic state governors called upon Stevenson at Libertyville and told him they supported his decision. Initially, Stevenson did not want to enter the state primaries (which in the mid-1950s were not as important as they became in later years). He felt that both ordinary Democrats and the party's chiefs overwhelmingly favored his candidacy and that that support was sufficient to obtain the nomination.

On September 24, however, President Eisenhower suffered a heart attack after playing twenty-seven holes of golf, which spurred W. Averell Harriman, Democratic governor of New York (one of the twenty governors who had called on Stevenson in Libertyville that August), to a renewed interest in the nomination for himself, since it was generally conceded that Ike, with his heart condition, could not run for a second term. Former President Truman and other liberal Democrats seemed to favor Harriman; thus, Stevenson reluctantly agreed with his advisers to enter selected primaries.

Stevenson formally declared his candidacy on November 15, 1955. Besides Harriman, his other rival for the nomination once again would be Senator Estes Kefauver of Tennessee. Disliked in the South for his liberalism, disliked in the North for his southern folksiness, and disliked by party chiefs for his renegade-Democrat past as a foe of big-city bosses, Kefauver knew that primary victories were his only road to the nomination.

The most critical issue the candidates had to confront was civil rights, particularly the integration of public schools in the South. On this issue, Stevenson and Kefauver held similar and moderate views. Harriman, on the other hand, was for aggressive federal action to implement the Supreme Court's May 17, 1954, *Brown v. the Topeka Board of Education* decision that outlawed segregation in U.S. schools. During the primary campaign, it became evident that Stevenson was a gradualist with respect to school integration.

During the Minnesota primary of March 1956, Stevenson campaigned lethargically. Even though he was supported by the governor and its two senators, his opponent Kefauver won twenty-six of the state's thirty delegates. It was generally believed that Republicans crossed over to vote for Kefauver in

Interior view of the International Amphitheatre during the 1956 Democratic National Convention. Chicago Historical Society.

Minnesota's "open" primary in order to embarrass their state's leaders.

Stevenson, mindful of Willkie's 1940 and 1944 defeats, sat out Wisconsin's primary when a private poll predicted he would do badly. However, he won in his home state of Illinois, in Alaska, the District of Columbia, New Jersey, and Oregon. His campaigning had taken on a zest it had lacked in Minnesota, but it left the candidate exhausted and on some evenings incoherent with fatigue. All the pollsters agreed that no candidate could win the nomination on the convention's first ballot.

In Florida, Stevenson and Kefauver both attempted to portray themselves as paragons of moderation on civil-rights issues. As a campaigner, Kefauver was far more effective. He would talk to older people about local fishing conditions while Stevenson talked about world issues that would eventuate, perhaps, twenty years in the future. Stevenson and Kefauver became the first major presidential candidates to debate over national television, but their face-to-face encounter proved little except that they found little to fault in the other's views. Stevenson won a narrow victory on May 29 in what was essentially a popularity contest.

The June 5 California primary was the last for Stevenson before the convention. At a Long Beach rally he delivered a hard-hitting attack on his opponent. He also said that the federal government should underwrite private health insurance plans and later endorsed expanding Social Security to include health care for the elderly. (A decade later the latter suggestion was written into law as Medicare.) He attracted noisy and enthusiastic crowds in California. Kefauver replied with a biting personal criticism of Stevenson but his hopes for attaining the nomination effectively ended in the Golden State when Stevenson overwhelmed him 1,139,964 votes to 680,722.

Three days after the California primary, President Eisenhower, who had recovered remarkably from his heart attack (and had announced on March 1 he would run again), was rushed to Walter Reed Hospital for major surgery for an abdominal obstruction caused by ileitis. There was fresh cause to believe he would not run for a second term. (A Gallup poll showed that his brother Milton would be the strongest Republican candidate if Ike retired.) But on July 10, a month after his surgery, Ike announced he would run again. The only question he left unanswered was whether or not he wanted Richard Nixon as his running mate. There were more than a few indications he did not.

On August 1 Estes Kefauver withdrew as a candidate and endorsed Stevenson. This move seemed to effectively terminate Governor Harriman's bid also, since he could no longer hope that Stevenson and Kefauver would battle to a deadlock that would force the convention to turn to him as a compromise candidate. On Saturday August 11, however, two days before the first session of the convention would be called to order, Harry Truman held a press conference at Chicago's Sheraton-Blackstone and endorsed Harriman. This unexpected jolt to Stevenson's candidacy was neutralized almost immediately by Eleanor Roosevelt, FDR's widow, who was an admirer of Stevenson. She intimated to reporters that Stevenson was better qualified to become president than Truman had been when he took over following her husband's death in 1945.

Inside the Amphitheatre, Stevenson's name was placed in nomination by Senator John Fitzgerald Kennedy of Massachusetts. The candidate from Illinois won on the first ballot with 905 1/2 votes. Harriman got 210; Senator Lyndon Baines Johnson of Texas, 80. The rest of the votes went to half a dozen favorite sons. When the roll call was completed, a motion was approved to make Stevenson's nomination unanimous.

Almost without exception the presidential candidate of a party selects his running mate. In a move that surprised and dismayed the Democratic chieftains, Stevenson threw the selection of the vice presidential nominee open to the convention. The forces of John F. Kennedy, Estes Kefauver, and Hubert Horatio Humphrey went frantically to work lining up delegates for their candidate.

In the first ballot, Kefauver led 483 1/2 to Kennedy's 304. Senator Albert Gore Sr. of Tennessee (father of Vice President Al Gore) had 178; Mayor Robert Wagner of New York City, 162 1/2; and Senator Hubert Humphrey, 134 1/2.

Kennedy took the lead in the second ballot (Stevenson privately favored him over Kefauver), with 618 to Kefauver's 551 1/2. But then Gore, still running third, withdrew in favor of Kefauver, and after other vote shifts the final tally was 755 1/2 for Kefauver and 589 for Kennedy. The Massachusetts senator then moved that Kefauver's nomination be made unanimous.

In his acceptance speech at the Amphitheatre, Stevenson declared:

When I stood here before you that hot night four years ago we were at the end of an era, a great era of restless forward movement, an era of unparalleled social reform and of glorious triumph over depression and tyranny. It was a Democratic era.

Tonight, after an interval of marking time and aimless drifting, we are on the threshold of another great era. History's headlong course has brought us, I devoutly believe, to the threshold of a new America, to the America of the great ideals and noble visions which are the stuff our future must be made of.

I mean a new America where poverty is abolished and our abundance is used to enrich the lives of every family.

I mean a new America where freedom is made real for all without regard to race or belief or economic condition.

I mean a new America which everlastingly attacks the ancient idea that men can solve their differences by killing each other.

Later in his address he made the following prophetic statements:

The truth is not that our policy abroad has the communists on the run. The men who run the Eisenhower administration evidently believe that the minds of Americans can be manipulated by shows, slogans, and the arts of advertising. And that conviction will, I dare say, be backed up by the greatest torrent of money ever poured out to influence an American election, poured out by men who fear nothing so much as change and who want everything to stay as it is, only more so.

This idea that you can merchandise candidates for high office like breakfast cereal, that you can gather votes like box tops, is, I think, the ultimate indignity to the democratic process. And we Democrats must also face the fact that no administration has ever before enjoyed such an uncritical and enthusiastic support from so much of the press as this one.

But let us ask the people of our country to what great purpose for the Republic has the president's popularity and this unrivaled opportunity for leadership been put? Has the Eisenhower administration used this opportunity to elevate us? To enlighten us?

To inspire us? Did it, in a time of headlong, world wide, revolutionary change, prepare us for stern decisions and great risks? Did it, in short, give men and women a glimpse of the nobility and vision without which peoples and nations perish?

The truth is that everyone is not prosperous. The truth is that the farmer, especially the family farmer who matters most, has not had his fair share of the national income and the Republicans have done nothing to help him, until an election year. The truth is that 30 million Americans live today in families trying to make ends meet on less than $2,000 a year. The truth is that the small farmer, the small businessman, the teacher, the white collar worker, and the retired citizen trying to pay today's prices on yesterday's pension, all these are in serious trouble. The truth is that in this government of big men, big financially; no one speaks for the little man.

The truth, unhappily, is not, in the Republican president's words, that our "prestige since the last world war has never been as high as it is this day." The truth is that it has probably never been lower. The truth is that we are losing the military advantage, the economic initiative, and the moral leadership.

Stevenson concluded:

It is time to listen again to our hearts, to speak again our ideals, to be again our own great selves. There is a spiritual hunger in the world today and it cannot be satisfied by material things alone, by better cars or longer credit terms. Our forebears came here to worship God. We must not let our aspirations so diminish that our worship becomes rather of bigness, bigness of material achievement.

The Republicans opened their convention in San Francisco's Cow Palace three days after the Democrats closed their assembly. The party slogan was "Peace, Progress, Prosperity," the same used by James Cox and the Democrats in 1920. The Republican convention was a Hollywood extravaganza, featuring a parrot brought from Missouri who kept repeating "Vote for Ike, Vote for Ike" and a kickoff gala for ten thousand of the party's faithful that cost $125,000 to cater. During floor deliberations, young women for Ike swung pompons and danced down the aisles followed by five hundred jubilant Young Republicans softly chanting "Ike, Ike, Ike." Old-time silver screen star George Murphy (later, Senator Mur-

Adlai Stevenson (*right*) and Estes Kefauver, the presidential and vice presidential nominees, raise clasped hands in a victory salute at the conclusion of the 1956 Democratic National Convention. A young John F. Kennedy looks on. Chicago Historical Society.

phy of California) managed the "entertainment" part of the convention. Later he admitted, "Politics and show business are getting closer all the time."

Ike received the votes of all 1,323 Republican delegates on the first ballot. His vice president, Nixon, who had implied in some of his public remarks that Harry Truman was a "traitor," was also renominated. The GOP platform called the Republican Party the "party of the young," but in the mid-1950s, it was more accurately a middle-aged party. Many observers felt the party was wrapped in a cocoon of complacency, wanting more freedom from the threat of disruption to the even, comfortable tenor of their lives.

The Democratic platform called for repeal of the Taft-Hartley Act, high rigid farm price supports, international control of the Suez Canal, and arms for Israel. It asserted that Supreme Court decisions were the law of the land but rejected "all proposals of the use of force to interfere with the ordinary determination" of desegregation disputes. The South was pla-

cated, but Harlem Democratic Congressman Adam Clayton Powell endorsed Eisenhower, as did several major African-American newspapers.

Stevenson's campaign focused on two major issues: ending the draft and stopping all hydrogen bomb testing. Both of these stands were taken against the advice of his advisers. Eisenhower contemptuously dismissed both proposals. Initially, public response seemed to favor Eisenhower's reaction but then it began to shift toward Stevenson's views, so much so that on October 18 Eisenhower was forced to put his military authority behind his rejection of the end-H-bomb tests proposal. He termed it a compound of "pie-in-the-sky promises and wishful thinking."

On October 21 the premier of the Soviet Union, Nikolai A. Bulganin, wrote a letter to Eisenhower stating: "We fully share the opinion recently expressed by certain prominent figures in the United States concerning the necessity of prohibiting atomic weapon tests." This bold interference in U.S.

domestic affairs was denounced by both Stevenson and Eisenhower, but it cost Stevenson votes. Nixon reprimanded the Democratic candidate for having blundered into a "communist mousetrap."

On Monday, October 29, a week before the election, an international crisis erupted in the Middle East. Convinced that Egypt was going to bar their use of the Suez Canal, which Egypt had seized in July, Britain and France attacked Egypt with planes and troops, and Israel, convinced that Egypt was about to attack her, thrust deep into Egypt's Sinai peninsula with tanks and paratroopers. By Friday President Eisenhower was forced to resort to calling on the United Nations, which he had heretofore ignored in his administration's maneuverings in the Middle East, to restore peace. In concert with the Soviet Union, the United States pressured Britain, France, and Israel to withdraw their troops from Egypt, which they ultimately did. Ironically, the crisis, which had developed as a consequence of numerous Eisenhower administration blunders over the years, resulted in additional votes for Ike.

On election day Eisenhower received 35,581,003 votes to Stevenson's 26,031,322. Eisenhower's plurality of 9,549,681 votes almost doubled the figures of his decisive victory four years before. He garnered 457 electoral votes to Stevenson's 73. But he also became the first president since Zachary Taylor in 1848 to begin a term with both houses of Congress in the hands of the opposition party. His coattails had not been sturdy enough to carry his party's other candidates to victory.

Stevenson's quixotic quest for the presidency had come to an end, though he did make an unsuccessful run at the nomination again in 1960. Stevenson's 1952 and 1956 campaigns had a long-lasting effect within the Democratic Party, however. His themes and rhetoric foreshadowed both John F. Kennedy's New Frontier and Lyndon B. Johnson's Great Society. In May 1957, less than a year after Stevenson's suggestion, a Pentagon task force called for the end of the military draft, and in October 1958, Eisenhower declared a moratorium on nuclear weapons testing in the atmosphere. Both actions vindicated Stevenson's two most controversial proposals during the 1956 campaign.

Adlai Stevenson had run against a myth, one created by the public's desire to believe in a hero and sustained by Republican control and effective manipulation of the new mass media. Stevenson's two failures at the polls perhaps were inevitable, but it is a truism long accepted that to lose in a political race does not guarantee that you were wrong or, for that matter, that your opponent was right.

Richard Milhous Nixon
1960 Republican Presidential Nominee

Henry Cabot Lodge Jr.
1960 Republican
Vice Presidential Nominee

Facts-at-a-Glance
★★★

Event:	Twenty-Seventh Republican National Convention
Dates:	July 25–28, 1960
Building:	The Stockyards International Amphitheatre
Location:	4300 South Halsted Street
Chicago Mayor:	Richard Joseph Daley, Democrat
Candidates for Nomination:	Senator Barry Goldwater, Arizona; Vice President Richard Milhous Nixon, California; Governor Nelson Aldrich Rockefeller, New York
Presidential Nominee:	Richard Milhous Nixon
Age at Nomination:	47
Number of Ballots:	1
Vice Presidential Nominee:	Henry Cabot Lodge Jr., Massachusetts
Number of Delegates:	1,331
Number Needed to Nominate:	A majority, 666
Largest Attendance:	15,000
Critical Issues:	The Republican platform, the "Missile Gap," civil rights
Campaign Slogan:	"Experience Counts"
Campaign Song:	"Merrily We Roll Along"

23
★★★

The 1960 Republican National Convention
Nuclear Divisions

Richard Nixon was as competent a vice president under Dwight David Eisenhower as he had been a relentless red-baiter for the House Committee on Un-American Activities in Congress during the late 1940s and early 1950s. The cocky, callow, aggressive, and sometimes brooding Nixon was admired by Republican Party bosses across the land and hailed by the rank and file for his loyalty, tenacity, and eagerness to learn and serve. He was equally despised by Democrats who saw him as both a forerunner and protector of Senator Joe McCarthy and the big smear tactic, and a conscienceless self-promoter who had crawled to power by character assassination, duplicity, lack of principle, and plain luck.

Ike himself had failed to denounce the Wisconsin senator and stop the red witchhunt that blacklisted so many Americans. The young Nixon had skillfully expressed the unofficial anticommunist hysteria that gripped the party of Dewey from 1944 onward. He also had attended thousands of local party functions, given pep speeches by the score, and had taken away a chest full of political IOUs he was ready to cash in at the 1960 Chicago convention.

Nixon had also endured anti-American riots in Latin America for his country and faced down Soviet Premier Nikita Khrushchev in the famous 1959 Kitchen Debate. He had sat in the president's vacant chair without problems during Ike's three prolonged sicknesses. So for most Republicans it was obvious Richard Nixon was the natural heir to the party crown when Ike retired, the man to steer America through the perils and promises of the new Atomic Age.

As hundreds of Nixon delegates poured into Chicago for a centennial celebration of the Lincoln Wigwam and to choose a leader of their own to confront the 1960s, they entered a city that gleamed with the polished luxury and power of American postwar affluence. The squalid pioneer town that had sent Lincoln to Washington one hundred years earlier to fight

for social justice now boasted a multimillion dollar lakefront with classy hotels, expensive department stores, and corporate glass towers. Monstrous steel mills breathed fire into the night sky along the lake's southern rim, and modern manufacturers and retailers by the neon mile produced and sold every item imaginable in the American consumer cornucopia.

Instead of horse-drawn wagons pulling up to the lumberyard or feed store, a steady stream of red, white, and blue Thunderbirds, Chevy Impalas, Chrysler Imperials, Cadillac Fleetwoods, convertibles and hard-tops, blasting the latest Elvis Presley and Everly Brothers hits from dashboard radios, rumbled with teenage drivers up and down Michigan Avenue, as hundreds of shoppers, secretaries, businesspeople, hustlers, and hipsters paraded in the summer heat.

When delegates arrived at their hotels, they were greeted by smiling "Nixon girls" adorned in scarlet dresses and white blouses, handing out Nixon buttons and palm cards. Sound-trucks blared the names of the candidates to delegates strolling into the Conrad Hilton and Blackstone Hotels, the two historic, twenty-story red brick and white terra cotta monoliths facing each other across from the lake on the corner of Michigan Avenue and Balbo Drive.

The 1960 convention was staged again at the Stockyards International Amphitheatre, scene of Ike's first nomination, along South Halsted Street on the outskirts of the Chicago stockyards, which had opened at the close of Lincoln's war and now helped to feed not just the nation, but the world. The telegraph of Lincoln's day had been replaced with live telecasts instantaneously reaching one hundred million Americans from coast to coast. Thousands of television, radio, and print journalists from around the world converged to capture images of the event. Little did they suspect that the key decision of the convention would be settled in the wee hours before the assembly opened and far away from the cameras and tape recorders.

In reality, Nixon had won the nomination on December 26, 1959, the day Governor Nelson Aldrich Rockefeller of New York unexpectedly withdrew from the race. Rockefeller, the biggest Republican winner in the otherwise disastrous 1958 midyear elections, was a fast-rising star in the tired old party of Ike. In capturing the New York governor's chair, he instantly vaulted himself into contention for the 1960 nomination. The fact that his name was Rockefeller amplified the possibilities and excitement that surrounded him. He was a darling of the press and a fine leader. But his travels around the nation to test the waters in 1959 ended in an abrupt cold shower. Potential financial backers and party bosses everywhere told him to put his ambitions on hold, that Nixon had their complete support. Although Rockefeller "hated the idea of Richard Nixon becoming president of the United States," he saw he had virtually no chance of winning.

So Rocky, as he was popularly known, told surprised reporters, "I believe . . . that the great majority of those who will control the Republican convention stand opposed to any contest for the nomination . . . therefore, I am not, and shall not be, a candidate for the nomination for the presidency . . . I am a Republican, seriously concerned about the future vigor and purpose of my party. I believe that we live in an age that challenges representative government and the two-party system that is its American expression . . . To the invigorating of this party's spirit, and to the clarifying of its purposes and policies, all of us who are Republicans should devote our thoughts and energies . . ."

Rocky added, "Quite obviously I shall not at any time entertain any thought of accepting nomination to the vice presidency." It was an arrogant dig at Nixon's status and qualifications that was not lost on the current vice president. Rockefeller concluded, "The decision is definite and final." New York's governor cited the need to attend to the upcoming legislative session. Then he immediately refocused his seventy-person precampaign staff, housed in two brownstones on West Fifty-Fifth Street in Manhattan, on the issues that would make up the party platform.

By late spring Rocky was having second thoughts about his decision, although all he could hope for was a miracle, a spontaneous draft in a convention solidly for Nixon. When he was asked by the press about his real intentions, he replied, "I didn't run for governor to become a party wrecker." Later he insisted that he had the right to speak out "with full freedom and vigor on issues that confront our nation and the world." The only response Rockefeller's plea elicited from party officials and the "statesman" Nixon was cold silence.

Nixon feared Rockefeller. He was everything that Nixon was not—charming, liberal, wealthy, philanthropic, easygoing, with an infectious smile and a big personality that made people instantly warm to him. In the 1940s Rockefeller had worked for FDR as coordinator for Latin American affairs and later as an international adviser to both Truman and Eisenhower, before resigning disillusioned by Ike's complacency when it came to world affairs. He was popular and could win elections. He had moved easily from big business to politics with his 1958 upset gubernatorial victory over W. Averell Harriman. And like Grover Cleveland and Thomas Dewey before him, he had sat but two years in the New York governor's chair before the powers of the presidency beckoned him. He willingly followed with a private fortune and army of staff workers that was unmatched in political circles. Vice President Nixon had only a handful of advisers he trusted; Rocky had whatever advice he needed.

In the early 1959 polls Rocky actually led Nixon, 40 percent to 38 percent, among potential primary voters. But the New York governor soon learned that the nation's corporate executives, Republican Party money men, and local bosses had been tightly organized by Nixon at least two years earlier. Wherever he traveled, it was "Nixon country." His hosts were cool to, even resentful of, a Rockefeller run. They warned him to stay out and wait his turn.

At first Rockefeller pleased them with his withdrawal announcement. But the multimillionaire was restless and had more on his mind than just a run for the presidency. "I know it is unconventional to mention lacks and lapses in one's own party," he acknowledged. "But the times we live in are not conventional." Like Stevenson before him, Rocky felt an obligation to warn the American public that its very existence was at risk. His impatience ultimately doomed his future presidential ambitions.

In the months before the Chicago convention, the Rockefeller forces went on the offensive again, demanding that the party use its platform to admit complacency and shortcomings under Eisenhower, to work on problems of civil rights that threatened social erosion, and to sound the emergency alert about Soviet atomic missiles that threatened utter annihilation.

In defeating the evil of Nazism, the U.S. had unleashed an atomic monster of its own that quickly came back to haunt its master, as the world for the third time in the century rushed toward a massive and terrifying armament. The Soviets had badly shaken the nation's sense of superiority and security with their 1957 launch of Sputnik, the world's first satellite. Now the nation felt vulnerable to surprise attack in a war that could, with atomic power, be over in a matter of hours. America's sense of security had been shattered. Although the Soviet Union did not have the capability to inflict nuclear devastation on the U.S., America could expect at least a million casualties if all-out war did erupt. Indeed, the race to build up nuclear arms led the USSR to gamble on installing nuclear weapons in Cuba within ninety miles of Miami a year after the election. It was deadly business.

Rockefeller, a domestic liberal and foreign affairs hawk, now warned of a "missile gap" that existed between the U.S. and Soviet Union and demanded that the party respond with new military options. U.S. B-47s and B-52s could be destroyed while still on the ground, he admonished. They needed to be supplemented by an arms buildup. Strategically, America needed to erect more and more missile bases of its own. On the civilian front, Rockefeller argued that the nation should launch a campaign to construct millions of fallout shelters to protect a vulnerable population that could be incinerated if left unprepared. Instead of Republican self-satisfaction, the nation needed to be brought to emergency red alert. If a Republican platform failed to follow through on these issues, Rocky could not support it. Nor could the governor accept the party's complacency on civil rights. Rockefeller demanded a national debate on these and other critical issues. Republicans owed it to America, he insisted.

After the Republican failure at the polls in 1958, President Eisenhower had already commissioned a Committee on Program and Progress, under the direction of Vice President Nixon, to reassess party strategy and action. Nixon chose Chicagoan Charles

H. Percy, the forty-year-old president of Bell and Howell, to coordinate the task force. The work of this committee fed directly into the first drafts of the 1960 platform that spring. Hence, Rockefeller's demands upset the spirit of cooperation.

Rockefeller kept Nixon on edge. On June 8 he released a memorandum that set the tone of the final conflict: "I am deeply convinced and deeply concerned that those now assuming control of the Republican Party have failed to make clear where this party is heading . . ." The governor challenged Nixon and the "new spokesmen of the Republican Party" to "declare what they now believe and what they propose to meet the great matters before the nation."

Nixon laughed off the summons, saying everyone knew his long public record and that it differed little from what Republicans everywhere wanted. He urged the platform committee to resolve the issues Rocky had raised and said he would be happy to answer Rockefeller on live television. Rockefeller retorted that Nixon had to clarify his positions first before any TV appearance. Over the next few weeks, the governor followed his assault with nine detailed policy papers. Percy met with Rocky in early July to try to work out a compromise. The governor resisted and instead called for open debate. And so it went, back and forth, until days before the convention.

On Monday July 18, 1960, a week before the convention, the Republican platform committee of 103 party regulars, under the skilled chairmanship of Percy, met in the Crystal Ballroom of the Blackstone Hotel. Percy had the difficult task of crafting a final document that celebrated the accomplishments of the lackadaisical Eisenhower years while pointing to a fresh approach to new American problems that Nixon would have to solve as president.

Rockefeller's Chicago affairs were managed by L. Judson Morhouse, the New York State Republican chairman; Lieutenant Governor Malcolm Wilson of New York; national Republican committeeman George Hinman; and Rocky's speechwriter and consultant, Emmet Hughes. The entire staff was headquartered in a wing of the Sheridan Towers on Michigan Avenue. Rocky was linked to the action by a sophisticated electronic command center. Communications trucks were parked outside the hotel, and two rooms were reserved for the press, which continually questioned him on whether he would accept the vice presidential spot. Rockefeller's aim, short of a presidential draft that he suspected would never come, was to shape America's policy and destiny. During the final week before the convention, he put out press releases expressing his deep concern over the platform drafts. Later, he would come to Chicago to lead the New York delegation.

Meanwhile, a "draft Rockefeller" drive was in full swing, working out of the Conrad Hilton and the Blackstone Theater and claiming as many as 275 delegates. His volunteers flooded hotel lobbies and the convention hall itself, handing out thousands of brochures and buttons. The "draft Rocky" committees placed appeals for support in newspapers throughout the nation. In response, an amazing 1 million letters and calls poured into Chicago, directed toward the various delegations, swamping hotels, and tying up switchboards.

The debate swirling around the 1960 Republican platform almost sent the convention reeling out of the control of Nixon forces who had, in the tradition of Hoover and Dewey, tried to carefully orchestrate and script events. The 1960 South Side wigwam served as a cold war council, marked by the clash of ideas representing the party's leading voices. Nixon tried to mold compromise, but his space for maneuvering was limited. The giant shadow resisting the drumbeat of change was retiring President Dwight D. Eisenhower. Although vacationing at the Newport Naval Base in Rhode Island, he was in constant touch with events that might mar his reputation.

Ready to pounce on any compromiser was a small contingent of conservative delegates who admired the other Republican star of the 1958 election, the outspoken Arizona senator Barry Goldwater. Nixon, with eight years of vice presidential experience behind him and nearly all the delegate votes in his pocket, tried desperately to prevent a party blowup that would wreck his chances of election in November.

The platform drafts developed by various subcommittees set off alarm bells in the Rockefeller suites. Percy tried to appease the New York camp by letting them add paragraphs of their own, but they resisted, giving the impression they wanted a floor fight instead. Finally, fearing the whole thing would unravel on the convention floor before a national televised audience, Nixon decided it was time for drastic action.

The vice president enlisted Eisenhower's former attorney general and Dewey's campaign manager,

Herbert Brownell, to contact Rockefeller on Nixon's behalf and set up a high stakes political powwow at the governor's 810 Fifth Avenue apartment. After a dinner befitting the country's second in command, Nixon got down to business. He wanted Rockefeller to become his vice president and form an unbeatable California/New York ticket. Naturally, Rocky refused to work for a man for whom he had less than full respect. Once Nixon was convinced that Rockefeller was truly uninterested in the second spot—something he found difficult to believe—and not just holding out for better terms, they turned to the platform itself and hammered out a deal. The governor took the offensive. Working until 3:00 A.M., the two top Republican contenders crafted a compromise. Both thought they had averted a party ruckus and satisfied important concerns.

The "Pact of Fifth Avenue," as the Nixon/Rockefeller truce came to be called, contained fourteen points: seven on foreign policy and seven on domestic problems. For the most part, it expressed the Rockefeller program in its entirety and was an extensive rewrite of the document that Percy and the platform committee had drafted in good faith during the previous week. Nixon agreed on principle about civil rights reform, hoping to broaden his appeal to independent and African-American voters. He pledged to get the fourteen points accepted by the platform committee if Rocky would agree not to challenge Nixon or raise a floor fight on the issues.

Later that morning, Sunday, July 23, on the eve of the convention, Rockefeller had the ultimate political pleasure of releasing a statement to the press: "The vice president and I met today at my home in New York City. The meeting took place at the vice president's request. The purpose of the meeting was to discuss the platform of the Republican Party. The vice president and I reached an agreement on the following specific and basic positions on foreign policy and national defense . . ."

By breakfast time word of the clandestine meeting broke in Chicago on an unsuspecting convention, including some of Nixon's top aides, such as Herb Klein, his media adviser, who had been kept in the dark about the summit. The reaction was both furious and bitter. Goldwater called the pact the "Munich of the Republican Party" and predicted a November defeat as a consequence. He charged that Nixon had not only "surrendered" party principle

Vice President Richard M. Nixon delivers his acceptance speech at the 1960 Republican National Convention at the Stockyards International Amphitheatre. Chicago Historical Society. Photo by Alfred A. Novick.

but, worse, had "humiliated himself" before the dreaded liberal Rockefeller, the symbol of Wall Street and its conspiracy of consolidated wealth. The platform committee was equally outraged that its hard work had been summarily scrapped by the arrogance of Rockefeller and the weakness of Nixon. The secret deal, instead of accomplishing unity, threatened complete dissension. The despised "Eastern liberals" had bought the party, they charged. Others suspected Rockefeller of political blackmail. Eisenhower was livid, Rockefeller was elated, and Nixon was stuck with the cleanup when the story became public.

Subcommittee members fought back by publishing their various planks in the press to undermine the pact. On Sunday the platform committee refused to make any changes. The convention was about to veer out of control. Nixon flew into Chicago on Monday, July 25, to launch the final offensive for the nomination from his second-floor suite at the Blackstone

and to soothe any hurt feelings. Acting unperturbed, he met with delegation after delegation, telling them all the same thing, that victory in November required party unity in July. Meanwhile, the Nixon/Rockefeller forces joined together to get the votes they needed to pass the platform. It wasn't easy.

The original platform statement on civil rights was a pragmatic one for the Republicans. The 1960 Democratic Party was torn over the issue of race. The Los Angeles convention that nominated John F. Kennedy two weeks earlier had drafted a tough civil-rights platform plank that endorsed student lunch counter sit-ins and freedom rides and urged strong federal intervention to end segregation. Many white southern Democrats were ready to desert their party rather than submit to federally-directed integration of key institutions, as ordered by the Supreme Court in 1954. In fact, Republican support in the South was rapidly growing in the postwar Eisenhower era.

Naming Texan Lyndon Johnson as Democratic vice presidential nominee mollified some Dixiecrats.

Conservative Republicans hoped to take advantage of the Democratic rift by drafting a softer civil-rights plank to encourage southern crossover votes. Eighty years earlier, James Garfield, although repelled by the failure of southern Democrats to set aside their racial hatreds, had seen a natural affinity arise between conservative southern business interests and the Republican Party. Now Republicans were ready to court them again, but this time with fewer moral qualms.

On principle, Nixon decided to side with Rocky and to fight party regulars for a tough civil-rights plank. Nixon had to call in IOU's to force the platform committee to redraft its original position. Barry Goldwater again protested. But Nixon had one eye on northern black voters who could swing key states, such as Illinois, Ohio, and Michigan. In fact, the black vote was now a critical component in eight industrial states.

Rockefeller was not appeased by Nixon's sacrifice on civil rights. He insisted Nixon follow through on revisions of the national defense plank, against the wishes of Eisenhower, whose endorsement Nixon desperately needed in order to win the White House. Rocky again threatened a floor fight. So all Monday night Nixon's aides negotiated with Eisenhower over wording that was acceptable to all. Rockefeller in turn adopted language more conciliatory toward the Eisenhower camp. By dawn they had an agreement that made reference to "intensified" missile production and "any necessary increased expenditures to meet the new situation."

On Tuesday, July 26, Rockefeller signed onto the party platform and notified the New York delegation that he was no longer a candidate for nomination. When Percy and the platform committee finally cooled down, it was ready to swallow the bitter pill. All fourteen of the pact's points became part of the platform. Rockefeller had his triumph and his headlines.

When Charles Percy read the 1960 Republican platform to the great assembly, no one could help but be struck by the scope of its concerns or the force of its preamble:

> The United States is living in an age of profoundest revolution. The lives of men and nations are undergoing such transformations as history has rarely

recorded. The birth of new nations, the impact of new machines, the threat of new weapons, the stirring of new ideas, the ascent into a new dimension of the universe, everywhere the accent falls on the new.

The Republican platform consisted of fifteen thousand words and encompassed all of Rockefeller's policy concerns in foreign policy, national defense, economic growth, labor, agriculture, natural resources, government finance and administration, education, science, and technology as well as the human needs of older citizens, health problems, juvenile delinquency, veterans, Native Americans, housing, consumers, civil rights, and immigration. It was thoughtful and provocative—and unpopular with delegates. But when it came up on the convention floor, it was unanimously adopted by voice vote. On the television screen there had been no platform debate at all; everything seemed smooth and reassuring to millions of viewers who had been excluded from the process. Besides, this TV election would revolve around candidates, not platforms; image, not substance—on how Nixon looked rather than what he thought or whether he had succumbed to the persuasive powers of the governor of New York.

When the convention got under way on Tuesday, July 26, the Stockyards International Amphitheatre was more than ready. Five hundred technicians had strung four tons of electrical and amplifying equipment, including closed-circuit television on a twenty-four-by-thirty-two-foot screen above the speaker's platform. Four television studios were available for the networks and independents. A helicopter landing site on top of the building was used to ship TV film to locations around the world. More than 4,500 newspeople worked out of pressrooms right next to the platform. Illinois Bell installed 3,500 phones as well as direct lines to Republican headquarters at the Conrad Hilton. Special suites were set aside for dignitaries, party officials, and candidate teams. The concession stands were ready to sell 5,000 pounds of steak, 6,000 hot dogs and soft drinks, 10,000 hamburgers, and 12,500 pounds of coffee per convention day. Delegates sat on padded folding chairs, while the audience was packed into three tiers of wooden stands.

Former president Herbert Hoover, now a Republican convention icon, instructed the party in the lessons of history. Then Congressman Walter Judd of Minnesota delivered a scalding keynote address that tarred and feathered Democrats with thirty-year-old charges. "Was it the Republicans who recognized the Soviet Union in 1933?" he bellowed. The audience reacted indignantly, "No, no." "Was it the Republicans who, at Tehran, against the urgent advice of Mr. Churchill, agreed to give the Russians a free hand in the Balkans?" "No, no." "Was it the Republicans who secretly divided Poland and gave half of it to the Soviet Union?" The crowd intensified its negative refrain. "Was it a Republican administration that divided Korea and gave North Korea to the communists?" "No, no, no." The Republicans had come to rely upon the twin themes of the Soviet threat abroad and the subversive menace at home to rally its troops into action and to scare voters into fleeing the Democrats.

On Wednesday night, July 27, the convention heard a stirring speech from its commander-in-chief, General Eisenhower. Then, finally, it nominated Richard Milhous Nixon to be its 1960 standard-bearer. The Arizona delegation nominated Senator Barry Goldwater, but he promptly withdrew his name, telling backers, "Let's grow up, conservatives . . . If we want to take this party back . . . and I think we can someday . . . let's get to work." It was a challenge Goldwater would soon fulfill, much to Rockefeller's discomfort. When the delegate votes were tallied at 11:13 P.M., Nixon sailed to victory, 1,321 to 10. The ten dissenting votes were cast by Louisiana delegates upset with the party's stand on civil rights. After the first ballot, though, Louisiana moved to make Nixon's nomination unanimous. Nixon was nominated for president of the United States in Chicago by the Republican Party celebrating its 100th anniversary of the Lincoln Wigwam.

Richard Nixon was a complex, capable, calculating, suspicious, and insecure vice president, just thirty-nine years old when he stepped into the office. But nominee Nixon was a shrewd student of electoral campaigns. He knew that despite Ike's popularity and eight years of power in the White House the Republicans were still the minority party of Dewey. In fact, Republican strength, as revealed in the midterm elections, indicated the Republicans were at their lowest point of popular loyalty since 1936. In 1958 just 43 percent of voters cast their ballots for Republicans. The party controlled only fourteen of forty-eight governors' chairs and only seven state legislatures. He knew that wooing independents,

African Americans, Southerners, and dissatisfied Democrats was essential to his victory.

In 1960 Nixon was a candidate with solid experience. He was the statesman running against the "amateur Kennedy." He had thought carefully about the role television would play in carrying his message to the voters. In fact, he was ready to book massive amounts of air time for the final days of the campaign. Most important, he had solidified his support with the party's financial backers and with the local Republican precinct workers in every state of the Union. Nixon knew this presidential election would be fought precinct-to-precinct in all fifty states.

Since the day the convention opened, Philip Willkie, Indiana state superintendent of public instruction and son of the 1940 nominee, flickered from delegation to delegation trying to drum up support for a vice presidential nod. To no avail; others, too, waited in the wings. But Nixon had his own well-thought-out plans. On Thursday morning, July 28, thirty-six party leaders traipsed into his Blackstone suite to designate a running mate. After Rockefeller rebuffed his overtures, Nixon settled on U.N. Ambassador Henry Cabot Lodge Jr., the former Massachusetts senator defeated by Kennedy in 1952. He needed further input to solidify his selection.

Nixon heard plenty of objections. Governor William G. Stratton of Illinois argued for a Midwesterner. "You can say all you want to about foreign affairs, but what's really important is the price of hogs in Chicago and St. Louis." Nixon argued that if the campaign was waged only on domestic issues, the Democrats would win. "Our only hope is to keep it on foreign policy," the new nominee insisted, convincing at least twenty party leaders. So Henry Cabot Lodge got the nod, and the convention unanimously endorsed him that day.

At the convention's final session Rockefeller introduced Nixon to the adoring crowds, who were certain he was on his way to the White House. The new nominee promised to campaign in all fifty states. Nixon was conversational yet somewhat awkward as he addressed the delegates he had spent nearly a decade courting.

Mr. Chairman, delegates to this convention, my fellow Americans, I have made many speeches in my life, and never have I found it more difficult to find the words to adequately express what I feel, as I find them tonight.

To stand here before this great convention, to hear your expression of affection for me, for Pat, for our daughters, for my mother, for all of us who are representing our party, is, of course, the greatest moment of my life. And I just want you to know that my only prayer as I stand here is that in the months ahead I may be in some way worthy of the affection and trust which you have presented to me on this occasion, in everything that I say, in everything that I do, in everything that I think in this campaign and afterwards . . .

This is truly a time for greatness in American leadership. I would like to discuss tonight some of the great problems which will confront the next president of the United States . . . One hundred years ago, in this very city, Abraham Lincoln was nominated for president of the United States. The problems that will confront our next president will be even greater than those that confronted Lincoln. The question then was freedom of the slaves and survival of the nation. The question now is freedom for all mankind and the survival of civilizations, and the choice each of you listening to me makes this November can affect the answer to that question.

Then Nixon criticized the goings-on at the Democratic convention held earlier in Los Angeles.

It was simply the same old proposition that a political party should be all things to all men, and nothing more than that, and they promised everything to everybody with one exception: they didn't promise to pay the bill. And I say tonight that with their convention, their platform, and their ticket, they composed a symphony of political cynicism which is out of harmony with our times . . . I pledge to you tonight that we will bring the facts home to the American people, and we will do it with a campaign such as this country has never seen before.

I have been asked all week long by the newsmen sitting on my right and left, "When is this campaign going to begin, Mr. Vice President? On Labor Day or one of the other traditional starting points?" And this is my answer: This campaign begins tonight, here and now, and this campaign will continue from now until November 8 without any letup.

Then the vice president turned to his own personal platform, defending "the best eight-year record of any administration in the history of this country and . . . goals of a better America." Nixon pledged better health care for older Americans, and for

younger Americans, "every boy and girl of ability, regardless of financial circumstances, shall have the opportunity to develop his intellectual capabilities to the full." Higher wages for workers, better prices for farmers, and revitalization of America's moral and spiritual strength were all a part of the Nixon vision.

And because "the communists are running us down abroad, it is time to speak up for America at home." So Nixon reminded his "listeners" that "America is the strongest nation militarily, economically, ideologically in the world." And that "when Mr. Khrushchev says our grandchildren will live under communism, let us say his grandchildren will live under freedom . . . When Mr. Khrushchev says the Monroe Doctrine is dead in the Americas, we say the doctrine of freedom applies everywhere in the world."

Nixon's solemn conclusion presaged the irony of his own political undoing a decade and a half later:

And my fellow Americans, I know that we must resist the hate, we must remove the doubts, but above all we must be worthy of the love and the trust of millions on this earth for whom America is the hope of the world.

Nixon was wrong about at least one thing. The campaign was very slow in getting off the ground. Both Kennedy and Johnson came from the U.S. Senate—a historic first—and were committed to staying in Washington until the upper chamber recessed late in August. To their dismay, Democratic civil-rights legislation did not pass. Meanwhile, Nixon spent two weeks in the hospital with a knee infection.

By September the contest finally hit the furious pace Nixon had forecast, with both candidates flying thousands of miles each week making speeches and attending campaign events. Wherever they traveled, they were cheered by huge crowds solicited by their advance staff and national organizations. Both campaigns were also guided by careful and extensive voter polling that indicated where they needed to shore up strength or make inroads.

Nixon and Kennedy had spent four years preparing for the fight. Nixon relied upon party regulars and his small loyal staff, while Kennedy supplemented the party organization with a large network of amateurs and intellectuals who brought enthusiasm and knowledge to the national debate. The 1960 election was hotly contested in the cities and towns of the nation and, for the first time, in the burgeoning suburbs. Kennedy's strategy focused on the big industrial states.

At the same time, the campaign was fought on television before millions of voters who had shared Rockefeller's concern for the future and showed renewed interest in this confrontation between the two young and dynamic candidates. Nixon emulated the Eisenhower media strategy of building broadcast time toward an election eve crescendo, favoring half-hour productions. Kennedy started strong with five-minute spots, but faded in the paid media as the Democratic coffers ran dry. However, Kennedy had the advantage of an admiring press corps that made much of his natural charm and quick wit.

The highlight of the campaign was the four nationally televised debates between the candidates in September and October 1960. Kennedy challenged, Nixon accepted, and Congress waived the equal time rule. More than seventy million viewers witnessed the first debate on September 26, televised in the studios of WBBM in Chicago, a CBS affiliate. The contest proved to be a decisive event that swayed voters toward Kennedy and gave the senator the stature he desperately needed to catch Nixon.

Nixon considered himself the superior debater and used classic debating strategies to score small technical points against Kennedy as though he were in a college debating club, while Kennedy effortlessly and knowledgeably played to the huge national audience. Radio listeners gave a slight edge to Nixon on content points. But on the small living-room screens of millions of American households, Nixon seemed dark and brooding, his face drawn, stark, and hard, his demeanor intense, almost disturbed. He was too hot, perspiring profusely through his "Lazy Shave" powder, on the ultracool medium. Kennedy was medium-cool from beginning to end, relaxed, tanned, aristocratic in manner and wit, the master of easy quips that left listeners chuckling. Kennedy was the big winner in the electronic eye, and momentum instantly shifted to his side in the razor-close contest. Enthusiastic crowds suddenly surrounded him wherever he went. Southern governors, stirred by his performance, fell into line and got their voters ready to "back Jack."

In subsequent debates, Nixon came out swinging, but first impressions endured. Though Nixon had been ill and tired before the first match, he now went on the offensive and looked much better. Kennedy insisted that the country needed to get "moving" again, while Nixon touted his experience and endorsement by Ike. Rockefeller's charges of a "missile gap" were turned around by Democrats against the Republicans. By the time the debates were over, more than 100 million Americans had viewed at least one of the epic sessions, events that dwarfed the earlier, though much more substantial, Lincoln/Douglas debates a century ago.

Worse yet for Nixon, as the summer faded into fall, the American economy slowed for the third Eisenhower recession. Kennedy was a whiz with the data and hit hard at the failure of the Republicans to hold onto old jobs or create new ones. Kennedy also won the African-American vote when his brother, Robert, arranged for the release of Dr. Martin Luther King Jr., who had been arrested in Georgia on a trumped-up traffic ticket charge. Further, Kennedy placated Protestant leaders at the Houston Ministers Association, who charged that the Vatican might run the White House on key decisions. Unlike Al Smith, victim of the anti-Catholic hysteria of 1928 that spelled the end to Smith's Democratic campaign dreams, Kennedy was given credit for his honesty, independence, and sense of humor that kept it all in perspective. His personality pleased people. They liked him.

Throughout the fall, Rockefeller vigorously campaigned across the country for Nixon and Lodge. Then in the final weeks of the canvass, Eisenhower hit the campaign trail, drawing huge crowds, striking out against Democratic policies he said would ruin the nation. Nixon saturated the nightly television screen with carefully scripted programs down the stretch. In the end, television contributed to the largest voter turnout to date.

On election night, November 8, the race was a photo finish. During the early morning hours returns from critical states, such as Illinois and Texas, seemed to guarantee victory for the young Massachusetts senator. The final count was Kennedy 34,227,069 to Nixon's 34,107,646, a plurality of just 119,450 votes nationwide, or just two votes per precinct. Again, charges of fraud were heard among Republicans. But Nixon himself never challenged the results. He knew how elections were won and lost, stolen or blown. Detailed analysis later showed a voter's religion influenced the turnout and voting patterns.

Nixon won twenty-six states, Kennedy only twenty-three. But Kennedy's big-state strategy worked, and he won a comfortable electoral college margin of 303 to 219. Senator Harry F. Byrd of Virginia snagged fifteen segregationist protest votes from Alabama, Mississippi, and Oklahoma. Kennedy took New York by 388,666 votes, despite Rockefeller's unwavering efforts, and swept twenty-six of the nation's forty largest cities; he held most of the South, with Johnson's help, and won twelve states by a margin of no more than 2 percent.

JFK also took Chicago by 450,000 votes—Illinois by fewer than 9,000 ballots. Every Chicago mayor knows politics begins and ends in the local precincts. When the votes were counted in the dark morning hours, Nixon was ultimately defeated by Mayor Richard J. Daley of Chicago, whose arithmetic was precise enough and voter lists padded enough to prevent the Republicans from gaining power. Republicans may have been out in force to police the polls, but Daley's experienced sleight of hand proved magical for the young Irish candidate. Daley had told Kennedy by phone on election night that "with a little bit of luck and the help of a few close friends, you're going to carry Illinois." America had elected its youngest president (Kennedy was just forty-three-years old), and the first New England Democrat in a century. Voters had failed to elevate another vice president to the top spot on his own merits. Republicans, bitter about the outcome and the behind-the-scene machinations, refused to return to Chicago to stage another national convention, forsaking for the rest of the twentieth century the city that had sent Lincoln and so many other Republican nominees on their way to the White House to touch the fate of millions.

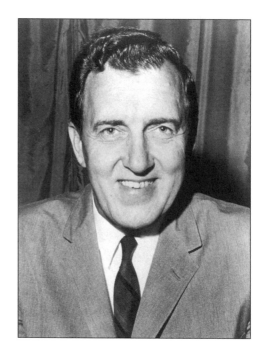

Hubert Horatio Humphrey
1968 Democratic Presidential Nominee

Edmund Sixtus Muskie
1968 Democratic
Vice Presidential Nominee

Facts-at-a-Glance
★★★

Event:	Thirty-Fifth Democratic National Convention
Dates:	August 26–29, 1968
Building:	The Stockyards International Amphitheatre
Location:	4300 South Halsted Street
Chicago Mayor:	Richard Joseph Daley, Democrat
Candidates for Nomination:	Vice President Hubert Horatio Humphrey, Minnesota; Senator Edward Moore Kennedy, Massachusetts; Senator Eugene Joseph McCarthy, Minnesota; Senator George Stanley McGovern, South Dakota; Daniel Killian Moore, North Carolina; Reverend Channing Emery Phillips, Washington, D.C.
Presidential Nominee:	Hubert Horatio Humphrey
Age at Nomination:	57
Number of Ballots:	1
Vice Presidential Nominee:	Edmund Sixtus Muskie, Maine
Number of Delegates:	2,989
Number Needed to Nominate:	A majority, 1,312
Largest Attendance:	15,000
Critical Issues:	Ending the war in Vietnam, civil rights and urban reconstruction, a nonracist and democratic delegate selection process, abolition of the unit rule, the future of the Democratic Party
Campaign Song:	"Happy Days Are Here Again"

24
★★★

The 1968 Democratic National Convention
With the Whole World Watching

The road to the 1968 Democratic convention in Chicago was bathed in blood. From the devastating casualties inflicted by the January 1968 Tet Offensive that rocked cities across South Vietnam to the assassination of the revered and feared civil-rights leader Dr. Martin Luther King Jr. in Memphis as he linked together the issues of discrimination and the war; from the angry riots, arson, and looting of a hundred U.S. cities from coast to coast in the explosive aftermath of King's assassination; to a second senseless murder, that of presidential hopeful Senator Robert Francis Kennedy of New York only moments after he won the California Democratic primary by promising to solve problems of discrimination and to end the devastating war in Vietnam; from beginning to end the route to the 1968 Chicago convention and the nomination of a new party leader was consumed by chaos and tragedy. Consequently, it is not surprising that in August 1968, the Democratic National Convention in Chicago witnessed the worst mass political violence in U.S. electoral history.

The Democrats were looking for a new party leader because on the evening of March 31, 1968, President Lyndon Baines Johnson had astonished the nation by announcing:

> With American sons in the fields far away, with America's future under challenge right here at home, with our hopes and the world's hopes for peace in the balance every day, I do not believe that I should devote an hour or a day of my own to any personal partisan causes or to any duties other than the awesome duties of this office, the presidency of your country.

Lyndon Johnson, the big-hearted, sweet-talking, fast-dealing Texan who was a "second Lincoln" with his legislative victories for civil rights and human dignity, hesitated and then sadly declared:

> Accordingly, I shall not seek and I will not accept the nomination of my party for another term as your president.

The 1964 landslide winner over Barry Goldwater, Johnson had unflinchingly enacted the historic Civil Rights Act of 1964 and Voting Rights Act of 1965, and he boldly attacked the problems of poverty and helplessness of the nation's weak, disinherited elderly and its disadvantaged young with his ambitious and inspiring Great Society programs. Nonetheless, the president had fallen prey to a fatal error. He had sent more than half a million U.S. soldiers to fight in a distant Asian civil war. His decision led to the agonizing death of, by the time of the convention, more than twenty-five thousand young Americans and tens of thousands more Vietnamese civilians and combatants in a seemingly endless clash of increasingly hollow ideologies.

The United States' involvement in Vietnam began covertly during the Eisenhower years in a policy panic after the defeat of the colonialist French army at Dien Bien Phu in 1954 by the Vietminh, the revolutionary nationalist army led by Ho Chi Minh that fought Japanese and French occupation. For six years, the secret American military commitment continued under Ike. Scheduled free elections were canceled in 1956. The U.S. commitment quickly escalated during the three years of the Kennedy administration. Thousands of strategic advisers and war materials were funded to prop up a teetering and far-from-democratic South Vietnamese government whose repression sparked a succession of suicides by self-immolating Buddhist monks. These harrowing incidents were broadcast on television worldwide. Then the Kennedy administration looked the other way during the assassination of South Vietnam president Ngo Dinh Diem, whose tyrannical behavior escalated dissent.

After Kennedy's assassination, Johnson felt compelled to outdo Kennedy in all respects, domestic and foreign. Within three months of his own election as a "peace candidate" against the "dangerous" Goldwater, he escalated the war. A U.S.-provoked attack by North Vietnamese patrol boats on U.S. ships led to the Tonkin Gulf congressional resolution in August 1964. Thus, the U.S. Congress "approved" the war for a "free and independent South Vietnam" even though the 1954 Geneva Accords that ended French involvement made no provisions for two separate Vietnams or military intervention. In February 1965 Johnson launched a three-and-a-half-year bombing campaign against North Vietnamese military and civilian installations that killed thousands on the ground. Scores of American pilots perished, too.

Almost from the beginning, Vietnam became an American policy apocalypse. By the summer of 1968 nearly half a million U.S. troops had been transported into a strange land of rice paddies that were studded with explosive mines and dense jungles where camouflaged Viet Cong snipers waited for their prey. The Viet Cong were indigenous independence fighters in the south formed to fight the U.S., who they saw as taking the place of the French. What started as an advisory and "counterinsurgency" support of the unstable South Vietnamese government exploded into a full-scale U.S. military operation designed to search out and destroy large numbers of Viet Cong soldiers and the North Vietnamese regular army. The latter adversaries turned out to be extremely capable as light infantry.

The goal of U.S. policy was not the conquest of territory, which the Viet Cong controlled, but rather a war of attrition that sought to kill or capture as many of the enemy as possible. But the enemy was evasive. War supplies poured through porous borders. Most Vietnamese were sympathetic to the goals of the National Liberation Front, the political arm of the liberation struggle that fought for unification and independence from outside domination, whether it be from China, France, or the United States. America's supreme advantage of technology and firepower, although decisive on the tactical battlefield, could not insure strategic victory without an invasion of the north, an option fraught with geopolitical, nuclear, and domestic nightmares. Operation Rolling Thunder, the strategy of bombing the North Vietnamese "back into the Stone Age," proved folly.

Thus the greatest military power in the history of humankind was trapped in a quagmire of unending casualties and unattainable goals. Although many military and government officials expected the enemy's will to break as a result of escalated military punishment, pragmatists among them, including those in the CIA, believed otherwise. In 1968 alone, 14,615 U.S. soldiers were killed in Vietnam. More than eighty thousand were wounded. Without a wholesale call-up of reserves and expansion of the draft, the United States was faced with defeat or withdrawal.

Hundreds of thousands of American and Asian lives were traumatized. U.S. civilians back home watched in dismay on their television sets, almost shell-shocked. Finally, the Tet Offensive, launched on January 29, 1968, placed all of South Vietnam under siege for two bloody weeks. Even the U.S. embassy in Saigon was embattled by Viet Cong. U.S. voters recognized the utter futility of Johnson's war policy and the vulnerability of American ideals, purposes, and personnel. Perception was everything. Although Tet was a brilliant psychological and political success for the North Vietnamese, from a strictly military point of view it was not. The Viet Cong in the south were decimated and no longer an effective fighting force.

Johnson's decision to wage war had sparked domestic opposition that cut across all walks of life and communities. Resistance spontaneously grew on more than five hundred college campuses across the land. Draft-age students readily followed the lead of the 1964 Berkeley "free-speech movement," which aroused a new sense of freedom and activism. With the support of some of their professors, members of the movement launched local Vietnam War "teach-ins," "educational campaigns," and demonstrations that dominated the headlines in college towns and then flooded the national news throughout the spring of 1968. Most of these students brought a sense of betrayed American idealism and patriotism to the forefront, determined as they were to "save" the country from what they considered blind obedience to failed governmental policy. Their goal was to stop the war before it destroyed their generation, a generation far more interested in making new music and cultural discoveries than killing.

Governor Harold E. Hughes of Iowa was an early Democratic proponent of the "dump Johnson" boom. However, resistance grew much more slowly in the halls of Congress than on college campuses or in churches. Senators Vance Hartke of Indiana, Wayne Morse of Oregon, and Ernest H. Gruening of Alaska were among the first to speak out against the misguided policy. Senator William J. Fulbright of Arkansas conducted congressional hearings on Vietnam in the long, hot summer of 1966 and gave further legitimacy to the protest.

Johnson's decision not to run again was complex, but was accelerated by the Democratic primary challenge of Eugene Joseph McCarthy, a senator from Minnesota, who came to represent the electoral wing of the antiwar movement in the early and later moments of the 1968 preconvention campaign. The fifty-one-year-old senator had come to Congress in 1948, two years after Richard Nixon, and had established a progressive record. His eloquent nomination of Adlai Stevenson for president in 1960 allowed him to claim a legacy with the Democratic idealist tradition of Wilson and Roosevelt. McCarthy announced his challenge to Johnson in November 1967 in order to "alleviate the sense of political helplessness and restore to many people belief in the process of American politics." He then recruited thousands of restless students who may have been too young to vote but who could propel his cash-poor campaign into contention. By the time of the New Hampshire primary on March 12, 1968, McCarthy had skillfully harnessed the undirected "student power." Committed young dissidents cut their hair and put on a tie to get "clean for Gene." McCarthy molded them into an unprecedented grass-roots force that descended upon primary states with a vengeance.

In the March New Hampshire primary, McCarthy showed startling strength, grabbing 23,280 votes to Johnson's 27,243 write-ins. Although Johnson was not even on the official ballot, the razor-thin write-in victory waged by his supporters was cast by the national press as a stunning loss for the president. Indeed, McCarthy ended up with twenty of New Hampshire's twenty-four delegates to the convention and a legitimate claim that he had beaten Johnson.

Within a week of McCarthy's New Hampshire upset, an impatient Senator Robert F. Kennedy of New York charged into the race. "I run to seek new policies," Kennedy proclaimed in his Boston accent, "policies to end the bloodshed in Vietnam and in our cities, policies to close the gap that now exists between black and white, between rich and poor, between young and old in this country and around the world."

Kennedy had been attorney general of the United States under his brother, President John F. Kennedy, and after JFK's assassination, under Lyndon B. Johnson. Although he had been an architect of the antiguerrilla war policies of the Kennedy administration, particularly in Latin America, Kennedy's experiences in the political arena led to a reconsideration and renunciation of some of the policies he helped shape. In late 1967 Kennedy became a dove, critical of the official Johnson policy. He had moved slowly and reluctantly into the presidential race. But he disliked McCarthy. His negative feelings extended back to 1960 when JFK beat Stevenson, who had been nominated by McCarthy. RFK felt little sympathy for McCarthy's complaint that he was dividing the peace vote. Robert Kennedy marched to his own drummer.

Later that month, on March 23, a meeting was held in a YMCA in the Chicago suburb of Lake Villa. One hundred student and antiwar groups, from the Students for a Democratic Society (SDS) to the National Mobilization Committee to End the War in Vietnam (MOB) to the Youth International Party (Yippies), gathered to plan demonstrations around the Democratic convention in August. Despite his problems, Johnson was expected to be renominated by his own party machinery. The coalition said it would recruit one hundred thousand students into the streets of Chicago to contest LBJ's policies and renomination.

At the forefront of the plan was SDS. Founded in June 1962 at a Port Huron, Michigan, convention of student activists, SDS was a radical, intellectual, nonviolent group dedicated to action. Its manifesto, the Port Huron statement, asserted, "As a social system we seek the establishment of a democracy of individual participation, governed by two central claims; that the individual share in those social decisions determining the quality and direction of his life; that society be organized to encourage independence in men and provide the media for their common participation." Its "subversive goals" centered on racial and social justice at home and national liberation movements overseas. Like Dr. Martin Luther King Jr., SDS linked the flaws of U.S. foreign policy and the plight of poor people to the actions of corporate elites and their government sponsors. SDS called for a decentralized "participatory democracy."

McCarthy and his "kiddie campaign" caught fire in Wisconsin. The senator drew thousands of volunteers over the spring break. Large crowds, converted by his message of peace, gathered wherever he spoke. Vice President Hubert Humphrey and other cabinet members flew into the Dairy State to try to save Johnson, whose name was required to appear on the ballot. But it was too late. A sitting president, the polls confirmed, was about to be defeated by Democratic voters who were heartsick over the war. The streets of Madison were already clogged with thousands of antiwar demonstrations, and conflict with police was intensifying.

Thus, on March 31, President Johnson preempted the voters and announced his resignation. That night, as he spoke to the nation in a solemn and agonized tone, he also announced a partial bombing halt. To his credit, Johnson had refused military requests for 200,000 more troops, and now wanted to begin negotiations with the Hanoi government to end the war on terms honorable to both sides. In the meantime, Johnson, the noncandidate, was defeated two days later in Wisconsin when McCarthy received 57 percent of the primary vote. The McCarthy grassroots campaign had stormed into New Hampshire and Wisconsin and driven a sitting president from his imperial throne. The antiwar movement, now more militant and determined than ever, claimed its first victory.

Four days after Johnson's bombshell announcement staggered the country, a single bullet inflicted even deeper damage on the national psyche and soul when Dr. Martin Luther King Jr., the country's moral conscience, was struck down by a sniper in Memphis. Civil rights was one thing, economic rights were another, his critics angrily complained. King and his Poor People's Campaign posed too great a threat in too unstable an environment. Was he killed on FBI orders, or by a secret southern elite, many wondered? Was his murder part of a racist conspiracy?

On that long and bloody night of April 4, and for several days and nights thereafter, America's capital city burned as it had not done since the British put it to the torch during the War of 1812. King was dead. The civil-rights movement he led was dead. Now from the darkness would emerge more angry and bitter voices, both black and white. Violence had won out; harmony seemed impossible; hatred took over. Los Angeles. Newark. Detroit. Chicago. Across the country, urban centers were on fire, lighting up with spasms of brutal violence. The National Guard

was summoned in state after state. Snipers emerged from behind windows. Rioters were shot. Whole sections of cities burned to the ground.

Vice President Hubert Humphrey moved into the leadership void left by Johnson's declaration and pledged to carry forward the policies of the Johnson-Humphrey administration. The war hawks swooped into line behind the vice president as he picked up endorsement after endorsement from labor unions and local party bosses. Humphrey officially announced his candidacy on April 27 with the blessing and support of President Johnson. Against the chaos of national tragedy and despair, Humphrey oddly dedicated his campaign to the "politics of joy." No one, however, felt elated or inspired. He later withdrew the slogan.

In an age suddenly dedicated to the exuberance of youth, Humphrey carried an aura of decay and distrust. Humphrey was on the wrong side of the "generation gap," which was growing wider and wider. In the eyes of many Democrats the "Happy Warrior," as Humphrey was called, had squandered his liberal credentials with his vehement advocacy of the war. Although the primary filing deadlines had passed, the vice president wasted no time playing the old-time politics he had spent a lifetime mastering. He courted the party's power sources and lined up more and more strength among those who found both McCarthy and Kennedy unpalatable.

Regular Democrats had another problem besides the war. Former Alabama governor George Corley Wallace threatened to cut heavily into their southern support with his own well-oiled campaign. The South was the origin and the heart of the Democratic Party. But issues of race were dividing the Democracy again as they had one hundred years earlier. At forty-eight years old, Wallace was best described by philosopher Thomas Hobbes's phrase, "nasty, short, and brutish." Wallace was loved by rednecks and racists alike for his defiance of a federal court order to desegregate the University of Alabama and for his ugly proclamation, "Segregation now, segregation tomorrow, segregation forever." In 1964 the former golden-gloves boxer had campaigned in the North against "integration" and "coddling" of common criminals by the courts. Wallace drew an incredible and frightening 40 percent in the Wisconsin, Indiana, and Maryland Democratic primaries against local candidates representing Johnson. The press called Wallace's showing a backlash against the civil-rights movement.

In 1968 Wallace created his own American Independence Party and collected enough signatures to get on the ballot in all fifty states. Wallace entertained his followers by bashing any protesters who got in the way: "Any demonstrator who lies down in front of my presidential limousine," he offered, "it will be the last one he lies down in front of." Wallace brought in $40,000 a day in unsolicited contributions to fuel his campaign.

Meanwhile, Robert Kennedy, who had been directing professional political campaigns since JFK first ran for Congress from Boston, sensed that McCarthy had cornered much of the antiwar vote. He reached out to Johnson, praising him for the courage of his decision to step aside, and courted some of the president's supporters, many of whom had been in the Kennedy administration. Kennedy exuded charismatic electricity that drew huge, optimistic crowds of whites, blacks, and browns wherever he ventured, whether Harlem or rural Mississippi.

On May 7 in Indiana, Kennedy battled McCarthy head-on for leadership of the Democratic Party's peace movement and scored an indecisive 42 percent plurality against Governor Roger Douglas Branigin, a Johnson supporter. McCarthy finished third. Kennedy won again in Nebraska. But his momentum was stalled by a whopping twenty thousand vote loss to McCarthy in Oregon. McCarthy's impressive win indicated that the peace movement was seriously split and offered an opening for Humphrey.

On June 4 the sun set on the Democratic Party's peace movement at the California primary. Heavy Hispanic and African-American turnout in the central cities and support from a "glamorous" California coalition of party regulars and Hollywood liberals carried RFK to a narrow 46 to 42 percent triumph over McCarthy. Then, after saluting his supporters in a wild and joyous celebration in the Los Angeles Ambassador Hotel, he quipped, "And now it's onto Chicago, and let's win there!"

Kennedy waved as he beamed at the packed room, turned, and retreated through the hotel's kitchen where he was cut down by the gun of Sirhan Bishara Sirhan, an unemployed Middle Eastern fanatic. Robert Kennedy died the next morning from a bullet to his brain, two months and two days after the assassination of Dr. King. The nation reeled backward in sickness, rage, grief, confusion, and disbelief. How could it happen again? Who could stop the madness of 1968? From whence had this tidal wave of irrational violence come? The nation mourned aloud that week as the body of its gallant, fallen senator was transported to Saint Patrick's Cathedral on Fifth Avenue in New York City and then by train to Arlington National Cemetery outside Washington to be interred beside his beloved brother, beneath the eternal torch that marks their promise and their misfortune. Their nation lay in disarray.

The preconvention campaigns of the candidates were put on hold while everyone reassessed the situation. But quietly Hubert Humphrey consolidated his support, with Johnson bringing along the reluctant South. McCarthy seemed strangely quixotic, not willing to fight for the nomination, thinking it should come to him by virtue of his political courage. Students, now on summer recess, discovered that even though the leadership was about to change, the policy was not. The Paris peace talks stalled. The wrath of the protesters grew as the peace alternatives narrowed.

The 1968 Republicans met during the first week of August in Miami Beach to nominate their candidate. He was far from a new political face, but he was the "new" Nixon. Richard Nixon had not only lost a close contest to Kennedy in 1960, he had gone down to defeat to Edmund Gerald Brown in the 1962 California gubernatorial race. He was a two-time loser, not quite like Stevenson, but he knew America disliked losers. So in the depths of those six years of political exile, a "new" Nixon was born, a softer, more mature, media-calculated candidate cultivated by Madison Avenue advertising techniques with a Southern California twist. The "new" Nixon was there to recast the shattered party left over from the 1964 Goldwater disaster, in which Democrats swept into the Eighty-Ninth Congress with the largest majority since 1936. By the end of the Miami convention, the "new" Nixon had successfully positioned himself as the only viable candidate who could "end the war and win the peace." As he later revealed, he had a "secret plan" to end the conflict. He also hoped to attract the support of voters who weren't interested in anything but "winning the war" and averting the first U.S. military humiliation since Korea.

For the vice presidency, Nixon chose Spiro Theodore Agnew, a former Baltimore executive and governor of Maryland since 1966, over New York's

John Lindsay and Governor John Volpe of Massachusetts. Nine years earlier, Agnew had been president of his local PTA. Agnew immediately became "Spiro Who?" to the press and admitted with wry humor that he was "not a household name." (He would eventually resign in disgrace.)

Nixon's nomination was topped off by a three-day riot in the African-American ghettos of Miami. Some delegates were trapped in Miami Beach. But the Republican riots came before the Democratic disturbances in Chicago, and the media was more cooperative in dispensing an image of Republican unity rather than urban disintegration. When Nixon arrived in Miami Beach, the polls pegged the national race as a toss-up between Humphrey, Nixon, and Wallace. When he left, Nixon popped into a 45 to 29 percent lead over Humphrey. As they headed for the Thirty-Fifth Democratic National Convention, McCarthy supporters argued that Humphrey was not electable. With a lame duck president at the helm, America was in a state of suspended anticipation.

Democrats converged on the Windy City during the last week of August 1968 with their party-splintered, delegates angry and uncertain, carrying all the burdens of the war on their shoulders. The 1968 convention, the first time the Democrats had been in town since the 1956 gathering, was supposed to have been a celebratory event lauding the great works of the Johnson administration. President Johnson had given Mayor Richard J. Daley the convention plum a year earlier as a reward for his long-term party loyalty and ballot box sleight of hand. Daley dissuaded him from choosing Houston, arguing that Johnson already had Texas in his pocket but that the race for Illinois votes in November would be more difficult. A convention would help. Chicago was now the world's largest convention city, and Daley was a political titan who had been in office since 1955.

As mayor, Daley had been reelected three times, most recently in 1967 by sweeping all fifty city wards with more than 70 percent of the vote. During his first thirteen years in office, the savvy political leader had built the city's system of expressways, reformed its fire department, and cleaned up the police department. Daley created a climate hospitable to big business. He was also seen as a model by other mayors around the nation for achieving a programmatic attack on urban problems. He was personally honest and beloved by most of the city's citizens and kept most of his partisan enemies under control with a respectable share of the political spoils, which in Chicago could be considerable.

But the mayor was increasingly autocratic and rigid, demanding loyalty above all else. And the city was rapidly changing. An African-American political and cultural revolution was transforming expectations and behaviors in the African-American community. Young people were marching for justice, not just new programs. But unbeknownst to the thousands of antiwar demonstrators about to descend on his city, Daley, the Johnson stalwart, had come to oppose the war in Vietnam as bad policy. He even had told the president of his misgivings and had advised him on how to end it. Nor was he particularly committed to Humphrey.

Mayor Daley located the convention at the same Stockyards International Amphitheatre that had nominated Eisenhower, Stevenson, and Nixon in an earlier era. Indeed, it had housed many a great event in its long history, from cattle shows and rodeos to a Beatles concert in 1964. The old and relatively small building, erected in 1934, now spruced up with a new coat of paint, stood on the edge of the aromatic stockyards, the giant slaughterhouse, the "jungle" immortalized to the world in Upton Sinclair's novel of the same name.

That "abattoir by the lake," however, was about to move out of Chicago altogether for Kansas City and Omaha, taking with it thousands of Chicago jobs and further eroding the city's tax base. Yet in 1968, Chicago, at 3.5 million people, was still the nation's second largest city with millions more in its sprawling and mostly affluent suburbs. Chicago was the nation's largest city for Southern-born Americans, African Americans, and Polish Americans. It was also an Irish city, a Lithuanian city, a Yankee city, a city of Germans, Italians, and Hispanics, all living in their own neighborhoods.

Chicago was still a manufacturing giant, too, hub of America's railroads and steel mills (250 million tons produced annually), its hog butcher, its speculative commodities pit. It had electronic manufacturers, universities, corporate headquarters, and jobs for all comers. The city spread along the emerald lake for twenty-three miles from north to south, with an elegant stretch of brand-new residential high-rise apartments gleaming out onto the distant waters of Lake

Illinois delegates cheer Mayor Richard J. Daley on the convention floor during the closing session of the tumultuous 1968 Democratic National Convention. Daley had spent much of the day defending the actions of the Chicago police department. George Dunne (*lower right*) and Roman Pucinski (*far left*) offer their support. AP/Wide World Photos.

Michigan. Its skyline was sprouting like summer corn. But behind many of its glittering facades lay mile after mile of rotting slums, dilapidated wooden three-flats, and overcrowded neighborhoods.

Mayor Daley spent half a million dollars decorating the city for his party and even constructed a "redwood forest" of wooden fences to hide the blight along the bus route from downtown to the Amphitheatre. After all, the "City that Works," as Chicago became known under Daley, was also "America's Number One Clean City." But little was pretty about the scene around the stockyards where the convention was about to be held. Democrats were meeting under strict security. In 1968 a coordinated effort of federal, state, and local armed forces were on constant alert.

Precautions included 11,900 Chicago police on twelve-hour shifts, 300 county riot police, 7,500 Illinois National Guards (with 5,000 more ready), 7,500 army troops, and 1,000 FBI and Secret Service agents. The numbers of armed personnel far exceeded the crowds of delegates and protesters and said little for the democratic process that the U.S. was trying to impose elsewhere around the world (with much greater force of arms). The very image of Chicago as an armed camp seemed to confirm the protesters' point that the war in Vietnam had corroded democratic values at home.

As powerful as these armed forces were, they did not outnumber the tens of thousands of sullen residents in the massive slums simmering on the South and West Sides of the most segregated city in the

North. Dr. Martin Luther King Jr. had been vilified and physically assaulted during his "open housing" marches through one of Chicago's white ethnic neighborhoods. King left, but not before the mayor agreed to pass an open-housing ordinance. Little seemed to change, though. In April, as the West Side burned following the assassination of Dr. King, Daley's order to police to "shoot to kill arsonists" who endangered the lives of innocent people and "shoot to maim or cripple looters" who destroyed property had been a stern warning. Everyone knew the mayor meant business.

Wherever delegates looked, they saw rifles, guns, jeeps with barbed-wire cowcatchers, armored vehicles, binoculars, and walkie-talkies. Helicopters hovered over the parks along the lakefront where protesters danced or listened to speeches or music. Airspace over the Amphitheatre was declared off-limits to all planes. Police were stationed throughout the Loop and inside and even underneath the convention hall. They guarded the downtown hotels where delegates and candidates stayed and pushed groups of youths and delegates alike along their way. After all, America was at war, even if it was an undeclared one, and the threat from foreign assault seemed as real to the city officials as the threat from domestic disorder. Chicago was under a state of siege.

"No one is going to take over the streets of Chicago," Daley insisted. Just to make sure everyone knew who was in control, the city denied parade permits and permission for antiwar group rallies at Soldier Field. Abbie Hoffman, founder of the Yippies and leader of the young contingent from New York, had insisted that the best way to prevent violence in 1968 was to give the youth who gathered special privileges for sleeping in the parks. Hoffman's pleas went unanswered, in part because they were accompanied by even more outrageous demands that the city could barely comprehend, much less meet, such as free food, free media, free marijuana, free sex, and "Free Huey," a reference to Black Panther founder Huey P. Newton, who was in jail on a murder charge in California.

Daley made it clear that his police would enforce the city's ordinance against sleeping in the parks. The first serious trouble occurred on the nights before the convention even opened. Small bands of early arrivals practiced snake dances to break through police lines, coordinated strategy, assembled first-aid equipment in case of trouble when the

convention began, and generally tried to "freak out" city officials. The police watched their antics with a mixture of amusement and resentment. At 11:00 P.M. on Saturday, August 24, and again on Sunday and Monday nights when Lincoln Park was scheduled to close, several hundred police in riot gear, which included helmets and gas masks, fired tear gas canisters into the crowds of defiant protesters and routed them with billy clubs.

The police assaulted whomever failed to vacate the park and struck with sudden violence. Seven reporters, including several from national newspapers and magazines, were beaten. The mood turned uglier on neighboring streets where young "new leftists" and police ran pitched battles. The skirmishes escalated throughout the convention week, intensifying each night. Each side became more and more angry and more and more ready to retaliate. But this action was far from the Amphitheatre.

On Monday night, in a repeat performance in Lincoln Park after the curfew, scores of demonstrators and twenty newsmen were beaten, many rushed to hospitals. The next day, police superintendent James Conlisk Jr. ordered police to desist from attacking journalists who were doing their work. But the mayor seemed to contradict him. "They think because they work for a newspaper that they can do anything, they can violate any law, they can take any action because they are newsmen. This shouldn't be. This isn't any prerogative of newsmen, television, or radio or anyone else."

Unlike McCarthy or Kennedy, Hubert Humphrey had not run in the primaries. Yet the party regulars, the bosses, the mainline union men and women, the public officials, the professional pols who made up the majority of delegates and who had known Humphrey for years, were on the verge of nominating him. In the eyes of peace delegates, he was a "me-too" prowar candidate, who like Richard Nixon was a rabid Cold Warrior. When the nation cried out for new leaders and new directions, the nominating process was serving up another old hat, making the sting of Robert Kennedy's loss even more devastating to his followers. To many student activists, Humphrey represented the bankruptcy of corporate liberalism that had come to control American life.

Humphrey's apparent lock on the nomination was no secret, despite President Johnson's criticism of his vice president in the weeks prior to the convention. But the vice president was edgy about Johnson, too. Humphrey's strategists were predicting 1,450 first ballot votes, enough to win. Yet they were worried that a wild convention could spin out of control and turn to a peace Democrat dark horse. HHH continued to straddle the fence on many issues when talking to reporters. He made proclamations on both sides of the war, as a hawk and a dove, so that neither group really trusted him. Both peace Democrats and antiwar protesters viewed Humphrey's attempt at party unity as hypocritical, but his nomination loomed like luminescent graffiti on a school yard wall.

As August waned, thousands of students and activists were drawn almost irresistibly to Chicago, urged on by antiwar groups, including SDS, MOB, and the Yippies, to demand that the Democrats nominate a peace candidate and adopt a peace platform. To contrast with the Democrats' "Festival of Death," the Yippies staged their own "Festival of Life," an anarchist masquerade of unrestrained rebellion, featuring nude swimming in the lake, pot smoking in the parks, and music in the air. Teenage boys and girls, older graduate students and professors, housewives and Vietnam veterans, musicians and artists, conscientious objectors and professional agitators, theater companies, and thousands of other young people came in cars, on motorcycles, and by trains, sometimes hitching or walking for miles to participate in a political carnival that sought to mock the legitimacy and legacy of Mayor Daley and Hubert Humphrey.

"We are the Second American Revolution," Abbie Hoffman, a specialist in black humor, declared. Hoffman and his Yippie demands included the abolition of money, elimination of pollution, a national referendum system, free cable television, and full employment. Machines would do most of the work. Hoffman was a utopian. The Yippies were far from dangerous in any military sense. Rather they threatened the cultural certainties that kept the children of the suburban middle class on the straight and narrow. To most young people, Yippie outrageousness actually softened the anger that had exploded all over America. Yippies were the intellectual heirs of dada and surrealism, performance artists in the medium of political subreality.

The Yippies knew what people of power feared most—not a tough fight, nor even defeat, but rather ridicule and mockery. Consequently, in the days before the convention, the Yippies started a near-

panic at city hall when they threatened to spike the city's water supply with LSD and to let loose greased pigs on the convention floor. Hoffman also passed out phone numbers of Chicago city officials.

In the Civic Center Plaza (now the Daley Center), across from city hall where the mayor sat in his fifth-floor office, the Yippies introduced the nation to their candidate for president, Pigasus, a huge pig. "Vote Pig in '68," their signs read. Some suggested a likeness to Humphrey, others to "his Honor" the mayor. But police, whom many protesters throughout the week called "pigs," hauled off Pigasus and several Yippies in paddy wagons.

Democratic delegates were greeted by muggy weather and a series of strikes that led to communication and transportation nightmares. Long a union town, Chicago was crippled by a communications workers' walkout against Illinois Bell that jammed telephone service at the hotels and made instantaneous coverage of anything but convention floor activity at the Amphitheatre impossible. The union made sure there was no live TV except at the convention itself and in the candidates' hotel rooms. Yellow and Checker cabbies were also on strike, so movement from the hotels on the lakefront to the Amphitheatre or elsewhere was difficult at best. Most often, delegates were brought to the Amphitheatre in chartered buses.

On August 25 McCarthy flew into Midway Airport with poet Robert Lowell, novelist William Styron, and essayist Shana Alexander and was greeted by five thousand adoring supporters. Meanwhile, Humphrey landed at Chicago's O'Hare airport with little fanfare. They both checked into the Conrad Hilton on Michigan Avenue. From the windows of their hotel rooms, the presidential candidates could safely look down on the thousands of protesters who gathered every day and night of the convention week chanting antiwar slogans.

Humphrey had a lock on the nomination as long as he could hold all his diverse pledges together. He counted on the party and the AFL-CIO for his base. McCarthy had faded as a serious candidate in the mind of the southern delegates. Although he still outpolled Humphrey and attracted big crowds wherever he traveled, he had failed to win the delegates. The whimsical McCarthy could not regain the momentum Kennedy had taken from him in California.

The Kennedy coalition was shattered. Arriving delegates looked around for a replacement. Sixteen days before the first gavel fell, Senator George Stanley McGovern of South Dakota, a war critic and Kennedy ally, stepped forward to rally the Kennedy and disillusioned McCarthy forces converging on Chicago. He won pledges from 150 delegates.

On Sunday night, August 25, in the informal gatherings on the eve of the convention, scores of delegates urged the nomination of thirty-six-year old Edward Moore Kennedy, the last surviving Kennedy brother. Even Mayor Daley, who was enchanted by the Kennedys and still officially uncommitted to Humphrey, made inquiries about Teddy. Daley wanted to be a Democratic kingmaker again, as he had in 1960 for Jack Kennedy. Daley delayed an endorsement vote by the Illinois delegation for Humphrey, adding to the vice president's anxiety.

Finally, the main show began. The convention was gaveled to order by Democratic National Chairman John M. Bailey, a former special adviser to President Kennedy, on Monday, August 26, at 7:30 P.M. (The chair was later given a gavel from timber removed from Jefferson's Monticello mansion.) After an invocation by Bishop William McManal of the Roman Catholic Archdiocese of Chicago and a syncopated rendition of the national anthem by Aretha Franklin, an unwieldy 5,011 delegates and alternates, the most ever at a Democratic convention, jammed the floor and made proceedings confused and order impossible. The facilities were simply too small, and aisles were clogged with delegates and alternates. Almost ten thousand spectators joined the ruckus.

Mayor Daley greeted his guests:

The people of Chicago and its mayor are proud to welcome a great political gathering of Americans who come here to shape the future of a nation, to choose a man to become our president . . . I would like to say it is an important sign of faith to the American people for this national political convention to be held here, not in some resort center but in the very heart of Chicago, in one of the greatest

Hubert Humphrey addresses the 1968 convention as chairman Carl Albert applauds.
AP/Wide World Photos.

neighborhoods of Chicago—my neighborhood. It is where people live and work and raise their families. The Democratic Party has always been a party and a place for all people.

When you in this convention consider the problems of our country, many of your decisions must involve the cities, for it is in the cities where most Americans live that we find our nation's greatest concerns. People do not come to cities to make problems, but they seek a better life . . . Everyone talks about . . . the challenges facing the cities, great and small . . . And they will never be solved in rioting and violence on the streets, and they will never be solved in anarchy. As long as I am mayor of this town, there will be law and order in Chicago.

The delegates loudly applauded the mayor's declaration.

Daley continued:

Let me say, with honor and pride, we have the finest police department and the finest fire department of any city in the United States . . . I believe, and I know every mayor agrees with me, that we must accept responsible criticism, but it is high time for the political leadership of this generation to reject the language of conflict and despair, and to speak out very loud in positive language of hope and human effort . . .

I welcome you to a great city. It is one of the greatest cities in the world. When we consider that only five generations ago it did not even exist, we get some notion of what the American people can do . . . It is the best possible place for a great convention to be held in our time. May we be proud of our country and proud of our city. And may we reject those who would burn our flag or desecrate those things that have always been great to all people who have come to this great country. We have no flag burners in this Democratic National Convention, and I don't think any of them would belong here. But you and I know that this country has given opportunity to all people, of all nationalities, of all race, of all creeds, and this 1968 convention is going to elect the next president who will carry on that program.

The mayor received a long and warm applause for his oration while the bagpipes of the Shannon Rovers played "When Irish Eyes Are Smiling." No one imagined the irony with which history would regard the mayor's speech.

Mayor Daley's address was followed by Illinois's Democratic governor Sam Shapiro, who reminded the delegates, "We are the militants of democracy, not just now, but for a long time, yes, and a long time to come." Chairman Bailey then told the convention,

In convention assembled, I cast my vote for Roosevelt, Truman, Stevenson, Kennedy, and Johnson . . . I must speak frankly to you about that work which you will perform in this convention. The work will be difficult, yes. But it will not be impossible.

He pointed out that 94 percent of the platform adopted four years earlier "is now the law of this great land. And that in itself set a new record for any party, at any time, in all of history."

He warned of trouble.

There are some who seek to rule by dissent, and who seek by dissent to ruin if they cannot rule. They will raise the voices of hysteria and hate, and they will attempt to persuade you that there can never be a better world and a better America. But listen not, I ask you, to the voices of hysteria . . . and heed those who have the voice of reason, and heed well the overwhelming cry of this great America. Then having heard, consult yourselves, and listen only to the voices of your own conscience.

Bailey introduced Senator Birch Bayh of neighboring Indiana, a young and dynamic figure who was a friend of the Kennedy family. Bayh got right to the heart of the dilemma facing his fellow delegates.

This is no ordinary convention. This will be no ordinary election. For these are no ordinary times. While American soldiers are struggling in Southeast Asia to secure the right of self-determination for a people who need it, half a world away in Eastern Europe Soviet troops are denying self-determination to a people who seek it.

Here at home, we are reminded of the unprecedented progress so vigorously pursued by the administrations of John Kennedy and Lyndon Johnson. But this progress has not been without its problems. Progress has opened new doors of opportunity for many who very frankly in previous years did not even know the meaning of the word "opportunity." But this progress unfortunately has not been shared by all Americans. In the injustices and suffering which have been endured for generations as inevitable, have all at once become intolerable for those who have been left behind.

For now it appears that there might be an escape, there might be a brighter tomorrow, and my fellow delegates . . . the very existence of our party is to provide a vehicle, a vehicle to which the promise of America, yes, the promise of America could have real meaning for each of our citizens, to every man, woman and child in this country, regardless of the color of his skin or his place of birth, for every man [a] golden opportunity, for every man the right to work, to live in decency, to live with dignity and self-respect . . . We bring to this convention in Chicago a sense of real impatience. We as Democrats are impatient because our business here is the unfinished business of our nation.

Senator Bayh introduced Senator Daniel K. Inouye of Hawaii, the convention's temporary chair. Senator Inouye was expected to deliver a typical rhetorical spellbinder of fluffy substance. Instead he rocked the convention without turning on Johnson and his achievements.

My fellow Americans, this is my country. Many of us have fought hard for the right to say that. Many are struggling today from Harlem to Da Nang so they may say this with conviction, "This is our country. . . ." The keynote address at a national political convention traditionally calls for introducing oratory. I hope to be excused from this tradition tonight . . . For even as we emerge from an era of unsurpassed social and economic progress, Americans are clearly in no mood for counting either their blessings or their bank accounts. We are still embarked on the longest unbroken journey of economic growth and prosperity in our history.

Yet we are torn by dissension, and disrespect for our institutions and our leaders is right across the line. In at least two of our greatest universities, learning has been brought to a halt by student rebellions. Others of the student revolution have publicly burned draft cards and even the American flag. Crime has increased so that we are told that one out of every

three Americans is afraid to walk in his own neighborhood after dark. Riot has bludgeoned our cities. The smoke of destruction has enshrouded the dome of our capitol. In Washington the task of restoring order drew more than twice as many Federal troops as were involved in the defense of Khe Sahn in Vietnam.

Voices of angry protests are heard throughout the land, crying for all manner of freedoms. Yet our political leaders are picketed and some who cry loudest for freedom have sought to prevent our president, our vice president, and cabinet officers from speaking in public. None go so far as publicly to condone [the] politics of assassination. Yet, assassins' bullets have robbed our country of three great leaders within five years.

The Hawaiian senator appealed to the great hall:

Why? What has gone wrong? . . . Some conveniently blame all our ills and agonies on a most unpopular commitment overseas. The Vietnam War must end, they say, because it is an immoral war. Of course, the war in Vietnam must be ended, but it must be ended as President Johnson said last March, by patient political negotiation rather than through the victorious force of arms . . . Just as we shun an irresponsible cause for total and devastating nuclear victory, so must we guard against the illusion of an instant peace that has no chance of permanence.

Here Inouye was quieted by loud cheers.

Of course, the Vietnam War is immoral. Whether by the teachings of Moses, or by the teachings of Christ, or by the teachings of Buddha, I believe that all wars are immoral. During the Crusades, Christians in the name of Jesus Christ slaughtered innocent men, women, and children, and plundered their cities because they were of another faith. These were immoral wars. In Vietnam we build schools across the countryside and feed the hungry in the cities and our president has pledged massive sums in aid of all Vietnamese, and yet this is an immoral war.

Perhaps by the time my four-year-old son is grown, men will have learned to live by the Ten Commandments, but men have not yet renounced the use of force as a means to the objectives. Until they do, are we immoral if there be such a degree to fracture our solemn commitments and see our word doubted not only by friends abroad, but by our enemies? Knowing that this could lead to tragic miscalculations, is it immoral now to take the easier course, and gamble the lives of our sons and grandsons on the outcome? These are not easy questions, and perhaps there are no certain answers . . .

But what should concern us is something far more fundamental. The true dimension of the challenge facing us is a loss of faith. I do not mean simply a loss of religious faith, although that erosion is a major contributor to our unease. I mean a loss of faith in our country, in the purposes, and in its institutions. I mean a retreat from the responsibilities of citizenship . . . there is a much larger number who, in the face of change and disorder, have retreated into disengagement and quiet despair.

Now, let us not deceive ourselves about the consequences . . . It is anarchy. It is a state in which each individual demands instant compliance with his own desires. And from there it is but a short step to the assumption by each individual of the right to decide which of his neighbors shall live and which shall not. And so it accelerates the sickening spiral of violence which has already cost us our beloved John F. Kennedy, our great leader, Martin Luther King Jr., and the voice of this decade, Robert F. Kennedy . . . Chaos and anarchy have never been more than preludes to totalitarianism . . . My fellow Americans, let us reject violence as a means of protest, and let us reject those who preach violence.

Then the senator articulated the social victories of the Johnson administration and the need to end racial discrimination. The crowd was thrilled by Senator Inouye's performance, and he left the platform in a swirl of attention.

McCarthy forces, under the direction of his campaign manager former Democratic National Chairman Stephen Mitchell, were committed to forcing a floor fight on as many issues as possible to try to fracture the convention. The credentials committee had been deluged with challenges against a record one thousand delegates in seventeen states by McCarthy and former Kennedy strategists, mostly for civil-rights violations. Postmaster General Marvin Watson exercised the will of the White House as chairman of the committee. When the administration's representatives on the committee rejected

challenges in Connecticut, Indiana, Michigan, Minnesota, and Michigan, antiwar and civil-rights reformers took their complaints to the convention floor, new Democrats against old Democrats.

In the Mississippi dispute, the convention simply rectified the wrongs against the Mississippi Freedom Democratic Party at the 1964 convention and seated an interracial delegation, with Humphrey's support. In Georgia, civil-rights activist Julian Bond and his delegation took on an all-white group headed by segregationist Governor Lester Maddox. The Georgia governor threatened to walk out rather than split his forty-three-member delegation in a compromise with a bunch of integrationists. But the spirited debate on the convention floor had been a long one, and the hour grew late. So the deliberations over Georgia were moved to Tuesday, and the first session of the 1968 Democratic National Convention was adjourned at 2:45 A.M. Delegates spilled out into the humid August night.

The second session, on August 27, was called to order at 6:00 P.M. by temporary chairman Inouye and blessed by Billy Graham, who reminded the throng, "We could not pray on this occasion without remembering that great American who led us in war and in peace, who lies ill in Walter Reed tonight. We pray that thy comfort and grace will sustain his family and that it be thy will that thou would spare Dwight Eisenhower."

Then Inouye shouted to clear the aisles, before again introducing Mayor Daley, who led the convention in singing "Happy Birthday" to "one of the greatest presidents of the United States, Lyndon B. Johnson." Anita Bryant followed, singing the "The Battle Hymn of the Republic" for the president. Meanwhile, "We Want Kennedy" banners were unfurled in the balconies.

Johnson originally scheduled the national convention to coincide with his own sixtieth birthday and as a national celebration culminating in his renomination. LBJ never relinquished control of convention events to Humphrey. In many respects, the event remained Johnson's convention. He even harbored notions of sweeping into the Chicago convention on his birthday after a successful international summit with Soviet leaders to stampede his own renomination by acclamation.

His vague plan might have worked, since the South and others were only reluctantly for

Humphrey, but the Soviets wrecked his scheme with a brutal invasion of Czechoslovakia to crush the government of Alexander Dubcek and its experiment with democratic socialism during the "Prague Spring of '68." Many a Czech flag flew among Chicago demonstrators, who symbolically drew ideological parallels between Washington and Moscow, the two combatants in the worldwide cold war. Even after the invasion, delegates from Tennessee and Texas still privately advocated a Johnson draft. But LBJ failed to show for his birthday party, fearing negative reaction in an already volatile political storm.

On Tuesday night, television cameras captured the walkout by the segregated Georgia delegation. In the process of trying to cover the story, CBS correspondent Dan Rather was punched in the stomach by security guards and pushed to the ground. Delegates and reporters alike were beginning to complain about the security "thugs," as news anchor Walter Cronkite called them. As the week progressed, security became more physical and by the night of nominations, reporters and reform delegates were jostled, shoved, and punched. Notebooks and newspapers were ripped from their hands. Cameras were jolted to the ground. Fights broke out on the convention floor while armed guards patrolled the catwalks overhead. On Wednesday morning, NBC's Chet Huntley announced to his radio audience, "The news profession in this city is now under assault by the Chicago police."

The convention floor was arranged to favor delegations friendly to Humphrey, such as those of Kentucky, Minnesota, Tennessee, and Pennsylvania, which were situated in front of the podium to give them an advantage. Antiwar delegates from New York, California, Massachusetts, New Hampshire, Oregon, and Wisconsin were isolated in separate and far-flung corners of the hall and routinely ignored by the chair. But the television cameras sought out their reactions anyway.

Humphrey forces repelled other credential challenges on Tuesday evening, many by delegates charging a racist selection process. But Humphrey was not badly damaged by the vociferous debate, since his record on civil rights had been a courageous one in the past, beginning with the 1948 convention. Regulars won when the minority credentials report was rejected 1,525 to 801 1/2. In the end, however, reformers won a big victory when they per-suaded the party to change how it selected delegates in the future by requiring more primaries and state conventions and a fairer shake for minorities and women delegates. In 1968 only 337 of the 5,611 delegates and alternates were African American. This would be the last old-style Democratic convention.

Another battle shaped up in Governor Shapiro's Committee on Rules and Order of Business. McCarthyites took on one of the Democratic Party's sacred cows, the unit rule, in which each state voted as one block based on the majority vote of that delegation, thereby eliminating dissenting votes. The unit rule favored boss decisions and had been another of the devices through which the party forged unity from its disparate factions over the generations. The antiwar and reform delegates wanted it to end, because they felt it was undemocratic and because many of their own sympathizers would be muzzled by it on the nomination vote. Here too, the Humphrey forces, fighting their own guerrilla war, yielded to further their power and diffuse dissent. Humphrey could spare the votes. The South and big-city bosses objected to any change, but when the issue came to the floor, the unit rule was abolished by a majority vote of 1,350 to 1,206. The reformers had their second victory, but it hardly seemed to matter to them compared to the larger issue of Vietnam.

Meanwhile, Governor John Connally of Texas had kept a close eye on Humphrey and his minions, warning him against "selling out" to the doves and peaceniks. But he was furious over the loss of the unit rule and the disregard he saw the party showing toward the South. Humphrey did not know that Connally planned to renominate Johnson if the right moment presented itself, although Humphrey feared Johnson might try to bamboozle him in the end. Connally eventually jumped ship and joined Nixon's cabinet as secretary of the treasury.

At 12:40 A.M. the debate over the 1968 Democratic platform opened on the convention floor. The Committee on Resolutions and Platform was cochaired by Ella T. Grasso, future governor of Connecticut, and Johnson's House Democratic whip, Hale Boggs of Louisiana.

Chairman Carl Albert called for Congressman Hale Boggs of Louisiana to present the platform committee majority report. The 1968 Democracy promoted a progressive platform expanding on the early successes of the Great Society. Democrats also endorsed findings of the Kerner Commission, convened after Dr. King's assassination, calling for massive aid to America's cities, despite a hefty price tag.

The 1968 platform solemnly pledged to reduce the growing abyss between white and black and rich and poor that threatened to tear the nation asunder. It called for the federal government to become the "employer of last resort" rather than padding the welfare rolls. Republicans simply wanted reinvestment by the very private enterprises that were fleeing the cities as fast as they could load their moving vans.

"Every American family whose income is not sufficient to enable its members to live in decency should receive assistance free of the indignities . . . that still too often mar our present programs." Boggs intoned. "We are firm in our commitment that equal justice under law shall be denied to no one. The duty of government at every level is the safety and security of its people." The 1968 Democratic platform of expanded social and economic justice contrasted sharply with the Republican demand for law and order.

Naturally, the most divisive controversy centered on Vietnam and how to end the war. The latest public opinion poll prior to the convention indicated popular support for the administration's position, with 61 percent opposed to any unilateral bombing halt. The peace position had been seriously harmed by the Soviet invasion of Czechoslovakia. "The triumph of the hawks in Moscow," observed Senator Claiborne Pell of Rhode Island, "has strengthened the hawks in Chicago."

At 1:10 A.M. the debate turned acrid and caustic. Antiwar delegates, outraged that the most important debate of the convention had been pushed back into the wee morning hours when most of the television audience would have retired for the night, demanded adjournment and booed relentlessly. Two hours for debate had been accorded to both the majority and minority positions. The chair denied a motion to adjourn, then had to repeatedly shout, "The convention will be in order, the convention will be in order," as chaos spread. Peace delegates staged a demonstration, chanting over and over, "Let's go home, let's go home." Albert refused to recognize them as their howls of protest grew louder and louder. Finally, Mayor Daley, sitting on the convention floor in the Illinois delegation just a few rows in front of the chairman, drew his finger across his throat to signal an end to the proceedings, and at

1:17 A.M., with anarchy ruling the floor, Albert was forced to adjourn.

Edward Kennedy had been the unknown factor during the first few days before the convention. Stephen Smith, Kennedy's brother-in-law, conducted negotiations on behalf of the Massachusetts senator from the posh Standard Club. Kennedy's admirers were many, and the family still had allegiances. By Wednesday Teddy Kennedy himself assured Vice President Humphrey that he was not and would not be a candidate. In seclusion since Robert's funeral, Teddy was just thirty-six, but cursed with a family name that courted tragedy. McCarthy told Smith that he would direct his votes to the Massachusetts senator after he made a first ballot appearance. But the bereaved senator was savvy enough to see that Humphrey had the votes. Kennedy finally withdrew his name from consideration altogether. On Wednesday August 28, 1968, Humphrey had breakfast with Mayor Daley, who at last offered his endorsement. Internal opposition to Humphrey's nomination, especially from the South, was drying up. Now Humphrey had a clear path to the laurel. The new leader spent the day working over his acceptance speech with his team of writers in a Hilton hotel suite.

The convention's third session promised to be even more tumultuous than the night before. Chairman Albert gaveled the gathering to order at noon. Finally, a national debate would focus on the war. Before entering the debate, the chair reminded spectators that the rules of the House of Representatives were in order and forbade "demonstrations of any kind on the part of guests of the convention either of approval or disapproval." Chairman Albert's admonition was totally ignored. Congressmen Boggs and Phillip Burton of California directed the debates for the majority and minority planks on Vietnam. First, Charles W. Davis, counsel of the resolutions committee, took up where Boggs had left off Tuesday night and again introduced the majority report.

> Our most urgent task in Southeast Asia is to end the war in Vietnam by an honorable and lasting settlement which respects the rights of all the people of Vietnam. . . . We reject as unacceptable a unilateral withdrawal of our forces which would allow that aggression and subversion to succeed. We have never demanded and do not demand unconditional surrender of the Communists. We strongly support

the Paris talks and applaud the initiative of President Johnson which brought North Vietnam to the peace table. We hope that Hanoi will respond positively to this act of statesmanship.

The majority plank advocated withdrawal from South Vietnam of all foreign forces, both United States and allied forces, and forces infiltrated from North Vietnam; election of a postwar government; acceleration of American efforts to train and equip the South Vietnamese army; promotion of social reforms in South Vietnam; a promise of substantial economic aid; and a confirmation of no bases or further military involvement by the U.S. of any kind.

"We have taken so many risks for war," Davis sadly admitted, "we must now take some for peace. The war must be ended now. It will not end in a military victory, surrender, or unilateral recall by either side . . . It must, therefore, be ended by a fair and realistic compromise settlement . . . the steps toward peace can be simply stated. First, an unconditional end to all bombing of North Vietnam while continuing to provide in the South all necessary air and other support for American troops." Davis ended the majority's opening statement by affirming, "We shall [not] assume the role of the world policeman . . . Above all, we shall avoid the unilateral use of military means where the issues are political in nature and our national security is not involved."

Senator Edmund S. Muskie of Maine weighed in for the majority with his firm and gentle reasoning.

Sometimes in the emotion of the debate on Vietnam, we overemphasize our differences and ignore our wide areas of agreement. No responsible leader wants unilateral withdrawal. None seeks to escalate the war. All major participants in this debate seek a negotiated political settlement, and an end to the war. All call for an end to the bombing, a cease-fire, and withdrawal of all foreign troops from South Vietnamese soil.

For the minority plank upon which the convention would soon vote, Congressman Phillip Burton of California stepped to the podium. He praised his committee, particularly Kennedy aide Kenneth O'Donnell of Massachusetts, and saluted the 174 voting Kennedy delegates from California who had made it to the convention after the assassination. He pointed out that the Illinois Democratic nominee for U.S. Senate, William Clark, along with Jack Kennedy's aides Ted Sorensen, Pierre Salinger, and Dick Goodwin, now working with Senator McGovern, had drafted the minority plank.

Burton began:

I view this war as an effort to resolve by military means problems that are essentially political, social, and economic. I view this conflict as essentially an indigenous one, where the people in Vietnam are just seeking to have the opportunity and the right to carve out their own destiny without the oppression or the dictation of the Japanese as they did in the 1940s, without the oppression or dictation of the French, as they did in the 1950s. And I am certain they view our effort in that area no different from those other two countries.

I submit, if we continue our effort in Vietnam, we are going to wander more and more into the jungleness of Asia. I fear that many more Vietnamese will be killed, many more brave Americans will perish, many more mothers and fathers will weep, and this great nation will be cast over by a shadow that only the passage of time will dispel. History will judge this nation and this convention, in my view, harshly, if we fail to act or contribute in any manner that we may to the prolongation of this war or its escalation.

His remarks were cheered by the noisy minority contingent of peace delegates and spectators throughout the packed Amphitheatre.

At a time when this nation, which still mourns the tragic death of one of its vital young leaders, seeks answers to the causes of violence within our society, is it not apparent to all but those who dare not see that this war bears great responsibility for the atmosphere in which we find ourselves? By our conduct, we have affirmed that in the affairs of nations, war and violence are acceptable instruments in solving differences. Is it any wonder that in the affairs of men, resorting to violence becomes more frequent?

Mr. Chairman, as the war in Vietnam continues and we find ourselves committed to more money expended in any given month to destroy the countryside some 10,000 miles away than we spend in a full year in our war on poverty at home. I would think that this is not acceptable. As we find we spend more in a year in Vietnam than we have spent in all the great income maintenance programs of this nation, I would think that that is not acceptable. And as we find, and we know, that education is a desperate problem in this land . . . we spend more money in two weeks in destruction in Vietnam than we spend under the Federal Elementary and Secondary Schools Act to educate the youth of our land . . .

So may I say: . . . How much more of the life blood of this nation must be shed? . . . How long must we wait before we heed the voices of the men and women of goodwill who, across this land, call for peace?

Many in the galleries rose in agitated agreement as Burton stepped down and the fighting picked up among other delegates. Senator Gale McGee of Wyoming, speaking for the majority, urged caution:

It behooves us to ask ourselves what happens if we withdraw so rapidly without any measure of consequences elsewhere? What happens to Laos when we leave? They are gone. What happens to Cambodia? What happens to the neighboring nations? . . . In my judgment the majority platform keeps open the most options for us.

New York Senate nominee Paul Dwyer retorted for the minority:

You are called upon not so much to listen to arguments about the minority report or the majority report because that is mere rhetoric. You are called upon to pass the majority report to actually approve four more years of the same. That is precisely what it is. It is altogether too late here for us to begin to discuss the merits of the war in Vietnam. That question has been presented to seven million Democrats across this nation. That question was presented in the states where there were primaries. And the people have found an indictment of that war.

They have returned an indictment that the war is unconscionably cruel, that it is highly immoral, that it is disastrously wasteful and that it is unbelievably savage.

The convention was tense.

We have a chance at least to eliminate the sickness and the faintness that has come over us. We have

failed once already. We have put the brand of racism upon this convention by failing to heed the minority reports already of those who would seek equality. Let us work for all. Let us prove to the young people of America that the difference between us and the Republicans is not rhetoric as they say it is, let us not give them an argument from this point on for leaving us as they will unless we pass a meaningful plank with respect to Vietnam.

Governor Warren Hearnes of Missouri countered for the majority:

I know full well that the delegates will be exposed in this debate to a great amount of oratory, a great amount of emotionalism . . . I would like to address myself, if I may, to the people back home who are listening by radio or watching on their television sets, and point out to them that we have two planks, a majority and a minority, of which we must take one or the other. I support the majority plank because I think it is the better of the two.

Jack Gilligan, Democratic candidate for the Senate from Ohio and a decorated war veteran, continued for the minority:

We must now consider not only what this long and tragic conflict in Vietnam has done to that tortured nation, but what it has done to America, to our plans, to our ideals, to our image of ourself as a people. We have not only devastated Vietnam, we have distorted the vision of America. We went to Vietnam to help, but now we remain to destroy. We did not intend it so, but as some one once said, we have created a desert and called it peace . . . We went to preserve freedom. Now there is no freedom in Vietnam, North or South.

So it continued, cheers and jeers from both sides splitting the Amphitheatre and the national airwaves. Congressman Matsunaga, Governor Sawyer, Congressman Hayes, Congressman Edmondson for the majority. Congressman Conyers, Senator Tidings, Governor Hoff, Pierre Salinger, Senator Moss, Senator Pell, Congressman Reuss, Congressman Pryor, Senator Gore, Congressman Fraser, Senator Morse, and Kenneth O'Donnell for the minority. They stirred the listeners of a confused and tormented nation with passion and logic; strong attacks and strong defenses. "The heart and the soul of this campaign should be for peace," thundered Vance Hartke, the heroic Indiana senator whose antiwar message made him an outcast in much of his home state. "Let us finally resolve to strike a blow for peace, and in so doing reaffirm our reverence for life."

President Kennedy's press secretary, Pierre Salinger, bellowed, "This is the moment of truth for the Democratic Party." Ted Sorensen summed up the minority argument. "The essence of the majority plank is its call to affirm and continue this nation's past and present Vietnam war policy. The essence of the minority plank, without attacking or repudiating anyone, is its call for a change toward peace. . . . The minority plank offers an honorable, reasonable plan to end the war. The majority plank, to be very frank, is one on which Richard Nixon, or even Barry Goldwater, could run with pleasure. The minority plank, is one on which any Democratic candidate for any office could and should run with pride."

After two hours of tumultuous and heartrending debate, Chairman Albert ordered the vote, shouting above the buzz of discord, "before we proceed . . . may the Chair respectfully, but earnestly and sincerely urge, first of all, that members maintain, and delegates maintain, that decorum which is so necessary to the exercise of the business of a parliamentary convention." The roll call began on the minority plank with shouts arising over every state's decision. At 5:00 P.M., the minority peace report was rejected 1,041 1/4 to 1,567 3/4. Albert then passed the majority plank on a quick voice vote of ayes.

Peace delegates and supporters in the galleries, many wearing black arm bands, instantly broke into song, "We Shall Overcome" followed by shouts of "Stop the war, stop the war." They swayed together, hands clasped as they sang. To drown them out, the convention band struck up a rendition of the Air Force theme "Off We Go into the Wild Blue Yonder" in ironic contrast. Then amid turmoil and disorder, Albert announced that there would be a two-hour recess. When delegates would report back to nominate their candidate for president. The hall slowly emptied as peace delegates with black crepe marched around the main floor. The great peace battle had been lost. Now what would the antiwar movement do? Would the peace forces bolt?

When word of the hawkish vote reached the Grant Park protesters, they became defiant and angry. Upset with the seeming inevitability of Humphrey's triumph on this day, they were distraught now that their long and extraordinary campaign had utterly failed. Somehow, these young activists, who had come by the thousands from throughout Chicagoland and all over the nation, had hoped for a political miracle, for a peace candidate and a peace platform to suddenly emerge from the convention as the "will of the people." Most were not Democrats anymore. They had renounced their former party months ago. Rather they had come to condemn the Democrats as perpetrators of war crimes, as guarantors of the corporate cold war state, as politicians who had "sold out" and would not "give peace a chance."

Their hopes seemed dashed now with the easy defeat of the Vietnam peace plank, and nothing remained for them but direct action, direct appeal to the convention itself before it made the final nomination, an appeal for peace, for an end to the war, for a new ethic of social compassion and reconstruction instead of destruction and destitution, of integrity and idealism instead of hypocrisy and hopelessness. They would do what they had always done, what they had learned from the civil-rights movement, from Dr. Martin Luther King Jr. They would march. And if they became martyrs to the cause, as King had in Montgomery and Selma, through arrests or beatings, so be it.

An afternoon rally in Grant Park was sanctioned by one of the few legal permits issued that week. It started at the modern band shell in the southern end of the park near the Field Museum. Speakers from SDS, MOB, Vietnam Veterans Against the War, the Yippies, and the Draft Resisters League made their angry complaints over a public address system. Authors William Burroughs, Allen Ginsburg, Dick Gregory, and Black Panther Bobby Seale, all incensed by the apparent inevitability of Humphrey's nomination that night and desperate in their denunciation of the continued slaughter in Asia, incited the growing crowd from the stage. Phil Ochs sang his antiwar anthem, "I Ain't A'Marchin' Anymore," and other protest favorites. Meanwhile radical groups danced under red, black, and Viet Cong flags chanting, "Ho Ho Ho Chi Minh, the Viet Cong Are Going to Win."

The large meeting of nearly fifteen thousand, culmination of a week's protests, was surrounded on three sides by Chicago police officers, now wearing blue riot helmets with protective face masks. Helicopters circled overhead.

The police were angry and weary from continuous duty. Protesters had taunted them all week, showering them with obscenities. Demonstrators, Daley later said, "used the foulest of language that you wouldn't hear in a brothel house." Everything was coming to a head. In one melee late in the afternoon, more than a dozen officers were injured by rocks and bottles as they tried to arrest a demonstrator who dropped an American flag from the flagpole at the band shell. By this time, undercover FBI and Chicago "Red Squad" agents and some provocateurs mingled among the activists and observers, seeking to spur the group to violent action.

Police moved in again when several demonstrators raised a red flag to replace the American flag that had been lowered earlier. The crowd shouted "Pigs, Pigs," before the police retreated under a hail of bottles. The police then charged again, this time firing tear gas into the center of the crowd. Demonstrators, scattering, retaliated by throwing smoke bombs. Several arrests were made.

Meanwhile, David Dellinger, editor-publisher of *Liberation* and chairman of the Mobilization, appealed for people to "sit down." Rennie Davis, one of the organizers of the Chicago protest, had argued that the purpose of the demonstrations was "to force the police state to become more and more visible." Now he saw just how visible it could become. He took a nightstick on the skull that later required nine stitches. Poet Allen Ginsberg tried to calm the crowd by leading it in choruses of "OM." The sacred syllables fell on deaf ears. The days of the "be-in" were over. Under police attack, the rally broke up late that afternoon and protesters splintered into many small groups. Tom Hayden, co-founder of SDS, called for spontaneous waves of action.

Dellinger led a nonviolent contingent of six thousand marchers from the park across Columbus Drive toward the Eleventh Street footbridge, which was also patrolled by National Guard. When stopped by police, the marchers sat down. Frantic negotiations for a parade permit made no progress. Upon threats of arrest, several thousand marchers suddenly disbanded. They walked and ran north through the park to the promenade at Buckingham Fountain. There

they joined other splinter groups that had been routed from the rally and chased north through the yellow and red rose gardens of Grant Park toward the fountain.

They spilled into Columbus Drive and Lake Shore Drive, bringing traffic to a rush hour halt before taking over the Congress Plaza and the expressway concourse in front of the fountain. The crowd began to move west up the four-lane highway toward the Congress Bridge that arched over the Illinois Central and South Shore railroad tracks chanting, "Freedom, freedom." Chicago's Loop lay just beyond the hill's crest. Horns were blaring, helicopters swooping, radios blasting. Determined at last to march to the Amphitheatre and demand a peace candidate or a confrontation, the demonstrators, divided and diluted by the police action, were still ten thousand strong.

But as the mass demonstration approached the Congress Bridge it met organized resistance. A long line of National Guard in khaki green combat fatigues, gas masks in place, rifles leveled, and bayonets unsheathed, blocked the bridge. The war in Vietnam had come home. Yippies, hippies, young men in shirtsleeves and ties, flower children, and former cheerleaders—committed young people of all kinds—marched toward the line and began face-to-face dialogue with the soldiers who were their own age or that of older brothers, asking why they wanted to fight for a corrupt system, for a war machine that cared little about them or anything except bottom-line profits. No one was listening, no one yielded.

The Congress Bridge was a gateway to the city's great expressway system. From Lake Shore Drive the traffic conduit took in thousands of cars at rush hour from the north and south sides of the city and directed them west, northwest, and southwest into the suburbs. Blocked by thousands in confrontation, the roads backed up with hundreds of drivers blaring their horns, rolling up their windows in fear, or turning off their engines in sympathy. Some joined in the demonstration. Others got into arguments. Seeking to unclog the highway, the National Guard attempted to let individual cars cross one at a time, but drivers invited demonstrators to ride with them past the armed lines. In turn, guardsmen threatened to puncture their tires with bayonets. Several protesters were dragged from the cars. Some kicked and punched back.

Conflict erupted on the frontlines. Protesters who tried to break through were met with rifle butts. The commander felt his troops were threatened. In riot shape since April, the Guard fired several rounds of tear gas, hoping to drive the surging crowd back. With stinging eyes and choked breath, the protesters retreated to Buckingham Fountain to wash out the vapors. Again the crowd was split, as some protesters doubled back along the lakefront to the south and north to work their way to Michigan Avenue. Several hurled gas canisters and rocks at the Guard. Many, including the rush-hour drivers stuck in the middle, were nauseous and fell on their knees, crying or gasping in the street.

The gas clouds thickened in the muggy blue August sky. But instead of disabling the demonstrators, the massive noxious cloud hung in the air momentarily and then was tossed back into the gas masks of the National Guard, back across the bridge, back into the city by a stiff northeasterly wind, the fumes filtering through the commercial streets. The gassing was a typical tactical error of unintended consequences so familiar in the Vietnam War itself. The haze drifted across the boulevards, choking tourists and cameramen, journalists and curious sightseers out shopping on Michigan Avenue, assaulting average citizens on the streets, involving everyone in the conflict America could no long avoid. The gas damage didn't stop there, but rising in curling clouds with the warm wind that swept off the lake, it twisted into the luxurious lakefront hotels of the conventioneers, turned upward to McCarthy's headquarters on the twenty-third floor of the Hilton and into Humphrey's ornate twenty-fifth floor suite where he was eating a celebratory meal with his aides.

As in the Vietnam War itself, the situation yielded to another strategic military error. In blocking the traffic bridges from Grant Park into the city over the Illinois Central railroad tracks, the coordinated security forces had failed to cover the footbridges at Harrison Street or to guard the exit two blocks north of Congress at Jackson Boulevard next to the Art Institute of Chicago. At nearly seven o'clock, the crowd running to escape both police and the National Guard poured through these crosswalks on to Michigan Avenue where they encountered no resistance until they raced two blocks south to the corner of Balbo

Drive. A large contingent of National Guard and Chicago police stood waiting for them. Protesters found themselves cornered on three sides. On the west stood the row of classic hotels from the Congress Hotel, where fifty-six years earlier Teddy Roosevelt had spoken from the second floor balcony to disgruntled delegates, south past the Blackstone to the Hilton. Across the street lay a thirty-five-foot drop-off on to the railroad tracks. Ahead more and more police were assembling.

The demonstrators were diverted by another surprise, a legal demonstration. The young, mostly white teenage protesters encountered the mournful mule train from Dr. Martin Luther King Jr.'s all-but-forgotten Poor People's Campaign, heading south on Michigan Avenue. On the corner of Balbo Drive and Michigan Avenue, the disinherited and directionless—survivors of two separate assassinations, King and Kennedy—were symbolically linked. Finally, police, fearful of sparking a race riot, allowed the mule train through at the request of Reverend Ralph Abernathy of the Southern Christian Leadership Conference.

Meanwhile, many of the demonstrators had been dispersed northward, away from the Hilton. Others pushed out of the crucible headed for Lincoln Park and Old Town on the North Side. Only five thousand protesters from the original afternoon rally had reached the Hilton. A separate crowd watched from the 100-yard strip of park in front of the Hilton. All week, police guarding the Hilton had been pelted from the hotel windows above with objects ranging from apples to ashtrays. Several had been injured, some seriously. Now a National Guard contingent separated the crowds. Some demonstrators waved Viet Cong and Czech flags. Smoke bombs were set off in the hotel lobby, filling it with the smell of vomit and tear gas. Firecrackers were popping like machine guns in the park.

Many who congregated on Michigan Avenue still wanted to march to the convention to be heard. As they waited in a standoff, the Chicago Police Department rushed busloads of reinforcements from police headquarters, just a few blocks away at Eleventh and State Streets, into the canyon between the Hilton and the Blackstone towers. The protesters chanted in unison, "End the war in Vietnam," their voices ricocheting off the glass and brick facade of the mammoth buildings, echoing across the city and the nation. "End the war in Vietnam," many holding up two fingers spread in the universal peace symbol of the Student Peace Union. With the television cameras of mobile trucks focused upon them, the demonstrators felt their message would be broadcast to the world and inside the convention itself. "End the war in Vietnam," they chanted defiantly. "Hell, no we won't go, hell, no, we won't go." Then the clarion call, "Let's go to the Amphitheatre."

Police commanders feared the restless crowd would storm the Hilton and endanger Vice President Humphrey. A police bullhorn repeatedly ordered them to disband and disperse. Bomb threats had been lodged against the convention site and the Hilton. Police loudspeakers informed the potential mob that it stood in violation of city laws. Demonstrators were ordered to leave immediately or face arrest. Skirmishes broke out. A police car in Grant Park was surrounded and plastered with McCarthy stickers while the officers inside radioed for help. Meanwhile, demonstrators sat down in the middle of Michigan Avenue and sang peace songs.

By 1968 the Chicago police were among the best trained and equipped anywhere in the world. Under the reforms of former police superintendent Orlando W. Wilson, who was brought in by Mayor Daley to clean up after the Summerdale police theft scandal of 1960, the department had recruited younger men, increased the size of the force, instituted new policing policies, and improved salaries. The changes made the Chicago Police Department a paragon of modern techniques. But the convention came just four months after the West Side was consumed in flames, an event more traumatic than any in the city's history since the Haymarket Affair. Police were tired and edgy. They had experienced crash courses in crowd control, but had little practice at it. Also, they were cut off from all communications.

On the front lines a palpable hatred seemed to separate the two groups. Chicago police had little understanding or sympathy for the idealism of the assembled youth. Most police officers were hard-working men with families to support, proud of their city, proud of their service to the city, and proud of their country. Many were Korean War or even Vietnam War veterans, extremely suspicious and resentful toward the "hippies" who they took to be traitors,

"commies," or just damn fools. The protesters were young and wild, and the police both disliked and envied them for their freedom. Protesters enjoyed taunting them, pushing them to the limit.

Earlier in the week, Abbie Hoffman had told demonstrators not to worry about "the pigs," since they had "small brains and moved slowly." Hoffman was wrong. The minds of the over-extended, spat-upon, ridiculed riot police remembered every insult of their mock-epic conflict, and now came their turn to retaliate. Police commanders passed an order to clear the streets. As soon as the SCLC mule train left the intersection, police, marching in lines three officers deep and fifteen across, advanced into the chanting crowd.

At 7:57 P.M. the first wave of officers caught the immobile mass of pacifists by surprise. People on the front lines were unable to retreat in the crush of bodies. Squadrons of Chicago's finest charged forward, firing tear gas, swinging away at protesters, long-haired Yippies, Democratic conventioneers, photographers, news reporters, pedestrians, and passers-by, knocking them to the ground as they stumbled on each other in the haze of choking gas. As they began making arrests, the officers were met by a hail of rocks, bottles, cans, and eggs. Since Chicago police were trained that it was illegal for demonstrators to resist or run from them, they escalated their behavior.

Police commanders gave the order to hold their position, but individual officers found themselves in confrontation and then surrounded. The police broke ranks. "The police lost their cool. They were totally out of control," Tom Foran, the federal attorney for northern Illinois, later admitted. Police phalanxes moved swiftly into the crowd of students and peaceniks with batons and nightsticks flailing away. Many fought back. One group of protesters was pushed through the plate glass window of the Hilton's Haymarket Lounge with the officers in pursuit. Some two hundred demonstrators pinned against the wall of the Blackstone Hotel were sprayed in the face with mace and then clubbed.

Other police officers chased demonstrators into Grant Park in front of the Blackstone, striking them on the backs and legs as they fell, dragging them by their feet, heads knocking, to waiting paddy wagons. Ghostly shadows of individual fights were caught in the haze of television lights filtered through clouds of tear gas. Sirens blared in eerie repetition, and the bright blue beacons of police cars flashed in surreal-istic rhythm. Only a few minutes had passed. Such mass political violence had never been witnessed before in the United States.

In the half hour of frenzy and sirens that followed, painful screams pierced Chicago's twilight air, and a fearful panic gripped the youngsters, the press, the police, the hundreds of bystanders, and those in the scores of hotel windows looking down on the side-walks and streets littered with injured demonstrators holding their bloody heads and broken limbs. Although the violence was widespread, no weapons were ever fired. Injuries were numerous, but none were lethal or even life-threatening. The great mass was uninjured, although astonished, angry, and agi-tated. Demonstrators shouted back "Sieg heil, sieg heil," at the officers. McCarthy angrily witnessed the attack from the Conrad Hilton in suite 2320. Humphrey, who had been eating dinner during the battle, now sadly shook his head as he watched from Room 2525A. He was sick at heart, but did nothing to try to halt it.

After the first few waves of police charges, the mass of protesters again pushed forward, chanting to the TV trucks with mounted cameras, "The whole world is watching. The whole world is watching," as indeed thirty million people would be when the tapes were developed and broadcast later. Chicago looked like Saigon at war.

By 8:15 P.M., Chicago police were back in control. The nearly five thousand demonstrators who had been isolated in Grant Park directly across from the Hilton since early evening remained, chanting anti-war and antipolice slogans. Elsewhere fires were set in the middle of intersections. Sporadic street demonstrations spread north with the dispersed protesters and continued until midnight. But the main "Battle of Chicago," as it was called the next morning, was over in forty-five minutes. By night's end, two hundred protesters had been arrested, most of them from metropolitan Chicago. Hundreds more groaned with busted skulls, glass splinters, broken arms, cuts, and bruises. A total of forty-nine newspeople had been assaulted. Almost two hun-dred police officers were injured during that week.

Although Mayor Daley had made all the major decisions on Chicago police policy, the day-to-day operations were left to the police command. Jim Rochford, the department's number two man, was in charge at the scene of conflict on the corner of Balbo and Michigan and gave the order to clear the streets. Following the principles laid down by former police chief Orlando Wilson, police were prepared to deal with any resistance by greater force than was used against them to insure success. The police officers in Grant Park felt they had been pushed to the limit. They simply lost their tempers and poise. For both sides, "push had come to shove." Protesters felt police had gone far beyond the realm of reasonable force, that their constitutional rights and personal safety had been badly violated—but that it was typi-cal of a "system" that solved problems in Vietnam or Chicago by violence. The psychic trauma was deep on all sides.

Meanwhile, the convention reassembled at 6:30 P.M., oblivious to what had happened in the streets. The chair set down the rules: Nominating speeches, tailored for television segments between commercial breaks, were not to exceed fifteen minutes for each candidate.

CBS television correspondent Mike Wallace tried to get through a crowded aisle with his equipment to interview a New York delegate who was having trou-ble with his credentials. Enroute, Wallace was blocked by Chicago police commander Paul McLaughlin. Wallace angrily protested that the police couldn't stop him from doing his job, shook his finger in the commander's face, and inadver-tently hit the officer, who immediately responded with a punch to Wallace's chin.

With all eyes upon them, McLaughlin and a group of officers whisked the reporter off the convention floor to a police command post inside the Amphithe-atre. A loud exchange followed, with CBS News presi-dent Richard S. Salant bitterly protesting Wallace's detention and treatment. Suddenly, the room fell silent as Mayor Daley walked in. The mood turned deferential. "Mr. Mayor," said Salant, "Things have gotten out of hand, but we can resolve them." Daley told Wallace to apologize or face arrest. Wallace shook hands with Commander McLaughlin, and Daley dashed off to deal with more serious problems.

At the podium, permanent chairman Albert now took the helm. "We are approaching the most impor-tant business of the convention, and it is necessary that delegates find their places." He warned them against demonstrations during the nomination of presidential or vice presidential candidates, something unimaginable in the early days of Chicago conventions. Then Albert got the immediate attention of the audience by reading two telegrams to the assembly. The first was from President Johnson, expressing "my appreciation to all those who might have wished me to continue. During the remaining months of my term as president, and then for the rest of my life, I shall continue my efforts to reach and secure those enduring goals that have made America a nation seeking peace abroad and justice and opportunity at home." The announcement was met with applause and scattered jeers.

The second telegram read: "in the event my name is placed in nomination at the Democratic National Convention for either the office of president or vice president . . . I respectfully request that the nomination be withdrawn." It was signed Edward M. Kennedy. Respectful applause rose throughout the hall.

Governor Dan A. Moore of North Carolina, a favorite son, was the first nominee for the 1968 Democracy. Then Albert temporarily handed over the gavel to Chicago congressman Dan Rostenkowski, who introduced Governor Harold Hughes of Iowa. Hughes nominated Eugene McCarthy to a loud and sincere ovation and chants of "We want Gene, we want Gene."

Hughes began slowly.

> I do not speak for myself alone, but for millions of Americans who believe that this man has brought new hope and new options to America. We are in the midst of what can only be called a revolution in our domestic affairs and in our foreign policy as well . . . and as the great President Kennedy once said, "Those who would make peaceful revolution impossible, make violent revolution inevitable."

McCarthy was seconded by Georgia legislator Julian Bond. John Kenneth Galbraith, the Harvard economist and Kennedy adviser, added his name to the nomination of the Minnesota senator. "Senator McCarthy has shown a different way. . . . He rejects the dogmas of the old cold-war priesthood which brought us to the Bay of Pigs, the Dominican fiasco, Vietnam, and is undoubtedly poised for yet greater things . . . He has shown that resort to violence first destroys those who employ it."

Then Mayor Joseph Alioto of San Francisco rose to nominate Hubert Humphrey. "I came here to talk to you about the man who has been for twenty years, right up to this present time, the articulate exponent of the aspirations of the human heart for the young, for the old, and for those of us in between." He recounted Humphrey's career of political triumphs from Minneapolis to the Senate, his defense of civil rights and his innovative ideas, such as Medicare.

Mayor Carl Stokes of Cleveland, a year earlier elected along with Richard Hatcher of Gary as the first African-American mayors of major American cities, seconded Humphrey and applauded his urban policy. Governor Terry Sanford of North Carolina argued, "the most original mind in American politics is the mind of Hubert Humphrey."

But the nomination roll call was interrupted by turmoil on the convention floor. Delegates near television monitors witnessed the first televised coverage of the violence on Michigan Avenue. Because of the communications strike, TV cameras downtown had not been able to transmit live coverage. Once the skirmish ended, news staff picked themselves off the ground and rushed the film to the Amphitheatre network editing rooms in a mad dash to get the footage on the air. Now the watching delegates responded in shock and outrage.

When he regained order, Chairman Albert called upon Senator Abraham Ribicoff of Connecticut, who nominated George McGovern:

> I have a speech here, as I look at the confusion in this hall and watch on television the turmoil and violence that is competing with this great convention for the attention of the American people, there is something else in my heart tonight and not the speech I intended to give. I am here to nominate George McGovern, just for that reason. George McGovern is a man full of goodness. He is a man without guile. He is a whole man . . . and because [he] has peace in his soul he can translate that peace to our cities, our states, the nation, and this world.

Loud applause welled up from the floor and gallery.

> George McGovern understood from the depths of his being that napalm, and gas, and 500,000 Americans in the swamps of Vietnam was not the answer to the people of Vietnam or the people of the United States.

The stately senator continued:

George McGovern is not satisfied that ten million Americans go to bed hungry every night. George McGovern is not satisfied that four and a half million American families live in rat-infested and roach-infested houses . . . The youth of America rally to the standards of men like George McGovern, like they had to the standards of John F. Kennedy and Robert Kennedy.

Then Ribicoff looked down directly at the Chicago contingent of the Illinois delegation and, in particular, Mayor Daley in the front row beneath the podium and bellowed:

And with George McGovern as president of the United States, we wouldn't have to have gestapo tactics in the streets of Chicago.

Instantly the mayor turned beet red and jumped to his feet, angrily gesturing for Ribicoff to get off the stage, shouting "Go home, go home . . . " Ribicoff continued, "And with George McGovern we wouldn't have a National Guard." The boos drowned out the senator's words. Again, staring at Daley, he boomed, "how hard is it to accept the truth when we know the problems facing our nation . . ." Ribicoff left the stage shaken.

The proceedings continued despite the rising turmoil on the floor. The national television networks repeatedly replayed the scenario of fist-to-fist combat between the defeated demonstrators and police, and news reports of injuries and arrests filtered in. Rumors swept through the hall that demonstrators had broken police lines of defense and were on their way to the convention.

Frank Mankiewicz, Robert Kennedy's former press aide, told the delegates:

Robert Kennedy said . . . that George McGovern was the senator who has the most feeling and does things in the most genuine way . . . He is a candidate . . . not of the clubhouse, but of the classroom, not of city hall, but of the people, not the nightsticks and tear gas, and the mindless brutality. Not of nightsticks and tear gas and the mindless brutality we have seen on our television screens tonight, and on this convention floor.

The boos and hisses and pushing and shoving continued, but they did not faze Mankiewicz.

Only in part because I know the affection Robert Kennedy had for him, but most of all, because I believe him to be the best and finest man to seek the presidency at this convention, I second the nomination . . . for George S. McGovern of South Dakota.

Philip Stern of Washington, D.C., then addressed the visibly agitated throng.

But for a single wanton senseless act, just eighty-three days ago, our delegation would tonight be casting votes for the sure nominee of this convention, and the next president of the United States, Robert Francis Kennedy. But we, and you, have been denied that opportunity. In his stead, we place before you the name of Channing Phillips. [Phillips was pastor of Lincoln Memorial Congregational Temple in the nation's capitol and a former basketball player at Virginia Union University.] To do so is not an act of presumption, but of profound respect to the memory of Robert Kennedy, for he sought to offer a voice for the voiceless, to represent the unrepresented, to encourage votes for the voteless, to open the doors of political opportunity.

Channing Phillips symbolizes those to whom and for whom Robert Kennedy sought to speak, for Channing Phillips is a member of that black minority in America that for so many decades has been voiceless and powerless . . . Tonight the presentation here of a black man qualified for the presidency must be the beginning of awareness that a man's race is as irrelevant to his fitness for high office as his religion.

Mayor Richard Hatcher of Gary seconded Phillips as did Congressman John Conyers of Michigan. Hatcher hammered at the delegates:

I say to you tonight that in an age that will come to be historically defined by its social crisis too often we have been too concerned with the political comfort of racists when we should have been concerned with the physical safety of the children who dwell in rat-infested slums . . . We have also been too concerned with the accommodation of every possible Vietnam posture and not enough concerned with ending an unjust and bloody war.

Said Conyers:

> We have already seen the politics of participation as
> envisioned by Mayor Daley. The supporters of peace
> and the supporters of equality for black people have
> been brutally attacked by the Chicago police. Dozens
> of young people, guilty of no crime other than
> greatly and strongly held convictions, have been cal-
> lously and cruelly wounded.

As the proceedings moved forward, most of the
American viewing audience was watching reruns of
the street confrontation and its aftermath, a dramatic
cinematic clash between generations and cultures.
Florida nominated its favorite son, Senator George
Smathers, but announced its intention to vote for
Humphrey. When Illinois was called, Mayor Daley
began to cast 122 votes for Hubert Humphrey, 3 for
McCarthy and 3 for McGovern, but the vote had not
yet been called. It was already 11:00 P.M., and the street
fighting had long since dispersed from the Hilton to
other neighborhoods. But the television depictions
continued, and some delegates who were electroni-
cally isolated on the convention floor were under the
impression that the reruns were live footage.

When the roll call reached Wisconsin, its chair
Donald Peterson announced, "Most delegates to this
convention do not know that thousands of young
people are being beaten in the streets of Chicago. For
that reason and that reason alone, I request a suspension of the rules for the purpose of adjournment
for two weeks at 6:00 P.M., to relocate the convention
in another city of the choosing of the Democratic
National Committee and the delegates."

"Wisconsin is out of order," shot back Chairman
Albert. Thousands booed his ruling. Mayor Daley
and much of his delegation walked out amid catcalls
and insults. Then the balloting began. When Georgia
was reached, it announced, "because of the atrocities
in downtown Chicago, Georgia's loyal national
Democrats cast their votes only with reluctance,"
and then gave McCarthy 13 1/2, Phillips 3, Ted
Kennedy 1/2, and the vice president 2 1/2 votes.
Indiana, where Robert Kennedy had won a tough primary, cast 49 votes for Humphrey, 11 for McCarthy, 2
for McGovern, and 1 for Reverend Phillips.

After the first ballot concluded, Chairman Albert
announced, "On this Call of the States, Vice President
Humphrey has 1,761 3/4; Senator McCarthy, 601;

Senator McGovern, 146 1/2; Reverend Phillips, 67
1/2; Senator Kennedy, 12 1/2; Governor Moore, 17
1/2. And the Chair declares that Vice President
Humphrey is the Democratic presidential candidate
for the United States." The remaining Illinois delegation then moved to make the vote unanimous amid
cheers and boos, but there could be no unanimity.
Rostenkowski called for the benediction, and at
12:10 A.M. the battered party recessed until the next
evening, reeling in shock and on the verge of disintegration. The peace delegates decided to stage a candlelight march to downtown in protest of the night's
events, but given the five-mile hike through darkened Chicago neighborhoods, they took buses
instead and symbolically walked the last few blocks.

Hubert H. Humphrey had always been a fighter,
and this would be just another tough fight, he
believed, no tougher than when he became the
mayor of Minneapolis at age thirty-four and took on
a corrupt police department, or when he had purged
the Minnesota Farmer-Labor Party of "communists,"
or when at the 1948 national convention in Philadelphia he forced his party to accept a progressive civil
rights plank, or when he had fought in the U.S. Senate for Medicare and the Peace Corps years before
they were enacted.

Only on Vietnam had he faltered, even then thinking he was pursuing principle. Humphrey was a
fighter who would die fighting, but he also knew how
to make peace among fighters. The vice president
had finally been nominated when Pennsylvania's 103
3/4 votes put him over the 1,312 votes needed. A triumphant Humphrey leaped up from his couch,
crouched before the TV set, and kissed the screen. It
was 11:47 P.M. on the longest day of 1968. Victory was
so sweet, yet bittersweet. He then took congratula-
tory calls from President Johnson and his rival
Richard Nixon.

That same night Richard Nixon must have kissed
his television set as well, although for altogether different reasons. The student/police violence was an
unexpected gift. Chicago Democrats had been part
of the Kennedy ring that he felt robbed him of victory in 1960, but now Chicago was wrecking
Humphrey in 1968. There seemed a cosmic, even
comic justice to it. Nixon would exploit it.

The next day, August 29, recriminations from the
night before were everywhere. The Battle of Michigan Avenue, not Humphrey's nomination, was the

top news story. Mayor Daley held a press conference and explained the city's position, "For weeks, months, the press, radio, and television across the nation have revealed the tactics and strategy that was to be carried on in Chicago during convention week by groups of terrorists. In the heat of emotion and riot some policemen may have overreacted, but to judge an entire police force by the alleged action of a few would be just as unfair as to judge our entire younger generation by the actions of this mob," he insisted. "Gentlemen," the mayor concluded, "get this straight once and for all. The policeman isn't there to create disorder, the policeman is there to preserve disorder." True to the mayor's malapropism, there was plenty of disorder to preserve. The nation was in an uproar, split down the age fault.

Daley and others hinted that assassinations had been plotted against him and three presidential nominees. Indeed, one man had been arrested on the roof of the Hilton, a rifle found in his car. Thus the heavy security was required, Daley insisted. At another news conference that morning Chicago Police Superintendent Conlisk also defended his men: "The force used was the force that was necessary." He argued that with 152 police officers injured, the violence had been initiated and inflicted by the demonstrators.

That final night of the convention, the hall was packed with city patronage workers and other Daley supporters waving "We Love Daley" posters. Soothing the raw nerves was a moving film tribute to Robert Kennedy that left many delegates in tears. When it was over the entire convention broke into choruses of the "Battle Hymn of the Republic" and then into thunderous applause.

But the real question on the final night was the vice presidency. Humphrey had offered the post to McCarthy and Ted Kennedy. Both had declined. So at Humphrey's direction the convention nominated fifty-four-year-old Senator Edmund Sixtus Muskie of Maine, a Polish American, former two-term progressive governor of a state where Democrats rarely won a senatorial seat. In protest Wisconsin nominated Georgia state representative Julian Bond, who successfully had led the challenge against the segregated Georgia delegation. But Bond, a veteran of the civil-rights movement, withdrew his name, noting that he was only twenty-nine years old, thus not able to meet the constitutionally required age of thirty-five. Mayor Daley moved that Muskie be nominated by acclamation, which was done.

Within minutes, Senator Muskie delivered his acceptance speech.

> The practice of freedom . . . has made possible tremendous advances in the lives of the average citizen of our country. But ironically, those very advances have highlighted our shortcomings, shortcomings which have denied hope for improvement to too many Americans; shortcomings which have concealed the reality of hunger, poverty, and deprivation for many under an illusion of prosperity and equality for all.

Then at 10:30 P.M., Vice President Humphrey was ready to deliver his acceptance speech, which he had considerably revised after recent events. He faced the perilous task of trying to unite not just a divided party, but a ruptured and emotionally distraught one. As he started his fifty-minute speech, he was greeted with both loud applause and several choruses of boos. He began solemnly.

> This moment is one of personal pride and gratification, yet one cannot help but reflect [upon] the deep sadness that we feel over the troubles and the violence which have erupted regretfully and tragically in the streets of this great city, and for the personal injuries which have occurred. Surely we have now learned the lesson that violence breeds counterviolence, and it cannot be condoned, whatever the source.

He was lauded loudly by the gallery, which was filled with Chicago city workers.

> I know that every delegate to this convention shares tonight my sorrow and my distress over these incidents, and may we for just one moment in sober reflection and serious purpose . . . pray for our country . . . But take heart, my fellow Americans, this is not the first time that our nation has faced a challenge to its life and its purpose. And each time that we have had to face these challenges, we have emerged with new greatness and with new strength. We must take this moment of crisis. We must make it a moment of creation.

The convention then listened to his vision for a Humphrey administration. He also saluted Lyndon B. Johnson, the man who made his nomination possible.

Mayor Richard J. Daley surrounded by well-wishers in front of his South Side home after a rally at a Bridgeport police station in September 1968. Chicago Historical Society. Photo by Jack Lenahan.

I truly believe that history will surely record the greatness of his contributions to the people of this land, and tonight to you, Mr. President, I say, "Thank, you, thank you, Mr. President." Yes, my fellow Democrats, we have recognized and, indeed, we must recognize the end of an era, and the beginning of a new day. And that new day belongs to the people, to all the people . . . of this Republic.

The vice president eventually addressed the question of Vietnam, the need for peace and justice in the cities, and the imperative of national unity.

Now I appeal, I appeal to those thousands, millions of young Americans to join us not simply as campaigners, but to continue as critical participants in the politics of our time. Never were you needed so much, and never could you do so much if you were to help now . . . I am aware of the fears and the frustrations of the world in which we live. It is all too easy, isn't it, to play on these emotions? But I do not intend to do so. I do not intend to appeal to fear but rather to hope. I do not intend to appeal to frustration, but rather to your faith. I shall appeal to Reason and to your Good.

The American presidency is a great and powerful office. But it is not all powerful. It depends most of all upon the will and the faith and the dedication and the wisdom of the American people . . . Believe in what America can do, and believe in what America can be. And with the help of that vast, unfrightened, dedicated, faithful majority of Americans, I say to this great convention tonight, and to this great nation of ours, I am ready to lead our country.

It was the speech of Humphrey's life. Amidst the cheers and demonstration, McCarthy was noticeably absent, refusing to come on stage with the nominee. "We have tested the process and found its weakness," said the failed peace candidate. "We'll make this party in 1972 quite different from what we found in Chicago." Mayor Daley received thunderous applause when he joined Humphrey on stage. Many delegates were thankful that he had kept the violence out of the convention itself. But party unity, the goal of every convention, was a severe casualty of the Vietnam War. Eventually, California Assembly Speaker Jesse Unruh, war critic Senator Wayne Morse, and others came to Humphrey's support. "I'm no fan of Richard Nixon," McGovern confessed after the convention, and he too joined Humphrey's campaign. So did Kennedy.

Chicago's reputation was badly tarnished. Mayor Daley was bitterly disappointed by the outcome of his convention, but became even more popular with his supporters and more in conflict with reformers. His local power continued to grow. But four years later, at the 1972 convention, the Daley delegation was displaced by another group, headed by the Reverend Jesse Jackson and lawyer William Singer. The day of the big-city boss in national conventions was over, at least for a while, and replaced by a more democratic and racially representative but less disciplined party that would suffer serious losses in the years ahead as it fragmented into single-issue factions. The Democrats would not return to Chicago for another generation.

The nation remained traumatized by the fury and frenzy of what was later called "a police riot." Polls showed strong national support for Mayor Daley and the Chicago police department. But a new hardness and cynicism overtook the American public, the police, the mayor, the Democratic Party, news reporters, and students. A week later, as the students filtered back to campuses around the nation, SDS meetings, which in the spring had attracted just a few hundred adherents on each campus, overflowed with scores of new recruits who had been radicalized by the Chicago drama played out on their television sets. The antiwar movement exploded in size and intensity.

Humphrey had won the nomination. The election was another question. The country was more divided than even before the convention. HHH left Chicago trailing Nixon by twelve points in the polls, with Wallace not far behind. Humphrey started the postconvention campaign without a clear strategy. Even after Kennedy's death, Humphrey had not sketched out his plan, had not mapped a media campaign, had not conducted adequate fund-raising.

Nixon's first campaign appearance after the Democratic convention was a forty-five minute open-car parade through the Chicago Loop. A large, enthusiastic crowd cheered him on. Nixon appealed to the "quiet Americans," Republicans, and working-class Democrats.

September was a disaster for the Humphrey campaign, the wounds of Chicago still festering with hostility toward the nominee. Humphrey was booed and jeered at every whistle stop. By the end of the month, he trailed Nixon by fifteen points and only led Wallace by seven. During the fall campaign, Nixon spent twice as much as Humphrey on television ads, $12.6 to $6.7 million, and controlled the pace of the campaign with carefully choreographed events and speeches each day, working the suburbs particularly hard. Nixon gave only one key speech each midday, in time to make the nightly news, targeting eight big industrial states. Fulfilling the dream of Garfield's southern strategy, he attracted crossover voters in states of the Old Confederacy. To appeal to Wallace supporters in the South and North, Nixon argued that "our schools are for education, not integration."

In October Humphrey began to articulate his own approach to Vietnam, calling for a bombing halt and "de-Americanizing" the war. (Nixon later picked up on the notion, calling it instead, "Vietnamization.") Coming to Humphrey's aid was a massive AFL-CIO field campaign that reached millions of union voters, emphasizing the antilabor biases of both Nixon and Wallace. At the same time, Wallace's support began to wane and, at least in the North, shifted to Humphrey.

By mid-October the race tightened. Protesters began to converge on Wallace and his running mate, retired Air Force general Curtis E. LeMay, former head of the Strategic Air Command. LeMay startled the nation by publicly mentioning the possibility of using tactical nuclear weapons to end the war. Wallace, also alarmed by his slippage, shipped LeMay off to Vietnam on a fact-finding tour. Meanwhile, negotiations to end the war were making headway. News leaks of a possible bombing halt in exchange for inclusion of the National Liberation Front, the political arm of the Viet Cong in the negotiations, gave Humphrey a glimmer of hope.

Nixon panicked. He implied that the timing of the possible peace breakthrough was politically motivated. Indeed, on October 31, 1968, Johnson finally called off the three-and-a-half-year bombings in North Vietnam and announced that formal peace talks were scheduled for November 6, the day after the elections. But the slim hopes of a Humphrey victory were slammed the very next day when the Saigon government denounced both the talks and President Johnson, refusing to participate. Saigon's reaction meant that Johnson's peace initiative was dead.

A week before the election Senator McCarthy finally endorsed Vice President Humphrey, the former senior senator of his own state. But on November 5, 1968, when more than 73 million Americans voted, Nixon edged out Humphrey, 31,783,783 to 31,266,006 in yet another close contest. Wallace held the remaining 9,898,543 votes. Richard Milhous Nixon would be a minority president, claiming just 43.3 percent of the vote. But in the electoral college, Nixon pulled in 302 votes from thirty-two states to Humphrey's 191, while Wallace won 45 electoral votes from five states. Wallace's strength translated into Humphrey's loss.

Humphrey lost to Nixon in states where McCarthy and Kennedy had scored victories, indicating that the scars from Chicago had not yet healed by November. But Nixon faced a Democratic controlled House and Senate. In the end, the "new" Nixon was not much different from the "old" Nixon. His fear and disdain of the antiwar movement and his paranoia about his "enemies" would eventually lead to Watergate and his own forced resignation from the presidency. Nixon's "secret plan" to end the war, which turned out to be remarkably similar to Humphrey's "de-Americanizing" policy, took another four years to reach fruition. In the meantime, an additional twenty thousand U.S. soldiers died in southeast Asia.

William Jefferson Clinton
1996 Democratic Presidential Nominee

Albert Arnold Gore Jr.
1996 Democratic
Vice Presidential Nominee

Facts-at-a-Glance
★★★

Event:	Forty-Second Democratic National Convention
Dates:	August 26–29, 1996
Building:	The United Center
Location:	1901 West Madison Street
Chicago Mayor:	Richard Michael Daley, Democrat
Candidate for Renomination:	William Jefferson Clinton, Arkansas
Probable Nominee:	William Jefferson Clinton
Age at Renomination:	50
Number of Ballots:	1
Vice Presidential Nominee:	Albert Arnold Gore Jr., Tennessee
Number of Delegates:	4,329
Number Needed to Nominate:	A majority, 2165
Largest Projected Attendance:	35,000
Probable Issues:	Protecting Social Security, Medicare, education, the environment, balancing the budget, economic development

25
★★★

The 1996 Democratic National Convention
Four More for Clinton and Gore

After an absence of twenty-eight years, the Democrats finally returned to Chicago in 1996. The old frontier town had become a world-class city, cosmopolitan in its architecture, renowned for its natural beauty, and secure in its commercial connections. But its status was not easily won. In the nearly three decades since the Democrats last convened, Chicago had seen hard times. Five hundred thousand of its workers had lost their jobs during the "rust belt" years of the 1970s and 1980s. Nearly three thousand of the city's seven thousand factories, from steel to electronics, had shut down. Jobs were exported overseas and to nonunion southern competition. Scores of the city's neighborhoods declined and, as a consequence, suburbanization drew away the fearful middle class. The school system collapsed, and the city's poverty rate escalated, along with its crime problems.

But in recent years Chicago rebounded and prospered as international trade and finance grew on the LaSalle Street markets, at O'Hare International Airport, and with the hundreds of small high-tech industries that grew in and around the city. Some schools turned around, and many neighborhoods had stabilized with the help of strong community organizations. Chicago political reformers finally triumphed with the 1983 election of Harold Washington as the city's first African-American mayor. After Washington's untimely death, Chicago managed to achieve a racial truce under Mayor Eugene Sawyer and Mayor Richard Michael Daley, son of Richard J. Daley. Immigration from South America and around the world enriched the city's racial and cultural diversity.

Chicago's famous "clout" was also at work in bringing the 1996 convention "home." Although raised in Park Ridge, Illinois, Chicago was birthplace to First Lady Hillary Rodham Clinton and a favorite city of President Bill Clinton himself. Mayor Daley's former campaign manager, David Wilhelm, a Chicago resident, had served as chairman of the Democratic National Committee and as President Clinton's 1992 campaign chief. William Daley, the mayor's brother, cochair of Chicago '96, the local convention group, had headed President Clinton's successful campaign to ratify the North American Free Trade Agreement. The Democrats had nothing to fear in holding their national celebration in a Chicago wigwam like the United Center, which stood across the street from the site of the old demolished Chicago Stadium where, Franklin Roosevelt was first nominated and twice renominated.

Meanwhile, Richard M. Daley, who had been handily reelected twice by the people of Chicago and elected by his peers as head of the U.S. Conference of Mayors, kept a low profile and strived for civic improvements to show off the city during the convention. Police superintendent Matt Rodriguez promised that demonstrators would be given space and time to protest without interference. He also requested special powers to bring back police infiltration and surveillance of potentially dangerous groups, particularly terrorists, domestic or foreign, like those who destroyed a government building in Oklahoma City in 1995. The threat of mass terrorism was far more dangerous than the mass demonstrations of the 1960s. And in 1996 the Chicago police department was much more sophisticated. But the city also opened its arms to visitors. Several thousand Chicagoland volunteers were trained to help the 35,000 anticipated guests, who were expected to stay in 17,000 Chicago hotel rooms and pump $100 million into the local economy.

The 1996 Democracy gathered to renominate an unopposed President Bill Clinton and Vice President Al Gore. Though ruthlessly pilloried by his opponents from his first months in office, President Clinton had withstood the attacks and carried on with his programs and policies. But a disastrous 1994

United Center, site of the 1996 Democratic National Convention, the modern "wigwam." The old Stadium is to the left. Bill Smith Photography.

mid-term election, "the Republican revolution," turned both the House of Representatives and the U. S. Senate over to the Republicans for the first time since Eisenhower. The president seemed politically vulnerable.

Under these adverse conditions, President Clinton showed his considerable skills as a conciliator and a fighter, standing firm on principles of "protecting Medicare and Social Security, fighting for education, the environment, and equal opportunity." In adversity, he had gained strength, and with a robust economic engine behind him (the Clinton stock market had done better than the Reagan market of the 1980s), the president gained steady favor with the voters, enough to put him ahead of potential opponents in 1996. With the California primary, Senate Majority Leader Bob Dole won enough delegates to become the Republican nominee. A bitter post-convention campaign loomed on the horizon.

The 1996 convention would be nothing like the 1896 gathering in the first Coliseum, when half the nation cried out for economic relief. But like William Jennings Bryan one hundred years earlier, the convention would hear a gifted speaker in William Jefferson Clinton.

Contentious national and international issues would be absent from the convention. The agenda promised a made-for-television entertainment extravaganza produced by Hollywood veteran Gary Smith, winner of twenty Emmy awards. This convention, like most renomination conventions, would be long on hoopla and short on drama. But once again the speeches promised to redefine the mission of the Democratic Party, trying to convince another generation of weary voters why they should elect Clinton and Gore for four more years. In 1996 the Democracy, gathered in a modern Chicago wigwam, would offer the nation a new agenda for the twenty-first century.

To follow the convention events, Internet users can contact the Ameritech Web page at:

WWW.Chicago96.org

This site will be in operation until September 30, 1996.

Major U.S. Party Presidential Nominating Conventions

Year	Party	Location	Presidential Nominee	Number of Ballots
1832	Democrat	Baltimore	Andrew Jackson	1
1835	Democrat	Baltimore	Martin Van Buren	1
1840	Democrat	Baltimore	Martin Van Buren	1
1844	Democrat	Baltimore	James K. Polk	9
1848	Democrat	Baltimore	Lewis Cass	4
1852	Democrat	Baltimore	Franklin Pierce	49
1856	Democrat	Cincinnati	James Buchanan	17
1856	Republican	Philadelphia	John C. Fremont	2
1860	Democrat	Charleston	None	57
1860	Democrat	Baltimore	Stephen A. Douglas	2
1860	**Republican**	**Chicago**	**Abraham Lincoln**	**3**
1864	**Democrat**	**Chicago**	**George B. McClellan**	**1**
1864	Republican	Baltimore	Abraham Lincoln	1
1868	Democrat	New York City	Horatio Seymour	22
1868	**Republican**	**Chicago**	**Ulysses S. Grant**	**1**
1872	Democrat	Baltimore	Horace Greeley	1
1872	Republican	Philadelphia	Ulysses S. Grant	1
1876	Democrat	St. Louis	Samuel J. Tilden	2
1876	Republican	Cincinnati	Rutherford B. Hayes	7
1880	Democrat	Cincinnati	Winfield S. Hancock	2
1880	**Republican**	**Chicago**	**James A. Garfield**	**36**
1884	**Democrat**	**Chicago**	**Grover Cleveland**	**2**
1884	**Republican**	**Chicago**	**James G. Blaine**	**4**
1888	Democrat	St. Louis	Grover Cleveland	1
1888	**Republican**	**Chicago**	**Benjamin Harrison**	**8**
1892	**Democrat**	**Chicago**	**Grover Cleveland**	**1**
1892	Republican	Minneapolis	Benjamin Harrison	1
1896	**Democrat**	**Chicago**	**William Jennings Bryan**	**5**
1896	Republican	St. Louis	William McKinley	1
1900	Democrat	Kansas City	William Jennings Bryan	1
1900	Republican	Philadelphia	William McKinley	1
1904	Democrat	St. Louis	Alton B. Parker	1
1904	**Republican**	**Chicago**	**Theodore Roosevelt**	**1**
1908	Democrat	Denver	William Jennings Bryan	1
1908	**Republican**	**Chicago**	**William H. Taft**	**1**
1912	Democrat	Baltimore	Woodrow Wilson	46
1912	**Republican**	**Chicago**	**William H. Taft**	**1**
1912	**Progressive**	**Chicago**	**Theodore Roosevelt**	**1**
1916	Democrat	St. Louis	Woodrow Wilson	1
1916	**Republican**	**Chicago**	**Charles E. Hughes**	**3**
1916	**Progressive**	**Chicago**	**Theodore Roosevelt**	**1**

Year	Party	Location	Presidential Nominee	Number of Ballots
1920	Democrat	San Francisco	James M. Cox	44
1920	**Republican**	**Chicago**	**Warren G. Harding**	**10**
1924	Democrat	New York City	John W. Davis	103
1924	Republican	Cleveland	Calvin Coolidge	1
1928	Democrat	Houston	Alfred E. Smith	1
1928	Republican	Kansas City	Herbert C. Hoover	1
1932	**Democrat**	**Chicago**	**Franklin D. Roosevelt**	**4**
1932	**Republican**	**Chicago**	**Herbert C. Hoover**	**1**
1936	Democrat	Philadelphia	Franklin D. Roosevelt	A
1936	Republican	Cleveland	Alfred M. Landon	1
1940	**Democrat**	**Chicago**	**Franklin D. Roosevelt**	**1**
1940	Republican	Philadelphia	Wendell L. Willkie	6
1944	**Democrat**	**Chicago**	**Franklin D. Roosevelt**	**1**
1944	**Republican**	**Chicago**	**Thomas E. Dewey**	**1**
1948	Democrat	Philadelphia	Harry S Truman	1
1948	Republican	Philadelphia	Thomas E. Dewey	3
1952	**Democrat**	**Chicago**	**Adlai E. Stevenson**	**3**
1952	**Republican**	**Chicago**	**Dwight D. Eisenhower**	**1**
1956	**Democrat**	**Chicago**	**Adlai E. Stevenson**	**1**
1956	Republican	San Francisco	Dwight D. Eisenhower	1
1960	Democrat	Los Angeles	John F. Kennedy	1
1960	**Republican**	**Chicago**	**Richard M. Nixon**	**1**
1964	Democrat	Atlantic City	Lyndon B. Johnson	A
1964	Republican	San Francisco	Barry Goldwater	1
1968	**Democrat**	**Chicago**	**Hubert H. Humphrey**	**1**
1968	Republican	Miami Beach	Richard M. Nixon	1
1972	Democrat	Miami Beach	George McGovern	1
1972	Republican	Miami Beach	Richard M. Nixon	1
1976	Democrat	New York City	Jimmy Carter	1
1976	Republican	Kansas City	Gerald R. Ford	1
1980	Democrat	New York City	Jimmy Carter	1
1980	Republican	Detroit	Ronald Reagan	1
1984	Democrat	San Francisco	Walter F. Mondale	1
1984	Republican	Dallas	Ronald Reagan	1
1988	Democrat	Atlanta	Michael S. Dukakis	1
1988	Republican	New Orleans	George Bush	1
1992	Democrat	New York City	Bill Clinton	1
1992	Republican	Houston	George Bush	1
1996	**Democrat**	**Chicago**	**Bill Clinton**	**1**
1996	Republican	San Diego	Robert Dole	

* A = By Acclamation

Bibliography

History necessarily builds upon the edifice of previous writers and interpreters of human events. In part that is what makes writing a history such a great adventure in learning. The authors wish gratefully to acknowledge the following primary and secondary sources, the pillars of our research, from which we have learned much. We recommend them to readers who wish to know more about any of the topics contained within these pages.

Abbott, Ernest H. "The Chicago Convention and the Birth of a New Party." *Outlook,* June 29, 1912.

Adler, Bill, ed. *The Stevenson Wit.* New York: Doubleday and Company, 1965.

Ambrose, Stephen E. *Eisenhower: Soldier, General of the Army, President-Elect, 1890–1952.* Vol. 1. New York: Simon and Schuster, 1983.

The American Experience: Chicago 1968. David Gruebin Productions, New York, 1995.

Bain, Richard C., and Judith H. Parris, eds. *Convention Decisions and Voting Records.* Washington, D.C.: The Brookings Institute, 1973.

Bernstein, Barton J. "Election of 1952." In *History of American Presidential Elections, 1789–1968.* Vol. 4. Edited by Arthur M. Schlesinger Jr., Fred L. Israel, and William P. Hansen. New York: Chelsea House Publishers/McGraw-Hill Book Company, 1971.

Biles, Roger. "Edward J. Kelly." In *The Mayors, The Chicago Political Tradition.* Edited by Paul M. Green and Melvin Holli. Carbondale, Ill.: Southern Illinois University Press, 1995.

Blum, John Morton. *The Republican Roosevelt.* Cambridge, Mass.: Harvard University Press, 1980.

Boller, Paul F., Jr. *Presidential Campaigns.* New York: Oxford University Press, 1985.

Broadwater, Jeff. *Adlai Stevenson and American Politics: The Odyssey of a Cold War Liberal.* Boston: Twayne Publishers, 1994.

Broder, David. "The Election of 1968." In *History of American Presidential Elections, 1940–1968.* Vol. 4. Edited by Arthur M. Schlesinger Jr., Fred L. Israel, and William P. Hansen. New York: Chelsea House Publishers/McGraw-Hill Book Company, 1971.

Burk, Robert F. *Dwight D. Eisenhower: Hero and Politician.* Boston: Twayne Publishers, 1986.

Burns, James M. *The Workshop of Democracy: The American Experiment.* Vol. 2. New York: Knopf, 1985.

Burns, James MacGregor. *Roosevelt: The Lion and the Fox.* New York: Harcourt, Brace, and Co., 1956.

Busch, Noel F. *T.R., The Story of Theodore Roosevelt and His Influence on Our Times.* New York: Reynal and Company, 1963.

Chicago American, June 28, 1932; August 14, 15, 1956.

Chicago's American, July 27, 1960.

Chicago Daily Journal, May 16, 17, 18, 1860.

Chicago Daily News, June 2, 4, 8, 1880; June 3, 5, 1884; June 25, 1888; June 22, 23, 1892; July 7, 9, 11, 1896; June 18, 20, 22, 1912; June 7, 1916; June 8,

10, 11, 1920; June 14, July 2, 1932; July 17, 1940; June 27, 28, July 19, 20, 1944; July 10, 11, 22, 25, 1952; August 17, 1956; July 25, 1960; August 26, 27, 1968.

Chicago Daily Sun-Times, July 8, 1952.

Chicago Daily Tribune, June 3, 6, 7, 1880; June 21, 1892; June 21, 22, 1912; June 7, 10, 1916; June 9, 12, 1920; June 16, 30, July 1, 1932; July 16, 18, 1940; June 26, 28, July 21, 1944; July 7, 9, 21, 23, 26, 1952; August 13, 17, 1956; July 26, 28, 1960.

Chicago Evening Journal, June 20, 1888.

Chicago Evening Post, July 10, 1896; June 19, 24, 1912; June 9, 1916; June 10, 1920; June 16, 27, 29, 1932.

Chicago Herald, June 8, 9, 1916.

Chicago Herald American, July 15, 17, 18, 1940; July 19, 1944; July 11, 23, 24, 1952.

Chicago History. Vol. 7., no. 1 (fall 1963–summer 1966).

"Chicago Lands Democrats with Empty-Pocket Pledge." *New York Times,* February 11, 1940.

Chicago Sun-Times, July 26, 28, 1960; August 27, 29, 30, 1968.

The Chicago Times, May 20, 21, 1868.

Chicago Times-Herald, July 8, 1896.

Chicago Tribune, August 29, 30, 31, September 1, 1864; May 20, 21, 1868; June 3, 1884; June 22, 1888; August 28, 29, 30, 1968; August 20, 1995.

Cohn, David L. *The Fabulous Democrats: A History of the Democratic Party in Text and Pictures.* New York: G. P. Putnam's Sons, 1956.

Coletta, Paolo E. *The Presidency of William Howard Taft.* Lawrence, Kan.: University of Kansas Press, 1973.

Congress of U.S. Government Printing Office. *Biographical Directory of the United States Congress 1774–1989.* Washington, D.C.: Congress of U.S.Government Printing Office.

Congressional Quarterly. *National Party Conventions, 1831–1988.* Washington, D.C.: 1991.

Cook, Frederick Francis. *Bygone Days in Chicago: Recollections of the "Garden City" of the Sixties.* Chicago: A.C. McClurg and Company, 1910.

Current History, June, July, August 1932.

Curtis, Francis. *The Republican Party: A History of its Fifty Years' Existence and a Record of its Measures and Leaders, 1854–1904.* Vol. 1 and 2. New York: Knickerbocker Press/G.P. Putnam's Sons, 1904.

Daily Illustrated Times, June 15, 1932.

Daily Inter-Ocean, June 5, 1880; June 4, 6, 1884; July 9, 11, 1884; June 19, 21, 23, 1888; June 21, 23, 1892; July 8, 11, 1896.

Davenport, Frederick M. "Preliminary Impressions of the Chicago Conventions." *Outlook,* June 14, 1916.

Davis, Kenneth S. *The Politics of Honor: A Biography of Adlai E. Stevenson.* New York: G.P. Putnam's Sons, 1967.

Dedmon, Emmett. *Fabulous Chicago: A Great City's History and People.* New York: Atheneum, 1983.

Democratic Party proceedings:

Official Proceedings of the Democratic National Convention held in 1864 at Chicago. James H. Goodsell. Chicago: Times Steam Book and Job Printing House, 1864.

Official Proceedings of the National Democratic Convention, held in Chicago, Illinois, July 8th, 9th, 10th, and 11th, 1884. New York: Douglas Taylor's Democratic Printing House, 1884.

Official Proceedings of the National Democratic Convention, held in Chicago, Illinois, June 21st, 22nd, and 23rd, 1892. Reported for the convention by Edward B. Dickinson, official stenographer. Chicago: Cameron, Amberg and Co., 1892.

Official Proceedings of the Democratic National Convention, held in Chicago, Illinois, July 7th, 8th, 9th, 10th and 11th, 1896. Reported for the convention by Edward B. Dickinson. Logansport, Ind.: Wilson, Humphreys and Company, 1896.

Official Report of the Proceedings of the Democratic National Convention, Chicago, Illinois, July 15th to 18th, inclusive, 1940, resulting in the renomination of Franklin D. Roosevelt of New York for President and the nomination of Henry A. Wallace of Iowa to Vice President. Washington, D.C., 1940.

Official Report of the Proceedings of the Democratic National Convention, Chicago, Illinois, July 19th to

July 21st, inclusive, 1944, resulting in the renomination of Franklin D. Roosevelt of New York for President, and the nomination of Harry S Truman of Missouri for Vice President. Chicago, 1944.

Proceedings of the Convention of the National Democratic Party held in Indianapolis, Indiana, September 2 and 3, 1896.

Unofficial Proceedings of the 35th Quadrennial Democratic National Convention, 1968.

"Democrats Cheer Keynote." *Chicago Tribune,* July 16, 1940.

Desmond, James. *Nelson Rockefeller, A Political Biography.* New York: Macmillan Company, 1964.

De Witt, Benjamin Parke. *The Progressive Movement: A Non-Partisan Comprehensive Discussion of Current Tendencies in American Politics.* New York: Macmillan Company, 1915; Seattle: University of Washington Press Americana Library edition, 1968.

Dictionary of American Portraits. Edited by Hayward and Blanche Cirker and the staff of Dover Publications. New York: Dover Publications, 1967.

Dillon, Mary Earhart. *Wendell Willkie: 1892–1944.* Philadelphia: J.B. Lippincott Company, 1952.

Ehrenhalt, Alan. "Civic Lessons." *Chicago Tribune Magazine,* August 20, 1995, 16–26.

Fehrenbacher, Don E. *Chicago Giant: A Biography of "Long John" Wentworth.* Madison, Wis.: American History Research Center, 1957.

Fite, Gilbert C. "Election of 1896." In *History of American Presidential Elections, 1848–1896.* Vol. 2. Edited by Arthur M. Schlesinger Jr., Fred L. Israel, and William P. Hansen. New York: Chelsea House Publishers/McGraw-Hill Book Company, 1971.

Foner, Eric. *Reconstruction: America's Unfinished Revolution 1863–1877.* New York: Harper and Row, 1988.

"Fortieth Congress: Second Session." *New York Times,* June 4, 1868.

The Forum, July 1932.

Fowler, Gene. *Beau James: The Life and Times of Jimmy Walker.* New York: Viking Press, 1949.

Freidel, Frank. "Election of 1932." In *History of American Presidential Elections, 1900–1936.* Vol. 3. Edited by Arthur M. Schlesinger Jr., Fred L. Israel, and William P. Hansen. New York: Chelsea House Publishers/McGraw-Hill Book Company, 1971.

Friedman, Leon. "Election of 1944." In *History of American Presidential Elections, 1940–1968.* Vol. 4. Edited by Arthur M. Schlesinger Jr., Fred L. Israel, and William P. Hansen. New York: Chelsea House Publishers/McGraw-Hill Book Company, 1971.

Frost, Lawrence A. *U.S. Grant Album: A Pictorial Biography of Ulysses S. Grant from Leather Clerk to the White House.* Seattle: Superior Publishing Company, 1966.

Fuess, Claude Moore. "Roosevelt: The Democratic Hope." *Current History,* August 1932, 513–33.

Gettleman, Marvin E., ed. *Vietnam: History, Documents, and Opinions on a Major World Crisis.* Greenwich, Conn.: Fawcett Publications, 1965.

Gibson, James W. *The Perfect War.* Reprint. New York: Vintage Books, 1988.

Ginger, Ray. *Age of Excess: The United States from 1877 to 1914.* New York: Macmillan, 1975.

Gleason, Bill. *Daley of Chicago: The Man, the Mayor and the Limits of Conventional Politics.* New York: Simon and Schuster, 1970.

Goldman, Ralph M. *The Democratic Party in American Politics: Franklin and Eleanor Roosevelt, The Home Front in World War II.* New York: Macmillan, 1966.

Goodwin, Doris Kearns. *No Ordinary Time.* New York: Simon and Schuster, 1994.

Graff, Henry F., ed. *The Presidents: A Reference History.* New York: Charles Scribner's Sons, 1984.

Harper's New Monthly Magazine, August 1864, June 1868, August 1880, July 1884.

Heise, Kenan, and Ed Baumann. *Chicago Originals.* Chicago: Bonus Books, 1990.

Howland, Harold J. "One Convention and Another." *Outlook,* June 29, 1912.

Hoyt, Edwin P., Jr. *Jumbos and Jackasses: A Popular History of the Political Wars.* Garden City, N.Y.: Doubleday and Company, 1960.

The Inter-Ocean, June 19, 1912.

Johnson, Curt, with R. Craig Sautter. *Wicked City: Chicago from Kenna to Capone.* Highland Park, Ill.: December Press, 1994.

Kane, Joseph Nathan. *Facts about the Presidents: A Compilation of Biographical and Historical Information.* 5th ed. New York: H.W. Wilson, 1989.

Kelly, Edward J. "Kelly's Story." *Chicago Herald-American,* May 12, 1947.

Kent, Frank R. *The Democratic Party: A History.* New York: The Century Co., 1928.

Koenig, Louis W. Bryan: *A Political Biography of William Jennings Bryan.* New York: G. P. Putnam's Sons, 1971.

Kogan, Herman, and Lloyd Wendt. *Chicago: A Pictorial History.* New York: Dutton Books, 1958.

Leech, Margaret. *Reveille In Washington, 1860–1865.* New York: Harper and Row, 1941.

Lewis, Lloyd, and Henry Smith. *Chicago, The History of Its Reputation.* New York: Harcourt, Brace, and Co., 1929.

Lippmann, Walter. "At the Chicago Conventions." *The New Republic,* June 17, 1916, 163–65.

Lorant, Stefan. *The Glorious Burden: The History of the Presidency and Presidential Elections From George Washington to James Earl Carter, Jr.* Lenox, Mass.: Authors Edition, 1976.

Low, A. Maurice. *Harper's Weekly,* June 29, 1912.

Lynch, Denis Tilden. *Grover Cleveland, A Man Four-Square.* New York: Horace Liveright Inc., 1932.

Lyon, Peter. *Eisenhower: Portrait of the Hero.* Boston: Little, Brown, 1974.

Mailer, Norman. *Miami and the Siege of Chicago: An Informal History of the Republican and Democratic Conventions of 1968.* New York: Signet, New American Library, 1968.

Martin, Michael, and Leonard Gelber. *The New Dictionary of American History.* New York: Philosophical Library, 1952.

Martin, Ralph G. *Ballots and Bandwagons.* Chicago: Rand McNally and Company, 1964.

Masters, Edgar Lee. *Across Spoon River: An Autobiography.* Urbana, Ill.: University of Illinois Press, 1936.

Mayer, George H. *The Republican Party, 1854–1966.* New York: Oxford University Press, 1967.

McCoy, Donald R. "The Election of 1920." In *History of American Presidential Elections, 1900–1936.* Vol. 3. Edited by Arthur M. Schlesinger Jr., Fred L. Israel, and William P. Hansen. New York: Chelsea House Publishers/McGraw-Hill Book Co., 1971.

McCullough, David. *Truman.* New York: Simon and Schuster, 1992.

McFeeley, William S. *Grant: A Biography.* New York: W.W. Norton and Co., 1981.

McNamee, Tom. "It's the Main Event, in Impact if Not Size." *Chicago Sun-Times,* February 5, 1996, 4.

Mencken, H. L. *Making a President: A Footnote to the Saga of Democracy.* New York: Alfred A. Knopf, 1932.

Miller, Kristie. *Ruth Hanna McCormick: A Life in Politics, 1880–1944.* Albuquerque, N.M.: University of New Mexico Press, 1992.

Minor, Henry A. *The Story of the Democratic Party.* New York: Macmillan Company, 1928.

Moos, Malcolm. "Election of 1956." In *History of American Presidential Elections, 1940–1968.* Vol. 4. Edited by Arthur M. Schlesinger Jr., Fred L. Israel, and William P. Hansen. New York: Chelsea House Publishers/McGraw-Hill Book Company, 1971.

Morgan, H. Wayne. *From Hayes to McKinley: National Party Politics, 1877–1896.* Syracuse, N.Y.: Syracuse University Press, 1969.

Morris, Dan, and Inez Morris. *Who Was Who in American Politics.* New York: Hawthorn Books, 1974.

Morris, Sylvia Jukes. *Edith Kermit Roosevelt. Portrait of a First Lady.* New York: Vintage Books, 1990.

Murray, Robert K. *The Harding Era: Warren G. Harding and His Administration.* Minneapolis, Minn.: University of Minnesota Press, 1969.

Mushkat, Jerome. *Tammany: The Evolution of a Political Machine,1789–1865.* Syracuse, N.Y.: Syracuse University Press, 1971.

Muzzey, David Saville. *James G. Blaine, A Political Idol of Other Days.* New York: Dodd, Meade and Company, 1934.

"National Affairs," *Time,* June 20, 1932, 10.

"National Affairs," *Time,* June 27, 1932, 9–13.

"National Affairs," *Time,* July 4, 1932, 8–12.

"The National Conventions." *North American Review,* July 17, 1916.

Neal, Steve. *Dark Horse: A Biography of Wendell Willkie.* Lawrence, Kan.: University Press of Kansas, 1989.

Nevins, Allan. *Ordeal of The Union.* 8 vols. New York: Charles Scribner's Sons, 1947, 1974.

"An Open Letter to Al Smith, from a Plain Citizen." *The Forum,* July 1932, 3–4.

Oshinsky, David H. *A Conspiracy So Immense: The World of Joe McCarthy.* New York: The Free Press, 1983.

Outlook, July 6, 1912.

Parmet, Herbert S. *Richard Nixon and His America.* Boston: Little, Brown and Company, 1990.

Peel, Roy V., and Thomas C. Donnelly. *The 1932 Campaign, An Analysis.* New York: Farrar and Rinehart, 1935.

Perkins, Dexter. *Charles Evans Hughes and American Democratic Statesmanship.* Boston: Little, Brown, 1956.

Peskin, Allan. *Garfield: A Biography.* Kent, Ohio: Kent State University Press, 1978.

Potter, David M. *The Impending Crisis 1848–1861.* New York: Harper Row, 1976.

"The Progress of the World." *American Review of Reviews,* June 1916.

Republican Party proceedings:

Official Proceedings of the National Republican Conventions of 1868, 1872, 1876, and 1880. Minneapolis, Minn.: Charles W. Johnson, 1903.

Official Proceedings of the Republican National Convention, held at Chicago, June 19, 20, 21, 22, 23, and 25, 1888. Minneapolis, Minn.: Charles W. Johnson, 1903.

Official Proceedings of the Thirteenth Republican National Convention, held in the City of Chicago, June 21, 22, 23, 1904, resulting in the nomination of Theodore Roosevelt, of New York, for President. Reported by M. W. Blumenberg. Minneapolis, Minn.: Harrison & Smith Co., 1904.

Official Report of the Proceedings of the Fourteenth Republican National Convention. Columbus, Ohio: Press of F. J. Herr, 1908.

Official Report of the Proceedings of the Fifteenth Republican National Convention, held in Chicago, Illinois, June 18, 19, 20, 21, and 22, 1912, resulting in the nomination for William Howard Taft, of Ohio, for President. Reported by Milton W. Blumenberg. Published under the supervision of the general secretary of the convention. New York: Tenny Press, 1912.

Official Report of the Proceedings of the Sixteenth Republican National Convention held in Chicago, Illinois, June 7, 8, 9, and 10, 1916, resulting in the nomination of Charles Evans Hughes, of New York, for President and the nomination of Charles Warren Fairbanks, of Indiana, for Vice President. George L. Hart, official reporter. New York: Tenny Press, 1916.

Official Report of the Proceedings of the Seventeenth Republican National Convention, held in Chicago, Illinois, June 8, 9, 10, 11, and 12, 1920, resulting in the nomination of Warren Gamaliel Harding, of Ohio, for President, and the nomination of Calvin Coolidge, of Massachusetts, for Vice President. George L. Hart, official reporter. New York: Tenny Press, 1920.

Official Report of the Proceedings of the Twentieth Republican National Convention, held in Chicago, Illinois, June 14, 15, and 16, 1932, resulting in the nomination of Herbert Hoover, of California, for President, and the renomination of Charles Curtis, of Kansas, for Vice President. George L. Hart, official reporter. New York: Tenny Press, 1932.

Official Report of the Proceedings of the Twenty-third Republican National Convention, held in Chicago, Illinois, June 26, 27, and 28, 1944, resulting in the nomination of Thomas E. Dewey, of New York, for President, and the nomination of John W. Bricker, of Ohio, for Vice President. Reported by George L. Hart. Washington, D.C.: Judd & Detweiler, Inc., 1944.

The Proceedings of the First Three Republican National Conventions of 1856, 1860, and 1864 as reported by Horace Greeley. Minneapolis, Minn.: Charles W. Johnson, 1893.

Proceedings of the Republican National Convention, held at Chicago, Illinois, June 2d, 3d, 4th, 5th, 7th, 8th, 1880. Reported by Eugene Davis. Chicago: Jeffery Printing and Publishing House, 1881.

Proceedings of the Eighth Republican National Convention held at Chicago, Illinois, June 3, 4, 5, and 6, 1884. Chicago: Rand McNally & Co.

Rhodes, Richard. *Dark Sun: the Making of the Hydrogen Bomb.* New York: Simon and Schuster, 1995.

Roosevelt, Theodore. "Thou Shalt Not Steal." *Outlook,* July 13, 1912.

———. "Two Phases of the Chicago Convention—The 'Steam Roller.' " *Outlook,* July 20, 1912.

Royko, Mike. *Boss: Richard J. Daley of Chicago.* New York: New American Library, 1971.

Sandburg, Carl. *Abraham Lincoln: The Prairie Years and The War Years.* New York: Harvest Book/Harcourt Brace and Company, 1982; New York: Galahad Books, 1993.

Sawyers, June Skinner. *Chicago Portraits: Biographies of 250 Famous Chicagoans.* Chicago: Loyola University Press, 1991.

Schultz, John. *The Chicago Conspiracy Trial.* New York: De Capo Press, 1993.

Sears, Stephen W. *George B. McClellan: The Young Napoleon.* New York: Ticknor and Fields, 1988.

Sibley, Joel H. *A Respectable Minority: The Democratic Party in the Civil War Era, 1860–1868.* New York: W. W. Norton, 1977.

Sievers, Harry J., S. J. *Benjamin Harrison, Hoosier Statesman: From the Civil War to the White House.* New York: University Publishers, 1959.

Smith, Page. *The Rise of Industrial America, Volume 11: A People's History of the Post-Reconstruction Era.* New York: Penguin Books, 1990.

Smith, Richard Norton. *Thomas E. Dewey and His Times.* New York: Simon and Schuster, 1982.

Sorensen, Theodore C. "The Election of 1960." In *History of American Presidential Elections,*

1940–1968. Vol. 4. Edited by Arthur M. Schlesinger Jr., Fred L. Israel, and William P. Hansen. New York: Chelsea House Publishers/McGraw-Hill Book Company, 1971.

Spector, Ronald H. *After Tet: The Bloodiest Year in Vietnam.* New York: Vintage Books, 1994.

Stanton, Shelby L. *The Rise and Fall of An American Army: U.S. Ground Forces in Vietnam, 1965–1973.* Novato, Calif.: Presidio Press, 1985.

Stone, Irving. *They Also Ran: The Story of the Men Who Were Defeated for the Presidency.* Garden City, N.Y.: Doubleday, Doran and Company, 1945.

"The Story of the Week." *The Independent,* June 19, 1916.

Strong, George, J. *The Diary of George Templeton Strong.* Edited by Allan Nevins and Milton Halsey Thomas. New York: MacMillan, 1952.

Swanberg, W. A. *Sickles the Incredible.* New York: Charles Scribner's Sons, 1956.

Time, June 20, 27, 1932; July 4, 1932; July 29, 1940; August 30, September 6, 13, 20, 1968.

Walker, Daniel. *Rights in Conflict: The Official Report to the National Commission on the Causes and Prevention of Violence.* New York: New American Library, 1968.

Warren, Harris Gaylord. *Herbert Hoover and the Great Depression.* New York: W.W. Norton and Company, 1967.

Wendt, Lloyd. *Chicago Tribune: The Rise of a Great American Newspaper.* Chicago: Rand McNally and Company, 1979.

Wendt, Lloyd, and Herman Kogan. *Big Bill of Chicago.* Indianapolis, Ind.: Bobbs-Merrill Company, 1953.

———. *Bosses in Lusty Chicago: The Story of Bathhouse John and Hinky Dink.* Bloomington, Ind.: Indiana University Press, 1967.

"What Was Demonstrated At Chicago." *The Independent,* June 19, 1916.

White, Theodore H. *The Making of the President, 1960.* New York: Atheneum Publishers, 1961.

———. *The Making of the President, 1968.* New York: Atheneum Publishers, 1969.

Whitney, Alan. "Hot Times in the Old Town." *Chicago,* July–August 1956, 36–42.

Wiebe, Robert H. *The Search for Order, 1877–1920.* New York: Hill and Wang, 1967.

Willkie, Wendell L. *One World.* New York: Simon and Schuster, 1943.

Index

Photo Credits

All photo credits other than the following appear with the photographs.